REBUILDING LABOR

ORGANIZING AND ORGANIZERS IN THE NEW UNION MOVEMENT

■

Edited by Ruth Milkman and Kim Voss

AN ILR PRESS BOOK

Cornell University Press
Ithaca and London

First published 2004 by Cornell University Press
First printing, Cornell Paperbacks, 2004

Printed in the United States of America

Library of Congress Cataloging-in-Publication Data
Rebuilding labor : organizing and organizers in the new union movement
/ edited by Ruth Milkman and Kim Voss.
    p.   cm.—(An ILR press book)
  Includes bibliographical references and index.
  "The chapters in this book were first presented at a conference organized by the editors under the auspices of the University of California's Institute for Labor and Employment, held at UCLA on May 17, 2001"—P.   .
  ISBN 0-8014-4265-6 (cloth : alk. paper)—ISBN 0-8014-8902-4 (pbk. : alk. paper)
  1. Labor unions—United States—History—20th century—Congresses. 2. Labor movement—United States—History—20th century—Congresses.   3. Labor leaders—United States—History—20th century—Congresses.   4. Labor unions—United States—Political activity—History—20th century—Congresses.   5. Industrial relations—United States—History—20th century—Congresses.   6. Working class—United States—History—20th century—Congresses.   I. Milkman, Ruth, 1954–   II. Voss, Kim. III. Series.

  HD5708.R43 2004
  331.88'0973—dc22

2004006703

Cornell University Press strives to use environmentally responsible suppliers and materials to the fullest extent possible in the publishing of its books. Such materials include vegetable-based, low-VOC inks, and acid-free papers that are recycled, totally chlorine-free, or partly composed of nonwood fibers. For further information, visit our website at www.cornell-press.cornell.edu.

Cloth printing   10 9 8 7 6 5 4 3 2 1
Paperback printing   10 9 8 7 6 5 4 3 2 1

CONTENTS

ABBREVIATIONS

ACORN	Association of Community Organizations for Reform Now
ACTWU	Amalgamated Clothing and Textile Workers Union
AFGE	American Federation of Government Employees
AFL-CIO	American Federation of Labor–Congress of Industrial Organizations
AFSCME	American Federation of State, County, and Municipal Employees
AFT	American Federation of Teachers
ANA	American Nurses Association
APWU	American Postal Workers Union
AWOC	Agricultural Workers Organizing Committee
CWA	Communication Workers of America
FAST	Food and Allied Service Trades
HERE	Hotel and Restaurant Employees International Union
IAF	Industrial Arts Foundation
IAM	International Association of Machinists
IATSE	International Association of Theatrical Stage Employees
IBEW	International Brotherhood of Electrical Workers
IBT	International Brotherhood of Teamsters
IUE	International Union of Electronic, Electrical, Salaried, Machine, and Furniture Workers
IUOE	International Union of Operating Engineers
LIUNA	Laborers' International Union of North America
NLRA	National Relations Labor Act
NLRB	National Labor Relations Board

NWU   National Writers Union
PACE   Paper, Allied-Industrial, Chemical, and Energy Workers
          International Union
SAG   Screen Actors Guild
SEIU   Service Employees International Union
UAW   United Automobile, Aerospace, and Agricultural Implement
          Workers of America International Union
UBC   United Brotherhood of Carpenters and Joiners of America
UFCW   United Food and Commercial Workers International Union
UFW   United Farm Workers of America
UMWA   United Mine Workers of America
UNITE   Union of Needletrades, Industrial, and Textile Employees
USWA   United Steel Workers of America

REBUILDING LABOR

INTRODUCTION

Ruth Milkman and Kim Voss

Organized labor's obituary appears regularly in the news as well as in scholarly commentary, and even union supporters tend to be pessimistic about the prospects for reconstruction. Over the past three decades, emboldened employers have redoubled their opposition to collective bargaining, helped along by deindustrialization, deregulation, and other types of economic restructuring. As a result, union density has fallen precipitously, especially in the private sector, in which only 9 percent of the workforce is organized today—about one-third the level that prevailed in the early 1970s (Hirsch and Macpherson 2003). Moreover, in the industries and occupations in which employment is expanding most rapidly, unions are conspicuous mainly by their absence. Similarly, key population groups like immigrants and women, whose share of the workforce is growing, remain underrepresented in the ranks of organized labor—despite evidence that such workers, especially those concentrated in low-wage jobs, are especially sympathetic to unionization efforts (Milkman 2000; Bronfenbrenner 1997).

These developments helped spur John Sweeney's dramatic ascension to the presidency of the American Federation of Labor—Congress of Industrial Organizations (AFL-CIO) in 1995, on a platform calling on unions to redirect resources toward "organizing the unorganized" on an unprecedented scale. Sweeney's election sparked widespread hopes that he would lead the Federation down the same road he had previously traveled as president of the

Service Employees International Union (SEIU): reversing the tide of de-unionization with imaginative strategies to rebuild union density in previously organized sectors where serious erosion had occurred, while at the same time establishing labor's presence in new and growing areas of the economy. The SEIU's iconic "Justice for Janitors" campaign of the early 1990s already had vividly demonstrated how new workers (in this case immigrants) in de-unionized building service jobs could be galvanized into action to restore union recognition and, against all odds, extract concessions from employers (Waldinger et al. 1998). And although they used more conventional strategies and tactics than in the janitors' drive, successful SEIU campaigns in nursing homes and other health care settings had also shown the potential for service sector unionization beyond the traditional strongholds of organized labor.

The SEIU's pioneering organizing initiatives, along with similar developments in the Hotel Employees and Restaurant Employees (HERE) and a few other highly innovative unions, raised hopes in many quarters that the lethargic "business unionism" that dominated postwar America could be supplanted by what has come to be called "social movement unionism"—hopes that gained momentum during Sweeney's initial years as AFL-CIO president. Drawing heavily on the staff who had helped revitalize the SEIU (some insiders quipped that the AFL-CIO was becoming the "AFL-SEIU"), Sweeney swept aside most of the old guard that had long run the Federation by installing younger, college-educated cadre, including many seasoned veterans of progressive social movements. This new generation of union leaders has been deeply committed to the project of labor renewal and has been prepared to use unorthodox tactics toward that end.

The Sweeney era produced some important breakthroughs. Indeed, in the late 1990s union density finally slowed its downward plunge. Given the rapid growth of the workforce in the late 1990s and the steady erosion of union membership through layoffs, retirements, deaths, business relocations and so forth, just keeping density stable—as the labor movement came close to doing in the late 1990s—has not been an insignificant accomplishment. Going beyond this to actually increase density, however, has proven to be an elusive goal. New organizing has produced membership gains, but these have been modest, concentrated in a few occupations and industries, and limited geographically as well. Examples abound of imaginative, successful campaigns that demonstrate the potential for change—several are analyzed in this volume—but thus far no one has been able to replicate them on a large enough scale to significantly impact the overall density problem. Moreover, as Kate Bronfenbrenner and Robert Hickey show in the first chapter of this volume, only a few AFL-CIO affiliates have acted on Sweeney's exhortations to refocus union efforts on organizing. The initial excitement of 1995 has given way to a more sober reckoning that is far less optimistic and in some quarters has led to deep demoralization.

Historically, union growth always has been uneven, with long troughs and occasional giant waves (Clawson 2003). The surges of growth have never been predictable—indeed, in the early 1930s, who could have imagined the rise of the CIO? It remains to be seen whether the embryonic organizing break-throughs of the past decade will generate a new wave of mass union growth, or whether the labor movement will remain hopelessly mired in the welter of employer resistance, internal bureaucratic inertia, worldwide neoliberal hege-mony, and an increasingly hostile domestic political environment. What are the prospects for a broader labor movement resurgence? What obstacles stand in the way of replicating the organizing gains that have been made over the past decade on a large enough scale to give unions real influence once again, of the sort they enjoyed in the 1940s? Those are among the questions posed by the chapters in this volume.

A STALLED REVOLUTION?

Many commentators have discussed the formidable external obstacles to union revitalization. For example, it is well documented that employers' anti-union strategies have become increasingly sophisticated in response to the new organizing approaches developed by the labor movement over the past decade, so that the bar unions must overcome is continually being raised (Bronfenbrenner 2000; Bronfenbrenner and Hickey 2002). Transnational cor-porations have developed especially potent and sophisticated approaches to countering union organizing efforts in their U.S.-based facilities, as Bronfenbrenner and Hickey note in this volume.

The political environment also presents major problems. Even under the relatively sympathetic Clinton administration, which was the context in which Sweeney's program was first launched, labor law reform proved impossible. And since the 2000 election, the political climate at the national level has dete-riorated dramatically, producing one of the most virulently anti-union administrations in many decades. The pervasiveness of neoliberal ideology, which undermines the legitimacy of *any* collective action project designed to affect the labor market, is another critical barrier that any union organizing effort must seek to overcome. Given these myriad external difficulties, at times it seems miraculous that any organizing successes are possible at all.

Yet the problems are not only external. Significant difficulties within the labor movement itself also have contributed to the present impasse. Most importantly, relatively few unions have seriously attempted to implement the Sweeney program. As Bronfenbrenner and Hickey's chapter in this volume demonstrates in compelling detail, only a handful of the AFL-CIO's sixty-five affiliates are actually engaged in organizing on any significant scale. Equally important, this analysis shows that even the most active affiliates do not consistently launch the strategically focused, comprehensive campaigns using rank-and-file-intensive tactics that have proven most effective in the current political and economic environment.

Bronfenbrenner and Hickey show that only about six Internationals have vigorously pursued the new organizing agenda that Sweeney promoted with such fanfare. Besides SEIU and HERE, which stand out as leaders even within this small group of unions, they identify the Union of Needletrades, Industrial and Textile Employees (UNITE); the Communication Workers of America (CWA); the American Federation of State, County and Municipal Workers (AFSCME); and the United Auto Workers (UAW) as the key players in the 1990s, each of which has achieved some major organizing victories. But few other unions have followed suit: most are hardly attempting to recruit new members at all. And even among those that are actively organizing, many fail in their efforts, largely because they continue to use obsolete approaches that savvy employers can easily neutralize. The result is that for all but a handful of unions, membership continues to hemorrhage, while their limited (or nonexistent) organizing activity makes the overall challenge of increasing density seem insurmountable, generating a vicious circle of demoralization and decline.

Why is it that so few unions, despite Sweeney's tireless encouragement, have followed the lead of SEIU and the other unions that have shown the way forward? One answer is that effective organizing consumes huge resources—money, staff time, intellectual and legal talent, and so forth. To organize a few thousand workers can take years, cost millions of dollars, and exhaust the capacity of already-stretched union staffers. Can the modest benefits of any single campaign really justify such enormous costs? Will the incremental membership gains that result have any significant impact on the density problem, for an individual union, industry, or sector—or for the labor movement as a whole? Not only outside commentators but also many progressive unionists ponder these questions regularly as they seek to maximize the impact of scarce resources, and to balance the work of serving their existing membership against the challenge of recruiting new workers into the fold.

The cost-benefit dilemma is a serious one for union leaders. Yet, union organizing efforts can be highly effective when key clusters of tactics are used in combination, as Bronfenbrenner and Hickey argue persuasively in this volume—offering systematic empirical evidence in support of the union slogan, "Si, se puede!" (Yes, it can be done!) If all sixty-five affiliates of the AFL-CIO were as active and strategically sophisticated in organizing the unorganized as the SEIU, the resulting quantitative gains in union membership might even translate into a qualitative leap forward. Moreover, if the alternative to expending major resources on new organizing is the slow (or perhaps not so slow) death of organized labor as a major social force, then investing all available resources in the project is simply imperative.

Yet, the daily reality on the ground is rather different—at least from the viewpoint of the individual labor leaders who are in a position to deploy or withhold resources for organizing. Most of these leaders are fully aware of the density crisis and of the fact that the very survival of organized labor is potentially at stake. But the decentralized structure of the American labor movement means that the lived experience of this crisis is highly fragmented. In some local unions—and it is at the local level that most organizing efforts are initiated—membership is stable, and the day-to-day work involves contract administration and other routine tasks. In such contexts, union officials may well be complacent about the larger crisis of the labor movement. Moreover, especially if they are elected (as opposed to appointed) leaders, they may be reluctant to bear the considerable risks involved in new organizing, even if adequate resources are available. From their perspective, while a major organizing success might have a large political payoff, a failure could be a career-breaker. In fact, even a success can be problematic if it overturns the political status quo of the local. In the absence of any attractive employment alternatives, most such officials, particularly the middle-aged (or older) functionaries who are at the helm of so many local unions, tend to be quite cautious in this regard. For them, avoiding the risks inherent in undertaking major organizing efforts is entirely rational, and this political calculus must figure prominently in any effort to explain why organizing activity is so limited.

Even when local leaders are prepared to take a chance on organizing, however, success is unlikely without extensive support from the International union (Voss and Sherman 2000). At the level of the International, union officials tend to be appointed rather than elected—and even when elected are unlikely to be deposed given the one-party-like systems that govern most Internationals. Even though in most cases they run little or no political risk by investing in organizing, International union leaders are nonetheless habitually cautious and wary. They tend to be even older than their local counterparts, and thus perhaps even less concerned about the long-term outlook for the movement as a whole. And for most of them, to impose change on reluctant local leaders is hardly the course of least resistance. Thus at the International level too, many union leaders are reluctant to invest the resources required for serious organizing initiatives. While they may echo the rhetoric of reform, few have taken the necessary practical steps toward implementing Sweeney's call to focus on rebuilding their base.

The AFL-CIO itself, while occasionally providing resources for its affiliates' individual organizing campaigns (in the shape of extra staff or funding), does virtually no organizing on its own. The fact that the Federation is plagued by a plethora of internal divisions and inter-union rivalries does not help matters (Lerner 2003, 26). Indeed, over the years some unions have disaffiliated entirely from the AFL-CIO, most notably the Carpenters. The fragmented and decentralized structure of the Federation, and the mistrust many individual locals and Internationals harbor toward one another, also makes it difficult to build multi-union organizing efforts, which in the abstract would appear to offer a promising strategy for large-scale sectoral organizing. In the exceptional cases where such efforts have been launched, they have proven difficult to sustain because of the internal tensions within labor's ranks (for an example, see Delgado 2000).

"Raiding" is a related problem, which involves one union persuading already-organized workers who are members of another union to switch their affiliation. This boosts the membership of the raiding union (and may even be presented as an "organizing" victory), though it has no impact whatsoever on the overall density problem. And of course raiding involves unions expending valuable resources fighting one another rather than focusing on the challenges facing the movement as a whole. Certainly this does not contribute in any meaningful way to the formidable task of redirecting resources into organizing the unorganized on a large scale.

Yet another obstacle to transforming the labor movement is the gender and ethnic mismatch between union leadership and that of the vast unorganized sector of the workforce. Despite the Sweeney administration's efforts to increase diversity at the highest levels of labor's officialdom, the majority of union officials are still older, native-born white males, who often have difficulty appealing to the nation's increasingly female, foreign-born and relatively youthful workforce. There are more women and minorities at all levels of labor leadership today than in the past, but in most cases their representation remains limited to that of tokens. Insensitivity or simple obliviousness on the part of labor leaders to the issues that can move women, immigrants, and young workers is the inevitable result, despite several initiatives Sweeney has launched to reach out to these groups.

Not only must the composition of union leadership change in order for organizing the unorganized to assume center stage, but the organizational structure and culture of unions must be overhauled as well. This is especially true at the local level, where the longstanding organizational focus has been contract enforcement and member services. The vast majority of local union staff positions remain dedicated to these functions, as do the overwhelming majority of funds and other resources (Milkman and Rooks 2003). And local union culture has reflected these priorities as well, so that many members have learned to view their unions as quasi-insurance companies or lawyers—calling on union representatives when problems arise at work, but otherwise not participating much in union affairs.

Ultimately, in order to recruit new members on a scale that would be required to significantly rebuild union power, unions must fundamentally alter their internal organizational practices to direct staff resources to organizing (Voss and Sherman 2000; Fletcher and Hurd 2001). This means shifting priorities away from servicing current members and toward unionizing new ones—creating more organizer positions on the staff; developing programs to teach current members how to handle the tasks involved in resolving shop-floor grievances, so that existing staff are freed up to work on external organizing; and building programs that train members to participate fully in the work of external organizing. Such a reorientation entails redefining the very meaning of union membership from a relatively passive stance toward one of continuous active engagement. For unions, as for any other type of organization, such a fundamental shift in orientation faces many obstacles—perhaps most importantly, confronting the formidable forces of bureaucratic inertia.

In the unions that *have* been successfully transformed, the process typically has been orchestrated from the top, contrary to the rather romantic view that only the rank and file can be the fount of democratic change (Voss and Sherman 2000). The prime example here is SEIU, and Stephen Lerner, one of the architects of the janitorial campaigns that have been so central to sparking the wave of union revitalization in the 1990s, unapologetically asserts that a key element of J for J's success was the institutional decision not to tolerate local leaders who did not want to organize. Lerner argues that in order for the labor movement to rebuild, it needs union leaders who are fully committed to putting organizing first, who are willing to focus all the institutional resources they control on that task, and who are willing to create moral and physical crises in the workplace in order to overcome employer opposition. Mass organizing, he contends, justifies a ruthless approach to purging any union staffers who refuse to go along with the program. This can involve forcing union mergers to rationalize collective bargaining regimes and ongoing organizing efforts, using trusteeships to bring resistant locals into line, as well as other seemingly undemocratic tactics (Lerner 2001). While this approach has engendered a stream of criticism from some quarters, no one can deny that the SEIU has by far the best record of recruiting new members and of advancing the difficult but crucial process of organizational change.

Yet lasting transformation *does* require genuine rank-and-file participation, so that members come to sense their ownership of the organization, a dilemma that Teresa Sharpe's chapter in this volume excavates in detail. This is the key strength of the HERE approach to organizing, which involves an intensive phase of training rank-and-file union members in a wide variety of leadership skills. These include: how to articulate the value and meaning of union building; how to persuade unorganized workers to commit themselves to that task, even at the risk of their (already precarious) livelihoods; and how to build confidence that union members themselves can successfully resolve problems in the workplace without relying on business agents or other experts. The process of worker empowerment is extremely labor-intensive, and HERE may be the only union to have fully developed the commitment and organizational capacity to implement such an approach across a range of different campaigns. Sharpe's chapter shows in rich detail just how complex this process is and exposes the tension between the inevitable reliance on the leadership and expertise of professional organizers, on the one side, and the urgency of transferring real decision-making power to the rank and file, on the other.

Yet another obstacle to new organizing is the unpleasant reality that in many contexts rank-and-file workers are not inherently pro-union, as the chapters by Steven Lopez and Robert Penney in this volume vividly demonstrate. Lopez's study of nursing home organizing in the "rust belt" exposes the very negative view of unions held by many workers who witnessed the devolution of industrial unions firsthand in the 1980s. That historical legacy is a major obstacle for the new unionism. Lopez shows that it can be surmounted, but that accomplishing this requires enormously nuanced strategic thinking and experienced leadership of just the sort that SEIU has developed. Penney, who also studied SEIU campaigns in the Midwest (although in hospitals rather than nursing homes), goes even further in emphasizing the conservatism of rank-and-file workers. He shows that in some circumstances hospital workers actively opposed unionism, which they viewed as a likely source of conflict and hostility in the workplace, and not necessarily as leading to any material gains. These workers, while skeptical about union organizers' claims, responded positively to employer promises of advancement through cooperation with management. Penney argues that the "No on Union" committees that many commentators dismiss as transparent vehicles of management manipulation are genuinely appealing to many workers, who actively embrace them and independently take on leadership roles in opposing union campaigns. If some ambiguity remains as to the relative importance of workers' own contributions to anti-union committees as compared to management's direct or *sub rosa* support for them, there is no doubt that they are a force to be reckoned with in many organizing campaigns.

This makes the role of professional organizers all the more central to rebuilding the labor movement, whether unions adopt an approach like that of the SEIU or that of HERE. Recruiting and training energetic and savvy organizers is critical—as is retaining them. As Daisy Rooks' chapter in this volume illustrates, the occupational culture of union organizing is extremely intense, and the high level of dedication it demands is often difficult to sustain, especially in the absence of day-to-day emotional support and a serious institutional commitment to organizers as the key agents of labor movement survival and growth.

Through initiatives like the AFL-CIO's Organizing Institute (OI) and programs like Union Summer, many talented young activists have been drawn into the labor movement in recent years. Indeed, for this generation labor organizing appears to be one of the few viable arenas in which to fight for social justice. But, as Rooks shows in rich detail, holding onto these young activists has proven difficult in the face of the grueling "cowboy culture" of 24/7 campaigning—easily justified by intransigent employer anti-unionism— and the uneven commitment to change within the labor movement itself. Thus unions may thoughtlessly squander precious human resources in the desperate battle for immediate survival, while the process of long-term leadership development recedes onto the distant horizon. This is among the many reasons that the recent organizing successes of the new labor movement have yet to be replicated on any significant scale.

BUILDING THE NEW LABOR MOVEMENT

If we put the question of scale to one side, there are many hopeful examples on the local level that show the potential for labor movement expansion. HERE and SEIU provide the leading models, as we have already noted. Those two unions and others have shown how effective creative and well-crafted organizing strategies can be. And these unions have also built impressive alliances in recent years, bridging divisions within the labor movement, as well as in the wider social and political community. In addition to coalitions with student activists, labor has built ties to immigrant rights groups, environmental advocates, the anti-globalization movement, and even the peace movement—breaking from the historic social isolation that for many decades had limited labor's vision and power (Clawson 2003).

When labor pursues social movement unionism, activists in these allied movements respond positively, attracted to its far-reaching vision of social justice and impressed by its institutional resource base and longstanding political influence. This dynamic recalls the historic influence of the United Farm Workers (UFW) on a whole generation of social movement activists. Many of those who initially got involved were attracted to the UFW because they saw it as part of a larger movement for social justice rather than simply as a labor union. They soon discovered, however, that unions themselves could be a vehicle of social change, as the chapter in this volume by Marshall Ganz, Kim Voss, Teresa Sharpe, Carl Somers, and George Strauss explains. More recently, immigrant union organizing campaigns have drawn in human rights and immigrant rights activists who have come to appreciate labor's potential contribution to a larger progressive agenda.

Many of the architects of new labor, then, have experience in other social movements, and this is indeed the source of many of the innovations that are guiding labor's transformation (Voss and Sherman 2000). Activists from the 1960s and 1970s generation, who cut their teeth in the New Left, the anti-Vietnam War movement, civil rights, and the women's movement, are now top leaders in many of the most innovative unions, as well as in the AFL-CIO. They have, in turn, worked to recruit a new generation of activists and to persuade them that labor is a viable arena for social justice efforts. The tactical repertoire of the earlier generation is palpable in AFL-CIO initiatives like Union Summer and the OI. As Leslie Bunnage and Judith Stepan-Norris recount in their chapter in this volume, Union Summer was explicitly designed to replicate the success of Freedom Summer—and it was most successful when student recruits were partnered with especially innovative and forward-looking union campaigns. The OI, similarly, seeks to teach young activists the techniques of nonviolent civil disobedience and other tactics honed in the social movements of earlier eras. The union-led 2003 Immigrant Workers' Freedom Ride is another deliberate echo of the 1960s.

Electoral politics, where unions retain far more influence than the density figures would suggest, has become another important arena for the new labor movement. California, and especially Los Angeles, has emerged as a site where labor has created a virtuous circle, whereby organizing success translates into political clout and vice versa (Meyerson 2001). On the municipal level too, as Preston Rudy's chapter in this volume shows, the SEIU has experimented with coalition-building, albeit with various degrees of success, increasingly recognizing the importance of the political arena in its efforts to recruit unorganized workers. In San Jose, Rudy shows, the janitors' campaign succeeded in part because it was able to tap into the political visibility and public legitimacy of a preexisting anti-growth coalition; however, the failure of a parallel effort in Sacramento suggests that alternative political strategies are necessary in certain contexts. In Sacramento, where a pro-growth coalition held power, SEIU activists experienced many setbacks before they found a way to define janitors' poverty as an issue of public concern, rather than as simply a private matter between workers and their employers. That SEIU activists were eventually successful in this effort suggests that labor is becoming much more savvy and effective in the political arena at both the municipal and state levels.

The same kind of careful strategic thinking is imperative for success in individual organizing campaigns at the workplace level. Not only, as Bronfenbrenner and Hickey's chapter shows, can comprehensive campaigns that draw on the full range of tactics in labor's arsenal be successful, even when faced with determined employer resistance, but in addition, and contrary to popular belief, there is no economic downside here. For as DiNardo and Lee's (this volume) analysis of more than 27,000 union certification elections between 1983 and 2000 reveals, successfully unionized establishments are no less likely to survive in the marketplace than their non-union counterparts. All this offers a basis for optimism: if the labor movement could effectively combine the successful strategies that Bronfenbrenner and Hickey highlight at the workplace level with those Rudy and others document in the political arena, and replicate both on a large scale, labor could emerge as a formidable social force once again.

OUTLINE OF THE VOLUME

We begin with Bronfenbrenner and Hickey's broad overview of the current state of union organizing in the United States. This analysis scrutinizes the organizing records of International unions in the late 1990s in extensive detail, emphasizing that the "New Labor" phenomenon is in actuality limited to a few key unions. The chapter provides both a sobering assessment of the accomplishments of this segment of the labor movement and a blueprint of the tactical repertoire that the innovative unions have successfully deployed to overcome employer opposition to new organizing.

The next three chapters look at the organizing process from a different vantage point, using qualitative data to evaluate campaigns launched by HERE and SEIU over the past several years. Sharpe's ethnographic study of a hotel organizing campaign exposes the complex process by which professional organizers create space for rank-and-file workers to become leaders, while still using their own expertise to guide the campaign strategy. She offers a very nuanced view of union democracy, going well beyond the standard focus on leadership turnover and the structure of union governance. This case study reveals the tension between building a participatory model of unionism and capitalizing on the accumulated knowledge of experienced organizers. That the hotel campaign deliberately avoided the traditional NLRB electoral road to unionization makes Sharpe's research of even greater interest, since there are so few studies of alternative organizing approaches.

Even less frequently examined is the reality of rank-and-file anti-unionism that is the focus of the next two chapters. Penney's study of workers who actively oppose union organizing campaigns is a pioneering analysis of a topic that few labor scholars are prepared to confront. It shows that unions are anathema to many workers—to the point that some will actively invest time and effort in assiduous resistance to union appeals. Penney takes the anti-union stance of these workers seriously, arguing that members of "Vote No" committees like the ones he interviewed are genuinely committed to the anti-union cause, even if they are being manipulated by management. Unpleasant as it may be, organizers need to understand this increasingly common phenomenon if they are to function effectively.

In other cases, workers may not actively organize against unions but they may nevertheless vote "no" in union elections. Steven Lopez documents an example of this in a context in which employer opposition was relatively mild. He compares two successive efforts to organize the same group of nursing home workers, one that failed and one that succeeded, confronting the reasons why even highly aggrieved workers often view unions as "do-nothing" organizations, as corrupt, or even as the cause of economic decline. Lopez shows that using the tactics Bronfenbrenner and Hickey recommend can indeed be effective, but argues that organizers must go even further by directly confronting workers' negative lived experience of unionism and by demonstrating with their actions that the new social movement unionism is distinctly different.

Recent literature on organizing tends to focus on the content of the campaigns themselves, paying less attention to the broader context in which they are embedded. However, Rudy's chapter highlights the role of the political environment and of the external forces that shape union campaigns. His comparative analysis of two SEIU janitorial organizing drives in northern California reveals the importance of framing labor struggles in broad terms that reach beyond the parochial, narrow definition of labor as a "special interest." Rudy shows that achieving this is far more difficult in some settings than others, depending on both the history of the local labor movement and on the skill of anti-union forces in defining labor as a narrow, special interest group. In one of his case studies, for example, Democratic politicians who might otherwise have supported labor were reliant on the targeted employers for financial and electoral support. Rudy also demonstrates the ways in which successful organizing campaigns can reshape the political context itself.

Taken together, these case studies expose many of the dilemmas confronting the leaders of the new labor movement. Not only must they face the challenges of building a more participatory democratic union culture, which traditionalists within the union officialdom themselves often resist, but they also are up against deeply entrenched anti-union sentiment from employers and the political establishment, as well as among workers themselves. How do unions recruit leaders who are prepared to confront these formidable obstacles? That is the subject of the next three chapters.

In the first, Ganz and his collaborators look at the generation of activists who entered organized labor in the 1970s and early 1980s, many of them veterans of the 1960s wave of protest movements. The data are drawn from a unique longitudinal study of California labor leaders who were first interviewed in 1984 and re-interviewed 18 years later. Today, several of them hold prominent positions in both state and national unions. This study not only highlights the reasons that this generation of leaders chose the labor move-ment as the arena for their work—well before the reforms of the 1990s—but also reveals the role some of them played in that transformation process. In addition, it examines in detail the ways in which individuals adapt to and help perpetuate established organizational cultures, as well as the reasons why some deliberately work to change those cultures.

The two chapters that follow shift the focus to a younger generation of labor organizers. Unlike the older leaders, the newer cohort was actively recruited into the labor movement through special outreach programs designed to attract student activists—part of New Labor's effort to break out of its social isolation and to make labor a social movement once again. Rooks' study of organizer retention focuses on the Organizing Institute, perhaps the most high-profile of these efforts. She shows that many factors conspire to erode the enthusiasm and commitment to social justice with which young recruits begin their labor work, highlighting the gap between the political ideals that motivate them and the reality on the ground in many of the local unions in which they are placed. Rooks documents the very high turnover typical of these young organizers and shows that one of the few effective means of reducing it is the presence of supportive peers—something that has received surprisingly limited attention, even from the leaders most dedicated to labor's new agenda.

Bunnage and Stepan-Norris examine another Sweeney-era program ori-ented to recruiting young activists: Union Summer. They trace the origins of the program and its implementation in 1996 and then turn to explore the experiences of the first group of student recruits. Whereas the Organizing Institute was designed to attract young people into labor movement careers, Union Summer had a somewhat different purpose: to engage students on a short-term basis in labor's struggles and to build bridges to other progressive movements on college campuses and in the wider community. Bunnage and Stepan-Norris attempt to sort out the circumstances under which students were successfully integrated into unions' organizing campaigns, as well as the factors that led some students to make a longer-term commitment to labor. Their chapter also includes an epilogue on how Union Summer has changed since it was first launched in 1996.

The volume concludes with a chapter that examines the effects of union organizing on the economic viability of the firms involved. Contrary to the view often repeated by employers (and at times echoed by workers themselves, as Lopez's chapter notes), Lee and DiNardo's rigorous quantitative analysis finds that union victory in an NLRB representation election has no effect on establishment survival. This important finding is powerful ammunition for the ongoing political debates about labor's future in the context of intensifying economic competition. Of course, even if unions did have negative economic effects, one might argue that their other social benefits are worth the cost, but this chapter suggests that this presumed tradeoff is nonexistent.

TOWARD A RESEARCH AGENDA FOR NEW LABOR

During the 1930s, which was the last time there was a giant wave of union growth in the United States, intellectuals and labor activists actively collaborated to address the dilemmas faced by U.S. workers, jointly challenging corporate domination, social injustice, and economic insecurity (Lichtenstein 2002). Many of the contributions in this volume suggest the potential fruitfulness of reviving this tradition of labor-academic cooperation, while once again labor struggles to renew its power. Thus research like that of DiNardo and Lee can be used by labor activists to counter the claim that unions serve only to undermine business survival. Studies like Bronfenbrenner and Hickey's can be used by union reformers to influence labor leaders who resist change. Findings like those of Rooks; Bunnage and Stepan-Norris; and Ganz and his co-authors can be a resource for both local unions and the AFL-CIO to design more effective programs to attract and integrate activists from other social movements into organized labor. And organizers can use research like Lopez's and Penney's to design campaigns that better address the concerns of anti-union workers.

However, the academic-labor relationship is a two-way street: active engagement with the new labor movement can deeply enrich scholarly research too, as the studies collected in this volume illustrate. It is no accident that many of our contributors were themselves former organizers: Ganz spent many years as the UFW's Organizing Director; both Rooks and Sharpe are former OI staffers; Bunnage was on the staff of Union Summer; Penney is a former SEIU organizer; and Rudy, Bronfenbrenner and Hickey all have labor organizing experience as well. In addition, Sharpe and Lopez volunteered or interned in the campaigns they studied. More generally, the recent revitalization of labor has sparked a new wave of research on organizing, after many years of neglect of the topic. This new scholarship is not only being undertaken by former organizers but also draws in researchers from a variety of disciplinary backgrounds and theoretical persuasions. A new generation of labor scholars has emerged, whose growing body of work is not only important in its own right, but may eventually contribute valuable new insights to our understanding of organizational change and to the advancement of democratic practices, not only in institutional settings but in the wider civil society as well.

Important as the contributions collected here are, they also neglect some important questions. Perhaps the most urgent of these is to explore more fully what happens *after* organizing drives succeed. How often do unions get contracts after winning recognition, and under what conditions? What are the costs of employers' anti-union campaigns and the polarization they cause within the workforce? DiNardo and Lee pose some of these questions, but their research thus far does not offer any definitive conclusions.

Another aspect of the aftermath of organizing campaigns also deserves more attention, namely, how to sustain participatory social movement practices after union recognition has been achieved? Sharpe's chapter suggests the importance of such practices, but the question of how to maintain them over the long haul is a pressing one that has barely been studied (one exception is Markowitz 2000). A related issue concerns the incorporation of immigrants and other underrepresented groups into union leadership positions. Even the legendary Justice for Janitors campaigns often have precipitated leadership struggles between newly organized immigrant workers and old-guard (native-born) union leaders. More broadly, unions have been much better at incorporating immigrants, women, and racial and ethnic minorities into membership than into leadership positions. This problem is salient even at the local union level, and far worse in the upper reaches of labor's officialdom.

Finally, successful organizing campaigns may have implications for broader efforts to democratize society. We know from the work of Robert Putnam (2000) and Theda Skopol (2003) that civic participation has declined sharply in the United States, and that there are precious few "schools for democracy" in America today. Can the empowerment generated by social movement unionism spill over into other aspects of social life? Will workers who learn to resolve their own problems at work also be more likely to intervene productively in the schools their children attend and in the communities where their families live? If so, social movement unionism can help rebuild not only organized labor itself but also democratic practices more broadly. In that case, not only those of us concerned about labor's revitalization for its own sake, but also anyone interested in fostering progressive social and political change, can profit from the insights of the new wave of research on organizing that is represented in the following pages.

■ ■ ■

The chapters in this book were first presented at a conference organized by the editors under the auspices of the University of California's Institute for Labor and Employment, held at UCLA on May 17, 2001. We thank the ILE for its support as well as the scholars who served as discussants for the gathering: Sanford Jacoby, Nelson Lichtenstein, and Margaret Weir. All the papers were improved as a result of their insightful critiques as well as the group discussion at the conference. We also are indebted to Richard Freeman and Richard Flacks, both of whom reviewed the manuscript for Cornell University Press, and whose comments and suggestions much improved the volume. Finally we thank Fran Benson, editor extraordinaire, whose support for this project went far beyond the call of duty.

1

CHANGING TO ORGANIZE

A NATIONAL ASSESSMENT OF UNION STRATEGIES

Kate Bronfenbrenner and Robert Hickey

In 1995 "changing to organize" became the mantra of a newly invigorated labor movement. There was talk of building a national organizing fund, recruiting thousands of new young organizers, and organizing millions of workers in new occupations and industries. In the years that followed, the AFL-CIO and its affiliates engaged in an aggressive effort to increase their organizing capacity and success. Staff and financial resources were shifted into organizing; leaders, members, and central labor bodies were mobilized to support organizing campaigns; and hundreds of new organizers were recruited from college campuses and the rank and file.

By 1999, it appeared that these efforts and initiatives were paying off when the media reported a net gain of 265,000 in union membership—the first such gain in more than twenty years (AFL-CIO 2000). But this would not last. Even leaving aside the tragic and unusual events of September 11, 2001, it is clear that despite all the new initiatives and resources being devoted to organizing and all the talk of "changing to organize," American unions have been standing still at best. The major victories have been highly concentrated in a few unions (SEIU, HERE, UNITE, CWA, AFSCME, and UAW) and industries (healthcare, building services, hotels, airlines, telecommunications, and higher education), while the majority of unions continue to experience organizing losses and declining membership (BNA PLUS 2001).

In this chapter we seek to answer the following questions: Why has it been so difficult for unions to turn the organizing efforts and initiatives of the last six years into any significant gains in union density? Why have a small number of unions been able to make major gains through organizing? And most importantly, which organizing strategies will be most effective in reversing the tide of the labor movement's organizing decline?

What our findings will show is that while the political, legal, and economic climate for organizing continues to deteriorate, and private sector employers continue to mount aggressive opposition to organizing efforts, some unions are winning. Our findings also show that the unions that are most successful at organizing run fundamentally different campaigns, in both quality and intensity, than those that are less successful, and that those differences hold true across a wide range of organizing environments, company characteristics, bargaining unit demographics, and employer campaign variables.

PREVIOUS ORGANIZING RESEARCH

Industrial relations research has provided important insights regarding the influence of environmental factors, company characteristics, and employer behavior on the outcome of NLRB certification elections (Farber and Western 2001; Kochan, Katz and McKersie 1994; Freeman and Kleiner 1988; Maranto and Fiorito 1987; Rose and Chaison 1990). This research has also deepened our understanding of the factors shaping attitudes toward unions and the individual union voter decision making process (Jarley and Fiorito 1991; Freeman and Rogers 1999; Weikle, Wheeler and McClendon 1998). Another stream of research has focused on the impact that institutional characteristics of unions have on organizing success (Fiorito, Jarley and Delaney 1995; Hurd and Bunge 2002). Yet, with the exception of a handful of studies, most quantitative organizing research has failed to capture the critical role played by union strategies in organizing campaigns (Bronfenbrenner 1997a; Bronfenbrenner and Juravich 1998; and Peterson, Lee, and Finnegan 1992).

A small but growing body of qualitative case study research does explore the role of union strategies in the organizing process, exposing the interactions between environmental factors, employer behavior, and union strategies (Hoerr 1997; Waldinger and Erickson et al. 1998; Sciacchitano 1998; Juravich and Hilgert 1999; Delp and Quan 2002). By capturing the dynamic role of union strategies, this research also provides much needed insight into how the organizing process actually develops. However, this literature suffers from the limitations of case study designs that can capture only a small number of organizing campaigns, representing the most dramatic or interesting cases (and almost all victories), and as such, are often unrepresentative of union organizing behavior.

Bronfenbrenner's survey of 261 private-sector NLRB certification elections in 1986 and 1987 was the first detailed study of the role of union tactics in organizing and first contract campaigns (Bronfenbrenner 1993; 1997a). The study showed that unions were more likely to win NLRB elections if they used rank-and-file intensive tactics such as person-to-person contact, active representative committees, member volunteer organizers, solidarity days, and building for the first contract before the election. This research also found that union tactics as a group had a more significant impact on election outcomes than other groups of variables that have been the traditional focus of industrial relations research, such as election environment, bargaining unit demographics, and employer characteristics (1993; 1997a). This was an important finding, because some researchers (such as William Dickens 1983) had argued that union tactics were entirely reactive—determined solely by management tactics. Subsequent quantitative studies of both private-sector NLRB elections and public-sector organizing campaigns have reinforced Bronfenbrenner's earlier research (Bronfenbrenner 1997c, 2000, and 2002; Bronfenbrenner and Juravich 1998; Juravich and Bronfenbrenner 1998).

However, in the more than ten years since this research was initiated, a great deal has changed in the economy, employer behavior, and the labor movement itself. Workers in almost every industry face more sophisticated employer opposition to organizing that is coupled with dramatic increases in corporate restructuring, foreign trade and investment, and shifts in work and production to other companies and other countries (Bronfenbrenner 2000, 2001). As Bronfenbrenner and Juravich found in their study of 1994 NLRB campaigns, traditional organizing approaches and the isolated use of innovative tactics have decreased in effectiveness (1998). Although some individual tactics, such as representative committees, workplace job actions, and media campaigns have a statistically significant positive impact on election outcomes, other tactics, such as house-calling the majority of the unit, holding solidarity days, staging rallies, or running a community campaign, did not have a significant impact. Yet, when these variables were combined into a single union tactics variable, adding one unit for each additional tactic, the probability of the union winning the election increased by as much as 9 percent for each additional tactic used. This suggests that the effectiveness of union tactics is strategically significant when unions combine tactics in a more comprehensive campaign.

In the years following the 1994 study, research by Bronfenbrenner and others has continued to show that comprehensive union tactics still hold the key to successful organizing efforts. Unions that use a broad range of union tactics as part of a multifaceted comprehensive strategy display greater organizing success across all industries, bargaining unit demographics, and employer characteristics and behaviors (Bronfenbrenner 1997c, 2002; Sherman and Voss 2000).

Sherman and Voss (2000), in their study of local union organizing in Northern California, argue that the implementation of innovative tactics, such as rank-and-file intensive organizing and strategic targeting, requires far-reaching organizational transformation. Without such organizational transformation, unions may use some innovative tactics, but are unlikely to integrate a comprehensive union-building strategy. Indeed, Sherman and Voss found that the locals using a comprehensive union-building strategy are also the most innovative organizationally. This challenge to transform organizationally in order to fully implement innovative tactics suggests one reason why the dispersion of comprehensive union-building strategies has been so limited.

RESEARCH METHODS

The data analyzed in this chapter were collected as part of a larger study commissioned in May 2000 by the United States Trade Deficit Review Commission to update Bronfenbrenner's previous research on the impact of capital mobility on union organizing and first contract campaigns in the U.S. private sector (Bronfenbrenner 1997b, 2000). Using surveys, personal interviews, documentary evidence, and electronic databases, we compiled detailed data on election background, organizing environment, bargaining unit demographics, company characteristics and tactics, labor board charges and determinations, union characteristics and tactics, and election and first contract outcomes for 412 NLRB certification election campaigns held in 1998 and 1999.

Our original random sample of 600 elections was derived from data compiled by the Bureau of National Affairs (BNA) of all NLRB single-union certification election campaigns in units with fifty or more eligible voters that took place in 1998–1999 (BNA PLUS 2000).[1] For each case in the sample we conducted in-depth surveys of the lead organizer for the campaign by mail and phone. We also searched computerized corporate, media, legal, and union databases, and reviewed Security and Exchange Commission filings, IRS 990 forms, and NLRB documents to collect data on company ownership, structure, operations, employment, financial condition, unionization, and employer characteristics and practices.

We were able to complete surveys for 412 of the 600 cases in the sample, for a response rate of 69 percent. Further, we were able to collect corporate ownership, structure, and financial information for 99 percent of the 412 cases. NLRB data were compiled from the FAST database for 65 percent of the

136 cases where NLRB charges were filed, while NLRB documents were collected for 46 percent. Summary statistics for the sample reveal that it is representative of the population of all NLRB certification elections in units over fifty that took place in 1998–1999 in terms of both industry and outcomes (BNA Plus 2000).

Descriptive statistics were calculated for a wide range of variables in order to capture the nature and extent of union and employer organizing activity and the broader context in which they operate. In addition, binary logistic regression was used to determine whether the number of comprehensive union-building strategies has a statistically significant impact on certification election outcome when controlling for the influence of election background, company characteristics, bargaining unit demographics, and employer opposition.

THEORETICAL MODEL AND HYPOTHESES

This research builds on the theoretical model developed by Bronfenbrenner (1993), and Bronfenbrenner and Juravich (1997) in previous organizing studies. According to this model, environmental factors plus union and employer characteristics and strategies combine to affect the election outcome both indirectly as they moderate the effect of other factors and directly as they influence worker propensity to vote for the union.[2] Under this model, union organizing tactics are an extremely important element of the organizing process. They play just as much—if not even a greater—role in determining election outcome than environmental factors and company characteristics and tactics.

This study tests two hypotheses. The first is that union success in certification elections depends on a comprehensive union-building strategy that incorporates the following ten elements, each of which is a cluster of key union tactics, that we argue are critical to union organizing success in the current environment: (1) adequate and appropriate staff and financial resources, (2) strategic targeting, (3) active and representative rank-and-file organizing committees, (4) active participation of member volunteer organizers, (5) person-to-person contact inside and outside the workplace, (6) benchmarks and assessments to monitor union support and set thresholds for moving ahead with the campaign, (7) issues which resonate in the workplace and in the community, (8) creative, escalating internal pressure tactics involving members in the workplace, (9) creative, escalating external pressure tactics involving members outside the workplace, locally, nationally, and/or internationally, (10) building for the first contract during the organizing campaign.[3]

This model expands upon Bronfenbrenner and Juravich's 1998 study by arguing that in the current organizing environment it is not enough to use as many union tactics as possible; rather, certain strategic elements, each comprised of clusters of key tactics, are essential ingredients for union organizing success. These strategic elements, which we will call comprehensive organizing tactics, may each be associated with higher win rates and/or have statistically significant positive effects on election outcomes. However, given the hostile climate in which unions must operate, we hypothesize that the use of these individual comprehensive organizing tactics will not be enough. Instead, union gains will depend on a multifaceted campaign utilizing as many of the ten comprehensive organizing tactics as possible. We hypothesize that the likelihood a union will win an election significantly increases for each additional comprehensive organizing tactic used by the union.

Our second hypothesis is that differences in the quality and intensity of the campaigns between unions are a better predictor of differences in election outcomes for those unions than employer opposition, bargaining unit demographics, or company or industry characteristics. We do not suggest that industry, corporate structure, unit type, worker demographics, or employer opposition do not matter. As our previous research has shown, all of these factors have a very powerful and significant impact on union win rates (Bronfenbrenner 1997a, 1997c, 2001; Bronfenbrenner and Juravich 1998). Indeed, it is more difficult to organize mobile industries, such as metal production and fabrication, garment and textile, food processing, and call centers, in the current global trade and investment climate. It is also more difficult to organize subsidiaries of large multinational corporations that have the resources to launch a full-scale counterattack against the union campaign. Furthermore, higher paid, primarily white male, blue collar, white collar, and professional and technical occupations are more difficult to organize in the current climate, because they tend to be more invested in the internal labor markets and more affected by threats of job loss or blacklisting that are typical in employer campaigns today (Bronfenbrenner 1997a; 2001). Although industry, unit type, worker demographics, and employer characteristics and tactics matter, union tactics matter more, because unions have so far to go before they live up to their full potential. While the majority of unions today run very weak campaigns with no underlying strategy, the majority of employers run very strategic campaigns, taking full advantage of the range of effective anti-union tactics available to them, and adapting and tailoring those tactics, depending on the organizing environment and the union's campaign.

If all unions were running aggressive comprehensive campaigns, and win rates continued to vary across the organizing environments in which individual unions operate, then these differences in organizing environment would play the primary role in explaining the variance in organizing success between unions. Instead, we hypothesize that the more successful unions owe their organizing victories to the nature, quality, intensity, and comprehensiveness of their campaigns, across a diversity of industries, companies, bargaining units, and employer campaigns. Similarly, unions with lower win rates lose more elections because of the lack of intensity, quality, and comprehensiveness of the campaigns they run, rather than the organizing environment in which they operate.

We first test the hypotheses by comparing means, frequencies, and win rates for each of the comprehensive organizing tactics that make up our model, both individually and as part of the additive comprehensive organizing tactics variable. This will allow us to see whether, in accordance with our first hypothesis, win rates improve as the number of comprehensive organizing tactics increases. We will also test different combinations of comprehensive organizing tactics in order to ensure that all of the elements of our model contribute to union organizing success when added together with the other elements of the model. Next, we will compare means, frequencies, and win rates for company characteristics, bargaining unit demographics, and employer behavior in campaigns where unions used a comprehensive union-building strategy, including more than five of the comprehensive organizing tactics listed above, as compared to campaigns where unions used five or fewer comprehensive organizing tactics.[4] This will allow us to see both the nature of the environment in which unions are organizing today and whether, in accordance with our second hypothesis, union win rates increase across different industry, company, unit, and employer characteristics when the union runs more comprehensive campaigns.

We then will use binary logistic regression to test the hypothesis that the odds of winning the election will significantly increase for each additional comprehensive organizing tactic used, when we control for election background, employer characteristics, bargaining unit demographics, and employer tactics. We will also standardize the logistic regression coefficient in order to further test the relative effects of each of the statistically significant variables. We will use two models. Model A will include each of the individual elements of the comprehensive strategy, while model B will substitute a number of union tactics adding one point for each additional comprehensive tactic used. As described in appendix 1.2, the following control variables (with their predicted impact) will be included in both models: number of eligible voters (+/−);[5] manufacturing sector (−); subsidiary of a larger parent company (−); ownership change before the election (+);[6] good to excellent financial condition (+);[7] board determined unit (−); other organized units (+); professional, technical, or white collar unit (−); unit at least 60 percent women (+); unit at least 60 percent workers of color (+);[8] and number of employer tactics used (−).

We will further test the second hypothesis by examining frequencies, means, and win rates across unions. This will allow us to evaluate the relative intensity and quality of union campaigns for each union and assess which unions are most likely to use each of the comprehensive organizing tactics in our model. It will also allow us to compare win rates across unions, depending on the number of comprehensive organizing tactics used, to see whether differences in union win rates are associated with the number of comprehensive organizing tactics they use.

ELEMENTS OF THE COMPREHENSIVE UNION-BUILDING STRATEGY

According to our hypotheses, each of the ten tactical clusters, or comprehensive organizing tactics in our model enhances the union's organizing power in a unique way. Unions that allocate adequate and appropriate staff and financial resources,[9] for example, make an institutional commitment to be more intensely engaged in the campaign, recruit staff who are demographically representative of the workers they organize, and run more campaigns. Unions that engage in strategic targeting have approached organizing as a means to build bargaining power within certain sectors and industries, in contrast to the non-strategic "hot shop" organizing approach. Perhaps the single most important component of a comprehensive campaign is an active representative committee that gives bargaining unit members ownership of the campaign and allows the workers to start acting like a union inside the workplace, building trust and confidence among the workforce and counteracting the most negative aspects of the employer campaign.

The use of member volunteers to assist in organizing campaigns reflects a combination of greater institutional integration of current and potential new members and an emphasis on a worker-to-worker approach to organizing. Person-to-person contacts made inside and outside the workplace enhance the union's organizing power by providing the intensive one-on-one contacts necessary to build and sustain worker commitment to unionization both at home and in the increasingly hostile election environment at work. The combination of benchmarks and assessments allows unions to evaluate worker support for the union at different stages of the campaign in order to better adjust their strategy to the unit they are trying to organize and to set thresholds to determine when, and whether, they are ready to move on to the next stage of the campaign.

A focus on issues that resonate with the workers and the community, such as respect, dignity, fairness, service quality, and union power and voice, is essential both to build worker commitment to withstand the employer campaign and to gain community support. Internal pressure tactics allow the

union to start acting like a union before the election takes place, building solidarity and commitment among the workers being organized and restraining
employer opposition. External pressure tactics, which exert leverage on the
employer both in the local community and in their national or international
operations, are essential to organizing in the increasingly global corporate
environment. Finally, building for the first contract before the election helps
build confidence in the workers being organized, showing them what the
union is all about and signaling to the employer that the union is there for
the long haul.

RESULTS: DESCRIPTIVE STATISTICS

Table 1.1 provides summary statistics on the election background and
outcome for the 412 elections in our sample. In an improvement over past
years, these data suggest that today's unions are beginning to target and win
in slightly larger units. With an election win rate of 44 percent, first contract
rate of 66 percent, and average unit size of 192 eligible voters, the percentage
of eligible voters who gain coverage under a contract has increased to 37
percent, compared to less than 25 percent in the early 1990s (Bronfenbrenner
2001, 2002).

Still, this progress must be put in perspective. At a time when union density
in the private sector has dropped below 10 percent and total private sector
employment continues to increase by an average of 2.1 million workers each
year (Bureau of Labor Statistics 2002), a 9 percent increase in the unit size of
elections won is simply not enough. If unions are going to reverse the tide of
union density decline, they will need to target units of 5,000, or 10,000 or
more; significantly increase the number of organizing campaigns; and dramatically increase the percentage of eligible voters who gain coverage under
a union contract.

The overall drop between the percentage of the unit who signed cards
before the petition was filed and the percentage of the unit who actually ended
up voting for the unit remains quite high (17 percentage points). However, in
winning units, where the percentage of card signers averages as high as 71
percent, the percent union vote is only five percentage points lower (66
percent).[10]

COMPREHENSIVE ORGANIZING TACTICS

Table 1.1 also lists the frequencies and win rates associated with the ten comprehensive organizing tactics included in our strategic model. As predicted,

TABLE 1.1
Comprehensive organizing tactics and election outcome

	Proportion or mean of elections	Proportion or mean of elections won	Proportion or mean of elections lost	Win rate*
Election background				
All elections	1.00	1.00	1.00	.45
1998	.49	.54	.51	.42
1999	.51	.46	.49	.47
Elections lost by union	.56	.00	1.00	.00
Elections won by union	.44	1.00	.00	1.00
First contract achieved	.30	.66	.02	—
Average number of eligible voters	192	201	185	—
Total number of eligible voters	79,167	36,706	42,461	—
50–99 eligible voters	.41	.39	.42	.43
100–249 eligible voters	.42	.43	.42	.45
250–499 eligible voters	.12	.12	.12	.45
500 or more eligible voters	.05	.06	.05	.50
Percent union vote	.49	.66	.35	—
Percent signed cards before petition filed	.66	.71	.62	—
Comprehensive organizing tactics				
Adequate and appropriate staff and financial resources	.14	.21	.09	.64 (.41)
Strategic targeting	.39	.45	.34	.51 (.40)
Active representative rank-and-file committee	.26	.33	.21	.56 (.41)
Effectively utilized member volunteer organizers	.27	.31	.23	.52 (.42)
Person-to-person contact inside and outside the workplace	.19	.23	.16	.53 (.43)
Benchmarks and assessments	.24	.35	.14	.66 (.38)
Issues which resonate in the workplace and community	.23	.25	.21	.49 (.43)
Escalating pressure tactics in the workplace	.37	.42	.33	.50 (.41)
Escalating pressure tactics outside the workplace	.17	.18	.16	.48 (.44)
Building for the first contract before the election	.35	.39	.31	.50 (.42)

TABLE 1.1—cont.

	Proportion or mean of elections	Proportion or mean of elections won	Proportion or mean of elections lost	Win rate*
Number of comprehensive organizing tactics used	2.60	3.11	2.19	—
Zero	.14	.10	.17	.32
One	.19	.12	.25	.28
Two	.21	.22	.20	.47
Three	.16	.15	.16	.43
Four	.15	.18	.13	.53
Five	.06	.08	.04	.63
Six	.06	.09	.04	.62
Seven	.02	.03	.01	.67
Eight	.01	.03	.00	1.00
Union used no comprehensive organizing tactics	.14	.10	.17	.32 (.47)
Union used one to five comprehensive organizing tactics	.77	.75	.77	.44 (.46)
Union used more than five comprehensive organizing tactics	.10	.15	.06	.68 (.42)

* Number in parenthesis equals win rate when characteristic or action is not present.

each of the individual elements in the model are associated with win rates that average between 4 to 28 percentage points higher than in campaigns where they are not used. Most dramatic are the win rates associated with adequate and appropriate resources (64 percent when present, 41 percent when not present), active representative committee (56 percent when present, 41 percent when not present), and benchmarks and assessments (66 percent when present, 38 percent when not present). The smallest differences are associated with issues that resonate in the workplace and community (49 percent when present, 43 percent when not present) and external pressure tactics (48 percent when present, 44 percent when not present). This is to be expected, given that escalating external pressure tactics tend to be only used in campaigns with aggressive employer opposition, while the effectiveness of issues is highly dependent on the tactics unions use to get their message across.

Although organizer training programs and materials have been emphasizing the importance of these tactics for more than a decade (CWA 1985; Diamond 1992), these data suggest that even today only a small number of unions are actually using them, and those that do so tend to use them in isolation, not as part of a comprehensive multifaceted campaign. Most significantly, in light of labor's much touted effort at "changing to organize," there has been only a minimal increase in the use of these tactics, both individually and in combination since 1995.

As shown in table 1.1, only 14 percent of all the union campaigns in our sample devoted adequate and appropriate resources to the campaign, only 19 percent engaged in person-to-person contact inside and outside the workplace, and only 17 percent engaged in escalating pressure tactics outside the workplace. Fewer than 30 percent had active representative committees or effectively used member volunteer organizers, while fewer than 25 percent used benchmarks and assessments or focused on issues that resonate in the workplace and broader community. The highest percentages were found for strategic targeting (39 percent), escalating pressure tactics inside the workplace (37 percent), and building for the first contract before the election is held (35 percent).

All of the comprehensive organizing tactics in our model were much more likely to be used in winning campaigns than in losing ones. For example, only 9 percent of losing campaigns devoted adequate and appropriate resources, compared to 21 percent of winning campaigns, while 33 percent of winning campaigns had active representative committees, compared to only 21 percent of losing campaigns.

Consistent with earlier research (Bronfenbrenner and Juravich 1998), the results for number of comprehensive organizing tactics used suggest that the overwhelming majority of unions continue to pick and choose individual tactics, in most cases without any coherent plan or strategy, rather than pulling them together into a more comprehensive, multifaceted strategy. Fourteen percent of all campaigns and 17 percent of losing campaigns used no comprehensive organizing tactics, while only 10 percent of all campaigns, and 6 percent of losing campaigns, used more than five tactics. This occurred despite the fact that, in accordance with our hypothesis, union win rates increase dramatically as the number of comprehensive organizing tactics increase, ranging from 32 percent for no comprehensive organizing tactics, to 44 percent for one to five tactics, to 68 percent for more than five tactics, and 100 percent for the 1 percent of the campaigns where unions used eight tactics.

We also tested a series of different combinations of six comprehensive organizing tactics from the ten elements of our model, making sure to include all of the different elements in an equal number of combinations so that, out of a total of 51 different combinations, each element was included in 31 combinations. As described in appendix 1.4, we found that for almost every different combination of six tactics, win rates increased for each additional comprehensive organizing tactic used.[11] The average win rates for all the combinations start at 32 percent, increasing to 38 percent for one tactic, 48 percent for two, 55 percent for three, 60 percent for four, 78 percent for five, and 93 percent for six tactics. Similarly, win rates range from a minimum 29 percent and a maximum of 38 percent for elections where no tactics in the combination were used, to a minimum of 67 percent and a maximum of 100 percent for six tactics. While some tactics, such as representative committee, have a greater impact on win rates than others, these data suggest that each of the ten comprehensive organizing tactics play a key role in improving union organizing success when used in combination with other comprehensive organizing tactics in the model. These findings also show that resources alone cannot be used as a proxy for comprehensive campaigns, because win rates increase as the number of comprehensive organizing tactics increase even for those combinations that do not include the resource variable.[12]

CORPORATE STRUCTURE AND COMPANY CHARACTERISTICS

Table 1.2 provides an overview of the characteristics of companies involved in certification election campaigns. The findings suggest that unions organizing today are operating in a much more global, mobile, and rapidly changing corporate environment. The majority of union private-sector organizing campaigns continue to be concentrated in relatively small units in U.S.-owned-for-profit companies. However, in the last five years there have been significant shifts in the industrial sector and ownership structure of private sector companies where organizing is taking place, reflecting both changes in union tar-

TABLE 1.2
Company characteristics, union tactics, and election outcome

	All elections			Elections with more than five union tactics			Elections with five or fewer union tactics		
	Proportion or mean of elections	Proportion or mean of elections won	Win rate*	Proportion or mean of elections	Proportion or mean of elections won	Win rate*	Proportion or mean of elections	Proportion or mean of elections won	Win rate*
Industrial sector									
Manufacturing	.33	.22	.30	.20	.19	.63	.34	.22	.28
Service sector	.43	.55	.57	.70	.70	.68	.40	.52	.55
Other sectors**	.25	.24	.42	.10	.11	.75	.26	.26	.41
Mobile industry									
Mobile	.47	.36	.34	.23	.19	.56	.50	.39	.33
Immobile	.53	.64	.54	.78	.82	.71	.50	.61	.51
Ownership structure									
Subsidiary of larger parent	.84	.77	.41 (.63)	.83	.78	.64 (.86)	.84	.76	.38 (.61)
Non-profit	.23	.30	.58	.40	.33	.56	.21	.30	.58
For profit	.77	.70	.40	.60	.67	.75	.79	.70	.37
Publicly held	.40	.30	.33	.35	.33	.64	.41	.30	.31
Privately held	.37	.39	.48	.25	.33	.90	.48	.40	.45

TABLE 1.2—cont.

	All elections			Elections with more than five union tactics			Elections with five or fewer union tactics		
	Proportion or mean of elections	Proportion or mean of elections won	Win rate*	Proportion or mean of elections	Proportion or mean of elections won	Win rate*	Proportion or mean of elections	Proportion or mean of elections won	Win rate*
Global structure									
U.S.-based, all sites U.S.	.33	.34	.45 (.44)	.20	.26	.88 (.63)	.35	.35	.43 (.42)
U.S.-based multinational	.31	.28	.39 (.47)	.33	.37	.77 (.63)	.31	.26	.35 (.45)
Foreign-based multinational	.12	.08	.29 (.46)	.08	.04	.33 (.70)	.13	.09	.29 (.44)
Any foreign sites, operations, suppliers or customers	.55	.56	.45 (.44)	.70	.67	.64 (.75)	.54	.54	.42 (.42)
Financial condition									
Good to excellent	.65	.63	.43	.53	.56	.71	.68	.64	.41
Fair to poor	.35	.37	.47	.48	.44	.63	.34	.36	.44
Unionization									
Other organized units as same site	.15	.22	.65 (.41)	.35	.33	.64 (.69)	.13	.21	.65 (.38)
Other organized units at other locations	.60	.63	.47 (.41)	.73	.67	.62 (.82)	.59	.63	.45 (.38)
Unit is located in AFL-CIO union city	.12	.16	.59 (.42)	.28	.33	.82 (.62)	.11	.14	.53 (.41)
Previous attempt to organize this unit	.46	.44	.43 (.46)	.53	.56	.71 (.63)	.45	.42	.39 (.44)
Pre-campaign company practices									
Threat of full or partial plant closing	.21	.17	.35 (.47)	.33	.33	.69 (.67)	.20	.14	.29 (.45)
Employee involvement program before election	.31	.28	.40 (.47)	.30	.29	.58 (.71)	.32	.28	.38 (.44)
Ownership change in two years before the election	.18	.22	.55 (.42)	.25	.30	.80 (.63)	.18	.21	.51 (.40)

* Number in parenthesis equals win rate when characteristic or action is not present.
** Other sectors include communications, retail and wholesale trade, transportation, construction, utilities, and sanitation.

geting strategies and changes in corporate ownership and corporate structure worldwide (Bronfenbrenner 2001).

These data confirm that unions are shifting their focus from organizing targets in manufacturing sector industries with high levels of capital mobility, such as garment and textiles, electronics, and auto parts, toward less mobile service sector industries such as health care, social services, education, and laundries. UNITE, for example, which in past years concentrated most of its organizing in textile and apparel manufacturing, where plant closing threats during organizing campaigns are universal and the number of plants closed and jobs lost has increased steadily each year, has shifted its focus to laundries and distribution warehouses where the ability of employers to move work out of the country is much more restricted (Bronfenbrenner 2001).

As shown in table 1.2, this shift by UNITE and other unions is also reflected in the frequency of elections in mobile (47 percent) versus immobile (53 percent) industries. The overwhelming majority of campaigns using more than five comprehensive organizing tactics are concentrated in immobile industries (78 percent). This suggests that unions are failing to utilize comprehensive organizing tactics in the especially difficult environment of mobile industries where these tactics are needed most.

Compared to five years ago, companies targeted for organizing campaigns are 50 percent more likely to be subsidiaries of large multinational parent companies. They are also much more likely to have foreign sites and locations, foreign suppliers and customers, and less likely to have all sites and operations based in the U.S. Today only one-third of all campaigns occur in for-profit companies with all sites and operations based in the U.S., while 23 percent take place in non-profit companies such as hospitals, social service agencies, or educational institutions, more than double the number of campaigns in non-profits in the early to mid-1990s (Bronfenbrenner 2001). This reflects both the surge in organizing activity among unions who normally dominate the non-profit sector, such as SEIU, and a renewed effort among traditionally public sector unions such as AFT and AFSCME to follow public sector work as it is shifted to the private, non-profit sector. It also reflects a continuing trend among industrial and building trades unions to branch out into the non-profit sector in search of organizing gains they have found difficult to achieve in their own industries.

The attraction of non-profit companies is not surprising given that organizing win rates average as high as 58 percent, compared to a 40 percent win rate for for-profit companies. Among for-profit companies, win rates are highest for U.S.-based companies with all sites in the U.S. (45 percent), and lower for foreign-based multinationals (29 percent) and U.S.-based multinationals (39 percent). Win rates are also much higher (63 percent) in the 16 percent of the companies in the sample that are not a subsidiary of a larger parent company, compared to a 41 percent win rate for companies that are subsidiaries.

As difficult as organizing in the for-profit sector has become, the findings described in table 1.2 suggest that, consistent with our second hypothesis, unions are much more likely to overcome the negative impact of capital mobility and corporate restructuring if they run a comprehensive campaign, incorporating more than five of the comprehensive organizing tactics in our model. While the overall win rate is only 30 percent in manufacturing and 34 percent in mobile industries, it increases to 63 percent in manufacturing and 56 percent in mobile industries when the union runs campaigns using more than five comprehensive organizing tactics. Similarly, the win rates increase twenty to thirty percentage points in campaigns in subsidiaries of larger parent companies, for-profit companies, and U.S.-based multinationals in which the union uses more than five comprehensive organizing tactics.

The exception is in foreign-based multinationals where we found just a minimal increase in win rates (from 29 percent to 33 percent) for campaigns where the union used more than five comprehensive organizing tactics. On closer inspection these findings are not surprising. Not only were foreign-based multinationals much more likely to run aggressive anti-union campaigns, but also the very fact that the company is foreign owned, with sites and operations in other countries, serves as an unspoken threat to workers that their employer might quite readily shift operations out of America if they were to try to organize. Neither are foreign-based companies as vulnerable to the community-based pressure tactics that have been found to be effective for U.S.-based companies. Instead, they may require a much more global and extensive campaign that takes the union's cause to the country and community where the company is headquartered. Yet not one of the campaigns in foreign-based multinationals in our sample ran a global campaign and only 10 percent ran any kind of external pressure campaign.

As would be expected, given that all of these elections occurred during the period of high corporate profitability in the late 1990s, 65 percent of companies in our sample were in good or excellent financial condition.[13] Overall, win rates were lower in companies in good to excellent condition than in other units, reflecting the fact that those employers have greater resources to improve conditions for workers and to devote to an aggressive anti-union campaign. However, consistent with our second hypothesis, this effect disappears entirely in units where the union used more than five comprehensive organizing tactics, bringing the win rate up in companies in good to excellent financial condition from 43 percent to 71 percent.

Table 1.2 also provides background information on the union environment in which these campaigns occurred. Only 15 percent of the units in our sample had other organized units at the same location as the unit being organized.

Consistent with previous research (Bronfenbrenner 1997a, 1997b), union win rates are much higher in such units (65 percent) both because of the greater access and information available to the union and because the unorganized workers have a ready-made example of what a union can accomplish in their workplace. A much larger percentage of companies in our sample (60 percent) had other organized units at other sites and locations of the company, either in the United States or abroad. Win rates were only slightly higher in these units. However, when the union used more than five comprehensive organizing tactics the win rate increased from 47 percent to 62 percent.

Twelve percent of the campaigns in our sample were located in one of the fourteen communities where the Central Labor Council (CLC) had met the criteria to be designated a Union City by the ʹAFL-CIO.[14] Not surprisingly, given the higher level of successful organizing activity and labor-movement support for organizing activity in Union Cities, win rates go up to 59 percent in campaigns in Union Cities, and to a more impressive 82 percent in campaigns with more than five union tactics. This suggests that Union Cities create a climate that serves to support and reinforce the effectiveness of most of the tactics in our model—including more union resources available to organizing, more training opportunities for organizers, and more community and union support and leverage to embolden workers to vote for the union and discourage the employer from running an aggressive anti-union campaign.[15]

For nearly half of the campaigns in our sample (46 percent), there had been a previous (unsuccessful) attempt to organize the unit. Overall, win rates are slightly lower in these units (43 percent) than in units where there was no previous attempt to organize the unit (46 percent). However, win rates in campaigns with previous organizing attempts increase to 71 percent if the union ran a comprehensive campaign using more than five of the tactics in our model.

Table 1.2 also presents findings on company practices before the organizing campaign took place. Nearly a third of the units already had an employee involvement or team system in place before the election, while 21 percent had had threats of full or partial plant closure, and 18 percent reported changes in company ownership. Consistent with earlier research (Bronfenbrenner 1997b; 2000) both pre-campaign employee involvement programs and pre-campaign plant closing threats were associated with win rates 7 to 12 percentage points lower than in units where they were not present. However, when unions ran aggressive campaigns that used more than five comprehensive organizing tactics, win rates increased to 58 percent for pre-campaign employee involvement programs and 69 percent for pre-campaign plant closing threats, as compared to win rates of 38 percent (employee involvement) and 29 percent (plant closing threats) in campaigns where the union used five or fewer tactics.

In contrast, changes in company ownership were associated with win rates 13 percentage points higher than in units where there had been no change in ownership prior to the campaign. This may be because changes in company ownership are more likely to be associated with practices such as job combinations, wage and benefit reductions, and increases in the pace of work which, in combination, may motivate workers to initiate a union campaign and vote for a union (Bronfenbrenner 2000). The positive effect on election outcome is intensified where unions are able to capitalize on worker dissatisfaction by running a comprehensive campaign, increasing from 55 to 80 percent when unions use more than five comprehensive organizing tactics.

BARGAINING UNIT CHARACTERISTICS

Table 1.3 summarizes the characteristics of the bargaining units in our sample, providing important information on the demographics of workers organizing under the NLRB. While today 44 percent of workers involved in NLRB election campaigns are in blue collar production, maintenance, and skilled trades units, 17 percent are in professional, technical, and white collar units, and 19 percent are in service and maintenance or non-professional units.

As expected, win rates are highest in service and maintenance and non-professional units (68 percent), while they average 33 percent in production and maintenance and skilled trades units, 44 percent in professional, technical, and white collar units. Consistent with our second hypothesis, these differences in win rates become much less significant in campaigns where the union used more than five comprehensive organizing tactics, increasing to 60 percent for production and maintenance and skilled trades units, 58 percent in professional, technical, and white collar units, 79 percent in service and maintenance and non-professional units, and 100 percent in drivers units.

While some research has suggested that more aggressive organizing tactics may be less effective among professional, technical, and white collar units than in production and maintenance or service and maintenance units (Cohen and Hurd 1998; Hurd and Bunge 2002; Hoerr 1997), the comprehensive organizing tactics in our model appear to be equally effective in improving win rates across a wide range of bargaining unit types, including clerical, technical, and professional workers. For example, although these studies have suggested that escalating pressure tactics in the workplace may be problematic for professional/technical and white collar workers, pressure tactics are associated with win rates 12 percent higher for professional, technical, and white-collar units relative to campaigns where they were not used. Of course, in any given campaign specific concerns and issues may apply, and tactics must be tailored and

TABLE 1.3
Unit characteristics, union tactics, and election outcome

	All elections			Elections with more than five comprehensive organizing tactics			Elections with five or fewer comprehensive organizing tactics		
	Proportion or mean of elections	Proportion or mean of elections won	Win rate*	Proportion or mean of elections	Proportion or mean of elections won	Win rate*	Proportion or mean of elections	Proportion or mean of elections won	Win rate*
Unit type									
Drivers	.10	.10	.46	.01	.07	1.00	.10	.10	.43
Production/maintenance/skilled trades	.44	.32	.33	.25	.22	.60	.47	.35	.31
Professional/technical/white collar	.17	.17	.44	.30	.26	.58	.16	.15	.41
Service/maintenance/non-professional	.19	.28	.68	.35	.41	.79	.17	.26	.65
Wall to wall	.10	.10	.49	.05	.04	.50	.10	.12	.49
Board determined unit different than petitioned for	.08	.06	.33 (.45)	.08	.07	.67 (.68)	.08	.06	.30 (.43)
Average wage	$10.94	$10.60	—	$10.27	$9.37	—	$11.01	$10.82	—
Average wage less than $8/hour	.22	.26	.53 (.42)	.30	.33	.75 (.64)	.21	.24	.49 (.40)
Average wage $8–$11/hour	.46	.47	.47 (.45)	.41	.46	.75 (.61)	.47	.31	.44 (.43)
Average wage more than $12/hour	.30	.26	.39 (.49)	.28	.19	.46 (.75)	.31	.27	.38 (.46)
Gender									
Percent women in unit	.46	.55	—	.69	.70	—	.44	.52	—
No women in unit	.10	.10	.45 (.45)	.05	.07	1.00 (.66)	.10	.10	.42 (.43)
1–49 percent women in unit	.40	.28	.31 (.54)	.10	.07	.50 (.69)	.43	.07	.31 (.51)
50–74 percent women in unit	.20	.20	.46 (.45)	.25	.22	.60 (.70)	.19	.21	.44 (.42)
75 percent or more women	.30	.42	.62 (.37)	.60	.63	.71 (.63)	.27	.38	.60 (.35)
Race and ethnic background									
Percent workers of color in unit	.39	.44	—	.56	.63	—	.37	.41	—
No workers of color in unit	.10	.09	.43 (.45)	.00	.00	—	.11	.11	.43 (.43)
1–49 percent workers of color	.51	.46	.40 (.50)	.40	.30	.50 (.79)	.53	.49	.40 (.46)
50–74 percent workers of color	.14	.14	.46 (.45)	.15	.19	.83 (.65)	.13	.13	.41 (.43)
75 percent or more workers of color	.25	.31	.56 (.41)	.45	.52	.78 (.59)	.23	.27	.51 (.39)
Percent women of color	.19	.26	—	.38	.47	—	.17	.23	—
No women workers of color	.19	.19	.43 (.45)	.05	.08	1.00 (.65)	.21	.21	.42 (.42)
1–49 percent women workers of color	.60	.51	.38 (.55)	.46	.31	.44 (.86)	.62	.55	.37 (.50)
50–74 percent women workers of color	.10	.14	.60 (.43)	.23	.23	.67 (.67)	.09	.12	.58 (.41)
75 percent or more women workers of color	.07	.13	.82 (.42)	.21	.31	1.00 (.58)	.06	.10	.75 (.40)
Percent undocumented workers	.02	.02	—	.04	.04	—	.02	.01	—
Percent recent immigrants	.05	.05	—	.12	.14	—	.04	.04	—
Percent non-English speaking	.15	.16	—	.27	.31	—	.14	.14	—

* Number in parentheses equals win rate when characteristic or action is not present.

adapted accordingly. However, our data suggest that, when we look generally across the diversity of workers and occupations who make up the professional/technical workforce—from nurses, to engineers, to basketball players—win rates increase, rather than decrease, when unions run more comprehensive campaigns.

Our findings in table 1.3 also confirm that organizing is increasingly concentrated in units with a majority of women and people of color. Only 10 percent of the units are all male or all white, while women make up the majority in half the units and workers of color make up the majority in 39 percent of the units.

Consistent with earlier research, win rates increase substantially as the proportion of women and people of color increases. The highest win rates are 82 percent for units with 75 percent or more women workers of color, while win rates are lowest in units where women (31 percent) or workers of color (40 percent) constituted a minority of the unit. Once again, win rates increase dramatically across race and gender groupings when the union uses more than five comprehensive organizing tactics in the campaign, suggesting that our model is equally appropriate across a diversity of demographic groups.

The higher win rates in these units mean that not only are women and workers of color (in particular, women of color) participating in union elections in ever increasing numbers, but because win rates are so much higher in these units, the vast majority of new workers coming into the labor movement today are women and people of color.

Win rates are also higher (53 percent) in the 22 percent of the units where the average wage was less than $8.00 per hour, while win rates are lowest (39 percent) in units with an average wage of more than $12.00 an hour. These higher wage units tend to include more white, male, blue collar, white collar, and professional and technical employees, all groups less predisposed to unions than their non-white, female counterparts in non-professional, largely service, occupations (Bronfenbrenner 1993; Freeman and Rogers 1999). As mentioned earlier, these highly paid workers are also more vulnerable to employer threats of job loss and blacklisting. While win rates increase from 39 to 46 percent, in the 24 percent of the campaigns in these units where the union uses more than five comprehensive union tactics, they might increase even further if more of the campaigns in these units utilized a more comprehensive organizing strategy.

Like the data on company characteristics, the descriptive statistics for unit characteristics support our hypothesis that the use of a comprehensive organizing strategy can greatly reduce differences in win rates across unit type, average wage, gender, race, and ethnic background.

EMPLOYER BEHAVIOR

As described in table 1.4, consistent with earlier research, the overwhelming majority of employers in our sample aggressively opposed the union's organizing efforts through a combination of threats, discharges, promises of improvements, unscheduled unilateral changes in wages and benefits, bribes, and surveillance. Individually and in combination, these tactics are extremely effective in reducing union election win rates. Fifty-two percent of all employers in our sample and 68 percent of those in mobile industries made threats of full or partial plant closure during the organizing drive. Approximately one in every four employers (26 percent) discharged workers for union activity, while 48 percent made promises of improvement, 20 percent gave unscheduled wage increases, and 17 percent made unilateral changes in benefits and working conditions. Sixty-seven percent of the employers held supervisor one-on-ones with employees at least weekly, 34 percent gave bribes or special favors to those who opposed the union, 31 percent assisted the anti-union committee, and 10 percent used electronic surveillance of union activists during the organizing campaign. Employers threatened to refer undocumented workers to the Immigration and Naturalization Service (INS) in 7 percent of all campaigns and in 52 percent of cases where undocumented workers were present.

Only 27 percent of the employers in our sample ran weak campaigns using fewer than five tactics. Forty-eight percent of the employers ran moderately aggressive anti-union campaigns using five to nine tactics, and 26 percent of the employers ran extremely aggressive campaigns using at least ten tactics. Employers ran no campaign whatsoever against the union in only 3 percent of the cases in our sample, 93 percent of which were won by the union.

Although most of the findings regarding employer behavior are consistent with earlier research, the percentages for some of the most egregious employer actions, such as discharges for union activity, have slightly declined (Bronfenbrenner 2001). However, rather than suggesting any reduction in employer opposition to union organizing efforts, these findings on employer behavior are primarily a function of the shift in union organizing activity toward non-profit companies. Although some non-profit employers, particularly hospitals and universities, have long been known for their opposition to unions and the substantial resources they spend on anti-union campaigns, the nature of their anti-union campaigns are quite different than those in for-profit companies, because non-profits are much more accountable and accessible to the clients they serve. Thus, while non-profit employers are more likely to use extensive unit challenges and public media campaigns, they are less likely to engage in more clearly identifiable illegal tactics such as discharges for union activity, bribes, or illegal unilateral changes in wages than their

TABLE 1.4
Employer campaign, union tactics, and election outcome

	All elections			Elections with more than five comprehensive organizing tactics			Elections with five or fewer comprehensive organizing tactics		
	Proportion or mean of elections	Proportion or mean of election won	Win rate*	Proportion or mean of elections	Proportion or mean of elections won	Win rate*	Proportion or mean of elections	Proportion or mean of elections won	Win rate*
Hired management consultant	.76	.69	.41 (.55)	.80	.82	.69 (.63)	.75	.67	.38 (.55)
Held more than five captive audience meetings	.46	.38	.37 (.51)	.53	.48	.62 (.74)	.46	.37	.34 (.49)
Mailed more than five letters	.17	.14	.38 (.46)	.30	.22	.50 (.75)	.15	.13	.36 (.43)
Distributed more than five anti-union leaflets	.42	.35	.37 (.50)	.65	.63	.65 (.71)	.40	.30	.32 (.48)
Held supervisor one-on-ones at least weekly	.67	.60	.40 (.54)	.85	.78	.62 (1.00)	.65	.56	.37 (.52)
Established employee involvement program	.17	.13	.33 (.47)	.18	.11	.43 (.73)	.17	.13	.32 (.44)
Made positive personnel changes	.34	.30	.39 (.47)	.50	.48	.65 (.70)	.32	.27	.35 (.45)
Made promises of improvement	.48	.37	.35 (.54)	.63	.59	.64 (.73)	.46	.33	.30 (.52)
Granted unscheduled raises	.20	.18	.40 (.46)	.35	.33	.64 (.69)	.18	.15	.34 (.44)
Made unilateral changes	.17	.16	.41 (.45)	.28	.26	.64 (.69)	.16	.14	.37 (.43)
Discharged union activists	.26	.24	.41 (.46)	.35	.30	.57 (.73)	.25	.22	.39 (.43)
Used bribes and special favors	.34	.29	.38 (.48)	.43	.48	.77 (.61)	.33	.26	.33 (.46)
Used electronic surveillance	.10	.10	.44 (.45)	.28	.26	.64 (.69)	.08	.07	.40 (.42)
Held company social events	.21	.18	.38 (.46)	.38	.37	.67 (.68)	.19	.14	.31 (.44)
Assisted anti-union committee	.31	.25	.36 (.48)	.38	.30	.53 (.76)	.30	.24	.34 (.45)
Used paid or free media	.07	.08	.56 (.44)	.20	.22	.75 (.66)	.05	.06	.47 (.42)
Laid off or contracted out workers in unit	.08	.14	.58 (.43)	.13	.15	.80 (.66)	.10	.14	.55 (.40)
Threatened to report workers to the INS	.07	.07	.43 (.45)	.13	.07	.40 (.71)	.07	.07	.44 (.42)
Involved community leaders/politicians	.06	.06	.42 (.45)	.13	.15	.80 (.66)	.05	.04	.32 (.43)
Filed ULP charges against the union	.02	.02	.50 (.44)	.05	.04	.50 (.68)	.02	.02	.50 (.42)
Threatened to close the plant	.52	.44	.38 (.51)	.63	.63	.68 (.67)	.50	.41	.34 (.50)
Number of tactics used by employer	7.21	6.27	—	10.18	9.59	—	6.88	5.70	—
Employer used 0–4 tactics	.27	.38	.64	.13	.11	.60	.28	.43	.64
Employer used 5–9 tactics	.48	.42	.39	.35	.48	.93	.49	.41	.35
Employer used at least 10 tactics	.26	.20	.34	.53	.41	.52	.23	.16	.29

* Number in parenthesis equals win rate when characteristic or action is not present.

counterparts in the for-profit sector. At the same time, for-profit employers
have maintained their aggressive opposition to union organizing efforts. For
example, employers discharged workers for union activity in only 14 percent
of campaigns in non-profits compared to a 29 percent discharge rate in campaigns in for-profit companies. Nine percent of employers in non-profits used
no anti-union tactics at all compared to less than 1 percent of employers in
for-profit companies. Similarly, only 15 percent of non-profits used more than
ten anti-union tactics compared to 21 percent of for-profit companies.

Overall, the win rate drops to 39 percent for units where employers used
five to nine tactics and 34 percent where they used more than ten, compared
to 64 percent where they used fewer than five tactics. At a time when unions
are running more aggressive and sophisticated campaigns, and workers' trust
in corporations is declining, in some units the aggressive anti-union behavior
of employers may reach a point of diminishing returns. This is particularly
evident in elections where the union uses more than five comprehensive
organizing tactics. Win rates for most of the individual employer tactic variables increase between 10 and 40 percent when unions used more than five
comprehensive organizing tactics, while unions won 100 percent of the campaigns with no employer opposition, 60 percent of the campaigns with weak
employer opposition, 93 percent with moderate opposition, and 52 percent of
the campaigns with aggressive employer opposition. This occurs despite the
fact that employers are much more likely to run aggressive campaigns when
they think the union is going to win, than in campaigns where the union campaign is weak, and there is little chance of union victory.

These data confirm that while the majority of employers run aggressive
campaigns taking full strategic advantage of a broad range of anti-union
tactics, the majority of unions continue to run fairly weak campaigns, even
when faced with aggressive employer opposition. Indeed, there were only two
campaigns in our sample, where, when faced with aggressive employer opposition, unions used more than six comprehensive organizing tactics. Both of
those elections were won. Thus, consistent with our hypotheses, although
employer anti-union campaigns can and often do have a devastating impact
on union organizing success, unions can increase their win rates, even in the
face of the most aggressive employer opposition, if they run comprehensive
campaigns.[16]

UNIONS AND COMPREHENSIVE ORGANIZING STRATEGIES

According to our hypotheses, unions that run comprehensive organizing campaigns, combining a large number of the tactics in our model, will achieve
higher wins across a wide range of employer tactics and industry, company,

and unit characteristics. Therefore, we would expect to see higher win rates for those unions that consistently employ comprehensive campaigns, relative to those unions that use only a few tactics in isolation.

Nevertheless, there are certain kinds of workers, in certain kinds of companies and industries, faced with different levels of employer opposition, who can be especially difficult to organize. Whether CWA in high tech and telecommunications, the UAW in auto-transplants and auto-parts, the USWA in metal production and fabrication, UNITE in garment and textile, IATSE in cable television, the IBT in national trucking companies, or the UFCW in food processing, some unions face much greater challenges when organizing in their primary jurisdictions, because they are confronted with more mobile, more global, and more powerful and hence effective employer opposition, and/or a workforce less predisposed to unionization (Bronfenbrenner 2001). Yet, our second hypothesis is that unions can improve their organizing success, even in the toughest industries, companies, and bargaining units, when they use a comprehensive union-building strategy.

Table 1.5 provides summary statistics for the most active unions organizing under the NLRB. The unions that dominate NLRB election activity continue to be IBT, SEIU, USWA, UAW, and UFCW. Among these unions, there are substantial differences in win rates.[17] Yet, as predicted, these differences fade, when unions use more than five comprehensive organizing tactics. For almost all the unions in our sample, across a diversity of industries and bargaining unit characteristics the win rates average above 67 percent or higher when the union uses more than five comprehensive tactics.[18]

What is perhaps most striking about these results is how few unions are actually running comprehensive campaigns. As shown in table 1.6, the unions tend to fall into three groups. The first group, which includes HERE, SEIU, and UNITE, averages four or more tactics in all of their elections. The second group, which includes AFSCME, CWA/IUE, UBC, LIUNA, UAW, and UFCW, averages three tactics per campaign. The third group, which includes IAM, IBEW, IBT, IUOE, PACE, and USWA, averages two or fewer tactics in each campaign. It is striking that even the most successful unions in our sample are still making only limited use of the comprehensive campaign model, while the majority of U.S. unions continue to run fairly weak, ineffectual campaigns.

Only the unions in the first group consistently run organizing campaigns that combine at least four strategic tactics. The overall win rate for this group is 63 percent, the highest for any group, increasing to 74 percent when they use more than five comprehensive tactics. These unions, SEIU, HERE, and UNITE have gained national reputations for effective organizing. And yet only 30 percent of their campaigns average more than five comprehensive organizing tactics. This suggests that these unions may be capable of winning

TABLE 1.5
Union, union tactics, and election outcome

Union	All elections			Elections with more than five union tactics			Elections with five or fewer union tactics		
	Proportion or mean of elections	Proportion or mean of elections won	Win rate	Proportion or mean of elections	Proportion or mean of elections won	Win rate	Proportion or mean of elections	Proportion or mean of elections won	Win rate
AFSCME	.04	.06	.59	.05	.04	.50	.04	.06	.60
CWA/IUE	.04	.02	.20	.03	.00	.00	.04	.02	.21
HERE	.02	.03	.50	.10	.11	.75	.02	.01	.33
IAM	.02	.02	.33	.03	.00	.00	.02	.02	.38
IBEW	.02	.03	.56	.00	—	—	.02	.03	.56
IBT	.20	.17	.37	.03	.04	1.00	.22	.19	.37
IUOE	.02	.02	.44	.00	—	—	.02	.03	.44
LIUNA	.02	.02	.30	.00	—	—	.03	.02	.30
PACE	.03	.02	.31	.00	—	—	.04	.03	.31
SEIU	.14	.20	.63	.40	.41	.69	.11	.16	.61
UAW	.06	.09	.64	0	—	—	.07	.10	.64
UBC	.02	.01	.25	.10	—	—	.02	.01	.25
UFCW	.07	.06	.33	.08	.04	.25	.07	.06	.35
UNITE	.02	.03	.67	.08	.11	1.00	.02	.02	.50
USWA	.09	.09	.43	.08	.11	1.00	.09	.08	.38
Other AFL-CIO building trades unions*	.03	.01	.18	.00	—	—	.03	.01	.18
Other AFL-CIO industrial unions*	.05	.02	.20	.03	.00	.00	.05	.03	.21
Other AFL-CIO service sector unions*	.02	.03	.56	.00	—	—	.02	.03	.56
Other AFL-CIO transportation unions*	.02	.03	60	.03	.04	1.00	.02	.03	.56
Local and national independent unions*	.07	.08	.48	.08	.11	1.00	.07	.07	.42
Unions that average four or more comprehensive organizing tactics	.18	.26	.63	.58	.63	.74	.14	.19	.57
Unions that average three comprehensive organizing tactics	.36	.35	.44	.28	.22	.55	.37	.37	.43
Unions that average two or fewer comprehensive organizing tactics	.46	.39	.38	.15	.15	.67	.49	.44	.37

* Other AFL-CIO transportation unions include ATU, ILWU, MEBA, SIUNA, and TWU. Other AFL-CIO building trades unions include BTCT, OPCM, and PPF. Other AFL-CIO service sector unions include AFT, IATSE, and OPEIU. Other AFL-CIO industrial unions include AFGW, BBF, BCTWU, GCIU, GMMPAW, NPW, SMW, and UMW. The national independent unions include ANA, IWW, NEA, NBPA, UE, UGSOA, and UTU. The remaining independent unions are designated by the NLRB as local independents.

TABLE 1.6
Comprehensive organizing tactics by union

Unions	Number of tactics	Percent of campaigns									
		Resources	Targeting	Rank & file committee	Member volunteers	1-on-1 contact	Benchmarks	Issues	Workplace pressure tactics	External pressure tactics	Building for first contract
Unions that average four or more comprehensive organizing tactics	4.07	.34	.71	.37	.30	.32	.41	.34	.46	.39	.42
UNITE	4.22	.44	.44	.56	.33	.44	.67	.22	.33	.33	.44
HERE	4.20	.90	.60	.10	.20	.50	.40	.00	.40	.40	.70
SEIU	4.02	.23	.77	.39	.32	.26	.37	.42	.49	.40	.37
Unions that average three comprehensive organizing tactics	2.93	.18	.44	.27	.27	.23	.27	.28	.44	.17	.40
AFSCME	3.24	.35	.53	.47	.29	.24	.29	.35	.41	.05	.24
Other AFL-CIO transportation unions*	3.20	.20	.40	.30	.20	.10	.50	.30	.40	.20	.60
LIUNA	3.10	.10	.50	.20	.10	.40	.20	.30	.40	.20	.70
UFCW	3.10	.30	.40	.27	.13	.43	.37	.17	.33	.13	.57
Other AFL-CIO building trades unions*	3.00	.00	.55	.09	.46	.27	.18	.09	.36	.09	.64
UAW	2.92	.08	.44	.32	.44	.08	.24	.32	.76	.16	.08
CWA/IUE	2.73	.07	.60	.13	.27	.20	.20	.20	.33	.40	.33
UBC	2.63	.00	.63	.00	.38	.25	.25	.13	.25	.13	.63
Local and national independent unions*	2.62	.17	.28	.24	.28	.14	.17	.41	.38	.17	.38

TABLE 1.6—cont.

	Number of tactics	Percent of campaigns									
Unions		Resources	Targeting	Rank & file committee	Member volunteers	1-on-1 contact	Benchmarks	Issues	Workplace pressure tactics	External pressure tactics	Building for first contract
Unions that average two or fewer comprehensive organizing tactics	1.75	.04	.22	.22	.25	.11	.14	.14	.28	.07	.27
USWA	2.38	.03	.32	.43	.38	.16	.19	.22	.38	.08	.19
Other AFL-CIO service sector unions*	2.33	.00	.44	.11	.11	.22	.22	.22	.22	.22	.57
PACE	2.08	.08	.61	.46	.00	.15	.08	.15	.31	.08	.15
Other AFL-CIO industrial unions*	1.95	.05	.25	.20	.30	.10	.25	.20	.20	.00	.40
IAM	1.56	.11	.11	.22	.11	.22	.11	.00	.33	.11	.22
IBT	1.41	.04	.13	.12	.27	.05	.12	.12	.24	.06	.27
IBEW	1.33	.00	.11	.11	.33	.22	.00	.00	.11	.11	.33
IUOE	1.33	.00	.00	.11	.00	.11	.11	.11	.56	.11	.22
All unions combined	2.60	1.4	3.9	.26	.27	.19	.24	.23	.37	.17	.35

* Other AFL-CIO transportation unions include ATU, ILWU, MEBA, SIUNA, and TWU. Other AFL-CIO building trades unions include BTCT, OPCM, and PPF. Other AFL-CIO service sector unions include AFT, IATSE, and OPEIU. Other AFL-CIO industrial unions include AFGW, BBF, BCTWU, GCIU, GMMPAW, NPW, SMW, and UMW. The national independent unions include ANA, IWW, NEA, NBPA, UE, UGSOA, and UTU. The remaining independent unions are designated by the NLRB as local independents, some of them based solely in the target company.

even more elections, if they used comprehensive organizing tactics more consistently.

The second group of unions, on average, uses fewer tactics and is less likely to combine them into a comprehensive campaign. Unions in this group average three comprehensive tactics per campaign, and have an overall win rate of 44 percent. Only 8 percent of campaigns run by unions in this middle group used more than five comprehensive organizing tactics. However, the win rate for those campaigns was 55 percent.

The third group of unions uses comprehensive campaigns even more seldom. Unions in this group average two or fewer comprehensive organizing tactics per campaign, and, not surprisingly, have the lowest average win rate (38 percent) for all three groups. Half of the unions in this group, including IBEW, IUOE, PACE, and other AFL-CIO service unions, did not conduct *any* comprehensive campaigns. Again, the win rate is much higher (67 percent), for the 3 percent of elections involving this third group in which unions used more than five comprehensive organizing tactics.

These data highlight three important trends. First, higher win rates are associated with campaigns that use five or more comprehensive organizing tactics for all three groups of unions. Second, higher win rates are associated with unions that consistently combine comprehensive organizing tactics in their campaigns. Third, there is a real mix of industries, companies, and unit types among the three union groups, yet comprehensive organizing tactics are consistently effective across the different union groupings.

It is important to note that for several of the unions in our sample—most notably CWA, HERE, and some of the building-trades unions—NLRB certification elections increasingly represent only a small portion of their recent private sector organizing efforts. Instead, their focus has been on bargaining to organize, voluntary recognition, and card-check neutrality. As the growing body of case studies of non-Board campaigns have shown, the utilization of a comprehensive union building campaign incorporating most, if not all, of the elements of our model has been critical to the success of many of the most significant non-Board victories (Juravich and Hilgert 1999; Waldinger and Erickson et al. 1998; Kieffer and Ness 1999; Rechenbach and Cohen 2000). Our organizer interviews suggest that, for these unions, NLRB campaigns are secondary and thus tend to be more locally based and that they involve smaller units with less strategic and less comprehensive campaigns. Thus, if we were able to include non-NLRB campaigns in our sample, unions such as CWA, HERE, and IBEW would likely display a higher average use of comprehensive organizing tactics.

Table 1.6 provides more detailed data confirming that the most successful unions are those that consistently combine comprehensive organizing tactics. The unions in the first group average at least 30 percent for all the tactics in the model and range as high as 41 percent (benchmarks), 42 percent (building for the first contract), 46 percent (workplace pressure tactics), and, most notably, 71 percent (targeting). The high targeting percentage for this group is particularly revealing, because it suggests that these are the unions that are most committed to a strategic organizing plan (organizing within their primary jurisdiction) and fully knowledgeable about their individual company's ownership structure, operations, finances, and vulnerabilities. At the same time, these data also reveal that, with the exception of targeting, even the most successful unions are using these tactics in fewer than half of their campaigns. Not only could an increase in frequency (and quality) of the use of all these tactics further increase win rates for these unions, but it also might facilitate getting more campaigns off the ground and winning them in larger units.

The results for the second group are much more uneven, ranging from 17 percent for external pressure tactics, and 18 percent for resources, to 44 percent for workplace pressure tactics and targeting. Overall, this group averaged lower than 30 percent for most of the tactics in the model. It is particularly striking that this second group rates low on resources (17 percent), one-on-one contact (23 percent), representative committee (27 percent), and benchmarks and assessments (27 percent), since these are fundamental elements of a comprehensive campaign. If unions do not devote adequate or appropriate resources, fail to build rank-and-file leadership among the workers they are trying to organize, and fail to reach the majority of the members through person-to-person contact in the workplace and the community, their campaigns may never get off the ground far enough to correctly identify issues, build for the first contract, or effectively mobilize workers for internal or external pressure tactics. And, if they do not use benchmarks and assessments, they have no way of evaluating the effectiveness of their strategy, or when and whether to move on to the next phase of the campaign. The findings suggest that while these unions have been taking new initiatives and organizing more aggressively than in the past, they continue to use tactics in isolation, without the interconnected, multifaceted union-building strategy required in the current organizing environment.

The third and largest group of unions average lower than 15 percent for half the tactics in the model (resources, one-on-one contact, benchmarks, issues, and external pressure tactics) and lower than 27 percent for all the remaining tactics. This suggests that nearly half of the unions involved in NLRB certification elections run campaigns not unlike campaigns in the late 1980s when we first started tracking the nature and success of union organizing efforts (Bronfenbrenner 1993, 1997). The findings are less surprising given that, on average, unions in this third group had adequate and appropriate resources in only 4 percent of their campaigns. Without such resources, it is difficult to pull together many of the other elements of the model.

For each individual tactic, these trends are consistent across the three groups, providing insight into the nature of current organizing efforts. For example, the frequency of targeting and external pressure tactics varies widely among the three groups, while the use of member volunteers shows much less variation. This suggests that while more sophisticated tactics, such as targeting and external pressure tactics, have yet to be embraced by many unions, even the least successful are comfortable with more traditional tactics, such as having members assist with organizing campaigns. Yet, even the most successful unions still do not make consistent use of such key tactics as adequate and appropriate resources, active representative committees, person-to-person contact, benchmarks and assessments, member volunteers, and internal and external pressure tactics.

RESULTS: REGRESSION ANALYSIS

In addition to examining the impact of comprehensive organizing tactics on NLRB certification election outcome through descriptive statistics, we used binary logistic regression analysis to control for the influence of election environment, company characteristics, bargaining unit demographics, and employer tactics.[19] Two models were used to estimate the predicted impact of comprehensive organizing tactics on the odds of the union winning the election. Model A includes each of the ten tactics that constitute a comprehensive union building strategy. Model B combines the individual tactics into a comprehensive union tactic scale variable, adding one unit for each individual comprehensive tactic used.[20]

As shown in table 1.7, while all ten of the comprehensive organizing tactics variables included in model A are associated with higher win rates, these positive effects were not statistically significant for the majority of the individual comprehensive tactic variables when controlling for election background, bargaining unit demographics, company characteristics, and employer opposition. The only exceptions were adequate and appropriate resources, rank-and-file committee, and benchmarks and assessments; these did have a statistically significant positive impact on the odds of the union winning the election, increasing the odds of an election win by 119 percent for resources, 89 percent for rank-and-file committee, and 162 percent for benchmarks and assessments.

The findings confirm that these three variables are fundamental elements of a comprehensive campaign, building blocks that enhance the union's ability to engage in any of the other tactics included in the model. Without adequate and sufficient resources, unions will be unable to staff and finance the labor-intensive, grassroots tactics that a comprehensive union building campaign requires. Similarly, a representative and active committee is necessary to develop rank-and-file leadership, build the union inside the workplace, and make connections between the workers and the community outside the work-place. Benchmarks and assessments are essential to evaluate when and whether to use each of the other tactics and when and whether to move on to the next phase of the campaign.

While these findings suggest that three comprehensive organizing tactics had an independent positive effect on election outcome, as we will see in the discussion of the findings from model B, their individual effect was not as great as the aggregate effect of using a combination of the comprehensive organizing tactics in the model.[21] Together, the descriptive and regression find-ings indicate that while resources, committees, and benchmarks and assess-ments are fundamental elements of a comprehensive campaign, they are not sufficient, in that they are most effective in combination with other compre-hensive organizing tactics.[22]

In accordance with our first hypothesis, the findings in table 1.7 confirm that most of the comprehensive organizing tactics that make up our model do not have a statistically significant effect when used in isolation of the other tactics. However, as shown in table 1.8, when these individual tactics are com-bined into a single variable, adding one unit for each additional tactic used, they have a strong positive impact on election outcome, statistically signifi-cant at .001 or better. After controlling for election environment and employer opposition, each additional comprehensive union tactic used by the union increases the odds of a union win by 34 percent. Thus, the unions in our sample who used at least six comprehensive organizing tactics increased their odds of winning the election by 204 percent (6 times 34 percent). The same logic demonstrates that unions averaging four or more tactics increased their odds of winning the election by at least 136 percent, while those averaging three tactics increased their odds by 102 percent, and those averaging two or fewer tactics increased their odds no more than 68 percent.

The findings from the election environment variables are also consistent with our hypotheses. In both models, manufacturing sector, subsidiary, and employer behavior had a strong, statistically significant negative impact on election outcome. The results for both model A and model B suggest that for each additional anti-union tactic used by the employer the odds of winning the election decline by 13 percent when we control for the influence of elec-tion environment and union tactic variables.[23] This finding confirms that employer behavior can have a devastating impact on union success. These results also confirm that the manufacturing sector is a particularly challeng-ing environment, decreasing the odds of a union win by 52 percent in model

TABLE 1.7
The impact of comprehensive organizing tactics on election outcome: Model A—Individual union tactic variables

Independent variable	Predicted sign	Mean or proportion of sample	Percent union win rate	Model A				
				Unstandardized logistic regression coefficient (β)	Estimated standardized coefficient	Standard error	Odds ratio exp$^{(\beta)}$	Predicted impact on odds of union win
Election background control variables								
Number of eligible voters	None	192.15	—	.000	.000	.000	1.001	
Manufacturing sector	–	.32	.29	–.732**	–.343	.296	.481	–52% if unit is in manufacturing sector
Subsidiary of larger parent company	–	.84	.41	–.648**	–.240	.327	.523	–48% if company is a subsidiary
Ownership change	+	.18	.55	.720**	.281	.308	2.054	+105% if ownership change before election
Good to excellent financial condition	+	.65	.43	.367	.176	.253	1.443	
Board determined unit	–	.08	.33	–.747	–.203	.463	.474	
Other organized units	+	.15	.65	.580*	.209	.350	1.785	
Professional, technical, or white-collar unit	–	.14	.48	–.458	–.172	.346	.632	
60 percent or more women	+	.43	.59	.534*	.264	.279	1.706	
60 percent or more workers of color	+	.32	.55	.443	.207	.286	1.558	
Number of employer tactics used	–	7.21	—	–.134***	–.559	.032	.874	–13% for each additional tactic used

TABLE 1.7—cont.

Independent variable	Predicted sign	Mean or proportion of sample	Percent union win rate	Unstandardized logistic regression coefficient (β)	Estimated standardized coefficient	Standard error	Odds ratio exp[(β)]	Predicted impact on odds of union win
							Model A	
Comprehensive organizing tactics								
Adequate and appropriate resources	+	.14	.64	.799**	.277	.391	2.198	+119% if adequate and appropriate resources
Strategic targeting	+	.39	.51	.011	.005	.262	1.011	
Active representative committee	+	.26	.56	.638**	.282	.279	1.893	+89% if active representative committee
Effectively utilized member volunteer organizers	+	.27	.52	.345	.155	.269	1.412	
Person-to-person contact inside and outside the workplace	+	.19	.53	−.033	−.012	.334	.967	
Benchmarks and assessments	+	.24	.66	.963***	.412	.287	2.621	+162% if used benchmarks and assessments
Issues which resonate in the workplace and community	+	.23	.49	.028	.013	.284	1.028	
Escalating pressure tactics in the workplace	+	.37	.50	.407	.198	.264	1.502	
Escalating pressure tactics outside the workplace	+	.17	.48	−.179	.140	.346	.836	
Building for the first contract before the election	+	.35	.50	.229	.109	.260	1.257	
Total number of observations				412				
Nagelkerke R square				.312				
−2 (log-likelihood)				457.038				

Significance Levels: * = .10 ** = .05 *** = .01 *(one-tailed tests)*

TABLE 1.8
The impact of comprehensive organizing tactics on election outcome: Model B—Individual union tactic variables

Independent variable	Predicted sign	Mean or proportion of sample	Percent union win rate	Unstandardized logistic regression coefficient (β)	Model B			
					Estimated standardized coefficient	Standard error	Odds ratio exp$^{(\beta)}$	Predicted impact on odds of union win
Election background control variables								
Number of eligible voters	None	192.15	—	.000	.000	.000	1.000	
Manufacturing sector	−	.32	.29	−.649**	−.304	.287	.523	−48% if unit in manufacturing sector
Subsidiary of larger parent company	−	−.84	.41	−.633**	−.233	.320	.531	−47% if company is a subsidiary
Ownership change	+	.18	.55	.669**	.261	.296	1.952	+95% if ownership change before election
Good to excellent financial condition	+	.65	.43	.317	.148	.246	1.373	
Board determined unit	−	.08	.33	−.691	−.188	.448	.501	
Other organized units	+	.15	.65	.587*	.212	.337	1.799	
Professional, technical or white collar unit	−	.14	.48	−.575*	−.218	.331	.563	
60 percent or more women	+	.43	.59	.535**	.267	.273	1.708	+70% if at least 60% women in the unit
60 percent or more workers of color	+	.32	.55	.553**	.257	.258	1.739	+73% if at least 60% women in the unit
Number of employer tactics used	−	7.21	—	−.137***	−.584	.031	.872	−13% for each additional tactic used
Comprehensive organizing tactics								
Number of comprehensive organizing tactics	+	2.60	—	.290***	.555	.070	1.337	+34% for each additional tactic used

Total number of observations   412
Nagelkerke R square   .277
−2 (log-likelihood)   470.723
*Significance Levels: * = .10 ** = .05 *** = .01 (one-tailed tests)*

A and 48 percent in model B. Similar negative effects shown for subsidiaries of larger parent companies, where the odds of winning the election decreases by 48 percent in model A and 47 percent in model B.

Ownership change in the two years before the election, as predicted, has a strong statistically significant positive impact on election outcome, increasing the odds of winning the election by 105 percent in model A and 95 percent in model B. Also as predicted, the number of eligible voters has no discernable (or statistically significant) impact on election outcome.

Good to excellent financial condition (positive), board determined unit (negative), other organized units (positive), and professional/technical or white collar unit (negative), all have their predicted sign, though with weak or statistically insignificant effects when we control for other variables, including the union campaign.

In model B both of the demographic variables (60 percent or more women and 60 percent or more workers of color) exhibit strong, statistically significant, positive effects. Sixty percent or more women in the unit increases the odds of a union win by 70 percent, while having 60 percent or more workers of color increases the odds by 73 percent.[24]

In addition to assessing the probable impact of the number of comprehensive organizing tactics on the odds of a union win, we also sought to examine the relative effects of the number of union tactics compared to the election environment and employer opposition variables in our model.[25] In model A the employer campaign variable, with a standardized ranking of −.559, appears to have a much greater effect on election outcome than any individual union tactic or environmental factor. The three comprehensive organizing tactics that were statistically significant in model A—benchmarks and assessments, active representative committee, and adequate and appropriate resources—also have a greater relative effect on election outcome than all of the environmental factors except manufacturing sector, which ranked third after benchmarks and employer tactics. The relative importance of manufacturing in model A suggests that union tactics used in isolation will not overcome the difficult challenges unions face in organizing in manufacturing.

However, in model B, where we substituted the number of comprehensive tactics for the ten individual comprehensive tactics, the number of employer tactics and the number of union tactics have a relatively equal rank (.555 for union tactics and .584 for employer tactics) followed by manufacturing (.303), at least 60 percent women (.267), ownership change (.261), at least 60 percent workers of color (.261), and subsidiary of a larger parent company.

Our results confirm the widespread view that manufacturing industries and subsidiaries of large parent companies are much more difficult to organize and that employer opposition continues to have a devastating effect on union organizing success in NLRB campaigns. The regression findings provide some new insights as well, suggesting that unions are much more likely to win in companies which have had a recent ownership change, despite all the negative changes in wages and working conditions that often accompany such changes. The findings also suggest that union success continues to be greatest in units with a significant majority of women or workers of color.

In brief, we found that the use of multifaceted, comprehensive union campaigns plays a much greater role in determining election outcome than individual union tactics. Our analysis also confirms that the more comprehensive organizing tactics used during the campaign, the greater the odds that the union will win the election, even when we control for industry, corporate structure, bargaining unit demographics, and employer opposition. Lastly, we found that although employer opposition and election environment all have a significant impact on election outcome, the number of comprehensive organizing tactics has as much impact as employer opposition and more impact than election environment. Given the consistency and strength of employer campaigns and the great potential for improvement in the quality and intensity of union campaigns, these results support our hypothesis that it is the nature and intensity of union campaigns, rather than the specific industry, company, and unit type in which they operate that plays the most critical role in determining differences in win rates among unions.

CONCLUSION

The coming years will be a period of enormous risks and challenges for the American labor movement. Almost all unions, locally and nationally, understand that both their political power and their bargaining power will be severely undermined unless they organize on a massive scale across every sector of the economy. Yet, as we have shown, this is also a time of great possibility for American unions. While unions face enormous difficulties in terms of changing themselves within the political, legal, and economic environments of organizing, their own organizing strategy is the one area they do control and has great potential for helping unions recapture power and leverage at both the bargaining table and the political arena.

Realizing this potential, however, will not be easy. Even as labor has struggled to regroup, the economic, political, and legal climate has only grown more hostile. Unions today are also much more likely to face a subsidiary of a large multinational parent company with the resources and structure to aggressively resist unionization. This is particularly true in manufacturing, where almost every union campaign must operate under the shadow of globalization and the attendant fear of plant closings, outsourcing, or major downsizing.

But it is too easy to simply blame employer opposition and the organizing environment. American unions themselves must shoulder a good portion of the responsibility for their organizing failures. Although our results demonstrate that even in the most difficult contexts, unions can dramatically increase their organizing success when they run more multifaceted strategic campaigns, the majority of unions organizing today still run weak, ineffectual campaigns that fail to build their strength for the long haul. They simply are not doing what is necessary to succeed in the current climate of mobile capital, aggressive employer opposition, and weak and poorly enforced labor laws. The most pressing question, therefore, is why the majority of unions, despite low win rates, are not choosing to run more comprehensive campaigns?

Part of the answer is rooted in the differences in history, culture, organizational structure, and leadership that influence whether, when, and how each union builds capacity for organizing and moves toward a comprehensive organizing strategy. For example, some of the most successful unions organizing today began building organizing capacity in the 1970's and 1980's starting with the recruitment of a new generation of talented young organizers who had come of age during the civil rights, anti-war, and women's movements. Many of the new recruits received their training as community organizers, welfare rights organizers, or working on the United Farm Workers' boycott, under an organizing model not unlike the comprehensive organizing model presented in this chapter.[26]

This contrasts sharply with more established industrial unions and building trades unions, who felt no pressure to organize until they faced massive membership losses in the 1980s, and, by that time, felt unable or unwilling to invest in the staff and member recruitment and training to organize on any scale. Several unions did not even have an organizing department or an organizing director until the 1990s. Only in the last few years have many of these unions recognized the critical importance of organizing and started the difficult process of shifting more resources into organizing, recruiting, and training more organizers.

This model of organizing is also extremely staff and resource intensive. Unions in the United States suffer from a critical shortage of trained and experienced organizers, as well as union and university labor educators with the knowledge and experience to train organizers in the comprehensive organizing model. But lack of resources cannot explain the failure of the majority of unions to organize more aggressively and effectively. For the costs of not organizing, to their current membership and to the survival of their union, are far greater than the resources and effort involved in utilizing a comprehensive organizing strategy.

Even the country's most successful unions cannot rest on their laurels. Despite notable victories, they too have yet to organize on the scale necessary for labor's revival and to fully utilize the comprehensive strategies that will allow them to expand their gains. At a time when unions need to be organizing hundreds of thousands of workers in order to simply maintain union density at current levels, they will, in addition, need to organize millions across every industry if they are going to make any significant gains in union density.

Nor can unions write off industries and bargaining units where employer opposition is more intense or workers are more hesitant to undertake the risks and challenges that organizing entails. For if unions fail to commit to the strategies necessary to win in manufacturing or other mobile sectors of our economy, they will lose their single most important hedge against the most negative effects of globalization that are fueling the race to the bottom in wages, benefits, and workplace rights and conditions for workers in every other industry. Similarly, if unions fail to more effectively meet the challenge of organizing among higher paid, production workers and professional and technical employees, they will find themselves isolated from a significant portion of the American workforce.

Even among those workers with the greatest propensity to organize— women and workers of color—higher win rates depend on the use of more comprehensive union campaigns, in particular, campaigns that include staff and rank-and-file leadership reflective of the unit being organized. Although women of color and immigrant workers are ready and willing to do what it takes to organize a union in their workplace, they will not endure the stresses and risks of an organizing campaign only to discover that they, and others like them, do not have a seat at the table, or a voice in the union, when the campaign is won.

Unions cannot wait—for labor law reform, for a more favorable economic climate, or more favorable political environment—before they begin to utilize this more comprehensive, multifaceted, and intensive strategy in all their organizing efforts, inside and outside the NLRB process. Regardless of sector or industry, the challenge facing unions today is to move beyond a simple tactical effort to increase numbers and to engage in the self-reflection and organizational change necessary to reverse the larger pattern of decline. Only then will "changing to organize" really bear fruit, and only then will American unions be able regain their power at the bargaining table, in the voting booth, and in the larger community.

APPENDIX 1.1

VARIABLE DEFINITION FOR COMPREHENSIVE ORGANIZING TACTICS

Comprehensive Union-Building Tactics	Variable Definition
1. Adequate and appropriate staff and financial resources	Equals 1 if there is at least one organizer for every 100 eligible voters in the unit; one woman organizer for units with 25 percent or more women; and one organizer of color for units with 25 percent or more workers of color.
2. Strategic targeting	Equals 1 if the union researched the company before the start of the campaign or the company was part of a union targeting plan and the union represented other workers at the same employer or in the same industry.
3. Active and representative rank-and file organizing-committee	Equals 1 if at least 10 percent of the unit is represented on the committee; there is at least one woman on the committee if the unit is 10 percent or more women; at least one person of color on the committee if the unit is 10 percent or more workers of color; and committee members met with workers one-on-one in the workplace and engaged in two or more of the following actions during the campaign: spoke at house meetings, spoke out at captive audience meetings, spoke at community forums, conducted assessments, assisted with preparing board charges, or helped organize job actions.
4. Active participation of member volunteer organizers	Equals 1 if the union used at least five member volunteers from other organized units and they engaged in one or more of the following: meetings outside the workplace, one-on-one in the workplace, leafleting outside the workplace, speaking at community forums, or assessments.
5. Person-to-person contact inside and outside the workplace	Equals 1 if the union house-called the majority of the unit or surveyed workers one-on-one about what they wanted in the contract and conducted at least ten small group meetings or house meetings.

Comprehensive Union-Building Tactics	Variable Definition
6. Benchmarks and assessments to monitor union support and set thresholds for moving ahead with the campaign.	Equals 1 if the union used written assessments to evaluate membership support for the union and waited to file the petition until at least 60 percent of the unit signed cards or petitions.
7. Issues which resonate in the workplace and community	Equals 1 if the union focused on two or more of the following issues during the campaign: dignity, fairness, quality of service, power, voice, or collective representation.
8. Creative, escalating internal pressure tactics involving members in the workplace	Equals 1 if the union used two or more of the following workplace tactics: five or more solidarity days, job actions, rallies, march on the boss for recognition, petitions rather than cards, and union supporters joined employee involvement committees.
9. Creative, escalating external pressure tactics involving members outside the workplace, locally, ationally, nand/or internationally	Equals 1 if the union involved one or more community groups during the campaign and also did at least one more of the following: corporate campaign, cross-border solidarity, involving other unions, using either paid or free media.
10. Building for the first contract before the election	Equals 1 if the union did one or more of the following before the election: chose the bargaining committee, involved workers in developing bargaining proposals, or surveyed at least 70 percent of the unit one-on-one about what they wanted in the contract.

APPENDIX 1.2

DEFINITION AND PREDICTED IMPACT OF CONTROL VARIABLES

Control Variables	Predicted Impact	Variable Definition
Number of eligible voters	No significant impact	Continuous variable measuring the number of eligible voters in the unit when the petition was filed
Manufacturing sector	Negative	Equals 1 if the unit is in the manufacturing sector.
Subsidiary of larger parent company	Negative	Equals 1 if the unit is a subsidiary.
Ownership change	Positive	Equals 1 if there was a change in ownership in the two years before the election.
Good to excellent financial condition	Positive	Equals 1 if the company was in good to excellent financial condition at the time of the election.
Board-determined unit	Negative	Equals 1 if the NLRB determined a different unit than the one the union petitioned for.
Other organized units	Positive	Equals 1 if there were other organized units at the same location as the unit being organized.
Professional, technical or white collar unit	Negative	Equals 1 if the election was in a professional, technical, or white-collar unit.
Unit at least 60 percent women	Positive	Equals 1 if there were 60 percent or more women in the unit.
Unit at least 60 percent workers of color	Positive	Equals 1 if there were 60 percent or more workers of color in the unit.
Number of employer tactics used[27]	Negative	Additive variable adding 1 unit for each additional employer tactic used.

APPENDIX 1.3

PERCENT WIN RATES ACROSS COMBINATIONS OF SIX COMPREHENSIVE ORGANIZING TACTICS

Combinations of comprehensive organizing tactics	Percent win rate						
	Number of tactics used from each combination						
	None	One	Two	Three	Four	Five	Six
Resources + targeting + committee + volunteers + 1on1 + benchmarks	.33	.35	.48	.62	.80	.75	1.00
Resources + targeting + committee + volunteers + 1on1 + issues	.36	.35	.50	.59	.61	.80	1.00
Resources + targeting + committee + volunteers + 1on1 + internal	.35	.35	.49	.54	.65	.70	1.00
Resources + targeting + committee + volunteers + 1on1 + external	.37	.36	.49	.61	.57	.83	1.00
Resources + targeting + committee + volunteers + 1on1 + contract	.32	.40	.47	.54	.64	.79	—
Resources+ committee + 1on1 + issues + external + targeting	.38	.36	.53	.53	.65	.60	1.00
Targeting + committee + volunteers + 1on1 + benchmarks + issues	.36	.33	.48	.60	.63	.86	1.00
Targeting + committee + volunteers + 1on1 + benchmarks + internal	.35	.32	.49	.53	.67	.80	.80
Targeting + committee + volunteers + 1on1 + benchmarks + external	.35	.37	.45	.63	.62	.80	1.00
Targeting + committee + volunteers + 1on1 + benchmarks + contract	.30	.40	.41	.56	.71	.82	.67
Targeting + volunteers + benchmarks + internal + contract + committee	.34	.30	.46	.54	.64	.82	.67
Committee + volunteers + 1on1 + benchmarks + issues + internal	.34	.34	.56	.47	.68	.86	1.00

Combinations of comprehensive organizing tactics	Percent win rate						
	Number of tactics used from each combination						
	None	One	Two	Three	Four	Five	Six
Committee + volunteers + 1on1 + benchmarks + issues + external	.35	.38	.49	.61	.65	1.00	—
Committee + volunteers + 1on1 + benchmarks + issues + contract	.32	.40	.46	.53	.73	.86	—
Committee + volunteers + 1on1 + benchmarks + issues + resources	.33	.38	.52	.60	.77	1.00	1.00
Committee + 1on1 + issues + external + resources + volunteers	.37	.38	.50	.64	.53	1.00	1.00
Volunteers + 1on1 + benchmarks + issues + internal + external	.32	.42	.48	.55	.67	.60	—
Volunteers + 1on1 + benchmarks + issues + internal + contract	.29	.43	.48	.48	.76	.70	—
Volunteers + 1on1 + benchmarks + issues + internal + resources	.31	.40	.51	.57	.65	1.00	1.00
Volunteers + 1on1 + benchmarks + issues + internal + targeting	.34	.35	.48	.53	.70	.69	1.00
Volunteers + benchmarks + internal + contract + targeting + 1on1	.32	.35	.47	.57	.55	.79	.67
1on1 + benchmarks + issues + internal + external + contract	.31	.46	.44	.57	.61	.71	—
1on1 + benchmarks + issues + internal + external + resources	.33	.43	.48	.61	.62	.86	—
1on1 + benchmarks + issues + internal + external + targeting	.36	.36	.50	.51	.72	.64	—
1on1 + benchmarks + issues + internal + external + committee	.34	.40	.48	.55	.66	.83	—
1on1 + issues + external + resources + committee + benchmarks	.34	.42	.46	.65	.79	.83	—
Benchmarks + issues + internal + external + contract + resources	.30	.42	.50	.51	.60	1.00	1.00
Benchmarks + issues + internal + external + contract + targeting	.33	.37	.49	.54	.50	.82	1.00
Benchmarks + issues + internal + external + contract + committee	.31	.43	.45	.52	.61	1.00	—
Benchmarks + issues + internal + external + contract + volunteers	.29	.44	.46	.56	.59	.75	1.00
Benchmarks + internal + contract + targeting + volunteers + issues	.32	.36	.44	.57	.60	.70	1.00
Issues + internal + external + contract + resources + targeting	.33	.40	.50	.55	.44	.75	1.00
Issues + internal + external + contract + resources + committee	.31	.43	.50	.54	.52	1.00	1.00
Issues + internal + external + contract + resources + volunteers	.31	.44	.46	.58	.52	.75	1.00
Issues + internal + external + contract + resources + 1on1	.33	.45	.49	.49	.60	.63	1.00
Issues + external + resources + committee + 1on1 + internal	.35	.41	.49	.61	.50	.80	1.00

Combinations of comprehensive organizing tactics	Percent win rate						
	Number of tactics used from each combination						
	None	One	Two	Three	Four	Five	Six
Internal + external + contract + resources + targeting + committee	.30	.40	.51	.53	.53	.60	1.00
Internal + external + contract + resources + targeting + volunteers	.34	.35	.55	.52	.45	.77	1.00
Internal + external + contract + resources + targeting + 1on1	.34	.39	.56	.48	.52	.57	1.00
Internal + external + contract + resources + targeting + benchmarks	.31	.35	.57	.52	.46	.80	1.00
Internal + contract + targeting + volunteers + benchmarks + external	.32	.35	.52	.53	.55	.71	1.00
External + contract + resources + targeting + committee + volunteers	.34	.37	.50	.57	.57	.78	1.00
External + contract + resources + targeting + committee + 1on1	.32	.44	.46	.54	.59	.75	.67
External+ contract + resources + targeting + committee + benchmarks	.29	.42	.45	.57	.68	1.00	.67
External + contract + resources + targeting + committee + issues	.34	.39	.48	.59	.48	.86	1.00
External + resources + committee + 1on1 + issues + contract	.35	.43	.45	.60	.62	.67	1.00
Contract + resources + targeting + committee + volunteers + 1on1	.32	.40	.47	.54	.64	.79	—
Contract + resources + targeting + committee + volunteers + benchmarks	.30	.35	.47	.59	.78	.78	1.00
Contract + resources + targeting + committee + volunteers + issues	.33	.36	.47	.60	.59	.86	—
Contract + resources + targeting + committee + volunteers + internal	.33	.33	.50	.53	.61	.73	—
Contract + targeting + volunteers + benchmarks + internal + resources	.31	.32	.48	.65	.48	.83	1.00
Average percentages for all combinations	.32	.38	.48	.55	.60	.78	.93
Minimum percentages for all combinations	.29	.30	.41	.47	.44	.57	.67
Maximum percentages for all combinations	.38	.44	.57	.67	.80	1.00	1.00

2

UNION DEMOCRACY AND SUCCESSFUL CAMPAIGNS

THE DYNAMICS OF STAFF AUTHORITY AND WORKER PARTICIPATION IN AN ORGANIZING UNION

Teresa Sharpe

Among those concerned with labor's decades-long decline, the election of John Sweeney's New Voice team to the highest union offices in the United States was cause for excitement. For union activists, Sweeney's call to "organize the unorganized" was a heartening mandate from an office that had been distressingly silent on the issue of declining membership and political power. There is no doubt that today's AFL-CIO looks different from before. Under Sweeney's leadership, the AFL-CIO devotes an unprecedented percentage of its budget to organizing, and it has instituted education and incentive programs to lure its affiliates into doing the same. Sweeney's old stomping ground, the Service Employees International Union (SEIU), has made the most impressive "change to organize," earmarking a full 50 percent of its international budget to organizing. Although institutional change has trickled down to the local level at a slow pace, it would be rare to find a union today that does not give at least lip service to the necessity of organizing.

Despite a growing consensus that unions must either increase their membership through new organizing or else risk extinction, both organizational transformation and successful union organizing have proved to be tedious and contentious projects. Elected leaders and staff, long accustomed to a bureaucratic style of "business unionism," commonly understand their industry as the particular exception to the organizing mandate, and oppose changes that threaten to make their servicing expertise obsolete. Unionized workers who over the years relied on paid union representatives to deal with their employers may also resent a unionism that replaces business agents with organizers, or transfers the work of paid representatives to volunteer shop-stewards. Internal resistance to change is a formidable impediment to union revitalization.

Research on the new unionism shows that labor resurgence involves significant movement in two areas. First, tactical innovation has a significant top-down dimension (Voss and Sherman 2001; Bronfenbrenner and Yuravich 1998; Bronfenbrenner and Hickey [in this volume]; Lerner 1991 and 1996). Rather than the desire for change bubbling up organically from the rank and file, experts play an important role in importing creative new tactics, at times against the wishes of the old guard (Voss and Sherman 2001). Organizing requires the strategic expertise of leaders with the experience and skills to navigate a complex field of struggle. Comprehensive campaigns, labor's best hope for organizing on an industry-wide scale, require the careful coordination of a competent staff.

Yet if the vision of revitalization often originates in the upper echelons of labor unions, neither the ideological commitment to change nor the practice of a new type of unionism can remain at the top. Leaders running for election on pro-organizing platforms must convince union members that allocating resources to organizing is ultimately in their best interest. Beyond eliciting the passive consent of the membership, leaders must also mobilize the rank and file to participate in actual organizing campaigns. Indeed, this is the second key ingredient in labor's revitalization. Previous research has driven home the point that the most successful new union tactics rely on extensive worker participation. In their chapter in this volume, Bronfenbrenner and Hickey find that unions are more likely to win certification elections when they use a comprehensive strategy built on "rank-and-file intensive" tactics, and involve workers in the organizing of their own work-places (see also Bronfenbrenner and Juravich 1998).

Ultimately, then, the new unionism demands not only the on-going participation of workers, but also the support of skilled leaders and staff capable of developing and carrying out strategic campaigns. Some argue that skilled leadership from the top and rank-and-file participation from below are compatible: workers participate in campaigns when leaders develop campaigns worth participating in (Lerner 1991). Yet while workers do make savvy choices about when to get involved, they are more likely to stay involved if they feel a sense ownership over the direction and outcome of the organizing drive (Markowitz 2000). Hence a necessary balance between a staff with the power to make strategic decisions and a rank and file empowered to take and sustain action.

This paper explores the issues that arise when these two components of robust unionism come together. Examining a local Hotel and Restaurant Employees (HERE) campaign to organize a hotel in a large California city, I explore the dynamics between staff authority and worker participation in the context of a new organizing campaign. While I argue that staff created a space for increasing participation, I also identify a tension between staff's efforts to build effective worker leadership, and their need to carefully manage and control the course of the campaign.

Given the dual demands of staff direction and worker participation, an understanding of the dynamics between the two provides an insightful window on some of the challenges facing contemporary unions. In union strategist Stephen Lerner's model, strategy is formulated in rooms that are closed to the rank and file, and workers participate primarily as part of an "army willing to risk arrest" (Lerner 1991). Staff leaders draft workers into this rank-and-file army through compelling campaigns. But what happens after the campaign ends and the army of workers demobilize? Devoting energies only to short spurts of worker mobilization risks engendering a fundamental separation between leaders and the membership—a split characteristic of bureaucratic unionism of the past. While such a separation may initially jump-start unions in which the membership opposes allocating resources to new organizing, merely institutionalizing new leadership at the top risks inhibiting the creation of rank-and-file leadership, the promotion of sustained activism, and the flourishing of social movement unionism. A focus on winning, in the absence of a radical reconception of the role of the rank and file, threatens the long-term viability of a more worker-centered model of unionism.

While some of Lerner's critics note his failure to envision more robust worker participation, none of them offer a viable alternative (Gruelle and Parker 1999; Slaughter 1998; Moody 1997). Gruelle and Parker, for example, condemn the staff direction of unions, arguing that unions are less powerful when paid officials run the program. They admonish Lerner for neglecting issues of union democracy.

> Lerner said not a word about rank-and-file initiative or control . . . Quite the contrary; Lerner clearly means officials and staff when he says "we" should build campaigns that "give our members reason to be involved." Workers are to be "activated," in Lerner's word—a cannon fodder version of organizing. In this view, member control is not relevant to rebuilding unions. But far from being a distraction, internal democracy is key to union power.

In this view, union democracy consists of member control, and democracy is incompatible with a leadership separate from the rank and file. Democracy exists when workers, rather than paid staff, set union priorities. Rather than relying on expert leadership to run campaigns, unions should give workers the space to learn on their own. Workers might not always make the most strategic decisions, but the process of learning is part and parcel of building strong unions capable of combating powerful employers. "If the rank and file can't even control their local union," argues Kim Moody, "how are they going to 'control' some aspect of a big corporation? Who'd dare to try?" (Moody 1999).

While Lerner's model is not beyond reproach, there are also serious flaws in the "democracy is power" line of reasoning, as well as in the concept of direct member control. First, what is to be done when the rank and file democratically opts for more servicing? (Voss and Sherman 2001; Lopez 2000; Fletcher and Hurd 1998.) The notion that member control equals union power not only assumes that workers will have the desire to run their union, if given the chance, but also that they will instinctively seek out ways to make their union grow. History shows that union members at times actively oppose efforts to increase their membership, especially to outsiders.

A second problem with the equation of democracy and power is the implicit assumption that strategic skills and new tactics arise spontaneously. Democracy advocates cannot explain how the rank and file creates winning campaigns in the absence of skilled leadership. Such leaders may eventually emerge from the rank and file, but without staff support and training at the front end, workers will find it difficult to generate effective strategy. The assumption that workers will figure out through trial and error how to combat an employer's sophisticated and well-funded anti-union campaign risks setting them up for failure. Such defeats are unlikely to provide an impetus for further activism; indeed, defeats and their interpretations have wide-ranging implications for social movements (Polletta 1998; Voss 1998). While understanding why a particular failure occurred is an important part of the learning process, in the absence of its positive interpretation the main lesson workers may learn from a defeat may be not to try. In order for defeats to be productive, they must be critically analyzed; they also must be interpreted in a way that boosts morale and encourages further participation. Otherwise, interpretations of defeat risk demobilizing the workers.

One illustration of the need for training and staff support comes from Lopez's (2000) ethnography of the SEIU in Pittsburgh. In the course of a nursing home contract campaign, staff had planned for workers at a handful of facilities to conduct job actions. Unfortunately, staff organizers had failed to anticipate obstacles that these workers might face when the time came to publicly show their support of the union, including fear of supervisors and wariness around less supportive co-workers. Without substantial support from union staff and dependable rank-and-file leadership, nursing home workers, long accustomed to business representatives dealing directly with their boss, found it hard to participate in confrontational actions. "The problem," Lopez argues, "was not with the workers themselves but in the fact that the union suddenly expected them to take on too much responsibility without providing the necessary training and support" (Lopez 2000, 169).

Other scholars have noted the importance of a vigorous connection between leaders and members. Marshall Ganz (2001) articulates a complex relationship between strategic leadership and the rank and file. He argues that the United Farm Workers (UFW) initially succeeded where the AFL-sponsored Agricultural Workers Organizing Committee (AWOC) failed, because the leadership core of the UFW was more closely connected and accountable to farm workers. A mix of insiders (farm workers) and outsiders (recruited from other social movements) made it possible for leaders to develop strategy in an environment of dynamic creativity and a wide range of experience. The UFW's ability to develop an effective strategy, one that addressed the real needs of farm workers, enabled them to successfully mobilize tens of thousands of workers in a relatively short time. A successful strategy developed out of the relationship of leaders and the rank and file, rather than being the result of a closed meeting of union staff who were skilled in campaigns but distant from the workers. Ganz's argument suggests that worker mobilization is not the end of the story, but the beginning out of which a vibrant connection between leaders and workers can be built, in turn enabling leaders to create relevant and effective strategy. The process can be a virtuous circle in which leaders' connections to the rank and file increase the union's "strategic capacity" (Ganz 2001), and good strategy in turn increases the level of participation of the rank and file.

Like Ganz, Linda Markowitz (2000) is concerned with the dynamic relationship between leadership and the rank and file. *How* workers are organized, Markowitz shows, affects the level of rank-and-file participation and workplace activism after the campaign ends. Looking beyond the period of election success, she finds that "worker activism experienced during organizing campaigns diffuses outside campaign settings" (Markowitz 2000, 45). The potential for activism is bounded by the structure of a campaign, specifically by whether or not the union campaign is based on worker participation. Comparing what she calls a participatory (ACTWU) and a non-participatory (UFCW) campaign, Markowitz finds that, in the course of the campaigns, workers in the two unions developed different cognitive frameworks of unionism—one that encouraged further activism and one that inhibited it. Participatory organizing builds a sense of self-efficacy, ownership, and solidarity, creating an institutional structure for sustained activism. Conversely, staff-driven organizing that fails to involve workers reproduces the "union as business" model and instills in workers the belief that the union exists merely to deliver the goods.

Markowitz illustrates the importance of involving workers in the process of organizing their workplace. She also shows that the meaning of a union in the minds of workers is not predetermined but created through experience. For instance, in the ACTWU campaign that she studied, workers came to believe that the success of the union depended on their on-going participation. Yet her thesis—that campaign activism drives further activism—fails to account for how workers come to participate in the first place. In her account, an ACTWU organizer comes to town and immediately begins talking to the workers about the union campaign.

> Employees first listened to the information that the organizers provided about unions and some did their own research to confirm that what the organizers said was accurate. Once workers believed that organizers gave them reliable information, they developed trust in the union, which gave them impetus to join together and use the information in original ways to collectively mobilize the entire workforce. (Markowitz 2001, 124)

Certainly the ways in which organizers convey information about the union and the campaign have enormous effects on whether or not workers will get involved (see also Lopez 2000). But Markowitz seems to suggest that the only obstacle in the election campaign was the initial establishment of trust. In the end, she notes that the workers felt a strong sense of efficacy and ownership. Just how that evolved remains vague.

A further problem is that Markowitz's descriptions of participation are often undeveloped, so that her conception of a participatory campaign remains fuzzy. She maintains that a structure of open communication is key. "Open communication means that participants have a place to discuss the goal, are allowed to disagree about the means of attaining the goal, and have the opportunity to voice new issues and concerns about the goal" (Markowitz 2001, 43). Yet she never discusses instances when organizers discuss strategy or goals with workers, much less moments when workers might voice opposition. Her examples of participation, which consist mainly of workers coming to meetings, fall short of her own definitions of participatory unionism.

Despite these shortcomings, Markowitz articulates the useful notion of a participatory democracy continuum, and contrasts this with what she calls "pseudoparticipation."

> Participatory democracy as a continuum means that, while not all workers participate all the time, information, open communication, and shared

decision-making are present at least from some members on some issues. Pseudoparticipation, however, occurs when there is not actual change in the authoritative organizational structure, but simply an alteration in the level of participation within it. (Markowitz 2001, 43)

Given the evidence Markowitz presents, however, it is difficult to evaluate where her participatory case falls on the continuum, or whether it became in the end—when staff shut workers out during the period of contract negotiations—an illustration of pseudoparticipation. Ultimately, she doesn't answer a seemingly important question: how do we know a democratic union when we see one?

Perhaps part of the problem lies in the effort to unambiguously label a union or union campaign as democratic or undemocratic. Rather than an either/or proposition, democracy might be better understood as a goal or ideal that a campaign is working toward. Democratic participation requires at least a basic understanding of what is to be deliberated; in the context of a union campaign, workers need to understand the basics of strategy and tactics before they can decide what might be the best course of action. Thus, educating and training workers facilitates the emergence of a more participatory democracy. One way to illuminate this is to closely examine the process by which staff organizers use their expertise to create a space in which workers feel able and willing to make decisions and become workplace leaders. Strong direction from the top of the union can constrain participatory democracy if strategic decision-making is monopolized by a few. Yet it is possible for workers to be genuinely engaged in the work of union building—participating in some levels of decision-making some of the time—even when they don't make all of the decisions all of the time.

Participatory democracy, then, is a complex and evolving process. With effort and over time, organizers can create structures that give workers increasing input and power within a campaign. When both campaign success (winning) and an active rank and file (activists and leaders) are conceptualized as goals, effective leaders are given the task not only of developing and overseeing winnable campaigns, but of facilitating the emergence of a participatory democracy. There are contexts in which democracy may arise *in spite of* an oligarchic leadership, particularly in corrupt unions. But, as I argue here, it can also emanate *from* a leadership genuinely concerned with worker empowerment and leadership development. In the case I observed, the president of the union and staff organizers prioritized on-going leadership development, which helped narrow a gap in knowledge and skills between leaders and the rank and file.

In the local I studied, elected leaders and staff organizers had a sophisticated and well-developed conception of leadership development. It involved the teaching and practicing of organizing skills, like how to do a house visit or speak at a city council meeting. Workers were never simply thrown into difficult situations without extensive training and role-playing. Organizers did their best to ensure that when workers took on new responsibilities and positions of leadership, the experience would be a positive one. But beyond this, leadership development entailed a more radical element of political education. Organizers taught about *power*. Primarily, the focus was on how to shift power at the hotel through mobilization and confrontation, and organizers framed on-going victories in the hotel—like winning the fight over wearing union buttons or backing management off from disciplining union activists over petty job infractions—as examples of collective power. Organizers also facilitated discussions of industry power, bringing workers from union shops to talk about the situation in their hotel or casino, and linking up higher wages and better working conditions with high union density, though not quite in these words. Whenever they could, and especially as the campaign wore on, organizers promoted a more expansive understanding of union power, one that was not limited to the notion of a contract in a single shop.

Staff at the local saw leadership development as a process. While they worked to empower union activists and increase their level of involvement in the campaign and the local, they did not see hierarchy as antithetical to either worker involvement or the training process. As Mark Warren (2001) points out in his discussion of the Industrial Areas Foundation (IAF), the very nature of leadership development rests on an assumption of authority. We might feel uncomfortable openly acknowledging the existence of power, particularly in working-class organizations, but "leadership *development* implies that there is an authoritative agency with the skills and knowledge lacking in others who need such training" (2001, 212). Leaders can teach practical and analytical skills in a way that fosters a type of democratic participation that bodes well for the possibility of a larger democratic revitalization. In this context, authority enables, rather than constrains, participatory democracy. Seeing authority as a productive force, rather than a repressive one, gives greater purchase on understanding the relationship between staff authority and worker participation in the campaign that I discuss below. Staff trained workers to organize and strategize, and encouraged a greater degree of decision-making, while workers practiced and perfected their skills.

This is not to argue that the dynamic between staff authority and worker participation was seamless, or without tension. Power and control were negotiated continually in interactions between organizers and workers. Organizers pushed workers into action. Workers were usually open and responsive to this type of agitation, but sometimes they pushed back—actively arguing strategy or passively withdrawing their participation. Sometimes organizers consciously overlooked or ignored this resistance, whereas other times they could not; after all, while organizers worked hard to push the agenda, the agenda could only be implemented with the consent of the workers.

HERE LOCAL B AND THE BAYVIEW CAMPAIGN

Rather than seeking an NLRB election, HERE Local B[1] ran a non-NLRB pressure campaign, the goal being a contract rather than recognition. After five months of covert committee building, organizers purposefully made the campaign public, and in the three days following about 80 percent of Bayview workers signed union cards. A few months later, Bayview workers authorized a boycott of the hotel. Close to a year later, Bayview workers had an impressive first contract.

Bayview Hotel is a moderately upscale waterfront hotel employing about 190 workers. The non-managerial workforce was largely immigrant and African-American; immigrants came from, among other places, Mexico, Central America, the Philippines, Tibet, and Laos. Employees were departmentally segregated by race or ethnicity, language and sex. Despite these work divisions, there was a strong sense of community across departments, particularly among older employees who had been at the hotel for many years. While there was rapid turnover in some departments due to the booming local labor market, average job tenure was high. Many Bayview employees worked at least one other job, often in the hospitality industry (the possibility of working only one job was an incentive for many workers to join the union). At the beginning of the union campaign, pay was far below industry standards for the region, and most workers had not received substantial wage increases in twelve years. Health insurance was prohibitively expensive, workers were routinely denied full-time hours, and the part-time nature of much of the work meant few employees were entitled to even the most basic benefits. For those who were employed full-time, benefits remained paltry.

Organizers devoted the first six months of the Bayview campaign to building the worker organizing committee. As much as they could, they targeted existing workplace leaders to join the committee. Secrecy was of utmost importance during this early stage. Local B had recently lost a new organizing campaign at a nearby hotel, and from this defeat staff had learned the hard way the importance of waiting to go public until the whole committee was fully on board. At this other hotel, management had found out about the union drive before there was a strong organizing committee, and, after a couple of outspoken activists were fired, many of the remaining committee members withdrew their support in fear of further management retaliation. In the Bayview campaign, until the first large committee meeting, after which organizers knew it would be impossible to keep the campaign underground, organizers were careful to house visit only those workers who were already union members from other workplaces, or those whom other committee members had solidly recommended.

Once located, organizers gave workers who were targeted for the committee small tasks to test their commitment and reliability, such as gathering the addresses of a couple of their co-workers, copying down the work schedule in their area (to help determine when co-workers might be at home), or investigating new hires in their department. Organizers met with workers in their homes and stressed in every visit the importance of staying silent about the union drive, even with closest friends at work. Once organizers were confident of a worker's support and commitment to the union, they explained in great detail what it meant to be a member of the organizing committee. Only then was the worker asked to sign a union card and join the committee. Workers usually showed at least a little reluctance at this point—claiming, perhaps, that they weren't really the leader type—but nevertheless almost every worker recruited for the committee during these early months agreed to join.

At any given time, the Bayview organizing committee consisted of about thirty-five workers representative of the different departments. Each committee member was responsible for continually organizing three to six of her co-workers, either while at work or during weekly house visits. Staff organizers planned with precision the structure of the committee in order to ensure that each of the hotel's 190 employees stayed in regular contact with a committee member and tracked this on huge charts on the walls of the union office. Organizers were in turn responsible for keeping in regular contact with the committee members they directed, communicating with each of them at least every couple of days. Committee members were required to attend the meetings and go out on house visits every week. The union did not pay members of the committee, but it did occasionally offer small stipends to workers who had their hours significantly reduced because of their union activity.

To accommodate different work shifts, the weekly committee meetings were held twice every Tuesday at a local Catholic Church. These meetings served a variety of functions. They were an opportunity to collectively review the week's victories and affirm confidence in the ongoing campaign. Organizers also used them as a venue to teach practical and analytical skills, often breaking the group down into smaller discussion groups. Lessons were not unidirectional; while organizers taught practical skills, such as how to talk to reticent co-workers, committee members kept organizers current on how management and other workers were responding inside the hotel. And, particularly as the campaign progressed, committee members suggested imaginative tactics; at times, in scenes reminiscent of Ganz's UFW meetings, collective brainstorms yielded a space of creativity that neither staff organizers nor committee members could have fashioned on their own.

LEADERSHIP DEVELOPMENT

As I briefly discussed above, Local B prioritized on-going leadership development in all its organizing projects and established union shops. Organizers assumed workers wouldn't magically emerge as full-fledged union activists and therefore would have to be trained in organizing and leadership skills. In the Bayview campaign, organizers worked with committee members to help them develop the skills they needed to effectively recruit their co-workers, confront management, and make decisions about the campaign. This focus on building worker leadership also served the pragmatic needs of the campaign, since it would have been impossible for organizers to stay in close contact with all 190 Bayview workers. Committee members articulated to their co-workers what came to be known as the "plan to win"; they also brought them out to union actions, gathered their signatures on petitions, and prodded them when they showed reluctance.

In general, developing a structure of worker leadership allowed the local to shift servicing responsibilities to stewards, freeing more union staff for organizing. In their union shops, stewards are the first to handle workplace grievances, taking over tasks that in the past were the domain of business representatives. Members are encouraged to envision union growth as beneficial to all workers in their industry, and organizers train activists to help organize at work sites other than their own. Workers at Local B's union shops sometimes came and spoke to the Bayview organizing committee and joined the regular picket lines.

Leadership development in the Bayview campaign involved teaching strategic thinking and concrete organizing skills. From the beginning, organizers stressed that the local had a strategic plan to win. Every chance they could get, organizers would explain that the local was waging a winnable campaign on multiple fronts. They also noted that the local's earlier haphazard attempts to unionize the Bayview hotel, which some of the older workers remembered, was entirely different from what the union was up to this time around. In the past, the union had simply set up shop in the restaurant in order to recruit workers and then casually left when this failed to yield any substantial support (at least this was the lore). Workers who were now pledging their support by standing up to managers were understandably nervous that the campaign would fail, as it had done earlier, and leave them vulnerable to retaliation. When this issue came up, organizers stressed that the local was not only waging a strategic campaign with the support of the larger community, but that they were promising to stick around until a good contract was secured. In the first committee meeting, the union president handed out a signed declaration to each committee member in which this was promised.

One of the first strategic lessons involved an explanation to the organizing committee of why the local wasn't organizing toward an election with the NLRB. This was important not just because staff wanted to explain the logic behind the pressure campaign, but because they predicted from past experience that management would accuse the union of denying workers a democratic vote. Anticipating that management would try to appropriate the language of democracy, organizers stressed that NLRB elections themselves were undemocratic. At the very first committee meeting, Frank, the president of the local, described the long and bureaucratic process of a labor board election. On over four pieces of butcher paper taped lengthwise to the wall, Frank drew out a likely time line of events in case the union were to organize around an election campaign. Outlining all the stages of possible court appeals, he described a process that was outrageously long and in the end uncertain. "Best case scenario," he told the assembled committee, "we would begin bargaining in [two years]. Is this what we want?" After workers shook their heads, he went on to ask, "Do you think the fight is in the courts or in the hotel? Where do you think the best place to fight is?" Finally, Frank inoculated workers against the notion that elections were the inherently democratic option by asking them, "Can you have a fair election under a dictatorship? Some of you are from the Philippines, could you have a fair election under Marcos?"

Instead, after a worker signed a union card, organizers emphasized that this act was the vote. Committee members adopted this logic as their own, and passed it on to their co-workers. The committee also told management about voting through the union card, asserting in all the early delegations—in which a group of workers dropped in at a manager's office unannounced—that "we've already voted, count the union cards." This became the committee mantra for the first few months of the campaign.

In mandatory captive audience meetings, management indeed tried to argue that the union's reluctance to an election was undemocratic, just as the organizers had predicted. But this argument never went over with the committee members and their co-workers who were well-steeped in the logic of the pressure campaign. The general manager did, however, use this tactic in the community. In a letter to the city orchestra, which had expressed concern over holding their event in a boycotted hotel, he wrote:

Congressional representatives, state senators are all chosen by secret ballot. For over 60 years, the NLRB has been conducting secret ballot elections for millions of employees . . . the best way to support our employees is to tell the union and the NLRB than an election should be conducted to protect the right of employees to make a decision without coercion. The hotel will honor the results in a secret ballot election.

Of interest was not that management employed this predictable rhetoric of democracy, but that they knew better than to use this tactic with workers.

Another example of leadership development involved teaching the committee how best to allocate a limited amount of organizing resources. In one meeting, organizers helped the committee evaluate how many "actions" the union could coordinate in any given month. Kyla, a staff organizer, drew three columns labeled "high resources," "medium resources," and "low resources." Written on post-it notes were dozens of familiar campaign actions, among them, "brunch picket," "leafleting outside the hotel," and "delegation to human resources." Workers assessed the kinds of resources each action demanded and stuck the different post-it notes in the appropriate column. Kyla explained that there were "different types of actions, ranging from four people delegating a manager—which we can plan in a day—to a 400 person rally like our boycott kick-off rally where we turned out over 60 workers and needed several weeks to plan." Holding up an "early AM picket" note, the organizer asked, "Where do you think this goes?" The room was quiet for a few seconds, until Sharon, a housekeeper, suggested "medium resources." Kyla nods, sticks the note in the middle column, and goes on to ask. "What about a cafeteria teach-in?" Workers brainstormed how this might work: "Would we do it in the morning?" "Wouldn't it be difficult to get workers to come to the teach-in with managers eating in the room?" "How would we get in there without managers noticing?" Laura, another staff organizer, interrupted the group to point out that the goal of the exercise was not to get bogged down in the details, but to think realistically about how much preparation each event required. "Four people to run the teach-in, a couple of days to decide what we should talk about. This is what we mean by resources," she explained. These exercises helped the committee learn to evaluate what they could likely plan in a given period of time.

More than anything else, organizers trained the committee to talk with their co-workers about the union, and to lead work-site actions. Workplace actions both strengthened the resolve of the organizing committee and deterred management's use of some especially egregious anti-union tactics. "Cultures of solidarity" (Fantasia 1988) emerged through such collective action and shared experiences of struggle. Support for the union increased over time as non-activist workers saw members of the organizing committee confront management and win real improvements.

The committee also learned to use confrontations with management to derail an anti-union campaign. If a manager unfairly disciplined a union activist, or tried to intimidate workers, organizers planned a delegation of workers to protest. Although these were committee-led work-site actions, the confrontations were meticulously premeditated and rehearsed in the weekly meetings. Creating a sense of conflict with individual managers was usually easy, since most workers were already frustrated with their managers before the campaign began. For organizers, the challenge was to inspire and empower the committee with an alternative vision of workplace power dynamics, and to convince them that challenging management face-to-face could lead to real change.

Early on, organizers had the organizing committee set the tone for how they would react to management's attempts to ignore or derail the union drive. Four days after the local president formally delivered the union petition announcing the organizing campaign, the general manager called for mandatory department meetings to discuss the results of recent employee surveys. Organizers assumed that management planned to talk about the union in these meetings, and they prepared the committee to respond. The goal was for the committee to turn the tables on management and use the first captive audience meeting as the stage for the committee's first show of strength.

Prior to the scheduled department meetings, staff organizers and committee members got together to plan their response. Workers spent two hours discussing and rehearsing the "take over" of the department meetings. Organizers explained the importance of standing up to management and appropriating management's space as their own, and in preparation they role-played what might happen. One of the organizers, pretending to be the general manager, began the mock meeting by lecturing on why a union would be bad at the Bayview Hotel. As planned, committee members began standing up and articulating why they supported the union and demanding that the general manager "count the [union] cards." Finally, the entire committee was on its feet, and workers finished by breaking into a round of excited applause. After this was over, organizers went around the room and asked each committee member for a commitment to stand up in the real meeting. To make it easier, two people from each department volunteered to stand first.

Over the next three days, the hotel buzzed with news of the meetings. Committee members from all the departments except one stood up to speak when managers and their hired consultants began talking about the union. In the restaurant and kitchen meeting I attended, management barely had time to say anything about the union before committee members started to respond. Raul, a committee member from the kitchen who was one of the first to speak, finished his speech by dramatically unrolling a union petition signed by an overwhelming majority of Bayview workers. Over half a dozen workers stood up to speak critically of the meeting—even one woman who did not yet support the union but who was clearly emboldened by what was happening in the room. After realizing that workers were "not going to act reasonably," and I would guess stunned by what was happening, the general manager abruptly ended the meeting. Committee members and their co-workers stayed behind to cheer, rehash the details of the meeting and mock the managers who had tried to silence them. Excitedly, they called organizers (who were waiting out in the parking lot) on their cell phones to report what had happened. Support for the union increased in the weeks after this, and more workers came to work with their union buttons pinned to their uniforms. Management never again assembled workers for large meetings; in fact, they avoided any type of gathering where actions like these might be repeated.

The committee pressed on with the workplace campaign, and its actions continued to be wildly successful. Organizers and committee members rehearsed delegations and confrontations in response to a whole host of tactics that management had tried in their attempts to deflate the momentum of the organizing drive. When the Human Resources manager asked several committee members for their immigration papers, organizers avoided the issue of undocumented workers by reframing the issue as one of intimidation, and by organizing a delegation in response. In one delegation I openly videotaped, a handful of restaurant and kitchen workers confronted two Human Resources managers in their offices, asserting that asking for immigration papers was a "scare tactic [that] wasn't going to work." After a series of these delegations from the different departments and community supporters from outside the hotel, Human Resource managers stopped demanding papers.

As time went on, the committee learned that delegations were successful in pressuring management and impressing their co-workers and these actions became part of the committee's regular tactical repertoire. Still, the process of leadership development was a gradual one—with ongoing intervention on the part of union staff. For example, when workers began complaining about Helen, an unpopular manager in housekeeping who was picking on union activists, organizers hoped committee members would suggest a delegation. But rather than simply telling the committee to organize their co-workers to confront this manager, organizers encouraged the housekeepers themselves to strategize a response in the evening committee meeting. After an update on the union's "recent victories," Kyla prompted a discussion of Helen. The housekeepers responded to the mention of her name with a barrage of angry comments.

"She's just rude to us," said one. "She won't even say hello in the mornings," added another. A third worker complained, "She wouldn't pass my room [for inspection] because the hairdryer wasn't straight. Can you believe that? The hairdryer?"

"She's been there for two weeks and she thinks she knows more than us. We don't need her telling us how to do our jobs. I'm not gonna take that from her, and I'll tell her that," another went on to say.

Laura, the organizer running the meeting, let the housekeepers talk amongst themselves for a couple of minutes, then tried to steer the conversation toward Helen's anti-union offenses and toward a committee response. "So what should we do about this?" She asked in a loud voice, attempting to refocus the meeting. "How should we deal with Helen?" There was a brief pause, then everyone started talking at once.

"I'll tell her to leave me alone the next time she says something."

"I'm not going to fix the hairdryer if she tells me to. I don't care if it's straight or not."

Becky, the lead organizer, had been observing the meeting from a chair on the sidelines. She let out an audible sigh and stood up. When she began talking, she brought up one of the senior housekeepers, a staunch committee member who had been having the most trouble with Helen. "Mary, one of the strongest leaders in the hotel, told me yesterday that she doesn't want to go to work because of Helen. Mary has supported you all in your struggles. What should we do?" After a long silence, one of the housekeepers spoke up.

"She should go in and tell Helen to leave her alone."

Most of the housekeepers nodded. But this wasn't the answer that Becky was hoping for. She wanted the committee to suggest collective action. She tried to nudge them in this direction by asking questions about earlier incidents that had prompted workers' delegations. "What did we do when Laurant was picking on Gabriel? What did we do when Quin and Sarah were written up? What did we do when Julie asked Alfonso and Carlos for their papers? Did they go in alone to talk to [the managers]?"

To the palpable relief of the organizers, one of the housekeepers made the right suggestion. "We should go in as a group to talk to Helen."

Laura nodded vigorously. "Yes, and should it just be housekeeping that goes in, or should the committee and supporters from other departments go with you?"

"Other departments should go with us. We've gone on their delegations, now it's their turn to come with us."

"That's right," Laura said. "If you want to see something changed you have to do it together. And you don't have to wait for us to talk about it in the meetings, you can organize delegations yourself if something comes up. This is what our members [at other union shops] do. This is what it means to be a union. You don't have to deal with these managers alone. Together you have power."

By the end of the meeting, housekeepers had planned and role-played a confrontation with Helen for the next morning. Although it took them a while to come around to the idea, once someone suggested a delegation the entire committee responded enthusiastically. And according to the housekeepers and maintenance staff who "marched on" Helen the following day, the delegation was a great success. Workers demanded that management stop harassing union supporters, and asserted that management's attempts to intimidate them only made the union stronger. Shortly after the delegation, Helen was transferred back to her old job as the general manager's personal assistant. At the next committee meeting one of the housekeepers described the decision to plan the action in a way that suggested it came from the workers: "We thought we needed to plan a delegation because Helen was bothering Mary, and when she picks on one of us, she picks on all of us."

This example illustrates not only the extreme care that went into getting the housekeepers to suggest a delegation, but the difficulty in assessing organizers' versus workers' control over the campaign and its tactics. Whose idea was the delegation? While the organizers clearly pushed the committee members to stage the action, the final decision and plan to delegate Helen was the product of dialogue. As a result of the learning process, the housekeepers themselves came to see the value of a delegation, and understood the action as one of their own making.

There were many less dramatic instances of skills teaching. Besides orchestrating confrontations, organizers taught committee members how best to organize their co-workers. Committee members were expected not just to take risks themselves, but to convince others to participate in on-going workplace and boycott actions. For the most part, this happened when organizers went with committee members to the houses of the their co-workers to talk about the union. Before and after the visit, organizers would discuss with their trainees the stages of a successful house call and ask them to reflect on the visit. Committee members sometimes teased organizers about these lessons, asking staff organizers in mock earnestness what they thought went well or bad with the visit before organizers could ask them this same question. These lessons worked, though, and with practice committee members improved their ability to convince their co-workers to participate in the union's ongoing activities.

As the campaign progressed, committee members grew frustrated with the tepid levels of union support from some of the workers in the hotel and suggested to organizers that some of their co-workers were never going to support the union. Organizers, however, assumed that with the right kind of organizing most workers could be brought around to the benefits of unionization. Thus, when committee members started regularly reporting hesitation among their co-workers, as well as their own frustration over their inability to change the minds of their co-workers, organizers intervened with a lesson on active listening. If committee members could just listen closely enough to the subtle protestations of their co-workers, organizers reasoned, they could get at the "real reason" why someone was against the union—and they then would be better equipped to respond.

In this meeting, organizers discussed the importance of active listening. "If you are doing most of the talking," Becky explained, "then there's a problem." Becky recognized that the impulse was to talk at people, barraging them with information in order to convince them to come to a rally or sign a petition. "We all want to do this, because we think we are right!" Becky said. "But when we talk at people, we don't hear their fears, and if we don't address their fears, they won't do what we ask of them." A few minutes later, the three staff organizers broke the committee up into small groups to role-play "listening for the issue"—that is, identifying the underlying reason why "the worker" was hesitant to take some action, and then responding appropriately. In each group, an organizer acted the part of the reticent worker, and a committee member attempted to convince them to participate in a boycott rally. This was a difficult exercise. When my own turn came, I completely overlooked that the worker I was trying to organize was worried about the campaign failing. Another committee member in my group caught on, and the debriefing of my mock house visit turned into a fruitful discussion of how to deal with the fear of failure.

In another meeting, organizers stressed that workers have different reasons for supporting the union, and that effective organizing entailed recognizing this diversity and then using it to better connect with people on the issues they found important. If someone supported the union because they wanted health insurance for their three kids, then committee members should bring up health insurance when they were trying to get their co-workers to take action for the union. Organizers told the committee that they should learn the "life stories" of the people they were trying to organize. "We are all fighting for different reasons," Becky explained, "so what moves me to action is probably different than what moves Carlos and Alfonso to action. And if I don't know why Carlos wants a union, what his history is, how can I organize him?" To illustrate the diversity of experience, organizers had each committee member draw a picture that showed what personally motivated them to "fight for the union," concentrating on their families, the hotel, and people who had been inspirational in their lives. Workers then shared these pictures with the larger group.

Interestingly, these lessons not only helped workers hone their organizing skills, but they revealed the same techniques the organizers themselves used on committee members. By teaching workers to organize, staff also taught these workers to recognize when they were *being* organized. Indeed, just as organizers discussed with committee members the best way to talk to their co-workers about the union, so did organizers discuss with their staff supervisors the best way to talk to members of the committee—sometimes, even, using similar role-plays.

As the organizing committee accumulated victories and new skills, their power to effect workplace change grew; conversely, management continued to flounder in their attempts to dissuade workers from supporting the union. Committee members exhibited a strong sense of ownership over the campaign and the union, the result of numerous workplace victories and organizers' constant efforts to get the committee to generate ideas in the meetings. Committee members talked frequently about how they were winning, constantly reminding their co-workers of ongoing victories and the overall plan to win. As Joanna, a young African-American housekeeper said in one meeting, "We might not win tomorrow or next week or even next year, but we *will* win."

TENSIONS IN COMBINING STRATEGIC LEADERSHIP WITH PARTICIPATORY DEMOCRACY

Local B leaders and organizers developed the larger strategy of the campaign. But the union could go nowhere without the support of the organizing committee. Organizers continually alleged that workers decided campaign strategy. This claim, another way of articulating the popular notion that "workers are the union," was partly a tactic employed to prevent management from claiming that the union was a third party that unjustly took away worker agency. But it was more than that. Workers voted with their feet, participating in union actions that they approved and endorsed, and, as time went on, the organizing committee took on increasing responsibility for the campaign. So when organizers insisted that workers were the highest authority in the union, this was not just rhetoric.

When organizers were able to transfer strategy from their closed-door meetings to the organizing committee—at times making it seem as if committee members were generating the ideas—the relationship between strategic leadership and worker empowerment was at its smoothest. After all, workers were advocating a course of action that mirrored the ideas of the campaign leaders, and organizers could easily invoke the notion of committee control. But there were also moments when committee members disagreed with organizers over tactical issues, or resisted lessons organizers wanted to teach, bringing tension to the forefront and exposing the power the union staff had over decision-making.

For Local B staff, a fierce commitment to winning a union contract could sometimes override concern with internal democracy. If committee dissent threatened to derail the process, organizers continued to invoke the language of democratic process even as they worked to eliminate all such dissent. Ironically, sometimes the language organizers used, ostensibly to generate discussion of the union plan, shut down any *possibility* of disagreement. This became transparent in one situation, as union staff unilaterally made a decision and tried to pass it off as committee-endorsed.

For weeks, union staff had been talking to the committee about a boycott picket in front of the hotel on the day of a large symphony orchestra dinner, *if* the orchestra refused to relocate to another hotel. The union had informed the orchestra of the boycott and requested that they move their fundraising event and pledge not to return to Bayview until workers had a contract. An organizer and three Bayview workers visited the orchestra to "inform" the musicians and administrators of the labor dispute at Bayview, and to warn them that they should expect a noisy picket line the afternoon of their fundraiser if they refused to move their event to another venue.

Two days before the weekly committee meeting, a union staff member met again with an orchestra administrator and was told that it was impossible to move the event at such late notice. As a compromise, the orchestra offered to print notice of the boycott on the front page of their fundraiser program notes, and agreed to let organizers speak at the event and distribute union flyers to the orchestra patrons. Without consulting the committee, the union agreed on this basis not to picket the day of the event.

How, then, to communicate this to the committee? One option was just to present the decision as a done deal. The committee was not likely to be overly concerned with this, since they trusted the judgment of staff organizers. Yet organizers approached it in another way. Laura brought up the orchestra situation during the section of the meeting devoted to recent victories. Framing it as a definitive victory, Laura told the committee that the symphony agreed "not only to do one thing, but to do *six* things." She only mentioned that the symphony did not meet the union's most important demand—to pull their event from the boycotted hotel—when she told the committee it was "too late to hold the fundraiser somewhere else." Laura explained that because the goal of the picket was to inform local residents coming to the event about the boycott, the action inside the hotel was even better than a rally outside. Laura wanted the committee to confirm the decision.

> But what do you guys think? We thought this was something great, but we always want to check in with you all. You call the shots. So you think even with all that the symphony is doing—letting us talk, putting us at the very front of their program, promising not to come back—that we should just keep going and have the rally? Or do you think, "let's play it smart and think about our strategy" and cancel the rally?

Organizers knew that going ahead with the rally after they promised to cancel it would not be the most prudent course of action. Laura described the two possibilities in order to shut down any questions committee members might have had about canceling the rally. If "playing it smart" meant calling off the rally, who was going to suggest otherwise? Organizers could present a façade of democratic procedure, "you call the shots"—while at the same time ensuring that the plan the committee supposedly developed was the one organizers had already decided.

On some occasions, organizers accidentally revealed a little more than they had meant to about behind-the-scenes planning. Once, in the middle of a meeting, Laura flipped through a tablet of butcher paper looking for a blank sheet on which to develop the weekly plan with the committee, only to flip to a page of an already written up weekly plan that organizers had made earlier that day. "Oops," Laura joked, "you weren't supposed to see that." And at the end of another meeting, after two hours of "developing the plan for the month of March," Laura pulled out a stack of flyers announcing the month's actions. "And what would you have done if we hadn't agreed to these actions?" one of the men from the banquet department asked. Laughing, Laura assured him that "we knew you'd agree."

Laura was right: the committee did agree that the actions listed on the flyers were good ones. Had they not, organizers would likely have reconfigured the March campaign plan in light of committee comments. One of the reasons Laura worked so hard to get the committee to think the actions were their own ideas was precisely *because* workers had effective veto power. Worker-intensive actions demand, by their very definition, the participation and vocal support of at least the most committed workers. Committee members who don't believe in the campaign won't participate, nor will they organize their non-committee co-workers to participate. Searching for where campaign ideas first originate, and using that as the touchstone of democracy, misses the distinction between staff's control of the agenda and workers' power to reject or reformulate it.

While the committee generally consented to or suggested a course of action that fit well into the larger strategy of the campaign, there were moments of resistance. The organizing committee's challenges to various aspects of the Bayview campaign came in two common forms. The first and more passive form was simply to not participate in scheduled union activities. Often this happened around house visits. Throughout the campaign, house visits remained a contentious topic. Committee members understood that they were effective, but no one enjoyed them. Again and again, organizers worked at convincing the committee of the necessity of the house visits, asking questions like, "How did we sign up 80 percent of our co-workers in three days?" Or, "Do we just give up on people, let them be scared?"

Mona, an outspoken committee member from the housekeeping department, argued most forcefully with organizers over the issue of weekly house visits. She believed that it was not worth returning again and again to talk with someone who refused to do anything for the union. "It's too much time to spend with grown people," Mona would say. At times she wouldn't budge from this position. When this happened, organizers, in their staff meetings, labeled her "off the program," and, humorously, tried to bring her back on the program by house visiting her. Dropping out of the campaign was unacceptable to organizers—"not an option," one of them told me—so the alternative was to try to convince her that the union plan was still a good one. When Kyla prepared me to go to the home of a committee member who had skipped a couple of meetings, she told me, "we have to ask him why he's not coming to meetings. We have to ask him if he thinks our program is a good one. And if he doesn't think that it is, we have to *tell him* that we're winning and that our program is working." Had all committee members resisted house visits as adamantly as Mona, organizers would have likely developed a more involved response. They were not, however, going to let a couple of the more errant and vocal committee members distract the larger group.

One way committee members exercised their authority was by suggesting alternative ways of doing things. Stan, one of the most active committee members, suggested creative organizing activities that the union regularly adopted. But there were some suggestions that staff refused to consider. Throughout the course of the campaign, a number of committee members suggested holding a mass meeting for all Bayview workers. Having experienced the weekly committee meetings as solidarity building, they hoped a meeting that brought in their more timid co-coworkers could generate more excitement about the union campaign. Organizers were against large meetings; they pushed instead for more one-on-one contact with hesitant workers. Occasionally committee members suggested the idea of a big meeting during strategic brainstorms. Organizers very rarely engaged the issue. "We don't think they are a good idea," Kyla simply said. Instead, organizers suggested occasional meetings where each committee member brought one co-worker who was a strong supporter of the union.

Another group of workers, led by Alfonso, a banquet worker from Mexico, would often bring up the idea of an employee walkout; they believed that the union was moving too slowly. Alfonso spoke very little English, and he relied on a translator in the meetings. Because the translator would have to translate his words into English before anyone could respond, back and forth interchange between the organizers and Alfonso was difficult in larger meetings. (Laura spoke Spanish with him when they were alone.) At times, the translating process assumed center stage—workers who spoke Spanish would respond directly to Alfonso, English speaking workers would go through the translator and, because of that, the translator would lag behind. Consequently, what Alfonso was trying to articulate would get lost in the confusion. If Alfonso advocated for a course of action with which organizers disagreed, as was often the case, the organizer running the meetings would not always have to respond.

While committee members tacitly and at times explicitly acknowledged the expertise of their trusted union staff, there were also times when committee members took seriously—more seriously than the organizers—their alleged responsibility for making decisions. A couple of months into the boycott, the union established a worker hardship fund to provide Bayview workers with financial support if they needed extra assistance when business in the hotel slowed down and their hours were cut. Organizers asked the committee to decide who should sit on the fund's committee, since the money belonged to them. Becky taped a piece of paper to the wall of the meeting room with the list of slots the committee needed to fill. On the paper were four Bayview worker slots, one union member slot, and one union staff slot. Choosing the Bayview workers was easy; one worker from each main department volunteered or was nominated by their co-workers. Once the Bayview workers were chosen, Becky started to move on. Mateo, a boisterous committee member from the banquet department, interrupted Becky to remind her that "we still have the staff and union member slots to decide." Becky laughed a little, then tried again to move on to the next part of the meeting. Mateo interrupted her again, this time more emphatically, reminding her that they needed to finish all business on one agenda item before moving on to the next. "No, no, no, we still have the other slots to decide," he told her. Becky, realizing he was serious, informed him that the other slots were "already decided." Mateo shook his head in frustration and mumbled that he thought Bayview workers were deciding on the "*whole* committee."

The process of choosing members for the hardship fund, and Mateo's understanding that the organizing committee was empowered to make the entire decision, illustrates two different forces at work. On the one hand, Mateo took seriously his job of picking the hardship committee; in this sense he believed that the organizing committee made the bulk of the decisions. Yet the fact that Mateo ultimately could not participate in the entire decision shows that workers who attempted to take their decision-making role too far would eventually bump up against the reality that part of the larger decision-making process was out of their hands. Still, it is important to note that while workers sometimes wanted more say than they were allowed in the campaign, it was much more common for the organizers to have to *prod* the committee into showing interest in making decisions.

There were moments when workers recognized the discrepancy between the language of democracy ("you call the shots") and the reality of a high level of staff control. During one particularly long meeting, Becky was trying to get the committee to agree that talking to the engineers should be the priority for the next week. (Engineering was the smallest department in the hotel, made up entirely of men who exhibited at best only weak support for their more active union co-workers, much to the frustration of the housekeepers.) Most of the committee was tired and cranky, and no one was responding to Becky's queries about the problems in the engineering department. Finally, after an awkward silence, Betty, the most senior housekeeper, replied in the most monotonous tone she could muster, "Ok, we'll tell you what you want to hear. We should all talk to the engineers," at which other workers chuckled under their breath. In another meeting when Kyla was discussing management's strategy and asking the committee how they wanted to respond, another housekeeper responded with the sarcastic comment, "You should just tell us, since you know all the answers anyway." Both Becky and Kyla responded to these remarks with laughter, with Becky adding, "But we want *you* to say it. It's your campaign."

Largely, committee meetings served pedagogical purposes, and in more lighthearted moments of tension organizers could poke fun at this—as Becky did when she admitted that organizers fish for the right answers. Workers were aware that organizers had an agenda, but they usually participated in executing that agenda. Fairly regularly, an organizer would pull a committee member or two aside before a meeting and ask them to bring up a certain point or suggest a particular tactic, so that other members could see their co-workers make suggestions.

If local B organizers worked hard to give committee members a sense of power and ownership—if the goal of the organizers was in some sense to make themselves increasingly useless—then orchestrating each step of the organizing committee (while pretending not to) could arguably end up being counter-productive. Yet workers were learning tangible new skills, and they were using these new skills to build workplace power and to participate more fully in developing the Bayview campaign. Over time, the committee became more adept at strategy and planning. Close to the end of the campaign, organizers tried an experiment. At the beginning of a meeting, they taped up a large blank calendar on the wall and asked the committee to come up with next month's plan of action. Then organizers left the room. In their absence, the committee developed a plan. While not perfect, it showed an extraordinarily high level of sophisticated strategic thinking—certainly a level that had not existed a year earlier.

HERE Local B's efforts to develop worker leadership and an activist-centered local are relatively rare among today's unions. Even unions that have given significant strategic attention and financial resources to organizing have not necessarily understood organizing to entail substantial leadership development. In the Bayview organizing drive, Local B prioritized worker involvement and leadership development both as a means to sustaining a lengthy non-election campaign, and as part of the process of building a strong worker-centered local. Union staff succeeded in building a competent and empowered group of workplace leaders who in turn effectively mobilized their co-workers in support of the union. Many of the workers on the committee stayed involved with the union when the campaign came to a close.

What can this tell us about the relationship between staff leadership and worker participation, or about union democracy? As I have suggested, union democracy can be understood as a goal a campaign works toward, as an ideal that—in the best of circumstances—develops richly over time, as workers come to be better versed in the tasks and goals at hand. Furthermore, union staff can play an important role not just in creating winning campaigns, but also in facilitating the emergence of greater and more sophisticated participation. While staff direction and worker participation work in tension, these two demands are not always at odds. In the case of Local B, strong direction from the top of the union sometimes strained its simultaneous emphasis on participatory democracy. But workers at Bayview were also genuinely engaged in the task of union building, expanding their sense of participation and active accomplishment as a result of the union's leadership development strategy.

Staff organizers for Local B used their expertise to create a space in which workers felt able and willing to make decisions and become workplace leaders. In this model of organizing, participatory democracy is perhaps best seen as a complex and evolving process. With effort and over time, organizers for Local B created structures that gave workers increasing input within, and power over, their own campaign.

The twin ideals of union democracy and campaign success—given flesh in the dual demands of staff direction and worker participation—were not simply manifested in creative tension, however. They also gave rise to contradictory moments, in which the language of pure worker democracy—"you call the shots"—was scraped away to reveal the hierarchical structure that lay just beneath it. These moments of tension, often laughed off by the staff, were also for the most part sloughed off by the workers themselves. What, then, do these moments really tell us?

The relationship between staff authority and worker participation that I have described is somewhat unique—given the nature of both the non-NLRB campaign and the local's on-going commitment to leadership development— and thus the moments of tension I witnessed in the course of local B's organizing campaign might have looked different in another context. In particular, the dramatic unfolding of worker participation and involvement in the Bayview campaign might not have happened to the same degree in a shorter campaign. In an election campaign, for instance, organizers often work under strict time lines. As a result, staff may not feel they have the luxury for continual deliberation or leadership development.

Looking beyond the idiosyncrasies of the campaign I described, however, I would argue that awkward moments alert us to an endemic tension in an organizing model that demands both skilled, expert leadership and robust participation, even when the two are working together for the most part quite smoothly. Indeed, the tension between authority and participation is one that exists in many forms of community-based organizing. Extremely hierarchical and rule-bound organizations are unlikely to garner much member participation. However, organizations that tend to get bogged down in dilemmas of process and democracy may not generate many concrete victories, which also discourages participation. Given Local B's commitment to both campaign success and participatory democracy, the tensions that arose during the Bayview campaign signaled the complicated relationship between staff authority and member participation that many organizations must negotiate.

3

WORKERS AGAINST UNIONS

UNION ORGANIZING AND ANTI-UNION
COUNTERMOBILIZATIONS

Robert A. Penney

Roger, an operating room nurse at Corporation Hospital, had never really been against labor unions.[1] His father had worked at a unionized grocery store throughout his life and even was on the union's board of directors for many years. "The whole time I was growing up," said Roger, "food was put on my table by union labor." But his feelings toward unionism changed in the winter of 1998 when he found himself in the midst of a contentious union organizing drive. One morning he read what to him was an unflattering article in the daily newspaper about the hospital that challenged his professional identity as a concerned caregiver.

> [The union] invited a reporter to a meeting and three or four nurses were willing to be quoted in the paper saying "they have to have a union at Corporation Hospital because the hospital has made such deep cuts that patient care is now being compromised." I thought it was a terrible thing to bite the hand that feeds you. General Motors might go on strike but the one thing you'll never hear a General Motors' employee say is, "Buy a Toyota." The union did that here. I was mad enough that I decided to do something to kind of balance the scales. Since they had gone in the [daily newspaper] and said "patient care at Corporation sucks," I went the other way. In my letter, I wrote that where I work, patient care is fine. We feel sorry for these other nurses that claim their patient care is not good, but we're doing just

great, thank you very much. In my letter, I never said I was anti-union. I did
not say anything about the union. But a lot of people assumed that obviously I must be anti-union. Which at the time probably wasn't even true.
(Roger, Corporation Hospital)

Reaction to Roger's letter was swift. While pro-union nurses at the hospital
immediately attacked Roger's position, other nurses shared his concern. Realizing a need to fight the union, Roger and a few co-workers formed the anti-
union "Our Choice, the Other Voice" committee. The anti-unionists recruited
like-minded people in numerous departments of the hospital and met regularly to discuss strategy, tactics, and organizing activity. Roger and a co-
worker, Carla, published a newsletter throughout the campaign that expressed
anti-union ideas and beliefs. With the help of a friend in the novelty business,
the committee produced anti-union pins and other accoutrements for solidarity actions. And finally, the committee organized collective actions such as
marches, rallies, and prayer vigils for the anti-union campaign. Their actions
were rewarded when eight months later the workers at Corporation Hospital
rejected the union in a 321 to 276 vote.

While conflict in labor relations is often understood in dualistic terms as a
division between workers and employers, there are also potential and actual
divisions within the working class itself. In union organizing drives, such divisions can result in a counter-mobilization by anti-union workers. Yet, self-
activity on the part of anti-union workers is seldom acknowledged in the
literature on organizing or declining union density. Instead, most explanations for the decline in union membership over the last twenty years have
focused on the increased hostility of employers toward unionization efforts.
Employers are more likely to harass, fire, and intimidate workers attempting
to organize unions and more aggressively pursue legal maneuvers to forestall
union certification elections and recognition procedures (Clawson 1999).
However, while this focus on the anti-union tactics of employers is important,
it has led to a blind spot in our understanding of worker action in union
organizing drives. Virtually absent from the literature is any serious examin-
ation of the counter-mobilization activities of anti-union *workers* such as
Roger.

Such anti-union mobilizations are not uncommon in union certification
election campaigns. Bronfenbrenner (2000) found that in almost one third of
union campaigns, worker "vote no" committees were "assisted" by management and mobilized for action.[2] But like the research on employer resistance
to union organizing, this otherwise valuable study gives the impression that
anti-union mobilization is simply a function of employer strategies and
tactics. Is this impression correct? Here I examine anti-union worker activity
in four union organizing campaigns launched between 1998 and 1999 at mid-

size, not-for-profit hospitals.[3] In all four campaigns, anti-union activists mobilized against the union organizing drive, although with varying levels of organizational strength and sophistication.

The similarities between the campaigns give credence to the idea that the actions by anti-union workers are a product of managerial manipulation. For example, in three of the four organizing drives,[4] anti-union workers attempted to create committees to become the "alternative" voice of workers during the campaign. Reflecting many of the same themes and ideas put forth by management's anti-union propaganda, these committees espoused a belief in the disempowering nature of unionism. In addition to being ideologically similar, the tactics and strategies used by the anti-union leaders were also comparable. In all four cases, the anti-unionists tried to create and distribute regular newsletters and leaflets that expressed their concerns about unionization and engaged in solidarity actions like "vote no" pins, gimmicks, or even marches and rallies in an attempt to defeat the union.

Yet despite such similarities, anti-unionists also distinctly expressed their independence from the parallel anti-union efforts of the hospital management. They were openly critical of their hospital and the current state of working conditions. They were disappointed by their employer's campaign to defeat the union, and angered that management had not "taken the union more seriously" at the beginning of the organizing drive. Asserting their own agency, the anti-union workers cast themselves as the key players in the countermovement to resist the union. Were such workers acting merely at the behest of the employer or did they oppose the union for independent reasons? If we assume the former, anti-union workers are reduced to the status of naïve victims of management manipulation, victims with no independent agency. If we assume the latter then what are the motivations for action among anti-union workers? How do workers' anti-union proclivities manifest themselves in union certification election campaigns, and what influences the ideology and organization of anti-union committees?

This chapter is an effort to explore such issues. Further contextualization of the ways in which employers influence worker anti-union committees is needed to understand the content and character of worker anti-union mobilization. Rather than presuming a direct link between employer desires and anti-union worker action, the relationship between the two needs to be problematized and empirically analyzed. Employers may augment anti-union sentiment, but they will not succeed in the absence of fertile soil in which to grow such sentiment. Workers' ambivalence toward unionism is deeply rooted in individualistic world-views and the negative overarching assumptions about unions and their place in society. Anti-unionists draw on these influences to create and frame their resistance to unionization. But the employer and the anti-union workers are not the only factors that shape this countermovement activity. The union also plays a crucial role in how workers view the idea of conflict and change. It is the unique combination of these three factors that influence the attitudes and behaviors of anti-union workers.

THE CASES

The first campaign was at Corporation Hospital where Roger helped form a well-organized, influential anti-union organizing committee. Amidst growing speculation about layoffs and wage freezes and in the face of ever-worsening staffing levels, nurses called on the local healthcare union for help in organizing their 600 person bargaining unit. Although starting off strong with over 60 percent of the nurses having signed union certification election authorization cards, that support dwindled during the eight-month campaign and the union ultimately lost.

The second campaign, also among nurses, occurred at United General, a larger facility of over 2,000 workers with 1,300 nurses. Widely regarded as one of the premier hospitals in the region, United General had for years been held up as a model for nursing education and training and was known for its generous benefits and wages. However, a few years earlier, the introduction of a new management team whom nurses felt was "unresponsive" to their needs led a small group of RNs to explore the option of unionization. After first contacting a number of state nursing associations, they finally settled on a healthcare union that was willing to commit the resources and time to organize a facility of their size. Other nurses at United General, however, were not impressed with the union or its message and chose to create a counter-mobilization effort. In contrast to Corporation Hospital, anti-union nurses at United General, although organized, could only manage sporadic activity and were generally ineffective at resisting the unionization effort. The pro-union nurses were overwhelmingly successful, winning the election 922 to 110.

The third and fourth cases involved service and maintenance workers rather than nurses. Both campaigns exhibited much lower levels of anti-union activity than the two nurses' campaigns. Over the last twenty years, Union City Hospital, a 372-bed facility with 800 service and maintenance workers, had grown from a "family" oriented community hospital to a major service provider for the area. Along the way, the once secure and comfortable hospital began to feel—to the service and maintenance workers—more like a "business" in which concern for the patients and employees was secondary to profitability and growth. Union organizers at Union City Hospital quickly gathered union cards authorizing a union certification election vote from a majority of workers and easily overcame anti-union efforts. While anti-union workers were present at Union City Hospital, their effectiveness was limited to one isolated area of the hospital—perhaps not coincidentally, the business office, where workers' contact with management was far more frequent than elsewhere, and where a particularly vocal anti-union leader emerged from its ranks. Although that area voted against the union, anti-union influence never spread much further.

The service and maintenance workers at Independence Memorial Hospital began organizing for similar reasons. Changes in the relationship between management and workers led to increasing dissatisfaction and resentment. Although a majority of workers signed union cards, the margin of support at Independence Memorial was much smaller than the other hospitals. And whereas the anti-unionists at Union City were well organized but isolated in one area, at Independence a larger and more diverse number of anti-union workers were spread throughout the hospital, but they acted independently and without coordination. This resistance, combined with a relatively disorganized pro-union campaign, led to a lopsided victory for management as the workers voted 243 to 105 against the union.

As will be discussed below, the anti-union campaigns at the four hospitals were influenced by three factors. First, the employer campaign and its messages of disempowerment and reconciliation provided themes and materials for workers to mold into their own frames of resistance.[5] Second, the workers' individualistic ideologies and their ability to turn these into collective frames of resistance, together with their access to resources, influenced their stance toward the union and the organizational manifestation of their beliefs. Finally, the actions and tactics of the unions both constrained and inspired anti-union workers' ability and opportunity to organize their own counter-mobilization.

Employer Campaigns and Anti-Union Framing

Given the current state of labor law and the increased hostility on the part of employers toward organizing, it is not surprising that the existing literature on anti-union activity focuses on the behavior of employers and their attempts to prevent unionization. Such research documents the tactics and strategies of employers and their effects on outcomes of union certification election campaigns. Such tactics include supervisory anti-union training, captive audience meetings, leaflet distribution, firing of worker activists, campaign delay tactics, and other unfair labor practices (Bronfenbrenner 1994, 1997, 2000; Freeman 1985; Grenier 1988; Hurd and Uehlein 1994; Kaufman and Stephan 1995; Kochan, McKersie and Chalykoff 1986; Lawler 1990). Labor law attorneys and management consultants have raised this process of anti-union campaigning to a science over the last thirty years (Levitt 1993). In order to guard against employer mistakes or non-productive illegalities, man-agement consultants often stick to a general pattern or blueprint of anti-union responses that has been "battle-tested" and proven effective. Thus it is not surprising that the themes and messages presented by management in the four organizing drives I studied were remarkably similar. This repertoire of coercive action has become increasingly sophisticated over time to the point at which such "strong-armed" tactics as firing and intimidation of pro-union employees becomes almost unnecessary.[6] Instead, employers utilize equally effective but more sophisticated and legal ways to defeat unions (Kaufman and Stephan 1995). These tactics and strategies revolve around a constant barrage of propaganda that can basically be divided into positive and negative incentives to vote against the union. Anti-unionists were clearly affected by this propaganda. Explaining their resistance to unioniza-tion, these workers would parrot back many of the same themes presented by management. The themes and messages contained within this propaganda can be described as a "carrot and stick" approach to union avoidance (Penney 2002).

The "carrot" involves pleas on the part of management for a "second chance" and promises to improve the conditions of work. "Carrot" leaflets and actions present management in a positive light as rational and fair, and as a potential victim of unionization—the benevolent provider of wages, benefits, and other rewards. Supporting this claim, employers may announce pay raises or new benefits during the union campaign that, although illegal, are strategically difficult for the union to challenge. In each of the cam-paigns, positive messages of the benevolent or rational employer found their way into the rhetoric or leaflets of the anti-union activists demonstrating the influence of management's campaign. In the anti-union newsletter at Corpo-ration Hospital, one nurse put it this way: "I believe the administration has had a 'wake-up call.' True—they made some stupid mistakes. I believe they are working to correct them. The presence of union activity has had some posi-tive effects. I plan to 'hold their feet to the fire' to make sure they continue to hear me. This woman will be heard but not through some union stooge" (Unidentified nurse in *Our Choice the Other Voice* newsletter). A similar call to respect the positive changes management had made and to give them another chance was voiced by Brenda, an anti-union leader at Union City Hospital.

There have been repeated problems with the present administration of Union City Hospital. However, we have received indications that this is about to change. This may be true or it may be false; the only way to know it to (sic) wait. At a time when other hospitals are removing salary and benefit packages, we have received several raises and an increase in our

pension fund . . . Changes have already been made in the Human Services
Department . . . and we have the administration's attention. We are asking
the union backers to take a step back and look at the whole picture . . . if
the administration does not deliver, the union will return. (Brenda, Op-ed:
"Union City Times," 1997).

While certain memoranda and leaflets by management laid out positive
messages, others, through subtle or not so subtle implications, hammered
home the potential pitfalls of unionization.

The "stick" involves employer attempts to persuade workers that unionization would have numerous negative consequences, disempowerment being
the overarching theme. This idea is typically developed through three different sub-themes: strikes, dues, and management rights. The strike theme was
articulated in numerous ways in the various hospitals. Newspaper clippings
from strikes involving the organizing local, International, or merely unions
in general were passed out to employees. These articles emphasized the
length of time the workers were out on strike, the economic impact, and the
failure of the strike to achieve its desired goals. In these propaganda pieces,
employers tried to convince workers that voting for the union meant voting
for the very real possibility of going out on strike. The strike threat not only
spoke to workers' anxieties about their material well-being and their loyalty
to the institution but also to issues of personal control. Management flyers
used phrases such as "if the union *takes you out* on strike" or "when *the union*
strikes" (emphasis added), thereby separating workers from the decision-
making. The message here was that workers do not have a choice about
whether they strike or not. If workers do not feel in control of that possibility, then the strike message becomes very difficult to defeat. Anti-union
workers often expressed fear of the possibility of striking. Reflecting the
same issues and concerns proffered by the employer campaign, anti-union
workers shared their encounters with strikes and the disempowering nature
of the event. In this leaflet at Corporation Hospital, a worker discussed her
husband's experience at a striking steel company. "My husband took a temporary job delivering beer for a company that was on strike. Even though he
paid his union dues, went on strike when his union called for one, and never
crossed the picket line at the steel plant, his personal property was vandalized
and people would drive past our house shouting "scab" and other obscenities
at all hours of the night. It was very frightening and I feared for his
safety when he went to work each day" (Tammy, Corporation Hospital).
Whether it was fear of conflict in general or the idea of striking and the accom-
panying violence and tension, strikes were at the forefront of workers' minds
and were constantly made the main topic of discussion by employer
propaganda.

"Union dues" was the second most common anti-union theme in the employer literature. This too was something that the union would *take* from employees without their control. Employer memos would calculate monthly dues, annual dues, and even the amount of union dues an employee would have paid to the union at the age of retirement. Beyond the personal costs of unionization, the dues message also questioned where the money went. The implication was that dues money is spent on lavish salaries of union officials or, at the very least, shipped off to Washington-based union headquarters, with no benefit to workers. In all four campaigns, anti-union flyers questioned the motives of the union trying to organize the facility. Reports of the declining number of union members were cited as the real justification for the union's interest in the hospital. This sub-theme would reappear in conversations with anti-union activists. "Unions have no interest in healthcare workers," they would say, "beyond their dues potential." To the anti-unionists, the union's inability to organize in traditional sectors had forced them to look in non-traditional areas like healthcare. In all these examples, the union was characterized as a "third party" or an outside bureaucracy coming in to take money without necessarily giving anything back in return. As Roger put it:

> If I had a message, my message was that this union tries to present themselves as our friends and if they were representing us, they might be our friends to some extent. But I said you got to remember this group is an outsider coming into our hospital and the only reason that they're doing it is so that they can make a profit. The bottom line is that the union is a business. They want our union dues to support their business. And is it worth our money to support them in hopes of what we might get back from them? I think my whole thing was, this is an outside group. We don't need them. (Roger, Corporation Hospital)

This message was very effective at Corporation Hospital. Genny, a pro-union nurse, complained that she could not convince people that the "union is us".

The final message or sub-theme found in the literature of the campaigns was probably the most powerful of all. That is the message of management rights or union impotence. Once again, in all four campaigns, memos and flyers were designed to remind workers about the "management rights" clause in union contracts. These clauses, a result of the Taft-Hartley Act, state that management has the sole right to hire, discipline, discharge for just cause, to lay off and promote, to schedule, to determine or change the starting and quitting time and the number of hours worked. The idea here is to convince workers that regardless of whether they unionize, management will always have the ultimate power over their jobs and working conditions. Carla, at

Corporation hospital, expressed this idea about downsizing and the power of unions. "Downsizing is going to happen, union or not. I hate to be like that but it's true. I am just lucky that I have a lot of seniority . . . If a facility is going to make cuts, then you can't stop them. The nurses are yelling, 'staffing, we need staffing,' but I felt the things that the nurses wanted could not have been helped by a union. It might have been a voice out there, but it wouldn't have accomplished anything" (Carla, Corporation Hospital). Anti-unionists had similar feelings about the overall changes in healthcare. When asked about the coming of managed care to the hospital, most anti-unionists expressed the opinion that larger structural changes in an industry could not be affected by workers, however numerous. This lack of belief in the power of workers led to their feelings that organizing was pointless.

While management clearly influenced workers' conceptions of unionism and their understanding of the organizing drive, less clear is how much direct support management offered to the workers' anti-union activities. As mentioned earlier, Bronfenbrenner found that a common tactic of employer anti-union campaigns is to "assist" vote-no committees and anti-union workers. Randy Shaw in his analysis of UNITE's Guess Jeans campaign found, for example, employers provided bus transportation and wages to anti-union workers for anti-UNITE rallies (Shaw 1999). But assistance also comes in less obvious and more sophisticated ways. Levitt (1993), a former labor/management consultant, describes his connections to anti-union workers in his memoirs of working as a union-buster.

> Through that handful of good soldiers [supervisors] I set to work establishing a network of rank-and-file employees who would serve as spies, informants, and saboteurs. Those so-called loyal employees would be called upon to lobby against the union, report on union meetings, hand over union literature to their bosses, tattle on their co-workers, help spread rumors, and make general pests of themselves within the organizing drive. I rarely knew who my company plants were . . . It was cleaner that way. Nobody could connect me to the activities, and the workers' "pro-company" countercampaign was believed to be a grassroots movement. (Levitt 1993, 181)

Levitt discusses numerous instances in which he used supervisors to act as leaders of anti-union mobilizations and to recruit other workers to their cause. This is the more typical characterization of such committees by labor activists and organizers. However, this may not always be the case. Indigenous anti-union committees can emerge from the agency of the workers themselves. Anti-union leaders in each campaign stressed that they had little to no contact with management or its representatives in regards to their activity, nor did they receive money for their activity. Roger explained how management specifically rebuffed him when he asked for help in his organizing.

> When we were doing the newsletter, at one point I went to see the president of the hospital to . . . I ran into a brick wall in my research and I was trying to find out a particular thing about the union, and I couldn't find it, and I thought maybe he could steer me in the right direction. And it was funny. He just said, "Roger, thank you for coming to see me. Now get the hell out of my office." I said, "What?" And he pointed out very quickly, he said, "Look, if I am advising you, as the president of the hospital that makes you an agent of management, which makes you subject to all the laws and rules that I am subject to." He said, "I can't help you. If I help you, you belong to me." He said, "As it is, you can go off and do whatever you want to without my help and you're a free agent to whatever you want." And I said, "Oh, I see your point." And after that he and I did not talk at all. (Roger, Corporation Hospital)

Bertha, a dietary aide at Independence Memorial, got the same treatment. When she asked management for help in combating the union, she was told that she would be on her own.

> My supervisor could see I was upset, so he said, "Do you want a personal meeting with me?" And I said, "Yes, if you have time." He said, "I'll take the time." So I went in and I was telling him how I felt about this union. I said, "I realize there are problems that employees have, but I don't think the union is the answer." I said, "Let's get this union out of here, what can employees do to fight back?" He says, "Bertha, I can't tell you what to do." So I said, "What do you mean you can't tell me what to do?" He says, "I can't tell you what to do . . . I'll tell you one thing, employees can say and do anything they want." (Bertha, Independence Memorial)

The assistance that Roger and Bertha did receive in these interactions was less tangible, but perhaps no less important: an indication that they should pursue their beliefs to the fullest and that they had plenty of space and opportunity to do what they wanted. Indeed, whether by design or by legal restriction, the anti-union workers at these hospitals indicated that they were very much on their own to develop and finance counter-movement organizations. Of course, one can not be sure whether these protestations reflect what anti-union workers and employers knew had to be the public face of their cooperation or a true representation of management's involvement. But in all four campaigns, anti-union workers told similar stories of limited relationship or even major disagreements between their groups and the employers' campaign.

For example, Danielle, a unit clerk at Union City Hospital, reported that she and Brenda, the main anti-union activist, felt management and their consultants were not doing enough to stop the union. "Brenda felt that they should have been doing things sooner. But I guess, from their experience, they felt that people would get tired of it if you throw it out there too soon. So they were waiting like until a couple weeks prior to the election to do the brunt of their work. I just wondered why, if they have these consultants, why aren't they doing, at least, equally to what the union was doing as far as getting information out?" (Danielle, Union City Hospital.) Cindy, at United General, felt similar and complained that the employer was not saying the right things and not being pro-active enough in stopping the organizing drive. Certain tactics the employers tried also irritated anti-union activists. When personalized letters from department supervisors were sent out to employees at Independence Memorial, Marcus said he was "insulted" and "very angry" at management for "invading his privacy." Roger related one story in which management had convinced an African American doctor to mail out a letter to employees reminding them of all the good Corporation Hospital had done for minorities in the hospital and the community. Roger said that "the moment he saw that," he knew it was a bad idea. "I think a lot of our black employees felt like they were being targeted. That management was trying to appease the blacks," and that it was too obvious a management ploy.

While management manipulation does influence the character of anti-union mobilization, these counter-movements can not be written off as solely a management ploy. The anti-union activity is representative of deeply held beliefs about unionization and power that go beyond what management can orchestrate. It is therefore important to understand the roots of this resistance and the agency of the workers involved in creating their own opposition.

The Roots of Resistance: Creating Anti-Union Ideology

Survey research data paint a complex picture of the extent and form of anti-union sentiment among workers. While 65 percent of the populace "approves of labor unions" (Gallup News Service 1999), 55 percent of workers would vote against a union if an election were held in their own workplace (Freeman and Rogers 1999). What drives this anti-union sentiment? In this volume, Lopez's work on union organizing in the rust-belt identifies three key influences that shape anti-union feelings—deindustrialization, union violence, and do-nothing unionism. Each of these ideas, Lopez argues, is the product of the "business unionism" that characterized AFL-CIO unions until very recently. Such ideas were certainly in evidence at the four hospitals where anti-union workers would describe unions as "dinosaurs" of a past industrial era. Marcus, a maintenance technician at Independence Memorial, saw unions as being a relic of the past. He had limited experience with unions prior to the organizing campaign, and neither he nor anyone in his immediate family had ever been a union member, although he remembers his father having the opinion that unions were no longer necessary in today's economy. That seemed to shape Marcus's viewpoint. "Granted my overall opinion of the unions is that back in the '20s, yeah, they were needed; 12-hour days, sweatshops, 7 days a week, men, women, and children, and unfair wages, unfair conditions—yes, unions were needed. But in today's day and age, there are so many laws in place to prevent that sort of situation, there is not, at least in our hospital's case, a need for a union" (Marcus, Independence Memorial). In this view, when working conditions were exploitative and dangerous in the past, workers absolutely needed to organize to improve conditions in the workplace. However, that project was largely completed in the minds of many anti-union workers. Today's workplaces are no longer so exploitative and in the few instances where they may be, there are more than enough labor laws and governmental oversight organizations to protect workers and their rights. As Marcus said, "the government can do things to stop it; although I'm not a big advocate of the government, there's places to call to make things stop." While these larger "meta-narratives" of unions afford powerful disincentives for organizing, they form just the broad contours of anti-union sentiment. This acceptance of the inefficacy of unionism is rooted in deeply held ideologies of worker individualism. Lack of a collective conscience provides fertile soil for management propaganda. For many anti-union workers this individualist consciousness was characterized by two different themes: a "grin and bear it" mentality toward work, and a "what's in it for me?" attitude toward unions. I now turn to explore these attitudes in more detail.

INDIVIDUAL IDEOLOGIES

The "grin and bear it" mentality is one common expression of free-market ideology. Work may be difficult and unpleasant, but that is just the nature of work, and if it is really bad, a worker always has the freedom to go elsewhere. Many types of workers in each of the hospitals expressed such ideas. Roger at Corporation Hospital took the position that although recent changes in healthcare had made things worse, there was little if anything that could be done about it. Therefore, workers and nurses needed to just "grin and bear it" and make the best of a bad situation.

> I guess that I do believe that the hospital business is changing. If you read about some of the things that are going on, like in California [where] staffing levels are even worse than they are here. The good old days of unlim-

ited staffing are gone. There was a time, twenty years ago, the hospitals were making money hand-over-fist. That's not true anymore. So now staffing levels have to be cut, and we're not getting reimbursed like we used to. Would I like to go back to twenty years ago? Absolutely. Do I think I ever will? No. Those days are gone. I'm sorry, but they're gone. (Roger Corporation Hospital)

Roger went on to add that nurses need to reorient their expectations about working conditions to take account of the financial considerations of the hospital.

Well, you know, I don't want to sound like I'm some "follow my leader blindly," I'm not at all that way, but the hospital's position was that yes they had made some money in the past, and yes they had put it in the bank, and yes there were plans for it long term. I bought that. It made sense to me. Should I be surprised that my hospital didn't say, "Hey, we made some money last year, here's a thousand dollars for every employee?" That doesn't happen in the real world. They pay us competitively. That's all they're ever going to pay us. The idea that the hospital had made a big chunk of money the year before, so what? (Roger, Corporation Hospital)

Other workers cited past work experiences to justify their belief that "there are a lot worse places to work," so whatever the conditions, one should just not complain. For example, Anna, a radiology clerk at Union City, used her past factory experience to justify her anti-union stance at the hospital. However bad things got, it was never as bad as the factory work, and "that is where unions need to organize, not here at the hospital." Even when workers perceive conditions as unfair, free-market ideology can inhibit a collective response. As Marcus at Independence Memorial suggested, if people are really unhappy at their place of work, "Why don't they just leave and go elsewhere, why do they stay? If things were that horrible, why are you still there? Have you put applications in at (the other hospital in town)? Have you put applications in at the grocery store? "Well, no." Why? "Well, I don't want to leave the hospital." But you're unhappy? So that's a catch-22. Although some people don't have a great education to fall back on. . . . if things are so bad there, why are they still there?" (Marcus, Independence Memorial)

This "grin and bear it" attitude is tied to skepticism about empowerment. Many of the anti-union workers just did not believe that workers, or at least workers in their hospital, had the power or ability to make changes in the healthcare industry. Cindy, at United General, believed in the "cycles of nursing," suggesting that with patience it could be seen that nursing shortages and problems were something that occurred regularly but would eventually swing back in the other direction. Similarly, managed care "just is," according to Cindy, and was not going to be changed, regardless of what the nurses did. Nurses need to adapt and "figure out how to change with managed care" rather than rail against the reorganization forced by it. Other workers also believed that the forces shaping change in the health-care industry were too far removed to allow worker involvement or that, as workers, they could not reasonably expect to be included in the decisions of the hospitals. Overall, the anti-union workers downplayed their collective grievances and expressed limited expectations of change.

In addition, most anti-union workers saw unionization as offering no concrete benefits, and some saw it as potentially harmful. This "what's in it for me?" attitude is exemplified by Marcus at Independence Memorial Hospital. He could not understand what the union could do "for him" and questioned organizers and co-workers about specific benefits he could receive.

> What would I be getting for the 25 dollars a pay period? Was I going to be getting anything for that? Representation that I don't want? What benefits were they going to get me? "If you're ever on the verge of getting fired, we could step in and do something" . . . if I'm ever on the verge of getting fired it's for a legitimate reason anyway. "We'll give you better benefits" . . . I'm happy with my benefits, good health, life, retirement, plus the hospital's chip-in for healthcare. "If you're treated unfairly by your boss." If I'm treated unfairly by my boss, I'm going to the vice-president or CEO. I will mouth off. (Marcus, Independence Memorial)

Other anti-union workers shared Marcus' individualistic attitude. They believed they could represent themselves at the workplace, have confidence in the fairness of employers, and generally were satisfied with their working conditions. Their ability to advocate for themselves negated the need for unions and for "having a voice" at work through the union.

Ultimately of more importance to the anti-union workers was the fear that a union win would mean an end to their employment. His "biggest fear," said Marcus, given the "quirks of my boss, and the quirks of the hospital," and the fact that the hospital had already been cutting benefits and costs previous to the union drive, was that his position would be cut if the union meant higher costs for the hospital. Carla and Roger at Corporation Hospital also felt that if the union came in, they would be "out the door." However, for them this was due to their general reluctance to work in a unionized facility. When the union drive became a reality at Corporation, Carla said it became "a really personal issue," because she "will not work in a unionized facility." Nor did she want to be a union member. Roger felt the same after a series of incidents that turned him off the union. "My job was on the line" in regards to the unionization campaign. But these personal philosophies of anti-unionism could not be used to fight the unionization effort.

Anti-union workers at the four hospitals advocating their position from solely a personal position rarely had any influence on other workers. The example of Stephan, a senior-level maintenance worker at Union City Hospital, is instructive. In the past, Stephan had been an advocate for the maintenance department to his supervisor and various managers at the hospital. Being well-spoken and educated, other workers looked to him when problems arose. However Stephan's influence waned when the organizing campaign began, because his arguments against the union rested entirely on his inability to see what the union could do for him personally. He had advocated for himself through numerous problems and concerns and his experiences with unions earlier in life left him with the belief that unions only protect bad workers. The last thing he was interested in doing was paying monthly dues to a union that could not do anything that he could not do himself. In his conversations with other maintenance workers, this seemed to be the main justification for his position, eventually making him a pariah in the department because of his "selfish attitude." More effective anti-union leaders went beyond such individually driven concerns to develop frames of resistance that resonated with those workers unsure whether the union was the best path for the hospital. Such leaders drew on management anti-union frames for the basis of their message, but then built on these ideas to create their own arguments.

CREATING COLLECTIVE FRAMES OF RESISTANCE

The uniformity of employer campaigns means that anti-union workers in a variety of workplaces draw on the same repertoire of themes in creating their own frames of resistance. These frames reflect but are not identical to those used by the employer. In all four campaigns, anti-union activists reshaped the employers' message to incorporate their own individual fears about unionization and a more collectivist anti-union orientation. They did not attempt to deny or diminish the problems that other workers saw at the hospital. On the contrary, they were quick to agree that changes at the hospitals had negatively affected working conditions. Their disagreements with pro-union workers were about the solution to the problems, not the problems themselves. The union, the anti-union workers argued, was not the answer. Other vehicles of change were more appropriate. This line of argument took two main forms: "working together" and "not *this* union."

Working Together

Many anti-union activists counseled their co-workers that all the existing avenues for improving the relationship with management had not yet been utilized and suggested that organizing was thus an unnecessary and over-reaching step. "What (the anti-union committee) kept saying was that there were mechanisms in the system. That . . . staff nursing council could have been mobilized and more done with that. That group could have been utilized more strongly to try to put more pressure on administration or to try to work more with administration, hospital administration to try to make more changes" (Cindy, United General). Each of the hospitals had used employee council programs in the past to increase worker participation in decision-making. Many of the anti-union workers pointed to these councils as a potential avenue for change. Although only one of the anti-union workers at United General and one at Union City had actually been on such a committee, and both recognized the limitations of the councils, nevertheless, these were often presented as a good alternative to unionization. Pro-union nurses believed that these committees had already been tried and had failed, whereas anti-union leaders felt that collective action was a lot easier than the union made it seem. If workers could come together and use collective action to build a union, why not just turn that energy on to management and pressure administration into change without the union.

> The union wasn't the way to go for the problems. I did suggest that some of the employees could work it out with the hospital without the need for a union. Basically, the "united we stand, divided we fall" [idea] seemed logical, but I felt if you had twenty, thirty employees writing a note to an employer saying that this is an intolerable situation, then it will be resolved. So that saying is true; we don't need to have you to come in and pay you to do what we can do for ourselves. (Marcus, Independence Memorial)

When questioned about how that organizational work would happen, proponents of independent action had little sense of the time and energy needed to organize their co-workers in potentially threatening situations. Although in theory workers do not need unions to act collectively, the fact that they never did so in the past is an indication of the remote likelihood of doing so in the future. Other leaders, like Brenda at Union City, believed that worker organization was not needed now that management had been "put on notice." She felt that since the issues and problems had been aired in the context of a union campaign, management was sure to start dealing with the grievances and open lines of communication. Other anti-union workers actually expressed tepid support for the union at the beginning of the organizing, but argued that "now that we have their [management's] attention, we don't need the union anymore."

The desire to work together with management to fix the problems in a facility has a powerful appeal among employees. Freeman and Rogers (1999) found that workers want "cooperative relations with management" (5) in dealing with workplace concerns. Although that does not necessarily preclude unions, workers generally prefer a relationship with management that minimizes conflict. Workers want a voice, but they also prefer to have that voice accepted as legitimate by employers. Workers fear that by "forcing" a voice on management, more restrictions and problems may result.

> I think it [the union] would have really disrupted my relationship with my boss. We now have set times we come and go, but there is certain flexibility to it. If I am going to be ten minutes late because my car won't start, I give my boss a call, say I'm running late and stay an extra ten minutes or something to that effect. With the way the hospital is, if the union made it in, there are these rules, these rules are written specifically, that's how it is, no exception, period. If you have to take your kid to the doctor's because he fell and hurt his arm, too bad. They would have taken all flexibility out just to be spiteful. The hospital would have. "Hey, you guys wanted these rules, your union presented them to us, we agreed on them, this is the way it is, that's it, no exceptions for nobody, never." (Marcus, Independence Memorial)

The call for further cooperation between management and workers was a powerful message, because it did not deny the existence of problems and legitimated the need for a workers' voice in decision-making, but presented an alternative with less potential conflict and ill-will. The idea of working together was the path of least resistance for workers to achieve their desired ends. The other major theme promoted by the anti-union workers also acknowledged the issues and problems of the hospital but again challenged the means by which the pro-union workers choose to address these issues.

Not *This* Union

Anti-union workers, using information provided by management propaganda regarding the union's strike record or militant activity, often suggested that "unionization" may not be a bad idea, but "this" particular union *is* problematic. This message recognized worker concerns and need for a voice but challenged the particular organization chosen to lead the effort toward empowerment. Marcus, for example, explained that although he had a certain amount of loyalty to the hospital for hiring him and "felt a need to defend them," he understood that many of his co-workers had serious problems, and that management was not dealing with those problems well. But Marcus communicated to his co-workers that this union was not the answer.

> I wasn't looking for any changes, anything specific, but at that point I guess I was looking out for the employees of the hospital. Had it been a union that had a good reputation for dealing with things without resorting to strikes very often, or presented themselves in the right way, where they hadn't been misleading in their propaganda, with all these things, then maybe that union would have been at least, if nothing else, a neutral impact on myself or people who didn't necessarily need it. But it would be there to help the employees that did need it. So, I like to keep an open mind, and a few years down, if it's a different union, I'll listen to what they have to say. So there is the possibility that there might be a right union. (Marcus, Independence Memorial)

Brenda at Union City used the same argument at her hospital. Having no union in her family, Brenda said she had no real opinion about unions one way or the other before the campaign. She did not consider herself anti-union when the campaign began. However, her transformation into an anti-union activist was based on her impressions of the union staff early in the campaign, impressions she first gathered at union meetings. Brenda became suspicious at a union meeting when an organizer was challenged by a worker about what they "get" for their union dues. The organizer "hemmed and hawed and tried to throw the question to a pro-union worker." Brenda felt that the organizers were subtly manipulating the workers at Union City by not actually promising anything themselves, but never correcting any inflated claims that pro-union workers said.

Dissatisfied by that meeting, Brenda then went home and searched on the Internet for information about the union. She found that this particular union advertised its commitment to organizing workers. "Rather than outline what the union could do for workers, all they talked about is what they were planning to do in the future. It seemed to me all this organizing was just about getting money." After a search of several anti-union web sites, she became convinced that this union was not good for the hospital and began to organize the anti-union workers. The problem was not unions in general, "just this union in this hospital at this time." She felt the union was too militant, aggressive, and untrustworthy.

The anti-union nurses at Corporation Hospital and United General also presented the "not this union" perspective. Cindy at United General was particularly torn. Identifying herself as "somewhat liberal" and usually the one to "support action" over acquiescence and progressive causes, she had difficulty seeing herself on the "other side" of the union fight. But ultimately she felt she could just not support the union, because the organizers were too "slick", "untrustworthy," and "disingenuous." She reported hearing from "other nurses" that this union was good at presenting itself one way during the campaign, but then acting a different way after the campaign was over. She, along with many other nurses in both campaigns, said that she would have been more comfortable with a "professional nurse organization" chartered through the American Nurse Association. Issues of "professionalism" arose frequently in these campaigns and were used as a wedge by anti-union nurses.

Although one can see the influence of the management campaign on the workers' frames, they used what resonated and was meaningful rather than uncritically accepting the employer's position. Combining their own sense of individual agency with the concerns and grievances of the pro-union supporters, the employer themes were reconstructed to fit the needs of the organizing drive. Hence, the positive "carrots" from management were translated into the broader notion that employers and employees need to "work together" to solve the problems of the hospital. The message was not simply to trust management to fix the problems, but instead a feeling that "now that management knows we are serious," we can work together on a more equal footing. And rather than proffering a blanket statement condemning all unions, the idea is that unionism is good; it is just "this union" that is the mistake. This re-articulation of anti-union themes was important in order for the anti-union committee to have an aura of neutrality as opposed to being a mouthpiece for the boss. In this respect, the anti-union committee can position itself as the "reasonable" party in-between the warring union and management.

> I felt that if I started being real preachy about [being anti-union] it would turn people away. People felt confident that they could come up to me knowing that I would give them an honest answer. What was really helpful was approaching people being open and honest, saying, personally I'm against it, but you have to make up your own mind. The hospital is throwing out all this information, they're throwing out all this information; hey, I'm playing neutral, here's the law and information, you interpret it yourself. (Marcus, Independence Memorial)

Unless the union can link the anti-union workers to management, these anti-unionists remain the only party in the dispute without institutional backing, something that gives them special credibility during the campaigns.

Thus, the anti-union workers clearly drew inspiration and clarification for their ideas from the propaganda of the employer campaign. But they did not adopt these ideas in total or without revision. Anti-union leaders transformed these messages into their own terms, combining past individual ideologies and the realities of the working conditions at the hospital. Rather than blatantly disparaging the idea of unionism, they instead looked to recognize the growing concern and grievances about the direction of the hospitals but sought to push those feelings into a direction other than unionization. Casting doubt in the minds of their co-workers, the anti-union activists confused the issue of change and provided an "out" through the "not this union" path of least resistance. The ideological battle of defining "who the union is" and what they can accomplish was not only a rhetorical process. Anti-unionists created "vote-no committees"[7] to press their beliefs at the worksites. Interestingly, the organizational manifestations of these committees were greatly influenced by the behavior of the union and its campaign tactics at each worksite.

UNION CAMPAIGNS AND THEIR IMPACT ON ANTI-UNION WORKERS

Although management may have influenced the content of anti-union ideology, the organizational manifestation of this ideology seemed more influenced by the union's campaign activity. The relationship between the union campaign and the activity of anti-union workers mirrors the "loosely coupled tango" (Zald and Useem 1987) between movements and counter-movements described in social movement theory.[8] Anti-unionists mirrored, to a surprising degree, the strategies and tactics of the union they were campaigning against. From "Vote No" pins to counter the "Union Yes" pins, to periodic leaflets challenging union claims, the anti-unionists deployed many tactics that they had already seen used by the union. The leaders of the anti-union committee at Corporation Hospital, for example, were not embarrassed to admit that they copied many of their ideas and tactics from the union campaign. Roger described how there was a lot of "tit for tat" between the campaigns.

> They were the professional organizers, so we let them go where they wanted to go and then we played their game. For example, the union was trying very hard to convince people that they weren't interested in the money. They were just interested in taking good care of the patients. Which I thought was crap. So the union came out with these buttons, big buttons that they passed out to nurses that said, "We Are United Because We Care." Well, the buttons came out on Monday. We had a meeting of the newsletter committee on Tuesday. Carla had a friend that was in the button making business. So we called and told them to start making buttons. And on Wednesday, the very next day, we're passing out our own buttons that say "We Care More." It made a lot of people mad. A lot of the union people were, like, "how dare

you take something we said and twist it." But, you know, let them take the first step and then we will counter it. (Randy, Corporation Hospital)

How the anti-union campaigns tried to spread their messages was also similar in each case to the pro-union campaign. Three of the anti-union campaigns, Corporation Hospital, United General, and Union City Hospital, developed and distributed a newsletter fairly regularly to inform their membership about issues in the campaign, just like the union had done. Roger and Carla made the newsletter the centerpiece of their organizing strategy.

> We tried to be consistent in a lot of ways in the newsletter. They were all printed on blue paper. The only reason for that was so that when someone saw it around the hospital, they would know what it was. Every newsletter started out with a quote from some famous person, a quote about choosing your friends or choosing your battles or something to kind of add light and at the same time with a message. We always carried a question and answer thing on the first page where people wrote us questions and we tried to get them an answer. Then we would have the articles. There was a consistency that after a while people who read the newsletter knew what to expect as far as what would be in column A and what would be in column B. (Roger, Corporation Hospital)

The United General nurses tried to pull a newsletter committee together, but their lack of organization prevented them from distributing more than a few issues. Because "everybody's volunteering their extra time" and "nobody has any time," keeping an organization going and maintaining a regular newsletter was more difficult than they had imagined. Instead, United General nurses tried to rely on an information table set up in the cafeteria. This too was copied from the union campaign. The union had gained permission to set up a cafeteria table and used it effectively to communicate with its activists. However this turned out to be a very ineffective method for getting the message out to the anti-union nurses, as they actually felt a bit intimidated by the "big" union table that was always present. That in turn led to less participation.

> We set up a table in the cafeteria. "Lead Your Own Way" had to move down the hall, because people felt very intimidated by the big union table. And there was some harassment coming over from there. Sometimes it was nasty, sometimes it was just intimidating, but it was never truly vicious. You have people flipping you off, but I mean it wasn't like really bad union, life threatening or any of that. It was a very different atmosphere than it would typically be in the lunchroom or in other areas. And a lot of the things that the union tried to present that was happening to them from administra-

tion, which I never saw at all going the other way, but I felt a lot of from the union. (Cindy, United General)

The anti-union committee at Corporation Hospital was sophisticated enough to not only pass out regular communications like the union, but also organized two solidarity actions to help build commitment to their cause. None of the other three campaigns reached this level of organization. Anti-union workers were told to gather during their lunch hour across the street from the hospital where they would proceed to march around the hospital and finish at a religious statue in a courtyard of the hospital. There, flowers were placed at the feet of the statue and index cards were distributed for people to write something that they loved about the hospital.

> We tried to make this rally more emotional. "This is Corporation Hospital! Look what this campaign is doing, it's turning friend against friend. I have friends that are not talking to me and I am not talking to them." So we wanted to try and really push let's have the union go away and work on things and return to the family atmosphere. What we did was kind of a symbolic thing, we presented roses to the statue on behalf of all the employees. It's one of those tear kind of things, I had to practice that speech a million times so I could get through it. It was real effective. I think, it got a lot of people revved up and people that came afterwards were like "Hey, that was really great!" (Carla, Corporation Hospital)

According to Roger, almost 400 people came to this rally, and it was widely talked about in the hospital afterward. At Corporation Hospital, such a high level of organization from the anti-union workers was more than the union could handle. Between management's resistance and the worker committee's counter-mobilization, the union could not maintain adequate support. Both Roger and Carla believed that their anti-union committee, not the employer, was the main reason Corporation Hospital was non-union today.

Although providing anti-union leaders with what amounts to a repertoire of collective action tactics to draw on, the union also has the ability to severely constrict the creation of anti-union organizations. Through either early success in its own campaign, or by effectively disrupting the counter-campaign, the union can influence whether an anti-union committee develops at all. Movement success can prevent counter-movements from ever arising, or can cause them to develop too late to make an impact. Zald and Useem (1987) suggest that "in the loosely coupled tango" between movements and counter-movements, an overwhelming early victory by a movement may stifle the emergence of counter-movements, for potential supporters of the counter-movement become "paralyzed" and see "little chance of success." This essentially was what occurred for the anti-union workers at Union City Hospital. Early in the campaign, the union held its first campaign-defining event at a local civic club that drew more than 500 workers over the course of three meetings. This became a defining moment for the supporters of the union as an overwhelming number of workers came out in support of unionization. The union quickly established a presence in many areas of the hospital and union supporters were free to openly speak their minds at work. The fear of isolation and reprimand rapidly lessened in the face of such solidarity. By the time anti-union forces began to mobilize within the business office of the hospital (whose workers did not participate in any significant numbers at the first big meeting), union dominance was entrenched.

> I think a lot of people were afraid. Like if you were in housekeeping, and you knew that group was pro-union and you might have felt, "Oh God, if I don't vote for the union, somebody might know it wasn't me, if they don't get in everybody's going to blame me." There might have been fear there, so they just went with the crowd. . . . It seemed like it was more accepted to be a pro-union person. Like, if you spoke out against the hospital that was more accepted than if I came out and said, "Hey, wait a minute, take a look at this." People were more accepting of you being pro-union than me being anti-union. So I think it was skewed toward the union. (Diane, Union City)

Unlike in the other union campaigns in which the pro-union workers often felt like the "minority" voice and were fearful about talking about the union and expressing their true opinions in front of co-workers, at Union City Hospital anti-union workers felt pressured to keep their opinions to themselves. Since the business-office workers were never really part of the initial unionization wave, they were insulated from the effects of the early victories and could establish an anti-union voice in their area, but it never developed into a broader effort.

In a different form of "victory" but a no less potent one, the nurses at United General severely hampered the growth of an anti-union committee by infiltrating the initial meetings and disrupting the process. Anti-unionists at United General made the mistake of openly advertising their first meeting for interested nurses. This allowed pro-union nurses to come to the meeting and prevented a collective voice from forming or an organizational strategy from developing.

> I got a call from somebody who said that there's a meeting for people who are not really sure that this is the direction they want to go and that they want more information or at least to present or explore what other options are out there. So I went to this meeting at the library. It was actually the first

meeting of [the Lead Your Own Way committee]—it didn't even have a name at that point. There were about seven people there with one agenda and the rest of them were from the union group that had seen the information about the meeting and came loaded for bear and shouted down anybody trying to talk about anything else. They were very abrasive and intimidating. "I want to make sure that the correct information gets out there!" they would say. It was like whoa, you know! (Cindy, United General)

Due to this initial stumble, it took a while for the anti-union nurses to re-contact each other and set up a private meeting at someone's home. The delay cost valuable time while the union was solidifying its support base. The situation intimidated anti-union nurses and created doubts about whether they wanted to get involved. This example highlights the importance of timing. The pro-union nurses at Corporation Hospital actually had a larger organizing committee than at United General, could mobilize more nurses for collective action events, and in the beginning were on much more solid footing, having signed up over a majority of nurse on union authorization cards. United General's union campaign started much more slowly with a lot less initial interest. Had the anti-union campaign reached the level of sophistication that it had at Corporation Hospital, the United General organizing drive may not have ever gained the necessary steam to finish as strong as it did. But because no alternative voice emerged in the hospital (other than management's) until four or five months before the election, the union was able to make up for lost ground, and the anti-union nurses were never able to really coalesce around a strategy or agenda.

CONCLUSION

In union certification election campaigns, management plays an important role in shaping the beliefs and actions of anti-union workers. But they would be far less successful in this effort if not for the pre-existing individual worldviews and notions of anti-unionism among workers, which are often reinforced by the actions and rhetoric of the union organizing campaign. We cannot overlook the agency of anti-union workers in shaping counter-union campaign activity. Neoliberal ideologies that characterize unions as relics of a by-gone industrial era influence many workers long before unions even arrive on the scene to organize the facility. The belief that unions are "dinosaurs" and responsible for working-class economic woes due to their intransigence in bargaining and violence to protect their interests is also widespread. Employers add to this impression by highlighting the possibility of strikes and union violence if workers unionize. Similarly, management typi-

cally attempts to characterize the union as an outside "third party" only interested in dues and membership numbers, rather than the needs and desires of
workers. In the four campaigns examined here, this contribution to the
message of anti-unionism was the main influence of employers on anti-union
workers. Although more insidious means of helping anti-union workers may
have occurred too, direct logistical, resource, and leadership influence do not
appear to have been present to any significant degree.

Workers' struggles for unionization, then, are not merely a contest between
employees and employers. Divisions among workers also can affect the ability
to create solidarity and power in the workplace. Anti-union workers are not
necessarily part-and-parcel of the employer's campaign. Indeed, their real or
apparent independence makes the message and rhetoric of anti-union workers
all the more powerful as a voice against the union. Regardless of how the anti-
union workers choose to disseminate their ideas and beliefs, their action opens
up ideological space for anti-union sentiment to grow among the workers. As
Carla at Corporation Hospital noted, the simple fact that they were "out there"
helped galvanize support.

> I don't know, maybe just getting out there to say that people aren't for it, to
> get them to look at both sides, I think that was the most important thing.
> I would say just getting out there and having a newsletter and saying, "Hey,
> there are people who just aren't for it." I think that was the big thing. (Carla,
> Corporation Hospital)

Moreover, it is not only management that has an influence on workers'
anti-union activity, for the union itself also had a strong influence on how the
anti-union sentiment manifested itself. The way the union initially sets up its
campaign and its organizational agenda can create many issues for the anti-
union workers to organize around. The union also provides examples of how
successful rank-and-file organizing can take place and directly affects the anti-
unionists through their own success and actions.

Among all these factors, it is the agency of the anti-union workers that is
most often ignored, though it is especially important to consider. Drawing on
a variety of influences, anti-union workers constructed their own frames of
resistance to the union campaign and then used those frames to mobilize their
co-workers. These frames acknowledged the feelings of the pro-union worker
by accepting that there were problems in the facility, but challenging them on
the vehicle for change. Rather than go through the union, anti-union workers
saw organizing drive as the perfect time to reinvigorate labor/management
committees and commit employers and the workers to solving their problems
on their own. Many workers disinterested in conflict, but tired of the wors-
ening conditions, latched on to this vision of reorganization within the facil-

ity. It justified the workers' sense of disgruntlement but spared workers the fear of the union. In addition, the messages of not "this" union validated worker concerns but argued that the particular union organizing was not the best pick for the workers.

The manifestation of these sentiments clearly also depended on anti-union workers finding leaders capable of gathering their co-workers together to fight the union. Sacrificing both their own time and money, anti-union campaigners characterized by inspired leadership built "vote no" committees that successfully mimicked the strategies and tactics of the union. It is significant that the campaign with the most aggressive organizing campaign (Corporation Hospital) also had the most aggressive anti-union mobilization, while the campaign with the weakest union campaign (Independence Memorial) had the weakest anti-union activity.

How should unions deal with these anti-union committees? Organizationally, this research shows that once the campaign is made public, early success on the part of the union can dampen anti-union activism. By "squeezing out" the ideological space and isolating anti-union workers, the union can give itself the needed time to cement its position in the workplace and gain the rhetorical high ground. In this regard, disrupting early anti-union meetings can also provide needed time to establish the "pro-union" line as the dominant frame within the facility. Ideologically, the response by unions to anti-union committees is more complex. Worker anti-union sentiment is not necessarily representative of undue loyalty to employers but may instead reflect misunderstanding, fear, and a lack of vision. Organizers and workers would do well to engage with anti-union activists, seeking opportunities to change their hearts and minds, rather than simply dismissing them as "bought and paid for" by the employer.

4

OVERCOMING LEGACIES OF BUSINESS UNIONISM

WHY GRASSROOTS ORGANIZING TACTICS SUCCEED

Steven H. Lopez

Rosemont Pavilion[1] sits well back from the two-lane blacktop, on a gently-sloping hill overlooking a wood-frame bungalow and a farmer's field. The nursing home is a single-story red brick building shaped like a capital "H," with one long side of the "H" facing the parking lot. Rows of identical windows above identical air conditioners mounted in the brick stretch out on either side of the main entrance. It is a modest but respectable-looking building in a modest but respectable industrial suburb of Pittsburgh, Pennsylvania.

On a warm spring day in late June of 1997, I found myself sitting with SEIU organizers, rank-and-file activists, and management representatives in the employee break room at Rosemont, watching an independent arbitrator count workers' votes for and against union representation.[2] As a doctoral candidate in sociology at UC Berkeley conducting a participant observation study of union organizing in the nursing home industry in Pennsylvania, I had just begun working for SEIU Local A as an intern.[3]

I was confident that the union would win this election. I knew that the SEIU had a successful track record of organizing nursing home workers in southwestern Pennsylvania. Moreover, Rosemont workers were very angry at management about the conditions in the nursing home. They earned poverty wages (most earned $6.40 per hour) for backbreaking, emotionally trying work. Their facility was seriously understaffed; each nurses' aide was expected to care for as many as twenty residents at a time on the day shift—an impossible task. And workers were routinely individually blamed, punished, and scapegoated by management for the predictable care problems that clearly stemmed from understaffing, poor training, and high turnover.

Also in the union's favor was the fact that management, distracted by a lengthy state investigation into the quality of care at Rosemont, had barely bothered to oppose the union's organizing campaign. Here, in contrast to many other union campaigns, there had been no firings, no serious unfair labor practices, no pressure or terror tactics. Operating under the terms of an expedited election agreement between the nursing home chain and the SEIU, management agreed to an election date just two weeks after the union filed its petition. Although the union's campaign had been rather lackluster (relying mainly on union meetings and several mass mailings) it seemed clear that workers' grievances, combined with the lack of strong opposition from management, spelled victory for the SEIU.

To my surprise, however, the workers voted 35 to 32 against unionization. As the union delegation left the building, I was stunned to hear Rosemont workers' cheers echo through the hallways and follow me out the door. Since I believed that unionization was the only way to address issues like low wages, understaffing, and arbitrary exercise of management authority, I could not understand why workers who were so disadvantaged and oppressed would not only vote against the obvious means of improving their situation but also cheer about it.

One year later, in 1998, Local A returned to try again, and once again I was able to observe the campaign as a participant. This time, the union did a much better job of implementing the SEIU's grassroots organizing approach. Organizers recruited and trained a volunteer rank-and-file organizing committee whose members played a crucial role in organizing their co-workers. Organizers and rank-and-file volunteers visited all 80 Rosemont workers at home at least once during the campaign. And unlike the year before, the 1998 campaign was organized not around a series of union meetings but around a series of escalating in-plant collective actions. Despite the fact that management mounted an intensive and sophisticated anti-union campaign, Rosemont workers this time voted by a two to one margin in favor of unionization.

The divergent outcomes of these two successive SEIU campaigns at Rosemont are consistent with Bronfenbrenner and Juravich's (1998) finding—based on quantitative analysis of NLRB election data and surveys of union campaigns—that grassroots union organizing tactics, when deployed in a coordinated way, are much more likely than "traditional" tactics to yield union victories (see also Bronfenbrenner and Hickey, this volume). But while quantitative research can tell us which tactics are statistically more likely to succeed, it cannot tell us much about *how* or *why* unions succeed. In particular, it cannot tell us what problems and obstacles social movement unionism must overcome in order to achieve success, or how these obstacles can be surmounted.

Comparing these two successive SEIU organizing campaigns at Rosemont nursing home can help us flesh out Bronfenbrenner and Juravich's quantitative finding with a more nuanced understanding of how and why grassroots organizing tactics succeed in the contemporary period. Specifically, the argument I make in this chapter is that the success of contemporary grassroots organizing approaches depends in part on its ability to deal with and transform working class anti-unionism. This anti-unionism is not merely a set of free floating attitudes or the product of misinformation and management pressure, but is rooted in workers' lived experiences of a half-century of business unionism. Without minimizing the very real dimensions of management repression and anti-union propaganda, I want to show that historically rooted working-class anti-unionism is a crucial obstacle to labor revitalization in its own right and cannot be understood simply as a reflection of management power.

WORKER RESISTANCE AND THE LIVED EXPERIENCE OF BUSINESS UNIONISM

The literature on union organizing has surprisingly little to say about the issue of worker resistance to unions. There is, of course, a huge literature on attitudes toward unions, including group attitudes (see Cornfield et al. 1998 and Weikle et al. 1998 for brief summaries). This literature has repeatedly found that about one-third of American workers say they would like union representation. However, the problem with surveys of union attitudes of various groups—as Weinbaum (1999) and Fantasia (1988) point out in different contexts—is that survey research ignores the way workers' "conflicting and contradictory views and questions" (Weinbaum, 47) can be suddenly transformed via organizing or episodes of collective action. Because they are abstracted from actual social relationships and processes, responses on attitudinal surveys can be very poor predictors of how workers are likely to respond to a real unionization campaign in their workplace.[4]

Studies of union organizing that raise the issue of worker resistance tend to do so indirectly or in passing. Voss and Sherman (2000) and Fletcher and Hurd (1998, 1999) discuss worker resistance in considerable depth, presenting evidence that existing union members' ingrained expectations about servicing lead them often to resist their unions' efforts to activate them—but these writers focus on *existing* union members and their resistance to union reform rather than on unorganized workers' responses to union organizing attempts. Researchers who have studied attempts to organize immigrants have observed that immigrants' divergent experiences shape their responses to union organizing. Waldinger and Der-Martirosian (2000) report that immigrants from former Eastern bloc countries may be ideologically hostile to unions, while Mexican immigrants are often strongly pro-union to begin with. Wells (2000), drawing on interviews with union organizers, discusses a variety of immigrant experiences, commenting on Chinese immigrant workers, for example, that because of their experience in China, "they think of unions as . . . arms of the government, rather than organizations formed by and for workers" (119). Writing about organizing American-born workers, Turner (1998) notes that in a United Mine Workers (UMWA) campaign, the union's failure to develop trust and close relationships with workers prevented organizers from being able to counteract its reputation for violence, a failure that management capitalized on by showing old films of picket-line violence in the Mine Workers.

Thus, while every good union organizer knows that contemporary workers are often highly skeptical of, or even hostile to, unions' motives, means, and ends, the literature on union organizing only hints at the roots of workers' ambivalence in different contexts, and so far has not really explained how or why grassroots organizing approaches can overcome it. This chapter's comparison of two SEIU organizing drives at Rosemont Pavilion adds to our understanding of contemporary union organizing by showing, first, how and why workers' negative experiences and images of business unionism can lead them to reject unions—even when grievances are bitterly held and when management does not mount a vigorous anti-union campaign. In particular, I argue that workers' perceptions that unions played a key role in Pittsburgh's deindustrialization; their association of unions with corruption, intimidation, and even violence; and their experiences of "do-nothing unionism" led them to be skeptical of, and even hostile to, union organizing campaigns. Second, this chapter suggests that social-movement organizing succeeds to the extent that it allows the union to create a new vision of participatory, powerful unionism that is understood—by workers—to be *different* from the old-style business unionism of experience and cultural memory. It is the re-interpretation of negative experiences and images of unions as belonging to an outmoded form of unionism that clears the way for workers to support the organizing effort.

LIVED EXPERIENCES OF BUSINESS UNIONISM

In the aftermath of Local A's 1997 organizing drive at Rosemont, the extent of rank-and-file opposition to unionization remained a mystery to me. Certainly, I could see that Local A had not fully implemented the SEIU organizing approach I had read about in the SEIU organizing manual during my training period. The union's small organizing staff had been overstretched by an attempt to run several campaigns at once, and, as a result, the Rosemont campaign had been a "quick and dirty" affair. There had been no serious attempt to build a functioning rank-and-file committee or to train rank-and-file volunteers to perform organizing tasks. There had not been a single collective action. Instead the campaign consisted of a handful of organizing meetings culminating in the circulation of interest cards. As soon as a simple majority of workers signed and returned their cards, the union petitioned for an election, which was held just two weeks later. But whatever the weaknesses of the union's organizing effort, it did not seem to explain the *intensity* of workers' opposition to unionization, especially when I considered (1) the seriousness of workers' grievances against management, and (2) the absence of a strong management response to the organizing drive.

The 1997 organizing drive at Rosemont did not fail because workers were insufficiently aggrieved. At organizing meetings, much angry discussion revolved around the issue of staffing. Staffing was so poor that workers were unable to attend to their residents' most basic bodily needs. As one worker complained, "Even when nobody calls off, I don't have time to bathe [residents'] legs every day and check their heels daily for [skin] breakdowns [as required by law]." But workers' complaints about the understaffing fell on deaf ears. "We told [the director of nursing] that we needed more staff. And she yelled at us and said that we were well above staffing requirements."

Rosemont's low wages translated into an annual turnover rate approaching 100 percent, and management also had continual difficulty finding a steady stream of new workers to replace those who left. "I see the ad in the newspaper every week," one aide said. "Most weeks, nobody applies. Why would they? You can make $6.40 an hour in lots of better ways than this. They're not going to be able to keep people unless they pay better." Desperate for staff, management often continued to schedule workers who frequently called off, or workers who had not turned up for scheduled work in days. This infuriated those who showed up faithfully and who often came in on their own days off to help ease staffing crises. "A lot of times you look on the schedule and you see names down there that you know are people who have quit, or haven't come to work in a while. I guess [the Director of Nursing] feels like her ass is covered as long as she's got a name to put down for that slot—but you know that day you are going to be working short for sure."

In addition to the staffing problems, Rosemont workers were also angry about what they perceived as management's indifference to the residents, the lack of respect for residents' dignity. One worker said:

Sometimes they make comments about the residents. Like the other day, some of the residents wanted to sit out in the hall, and the supervisor said to the aide who asked about it, "No, we can't have them cluttering up the place like firewood." And the residents could hear how they were being spoken about, you know. It just wasn't handled in a nice way, a caring way. That's the kind of stuff that really burns me.

Every aide I talked to had her own angry stories about residents whose medical needs had been ignored by management, sometimes for weeks. I heard about residents falling out of broken chairs; I heard from aides who had been ordered to roust residents in the middle of the night for showers; and I heard about management's indifference to aides' reports of resident injuries. "If you find a broken bone, or a skin tear, or a bruise," said one aide, "and you tell management about it, a lot of times they don't do anything right away. They don't like calling the doctor in too often, because it costs money. And they never investigate injuries like they're supposed to.[5] A lot of times they'll just blame it on you."

Finally, all the workers I talked to were upset about the way management exercised arbitrary authority, targeting some workers for discipline (often unfairly or on unfounded charges) while letting others slide. Part-time workers were routinely scheduled to work just a few hours short of full-time in each pay period, so that they worked essentially full-time hours but received no benefits. Long-awaited vacations were often cancelled without notice or recourse. And workers were particularly outraged over how a series of abrupt scheduling changes had been handled. Workers were shuffled to new shifts with only a few days' notice and told to show up for their new shifts or consider themselves fired. Those with transportation or child care dilemmas were not permitted any time to make alternate arrangements. Every worker had his or her own story of management injustice.

The SEIU's 1997 campaign also did not fail because of strenuous management campaigning against the union. Rosemont essentially lived up to its obligations under the election agreement. Management limited its anti-union campaign to the two-week period between the union's petition for election and the election itself, and its efforts were remarkably restrained. No workers were targeted or fired for their union activity, and no individual threats were made. There were rumors that some workers had been promised raises if they agreed to vote against the union, but the union was not able to pin these rumors down. The closest thing to a documented case of unlawful anti-union communication during this period was one incident in which Rosemont's administrator wrote a sarcastic note to a strongly pro-union worker: "Union meeting today at [a local diner]—how come I'm not invited?"[6]

Given the intensity of workers' grievances and the absence of a strong anti-union effort by management, why did so many workers not only vote against unionization but actually cheer out loud upon hearing the outcome? The nature and meaning of rank-and-file opposition to unionization at Rosemont did not begin to become clear to me until 1998 when the union returned for a second try with a more grassroots approach. This time the union made a strong effort to build an effective, representative rank-and-file committee, and to train committee members to organize their work areas. Organizers and rank-and-file activists house-visited every worker in the proposed bargaining unit. And unlike the previous year's effort, in 1998 the campaign was organized around a series of escalating shop-floor actions rather than a series of static union meetings. During this second campaign, I was able to participate in 36 house-visits (more than one-third of the total). Discussions with workers during these 1998 visits convinced me that three distinct sets of union experiences were functioning as a barrier to the SEIU's organizing efforts: experiences and images of "do-nothing" unionism; experiences of deindustrialization and job loss; and experiences of union violence, intimidation, and corruption.

Deindustrialization and the Fear of Job Loss

At the town hall, red dots on a wall map show the location of more than a hundred mines in and around the township in which Rosemont is located. Every one of these mines is closed. By 1990, there were no workers at all employed in the mining sector in the township (U.S. Bureau of the Census, 1990). A few miles closer to Pittsburgh, the signs of a vanished industrial world are more visible in the bizarre landscapes of rusting and twisted metal and broken glass that line the Monongahela River. In nearby industrial suburbs of Pittsburgh, communities that were sites for large-scale steel manufacturing for a century do not have a single working mill.

These economic changes loomed large in the lives of workers at Rosemont. Many older workers had been directly affected. Men who lost industrial jobs in the 1980s rarely found new work at equivalent wages; their wives were among Rosemont's older female employees, who had gone to work in the 1980s or early 1990s to help cope with their families' sinking standard of living. This older worker's story was typical of many others I heard:

> My husband and father both worked for Westinghouse. My husband was laid off from Westinghouse years ago when my daughter was little. Those were bad years. I worked two jobs, and one of them was sewing piecework. I hated that job, but I was there for the benefits—I needed hospitalization for two children and a husband. Finally he got a job at the prison. He still wasn't making great money but at least he had benefits. I quit the sewing job within a week of his benefits kicking in.

Older workers like this one, who had lived through the collapse of industrial unionism in the Monongahela valley, interpreted their experiences in a variety of ways. Some remained strongly pro-union, blaming the companies for deindustrialization and viewing the decline in unions as a major reason that times had gotten so much harder than they used to be. Many of these women had husbands who felt the same way, and who believed that their wives' job conditions would never get any better unless they organized a union. During organizing visits to a number of workers' homes, I met several strongly pro-union men who welcomed me warmly and often sat in on the discussion about Rosemont, chiming in with strongly worded comments about the need for a union there. Rosemont women with this kind of support were almost always pro-union themselves and tended to interpret the economic disaster they were living through as something that had been perpetrated against the unions rather than something that the unions had caused.

However, this interpretation was far from universal. Equally common were workers who bitterly blamed the unions as much as the companies for what had happened to the industrial economy of the region. Several workers I spoke with were particularly angry about decisions their husbands' unions had made in the 1980s to go on strike even while management was planning or threatening to close or relocate their plants. "What were they thinking?" one woman said. "[Management] was just looking for an excuse to relocate the plant. And the union went out on strike just to get another dollar an hour. Hell, my husband was making $19 dollars an hour already. They didn't need that extra dollar an hour, not really. Management didn't care if they went on strike— they just closed the plant up for good. If the union hadn't gone on strike we might have kept the plant for a while longer, anyway."

This view was not limited to just a few workers. In one of the early organizing meetings I attended in June of 1997, those present were talking about the views of their co-workers. One worker said, "If I hear one more time that so-and-so's husband lost their steel job because of the union, I'm gonna scream!" There was a chorus of agreement from the others, and Joan Hardy, the union organizer who was running the meeting, asked people to elaborate. "People say that the unions put the plants out of business because of the high wages," one said. "We hear that all the time."

During my home visits the following summer, this issue was raised again and again by anxious workers, who were worried that forming a union might ultimately lead to the shutdown of the nursing home. How the union addressed these questions in the 1998 campaign will be discussed below, but the point here is that the union's arm's length campaign tactics in 1997 had prevented it from dealing with the widespread view that unions were largely to blame for deindustrialization and that unionization might force the nursing home out of business.

Union Violence, Intimidation, and Corruption

The stereotypical images of the corrupt union boss and the thick-necked labor goon have become standard fare in movies and television shows (Puette 1992), but like most stereotypes they do contain a kernel of truth. Unions have always been less violent than their corporate opponents, especially if one defines violence to include forms of economic violence. However, the fact remains that some industrial unions have a reputation for using strong-arm tactics to intimidate bosses and to keep workers in line. Even worse, sometimes these tactics have been deployed by corrupt union officials against workers who have tried to democratize their unions. The cases are rare, but they tend to be famous. In one of the most widely known, the president of the United Mine Workers ordered the murder of the leader of a UMW reform movement in 1969 (Armbrister 1980). In the mining country of southwestern Pennsylvania, older workers remember these events vividly. Nothing makes contemporary organizing more difficult than these images of unions as not only corrupt but violent organizations.

At Rosemont nursing home, this view of unions was grounded in the experience of a core group of kitchen workers who had worked at the nursing home for nearly two decades. In 1980, the Teamsters union had organized the facility and won a certification election. However, the president of the Teamsters' local apparently believed that strong-arm tactics were the best way to win a good contract. Instead of negotiating in good faith, the Teamsters' president began threatening the nursing home administrator with bodily harm if management would not accede to the Teamsters' demands. He refused, and the Teamsters escalated their attack. According to several workers I spoke with who had worked at Rosemont during this period, Teamsters came to the facility on several occasions and threw rocks through windows, terrorizing residents and angering workers. At first, I dismissed these stories as exaggerations. However, local news reports from the early 1980s reveal that matters had become even graver. In October of 1980 a homemade bomb was found underneath a car in the parking lot. According to local newspaper reports, the bomb, equivalent to three to five sticks of dynamite, failed to detonate only because the timing device was faulty. Police and FBI investigations failed to yield a suspect, but two months later a similarly constructed device—this time filled with mud instead of explosive—was disguised as a gift and left under a Christmas tree inside the nursing home. The president of the Teamsters local made an anonymous telephone call to the facility to warn them that there was a bomb in the facility. His message was captured on tape and his voice identified by the FBI. According to a UPI news report, he was eventually indicted and convicted on charges of making bomb threats, but no one was ever definitively connected to the October bomb.[7]

As a result of this debacle, many workers at Rosemont remained staunchly anti-union for years afterwards. In 1997, a group of kitchen workers who had seen these events firsthand still vociferously opposed the union and went to great lengths to persuade their co-workers that forming a union could only lead to trouble. This group formed a vocal opposition to the small group of workers that was actually involved with the union in 1997, shouting down union supporters in break-room discussions. With encouragement from management, they formed a "just vote no" committee that held regular meetings, put up anti-union posters around the facility, and helped management distribute anti-union literature.

These anti-union workers formed networks that militated *against* unionization and exerted social pressure on anyone who dared venture the opinion that a union might be a good idea, thus raising the costs of being pro-union—especially in the kitchen, where the leaders of the anti-union group worked. In the summer of 1998, I visited two kitchen workers who had disagreed with the "just vote no" committee. However, both had been intimidated into silence. "I couldn't speak up," one said. "You don't understand what it's like in there. The kitchen is a closed environment. I have to deal with these people every day. They would have made my life miserable if I had said anything against them. I didn't agree with them but I just kept my opinions to myself." The other pro-union kitchen worker I talked to in 1998 felt the same way. She had been cautiously supportive of organizing a union but was terrified of her anti-union co-workers. "Please don't tell anyone that you visited me," she begged. "I believe in the union but if they find out I was talking to you they'll all be after me."

Of course, the events associated with the Teamsters' organizing campaign represent an extreme case. But they spoke to stereotypical images that do contain a kernel of truth. And they illustrate that even if rare, incidents of union violence or corruption can poison workers' views of unions for decades. Even campaigns that do not involve violence, intimidation, or corruption can leave an anti-union legacy in their wake. Markowitz's (1995, 2000) comparison of a top-down, business-union United Food and Commercial Workers (UFCW) campaign with a more participatory, grassroots-oriented Amalgamated Clothing and Textile Workers Union (ACTWU) campaign shows that workers who initially support a union can emerge from successful organizing campaigns feeling bitter and disappointed, and even anti-union, if the union does not live up to its promises or their expectations. Interestingly, Markowitz found that workers who had been involved in the ACTWU's grassroots, participatory, "workers are the union" campaign were even more bitter than their UFCW counterparts when the participatory ideals of their campaign were replaced by the realities of post-contract servicing. These findings highlight how crucial it is for union organizing campaigns to be honest and open with rank-and-file workers—and to follow through on promises. Campaigns that treat workers as votes, marginalize workers' concerns and issues, or fail to deliver on their promises can poison the well for years to come.

"Do-Nothing" Unionism

The fear of many workers, quite plainly, was that the union was only interested in their dues money; that if they voted to unionize, the union would take their dues and not help them, leaving them perhaps worse off than before. These workers were intimately familiar with the workings of one organization—their employer—that exploited them and turned a deaf ear to their complaints, grievances, and problems. They feared that the union would be no different.

This fear was something I encountered over and over again as I visited people at their homes. Their overriding concern was how much, and what kind of, representation they would get for their dues. Like wary and skeptical consumers, workers tried to figure out exactly what they were being asked to buy, how much it would cost them, and what guarantees they would have that they would actually get what they thought they were buying. How much were the dues? How did the union spend the dues? What if the union spent their dues money on things—like political candidates—that they didn't support? How much did the president of the local make? How could they be sure the union would fight for them? How could they be sure (as one worker put it) that the union wouldn't "take my money and run"? "What kind of raises will we get if we vote the union in?" was a common question. The following worker's question was also typical: "They said that we could end up with no more than we have now, or less. What guarantee do we have that we'll get anything out of it?" Workers also worried about the possibility of a strike. "What if they don't agree to anything and the union calls us out on strike?" I was asked. "What will happen then? We can't just abandon these residents in here."

On the one hand, these kinds of questions highlight something that theorists of social movement participation have long emphasized: that people usually weigh the costs and benefits of participating—or at least, they weigh their *perceptions* of costs and benefits—before they commit themselves (Olson 1965, Oberschall 1973, Klandermans 1984, Klandermans and Oegema 1987). On the other hand, the workers' assumption that they were being asked to purchase a service, as opposed to being asked to join in a collective effort to change their workplace, also reflected their experience with the norms and expectations of servicing-oriented business unionism. As numerous critics of business unionism have pointed out, the ideology of "servicing" discourages rank-and-file participation and creates dependence on professional union staff (Aronowitz 1992, Buhle 1999, Moody 1988, Eisenscher 1999). Workers were certainly right to be wary and careful in their decision making—but their assumption that the role of the union was to "fight for me" reflected a pre-existing normative expectation, rooted in the ideology and reality of business unionism, that their role in the union would be a passive one.

Many workers I talked to had stories to tell about how they or people they knew had been "shafted" by their union. Either the union hadn't listened to their views or the union had failed to represent them in some way. One woman I visited was particularly blunt. "Y'ins are buggers," she said. "You can make your promises but they don't mean shit to me." She went on to complain about her experience as a member of a factory union in the 1970s. "That was an old-boy network," she said. "I was one of the only women there. They didn't listen to what I had to say because I was a woman. I didn't get the same raises [as the men] and when I had a grievance they didn't do anything with it. So as far as I'm concerned, your unions are just for the ones that run 'em."[8]

There were also other kinds of complaints. One woman's husband had been injured on the job, and he was fighting for his settlement when his plant closed. She was bitter because in her view the union hadn't done enough to get him a fair settlement. And some workers with direct experience in business-union settings simply felt that the union had not been a significant factor in shaping the quality of their work life. Consider the case of a house-keeping worker, Gene, I spoke with early in the 1998 campaign. The union had learned from another worker that Gene, a quiet person who would not necessarily be influenced by others' loud opinions, was undecided about the union. He had told the union's informant that he didn't want to be visited at home, but that he would like someone from the union to call him. When I spoke with him on the phone, he was pleasant but he made it clear that he was completely indifferent to the union. "I don't care whether it's voted in or not," he said. He explained that he had been working part-time for a number of years at a local supermarket where he was represented by another union. "The union there doesn't mean a lot," he said. "Our wages there are not much more than minimum. The union makes no difference to my life there. So I don't see how it's really going to change much for me here either." Gene was respected by other workers in his department, and when he spoke up his co-workers listened. Gene's views thus hurt the 1997 campaign quite a lot, but the union hadn't known anything about him during that campaign. Gene had every reason to be dissatisfied with his supermarket contract. Local Z, the largest local union in southwestern Pennsylvania, was notorious for contracts that paid only nickels or dimes above the minimum wage. Gene and his fellow supermarket workers represented by Local Z have had to accept bad contracts negotiated by union bureaucrats with little or no rank-and-file involvement. Little wonder that such workers are unimpressed by the benefits of union membership.

FACE-TO-FACE ORGANIZING AND COLLECTIVE ACTION IN THE UNION'S SECOND CAMPAIGN

The analysis above identified three kinds of lived experience that contributed to workers' ambivalence about unionism. The union's 1997 campaign failed primarily because it had done nothing to address these issues or modify workers' views of unions as remote, top-down organizations, possibly corrupt or criminal, interested in their dues money more than their welfare, and probably incapable of helping them improve their job situations.

In 1998, the union had to contend not only with workers' negative lived experiences of unions, but also with a much more extended, intense, and sophisticated anti-union campaign from management. In 1998, Rosemont hired an anti-union consulting firm, brought in anti-union speakers, held one-on-one and captive-audience meetings, distributed anti-union literature, and targeted pro-union workers for disciplinary action. Despite this intensified management resistance, however, this time the union won the certification election by a two-to-one margin. The union's 1998 campaign succeeded where "traditional" tactics had failed, primarily because face-to-face organizing and collective action tactics enabled it to neutralize workers' negative experiences of unions, building a positive vision of a participatory and empowering form of unionism that defined itself in opposition to traditional business unionism.

Overcoming Fears of Job Loss

Local A's 1998 organizing campaign addressed Rosemont workers' fears about job loss primarily through one-on-one discussion during house-visits (by rank-and-file committee members and organizers) and via one-on-one work by rank-and-file activists on the shop floor. It was fairly common for workers I visited at home to say, "I've heard we could all lose our jobs if the union gets in," and then wait for a response. In 1998, management (illegally) suggested that if the workers at Rosemont formed a union, the company might be forced to close or sell the nursing home. This played on the association many workers made between unions and the deindustrialization and job loss that had previously affected the region. In addition, the union campaign had to deal with some real bitterness on the part of workers who blamed unions (at least in part) for deindustrialization more generally and the decline in living standards that they had experienced.

Like other house-callers, I spent a lot of time during house-visits listening to workers' views on these subjects and discussing these issues with them. When workers argued that unions' blind pursuit of higher wages had made the steel industry uncompetitive, organizers and committee members responded by initiating a discussion about the forces of economic globalization which pitted American manufacturing workers against highly exploited low-wage workers abroad. Rosemont workers could easily see that these forces, however disastrous for manufacturing workers, do not apply in the same way to most in-person services, especially health care services that must be delivered in local communities. They could see that while steel mills could be located somewhere else, and mines could be shut down while coal was bought from other places, nursing homes have to serve the communities in which they are located.

House-callers also pointed out that the Hewitt Group,[9] the nursing home chain Rosemont belonged to, hadn't closed any of the five other facilities where Local A represented workers, and that the chain was still making a profit at those facilities even though wages were higher and benefits better than at Rosemont. The house-callers also brought with them copies of the facility's financial statement, a publicly available form that all nursing home operators are required to file with the Department of Health. This document showed that with an initial investment of $400,000, the chain's owners had taken out a loan to buy Rosemont. Even after making their loan payments—and despite the fact that the state had suspended admissions for more than two months during the summer of 1997—the partners had earned approximately $350,000 in profits at Rosemont during that year. This figure did not include money the company hid through the subterfuge of contracting the management of the facility out to a company that was actually owned by the Hewitt Group. The facility paid the management company several hundred thousand dollars for "management fees" over and above the salaries of the administrator and the management staff, thus allowing Hewitt to report lower profits. Discussion of these issues convinced most workers that management's threats about job loss were bogus. One-on-one face-to-face organizing was crucial in this respect not only because it enabled union activists to make sure that everyone knew the facts about the nursing home's profitability and the status of the other unionized homes in the chain, but also because it helped Rosemont workers put their struggle in the context of a sectoral analysis of the economy.

Building Trust: Combating the Image of Violence and Corruption

Workers who may have been worried about a repeat of the Teamster debacle were encouraged by the kinds of actions organized by the SEIU, and by the growing camaraderie, excitement, and fun that workers were having, especially during impromptu meetings and rallies on the lawn just off Rosemont's property. Instead of intimidation or negativity, all of these actions emphasized nonviolence and positive themes. House-calling also helped alleviate workers' fears about union violence and intimidation. House-callers were carefully trained by the union to make the contact a positive one, even when encountering a hostile response. They were polite, they were respectful, and they listened carefully to what people had to say.

The house-visits were a hot topic of conversation inside the facility according to members of the organizing committee. "Everybody knows who got visited the day before," one committee member said. "It's something different to talk about, that's for sure." Initially, some were nervous about being visited, and let it be known that they did not want anyone to visit them. "They better not visit me," one worker said, "cause I'll call the cops." Whenever organizing committee members heard that someone had expressed a preference not to be visited, they held off and respected their co-workers' wishes. But as more and more workers experienced the visits as positive events, some of the workers who initially said they did not want to be visited changed their mind and told organizing committee members it would be all right if someone came by. The positive nature of the interactions people experienced during house-visits broke down workers' fears about intimidation or violence by convincing them that whatever the Teamsters had done in the past, Local A was a different kind of union.

The substantive communication that took place during the house-visits was also important in this respect, because workers' perceptions that union organizers were being "straight up" helped build trust. Workers feared unionization, in part because they initially viewed the union as an external organization and did not necessarily trust it. Because lead organizer Joan Hardy understood the importance of trust, she emphasized that if the house-callers didn't know the answer to something, we were not to pretend. "Whatever you do, don't bullshit people," Hardy instructed. "If you don't know, say you don't know, but you can find out. Then find out and follow up. You'll be amazed at how grateful people will be if you actually do what you say you will." It was also important to be honest when the answer wasn't what people wanted to hear. For example, a common question was, "What can the union do about the staffing in this place?" The answer was that staffing was the most difficult issue to deal with directly, and that it was almost impossible to negotiate staffing guarantees into a contract. Of course, it helped to mention that the SEIU was at the forefront of political efforts at the state and national level to change the legal minimum staffing requirement, but we had to admit that forming a union was not necessarily going to translate into an immediate improvement in staffing. I found, as Hardy predicted, that giving straight answers on issues like this one was much better than making promises upon which the union could not deliver. People appreciate being told the truth, and their respect for the union usually went up, not down, when they received an honest answer.

House-callers were careful not to promise specific raises. As I noted earlier, sometimes I was asked, "How big a raise will we get if we vote for the union?" I was trained always to answer this the same way: "I can't promise that you will get a specific wage increase. How much you can improve things is going to depend on how united you are, how much you stick together, and what you're willing to agree to in the end." Organizers and committee members on house-visits emphasized that it was unrealistic to think that Rosemont workers would get a huge wage increase in their first contract. Workers at Rosemont's sister homes had gradually won substantial increases over several contract rounds. The goal would be to gradually equalize Rosemont with the other nursing homes in the chain through coordinated bargaining. "There's no way they're going to get a dollar an hour more in their first contract," said Hardy. "We have to make sure they understand that. They'll get more if they stick together, but it's going to be a gradual process."

Because nearly everyone had personal, positive contact with union staff during the second campaign, when management showed anti-union movies with old news footage of violence during Steelworker or Teamster strikes, few workers were impressed. "All they have to show us is stuff that happened in the past," one worker said. "This here union is completely different from all of that old-time stuff. What I want to know is why they can't come up with any examples [of violence] that are recent or from this union."

Overcoming Do-Nothing Unionism

Workers' fears about the union "taking our dues money and running" were much lessened by the opportunity house-calling gave to explain clearly how dues worked. During mandatory anti-union meetings in 1998, management representatives claimed that union dues would cost workers more than $500 per year, and had left workers with the false impression that dues deduction would begin immediately if they voted to form a union. House-visits were an ideal way of combating this misinformation, since the first question people asked would often be, "They told us that union dues were $500 a year. No way can I afford that. Is that right?" Conducting house-visits enabled organizers to explain carefully that Local A dues were $11 a month for the first year of the initial collective bargaining agreement; thereafter, any workers earning less than $13,000 annually would continue to pay $11 per month, while those above $13,000 paid 1.4 percent of their monthly base wage ($18.66 per month, or $224 per year, for a full-time worker earning $8 per hour).

Organizers and committee members doing house-visits used these opportunities to drive home the point that the union did not collect any dues until *workers* approved the first contract. In other words, workers would not pay a dime until they approved a contract they were happy with. There was, organizers told workers, no reason they should approve a contract that did not at *least* provide raises sufficient to cover the cost of their dues. How big a raise would be required to do that? A ten-cent raise in the first contract would cover the cost of dues. Any increases above that would be theirs.

But overcoming images and experiences of "do-nothing unionism" required more than talk. It was here that collective actions contributed something that face-to-face organizing alone could not: a growing feeling of solidarity and power, a sense that the workers were symbolically taking control of the nursing home. The way that the actions built on one another over time transformed the union from an abstract notion of an external organization into an assemblage of visibly active nursing home workers that became impossible to ignore or dismiss as an external "third party." This growing sense of collective identity and power made the initial objections of people who worried that the union would not change anything seem palpably absurd.

The building process began with "button days." During the first few button days, only the strongest union supporters would wear pro-union buttons; everyone else was afraid to put them on. But the bravery of the leaders was catching: each day, more and more buttons appeared until nearly everyone but the staunchest union foes was wearing them. Next came union tee-shirts. By a lucky coincidence, the nursing home's uniform included purple tee shirts, the same color as SEIU shirts. Therefore workers could come to work in SEIU shirts and still be in uniform.

The petitions were a third step, and the marches on the boss that they led up to became turning points in the campaign. Rank-and-file workers presented several petitions to management during the campaign, but the first petition—asking for air conditioning or at least adequate ventilation for workers who toiled in the heat of the kitchen and laundry rooms—was the most important. I stood outside with rank-and-file committee members who were about to go in at shift change and deliver their petition on behalf of laundry and dietary workers to the facility's administrator. A large majority of their co-workers had signed the petition, and their excitement was visible as they discussed the logistics of how they were all going to drift toward the boss's office at the same moment. This effort to confront the boss together was something no group of workers had done in living memory at Rosemont. When the time came, they went inside, and about fifteen minutes later two cars—one belonging to the administrator, the other to the Director of Nursing—came tearing out of the parking lot. We later learned that the bosses had been so petrified of the delegation that they had fled the facility rather than receive the petition!

At first some in the delegation were upset and disappointed—until they realized that the bosses had fled because they had been *afraid* of dealing with the workers all together in a group, on the workers' terms, rather than in a management-controlled meeting. This self-recognition of the ability to wield collective power was electrifying, and it transformed the members of the delegation into authentic leaders of a real movement—despite the fact that at least some of the dietary and laundry workers on whose behalf the petition was made had initially viewed it with skepticism as a cynical and manipulative attempt by the union to curry favor in the most anti-union departments. (Indeed, in some respects this was an accurate view of the petition—but this did not subtract from the undeniable courage of rank-and-file leaders in confronting management with their petition or the effects of management panic on the sentiments of the rank and file more generally.)

After this, rank-and-file workers were able to lead even more daring actions, like taking control of management's anti-union meetings. Instead of listening quietly to management's anti-union presentations, the idea was to use these mandatory meetings as a forum for fighting back. The committee helped prepare a list of "awkward questions for management," such as, "Why are you wasting time and money with anti-union meetings when you know we don't have enough time or staff to give the kind of quality care we want to give?" And, "Could you do the work we do or live on the wages we make?" They divided the list up so that each question would be posed by a different worker. Then they decided to make their point in an even stronger way. When management was about to begin one meeting, a worker put up her hand and asked, "Do you mind if we get comfortable first?" Upon receiving the affirmative answer, workers began turning their chairs around and facing the back of the room, turning their backs to the boss. This meeting ended up in bedlam, with the administrator losing his cool and yelling at the workers, while they simply kept demanding answers to their questions.

These actions turned the tide. Shift-change leafleting sessions turned into regular but impromptu union rallies, as people coming off their shift joined the leafleters on the lawn by the roadside instead of driving off. In the weeks preceding the vote, leafleting days usually meant that fifteen or twenty people would be hanging out on the lawn in high spirits, cheering and exchanging 'V' signals to those workers going in for the next shift. By the time the election was held, the only question was how large the union's margin of victory would be.

CONCLUSION

Local A's first Rosemont campaign failed not only because it was unable to convey basic information or counteract management claims, but also because it was unable to defuse or refute anti-union sentiments among the workers themselves. Campaigns relying on arms-length organizing tactics like mailing lists or mass meetings are not able to effectively deal with workers' lived experiences of the labor movement itself. Workers have deep concerns and anxieties about unions drawn from those experiences, which, particularly in rustbelt areas like Pittsburgh, can be quite negative. As a result, anger at management is not enough to guarantee union victory, even when management opposition to unionization is weak.

The success of Local A's 1998 campaign at Rosemont confirms the importance of utilizing multiple tactics in a coordinated way (Bronfenbrenner and Hickey, this volume); demonstrates the importance of involving rank-and-file volunteers in member-to-member organizing (Turner 1998, Nissen 1998, Early 1998); and highlights the ability of disruptive tactics to build workers' confidence, sense of collective power, and solidarity (Waldinger et al 1998; Acuff 1999; Cohen and Early 1999). But it also shows that these elements cannot be viewed as a formula. The virtue of a grassroots approach is not simply that it represents a more efficient or effective organizing model. Rather, what I have tried to show is that grassroots organizing tactics succeed to the extent that they enable union campaigns to overcome the negative legacies of business unionism. Face-to-face organizing and collective action allow organizers and rank-and-file activists to confront workers' servicing expectations and deal with workers' ingrained fears about organized labor. They achieve this not merely by talking about unions—although that is important—but by building a rank-and-file campaign that puts into practice a different sort of unionism. The new and positive union experiences that result, as the experience of these campaigns shows, are more crucial to success than any specific tactic, or set of tactics.

5

"JUSTICE FOR JANITORS," NOT "COMPENSATION FOR CUSTODIANS"

THE POLITICAL CONTEXT AND ORGANIZING IN SAN JOSE AND SACRAMENTO

Preston Rudy

The Justice for Janitors (JfJ) campaign is the basis for Ken Loach's film *Bread and Roses* and is the first labor struggle in the last twenty years to be depicted on movie screens across the United States. The California campaigns of JfJ have pitted immigrant Latino workers against large real estate companies and property owners in the most unexpected places, such as the corporate landscapes of the Silicon Valley and the Wilshire corridor in Los Angeles. Much of the attention from the press, the movies, and academics has resulted from the consciously staged public demonstrations and marches that have taken over the streets, what one journalist called "Burlesque Hall tactics" (Ybarra 1994). The innovations of the Justice for Janitors center on their tactics and strategies and include organizing tactics that have been identified by Kate Bronfenbrenner and Tom Juravich (1998) as singularly important to ending the decline of unionized labor (see also Bronfenbrenner and Hickey in this collection). These methods of organizing include house-visits, face-to-face organizing, member-intensive organizing and strategic analyses of the political and economic contexts, and organizational renewal of moribund locals. Most of the recent studies of JfJ innovations have been directed at these repertoires of recruiting new members and winning new contracts (Banks 1991; Fletcher and Hurd 1999; Howley 1990; Mines and Avina 1992; Piore 1994; Savage 1998; Voss and Sherman 2000; Waldinger et al. 1998; Williams 1999). Indeed my own research on JfJ in California has been concerned with how these tactics are deployed in different settings. To supplement existing research, I want to show that by comparing JfJ campaigns in San Jose and Sacramento, where the same methods of organizing and many of the same organizers were working, we can discover the significance of the political context in shaping the trajectory of the campaigns and their successes. So long as the focus of research is exclusively on the internal organizational renewal of unions, we miss how the interaction of repertoires and the political context explains outcomes. The claim I am making in this paper is that it is the "resourcefulness" of unions in strategizing their relationship with the political context, and not simply the resources they bring, that determines the fate of organizing campaigns (Ganz 2000). In fact, an early failure to account for the importance of political context nearly resulted in a disastrous loss in Sacramento for the Justice for Janitors.

In this essay I will examine JfJ's campaigns to establish initial contracts and rebuild their presence in San Jose and Sacramento during the 1990s. In both cases, the important elements of the political context were the issues being debated in local politics and the political participants. By political context I am referring to the political power in an urban region, the players who participate in the political game, the issues around which the game is organized, and the legacy of prior struggles over power. In San Jose, as an established presence in the area, the SEIU local confronted a political context in which neighborhood groups ousted a pro-growth coalition of developers by highlighting the social problems created by unchecked urban expansion. Within this context the JfJ was able to build a community coalition that was focused on problems of growth, thereby creating an opportunity for casting the janitors as exemplars of problems created by urban and suburban growth. Moreover, the initial campaign was against both Apple computer and their janitorial firm, Shine Building Maintenance, thus combining an international corporation and a local cleaning firm. By contrast, in Sacramento JfJ was a new entity with no history in a city that made a virtue of well-established connections among a parochial group of players. Power was in the hands of a coalition that was pro-growth and in which the social problems of growth were not yet evident or debated. The initial campaign was directed against a locally owned cleaning firm, Somers Building Maintenance, whose client base was largely local developers and owners, as well as the State of California. To succeed in this political context, the JfJ campaign faced greater challenges in establishing the janitors' struggle as a public issue in which the real estate interests were closely tied to elected officials.

In both San Jose and Sacramento, the JfJ campaigns needed to create crises in the political context in order to draw the political players into the dispute with their employer. That is, as Schattschneider (1960) put it, the "audience" was important in determining the outcome of this dispute, and as the weaker party initially, the union was more intent on bringing in politicians and community activists who would help them pressure the employer and the client. The way to draw in these other players was by creating a crisis that cost the local municipality money and disrupted the normal, regulated life of the community. Nevertheless, given the history of Local 1877 in San Jose and its embeddedness within the community, creating a crisis was not nearly as difficult as it turned out to be in Sacramento, where for the first two years the unionization campaign remained a limited dispute between employees and their employer. As Piven and Cloward (1977 and 2000) have argued, disruption of electoral coalitions creates opportunities for change, because issues, such as the place of organized workers in community life, are avoided, except at election times when money and votes are needed by politicians to stay in office. Indeed, without disruption, justice in the workplace is not likely to be raised in American politics, nor the larger "labor question" which has so effectively been eliminated from public discourse in twentieth-century politics (Lichtenstein 2002; Clawson 2003). Raising these issues through disruptions is exactly what the JfJ campaigns have done in each urban region.

To complete this research I was a participant observer in the Sacramento JfJ campaign from the fall of 1997 through 1999. From 1995 through 1996, I had participated in a variety of demonstrations and actions, given that the union had called me to help, since I was already on a list of area activists before being engaged in this research. In the course of my research, I conducted numerous informal interviews with organizers, workers, and community participants while on picket lines and attending various marches through Sacramento. Most of the organizers in Sacramento had participated earlier in the San Jose campaign and, therefore, I was able to collect data from them about both campaigns. In addition to these informal interviews, I conducted thirty formal semi-structured interviews with organizers.[1] These interviews were mostly sixty to ninety minutes in length, although a few were longer. I was also given access to the union local files and spent two months in the Sacramento office reading through their collection of documents and two days in the San Jose office photocopying materials which enabled me to read them once I returned home. In addition, I have collected archival material at public libraries, Sacramento City Hall, and made use of Lexis-Nexis and other electronic searches.

CLEANING UP SILICON VALLEY

During the 1970s, San Jose's politics were transformed as a result of the growth policies of the prior twenty years. Not only were neighborhoods organizing to limit growth in favor of resolving issues in existing neighborhoods, but the city became a center for women workers' struggles for comparable worth (Johnston 1994; Trounstine and Christensen 1982). Following the long struggles over growth, a coalition of groups successfully elected Janet Gray Hayes as mayor in 1975 on a platform that called for limited growth. Hayes was the first female mayor of a large American city. Her election coincided with the fight by female municipal employees—especially librarians—who successfully fought for comparable wages in their city contract. These employees had defeated not only the opposition by the city manager and his staff, but also the opposition by the male leaders in their union. The effect of their collective action was to revive contentious repertoires as methods of securing policy changes in San Jose politics.

By the 1980s, Mayor Hayes was succeeded by Mayor Tom McEnery, who continued the limited growth programs and shifted the emphasis to renewal of the central city under the slogan of making San Jose the capital of Silicon Valley. Simultaneously, the problems of a growing region continued to be politically potent, and attention was shifting to the disparity of incomes and life chances. The social problems of traffic congestion, environmental degradation, increasing housing prices and rents, and the growing population of immigrant low wage workers were drawing the attention of business leaders and community activists. The corporate executives of the high tech industries, led by David Packard, were dissatisfied with the chamber of commerce and created the Santa Clara County Manufacturing Group to address the area's social problems, while sustaining growth to accommodate their business interests (Saxenian 1989, 46–47). This new group was particularly concerned with the fate of the region and their ability to continue to attract highly qualified employees.

Beginning in 1990, the Service Employees International Union (SEIU) Local 1877 began to organize workers employed by Shine Building Maintenance and its major client, Apple Computer, in Cupertino. The public campaign to win a contract was built on the opportunities created by the legacy of prior collective action and the relationships the local had developed with civil society and the labor movement in the South Bay. Local 1877 organizers were able to define the janitors as low wage workers being paid poverty wages, and as such were exemplars of the social problems of growth in the Silicon Valley. Unionization seemed a viable solution which would alleviate cost burdens for various social programs funded by fiscally strapped local governments.

By 1990, Local 1877 had begun a process of organizational renewal, following a succession of contentious trustees imposed by the International. Throughout the 1980s, the local had been poorly managed and the trustees leading the local had negotiated tiered contracts that had created lower wages for newer employees, largely Latino immigrant workers (Johnston 1994: 155–175). Trustee Susan Sachen, who had experience with the United Farm Workers (UFW), was sent to lead the local in 1987 and was able to begin to repair the damage, initially by hiring organizers who also had training in the UFW and who spoke Spanish. Under her leadership the local launched an aggressive campaign in 1988 to win a new contract with the shrinking number of unionized janitorial firms, using the slogan of "Justice for Janitors." The public campaign mobilized supporters among churches, civil rights organizations and other unions to pressure employers to agree to a contract with limited concessions. At a key moment in the campaign, the union discovered a connection between one of the more important contractors and City Councilor Blanca Alvarado. To avoid an embarrassing protest at her offices from Latino janitors and their supporters, Alvarado helped move the negotiations to a favorable resolution.

The South Bay Central Labor Council, a central player in local politics, helped Local 1877 in its subsequent political activity. While still tending to be dominated by the building trades in the late 1980s, the council was a progressive and significant player in local politics. At this time in the SEIU local's history, the janitors shared the same building with the Council. Under the leadership of Richard Sawyer, himself an SEIU member who had come to the Silicon Valley from the state of Washington, the CLC continuously supported the janitors in their efforts to win new contracts.

Sachen's tenure as trustee was short lived, in part because of opposition to her from the Mexican janitors who demanded a Latino leader for their local. In 1989 Mike Garcia was installed as trustee, having worked in this local before in the mid 1980s. His advocacy for the dignity of the janitors and support for the Latino janitors, in particular, especially during a doomed Christmas strike in 1984 (Johnston 1994, 163), had resulted in his being removed from the local to spend several years in Southern California and then in Denver, working with the new Justice for Janitors campaigns. On returning to San Jose as trustee, Garcia and his staff proceeded to rebuild the local, initially by combining the Silicon Valley local with the Alameda and Contra Costa counties local to form Local 1877.

By 1990 it became clear to the Local that they needed to organize on a new basis, and they fully adopted the Justice for Janitors strategies and tactics. Following the loss of an NLRB election at Loma Building Maintenance, the Local held a series of meetings to assess the union's position and choose a target for their organizing. According to an organizer I interviewed, the debate was fairly contentious, divided between those who advocated going after Hewlett-Packard (HP) and those advocating Apple Computer as the better target. Although workers cleaning HP had approached the union for help, Local 1877 decided to target Apple, because they had a single contractor, Shine Building

Maintenance, cleaning a majority of their buildings. Reciprocally, most of Shine's janitors worked for Apple. The dependence of each on the other created a vulnerability that the union thought they could exploit. An added Apple vulnerability was its cultivated image of corporate responsibility and progressiveness.

The first two actions by the Local and the janitors were protests at the 1991 MacWorld Expo in San Francisco during Apple CEO John Sculley's speech and then a protest at the annual Apple shareholders meeting a month later when a janitor was able to ask Sculley a question. Each of these events gained the workers and the union a great deal of media coverage, raising the profile of the developing struggle for a contract.

Soon after launching the "Apple campaign," Local 1877 received an advisory memo from a national SEIU leader on the importance of forming a community coalition. Building a coalition was deemed singularly important in regaining control over the local labor market. The coalition would be able to pressure employers and their clients, and it was to include local state actors as well as civil rights and religious leaders and organizations. Quoting from the memo, the overall purpose was to "build a movement among janitors and the community as a whole to support low wage immigrant workers" which could win victories that would then build "credibility among workers, community leaders, and lessen employer opposition" (memorandum, author's personal archive). The recommendation was for a political movement that would assert electoral and moral pressure on elected officials and state agencies to resolve the Silicon Valley's social problems that were partly being created by subcontracting and the low wages that resulted.

Forming a coalition was facilitated by the prior contacts the union had as a result of the contract campaign in 1988. Calling the coalition Cleaning Up Silicon Valley (CUSV), SEIU launched the group with an accountability session in June 1991. This accountability session was also preceded by a series of resolutions supporting the Justice for Janitors goals from the Santa Clara Human Concerns Commission and other public bodies that the union had petitioned with the help of the Central Labor Council. This earlier organizing established the relationships and support that the union used to secure the attendance of numerous political leaders at the accountability session. Apple CEO Sculley was also invited but declined to come. The list of attending officials included Congressman Norm Mineta, State Senator Alfred Alquist, Sunnyvale mayor Richard Napier, Santa Clara County Supervisors Rod Diridon, Mike Honda and Zoe Lofgren, and San Jose Councilors Blanca Alvarado and George Shirakawa (Medina 1991). Representatives from the offices of San Jose mayor Tom McEnery and other officials also attended, as did a representative of the Catholic Archdiocese and Father Bill Leninger.

In this event, the political and community leaders sat at the front of the room at a long table with only a couple of microphones, while several microphones were placed in the "audience." These leaders listened to the testimony of janitors recounting their daily work experiences and humiliations. In addition, the union presented a statistical report on the general conditions of low wage workers, which they had written for this occasion, as well as testimony from social service agency representatives who were working with many of these low wage workers in Santa Clara County (Medina 1991). In the last hour of the three hour forum, the political and community leaders were asked to pledge their support for the janitors by agreeing to meet in delegations with Sculley. According to the event's organizers that I interviewed, Sculley would find it more difficult to refuse to meet a delegation of city councilors from San Jose or Sunnyvale than a delegation of union officials and janitors.

The goal of an accountability session is to inform leaders about the actual living conditions of low wage workers and to make the case that the low-bid system of contracting creates a social problem for elected officials and social service agencies. First, testimony at this session described how low wage workers lived in the poorest neighborhoods, in run-down buildings, many times ten people to a two bedroom apartment, sometimes hot-bedding[2] to save money (Zlolniski 1994). These neighborhoods were a perpetual problem for local officials, which might be resolved by better wages for the residents. Secondly, as poor city and county residents, these workers made use of rent subsidies, food banks, and other social services. Especially noted at the June hearing were the cost overruns at the county hospital whose emergency room was used for health care by low wage workers without health care benefits. A third point brought out in testimony was that most janitors were Latino. Therefore, the low-bid system appeared to discriminate based on ethnicity, and this dimension was used to pressure elected officials who were sensitive to accusations of racial discrimination (Voss and Sherman 2000). In a political context in which the social problems created by growth were taxing municipal resources, a union contract that potentially reduced expenses to public budgets by displacing costs onto the major regional employers—transnational corporations in computer and electronics—seemed like a favorable solution to politicians and community leaders. The appeal was not just one of moral suasion either, as elected officials were also feeling pressure from the Central Labor Council, which made the janitors' struggle an important issue in their support for politicians.

The accountability session had its desired effect in securing the support of local politicians and isolating Apple. According to another organizer I interviewed, the forum was "an enormous success; we got a lot of press coverage." This did produce initial negotiations with Shine, but no resolution to the dispute. Therefore the local continued its protests. In the process, the union and its coalition of supporters were creating a crisis for Apple, and costing local municipalities money to pay for police patrols and interventions at demonstrations. The coalition organized a boycott by Latino families whose children were attending schools that were using Apple computers. In response to the union's collective actions, Apple was able to win a restraining order against Local 1877 in the summer of 1991. While this was a potential major setback for the union, their work building community support enabled the campaign to proceed. The Cleaning Up Silicon Valley coalition took over the work of organizing protests and press conferences, and by fall 1991, the newspapers reported that CUSV was the group organizing events in support of the janitors at Shine.

As Apple prepared for the renewal of their janitorial contract in November 1991, the coalition organized a Fast for Justice on the grounds of Apple corporate headquarters in Cupertino. For one week a group of half a dozen janitors, including Local president Mike Garcia, fasted to appeal for a union contract. Numerous local labor leaders and community leaders participated in the fast for one or two days, including leaders of the AFL-CIO in California. Dolores Huerta, Vice-President of the United Farm Workers, helped launch the fast, while Cesar Chavez participated in the ceremony that ended the fast, calling for a boycott of Apple products (Bailey 1991). The event generated tremendous media coverage and seemed to add to the pressure on Apple to sign a contract with a union janitorial firm or pressure Shine to sign a contract with SEIU.

Pressure from the growing coalition of supporters for the janitors did not result in Apple changing contractors, let alone choosing a unionized firm. But Apple was increasingly isolated from the other computer firms in the San Jose area and from elected officials. In the new contract with Shine, however, the 165 janitors cleaning Apple were awarded health benefits and higher wages. Garcia, in a letter to the editors of the San Jose *Mercury News*, rejected these changes in the Shine contract and promised to increase the pressure on Apple and Shine. The Shine workers also understood that any improvements in their working conditions resulted from the pressure that the union had organized, and they stayed loyal to the union. So the union and their supporters continued to pressure Apple and Shine on multiple fronts. At the end of 1991, Local 1877 organized an international support network that pushed for a boycott of Apple products. In January 1992, two janitors filed sexual harassment charges against Shine and their supervisor. During the next couple of months, however, the CUSV, rather than the union, negotiated with Apple and Shine. The union and the employers had developed too much animosity to be able to meet for negotiations. As recounted to me by two different organizers, while the coalition members sat with the Shine and Apple personnel, union negotiators were in the Local 1877 offices conferring by phone over the terms of the contract that was eventually signed in March 1992.

In quick succession after the Shine contract, SEIU went to Hewlett-Packard to pressure them to choose a union contractor, which they did in 1992. HP wanted to avoid the "circus" that had confronted Apple. They were able to build on the reputation they had developed through the Apple campaign to win contracts for a majority of janitors in Silicon Valley by 1994. The coalition they had helped form persisted and continued to help with labor organizing as well as other issues such as an eventual living wage campaign. Moreover, they had developed a powerful set of networks with the local elected officials who sought out the support of Local 1877 and other unions. By 1994 the union developed another campaign in coordination with the community and three other unions, "The Campaign for Justice," which for SEIU was geared to organize gardening and landscape workers. This campaign eventually foundered, however, because the other unions were unwilling to continue to spend money on the organizing with no clear influx of new dues paying members, and for SEIU they were unable to make much headway with the landscaping employers.

Early in 1994, in part as a result of the organizing of janitors and the "guerrilla legal tactics" (Waldinger et al. 1998), the U.S. Department of Labor (DOL) announced an initiative to pressure high tech firms over the use of subcontracted janitorial companies that were not paying their workers for all the hours they worked. This initiative by the Department resulted also from the high number of labor law violations in Silicon Valley, and the concentration of the high technology industry that could be held responsible for these violations. The Department indicated that they were going to seize products of computer and chip companies, considered "hot goods," if violations in the janitorial service persisted (Levander 1994). For most of the large computer and electronics firms, it was relatively easy to make the case that the production process itself requires high levels of cleanliness and that the work of janitorial contractors was central to production. At the same time, as one of the organizers I spoke with told me, the costs associated with the building maintenance contracts were relatively insignificant for these high tech firms, and unionized janitors were marginal to their main business. Had the Department of Labor been mobilizing to change the employment practices of the production workers employed by the high tech firms, the response would have been much different. This initiative by the Department would last for a couple of years and DOL made use of union organizers to help them discover violations.

The lesson from Silicon Valley should have been the importance of the political context to successful outcomes. The facility in organizing a community coalition resulted from the legacy of a politics to limit growth and address the social problems created by urban and regional growth in Silicon Valley. The political activism of the local labor movement was part of this political context which had its own dynamic. JfJ had worked with the South Bay Labor Council's political director, Amy Dean, since 1990, and in 1994 she was appointed head of that organization. She used her experiences to transform the council into one of the most innovative organizations in the U.S. labor movement. With these supporters and the history of contentious collective action, JfJ was able to win a new contract with the largest non-union firm and begin to unionize the rest of the Valley's janitors. The other part of the political context concerned the size of the clients and their relationship with the janitorial contractors. In Silicon Valley, the main clients were the corporate high tech firms, for whom the costs of their janitorial contracts were not so large that they were unwilling to compromise by agreeing to hire a union firm, rather than go through what Apple endured in their effort to avoid taking responsibility for their subcontractor. The same would be the case in 1993 when Oracle and Solectron pressured their subcontractor, Service by Medallion, to sign a contract with SEIU rather than continue to be "hosts" for Justice for Janitors demonstrations and the resulting press coverage. In looking at Sacramento in 1994 to prepare for an organizing campaign there, the organizers at Local 1877 thought their reputation and the political profile of the capital would result in a quick twelve month campaign.

SOMERS IN SACRAMENTO: THE IMPORTANCE OF POLITICAL CONTEXT

When Local 1877 took over the representation of the Sacramento janitors from SEIU Local 22, they confronted a different political landscape. According to conversations I overheard among union organizers, which were confirmed by internal union documents and interviews, the lead organizers thought that because Sacramento was a town dominated by Democratic party officials who had a record of supporting labor, the union would have an easy campaign. The largest janitorial company had a board of directors with members who were active in Democratic politics, and their largest client was HP's facility in Roseville, a suburb of Sacramento, with whom the union had developed cordial relations in San Jose. But during the first two years in Sacramento (1995–97), the union did not develop an effective coalition, and they confronted a near disaster for the statewide movement to organize janitors.

The political context in Sacramento was more conservative and had no history of contentious repertoires as part of accepted political activity. Moreover, in contrast to San Jose, a debate about growth's problems was only beginning to take shape in Sacramento when Local 1877 arrived and the fate of low income workers in a new booming economy was not part of that debate. Therefore the union had to create the narrative about the plight of workers earning less than the poverty rate, and had to create the coalitions without these narratives having already generated an interest from existing civic groups. For its part, local labor was dominated by the building trades who were part of the pro-growth coalition and whose politics was business unionism. An additional difficulty for JfJ consisted of the structure of the real estate industry and its associated services. Sacramento was still dominated by local developers and owners, although by the late 1990s it was becoming a more attractive market for national and international institutional investors. The local developers were part of the growth coalition, as was the largest janitorial firm against whom JfJ fought from 1995 to 1999. This made the struggle much more personal in Sacramento and increased the resistance from the whole industry to pressure from SEIU.

The initial organizing by Local 1877 in late 1994 consisted in collecting information from the employees of Somers Building Maintenance about violations of wage and hour laws. Given the Department of Labor initiative in Silicon Valley, this seemed like a plausible direction for organizing, and initially the Sacramento Wage and Hour office was interested in receiving this information. Violations discovered by union organizers in their interviews of workers included not paying workers for the time they worked, having "ghost" employees doing the work, employing under-age children, and not paying overtime. One of the violations they documented in the files at the union offices involved a young man named Ramon.[3] Ramon's mother cleaned offices for Somers in the Arden Fair area of Sacramento and had complained to her supervisor that she could not finish all the work assigned to her in the time given. Her supervisor told her that if she could not do the work herself, she should have her husband or son help her out. This is how Ramon came to work cleaning buildings for Somers from July 1991 to February 1993. At the time Ramon was twelve to fourteen years of age, and worked from 5:30 to 9:30 on school nights, depending on when his father could pick him up. Ramon was what the DOL refers to as a "ghost" employee, because he was performing work though not an employee and not getting paid. While at first the DOL was interested in learning about cases like Ramon's, by February 1995 DOL investigators were no longer responding to phone calls. Thinking that perhaps they did not believe the union, a Local 1877 organizer told me that they brought a few workers directly to the DOL offices to allow their investigators to interview them directly, but they were shunned and told to leave.

The DOL's decision not to pursue an investigation of Somers had, in fact, resulted from pressure against the DOL investigators by Somers' lawyers. According to an account of a conversation between an SEIU organizer and the lead DOL investigator, a 1991 investigation of Somers had been one of the more difficult and contentious investigations for the investigator. At the time, Somers, through their legal representatives, Littler, Mendelson, Fastiff, Tichy, and Mathiason (aka Littler Mendelson), had successfully reduced a fine to $70,000 in back pay, half the original amount, after exerting intense pressure on the local DOL office (U.S. House 1996). The investigator was hesitant to go through a similar experience in 1995. To push along the investigation, Local 1877 organizers called Richard Sawyer, formerly of the San Jose CLC, who by 1995 was the Western Region Representative of the Secretary of Labor, Robert Reich. While this seemed reasonable, given the Bay Area initiative and the violations of the law, in Sacramento this aggressive use of the DOL upset Somers. One of Somers' directors contacted Republican Congressman John Doolittle, who was able to engineer a congressional hearing into the DOL investigation and Sawyer's role, in particular. More specifically, the chairman of the sub-committee before which the hearing was held, Republican Pete Hoekstra from Michigan, was exercised about an apparent partnership between SEIU and the DOL: ". . . it appears that Mr. Sawyer thought that he could create a sort of partnership between the Department of Labor and his former employee [sic], the Service Employees International Union, to organize and unionize Somers Building Maintenance" (U.S. House 1996, 52). By the time of the hearing, Sawyer had been removed from DOL employment as he had refused to resign,[4] and Somers had to pay only $347 in back-pay to eleven workers, although Local 1877 had discovered $49,000 due in back-pay to a sample of workers.

However, this use of a Republican congressman backfired on Somers and was helpful in the long run for the janitors and Local 1877. The Somers' director responsible for contacting Doolittle had been president of one of the Democratic Party clubs in Sacramento, one formed specifically to support the Democratic opponent in Doolittle's congressional district. When the local press published this connection that resulted in the hearing, the Somers director was ousted from his position of club president. More significantly for the developing JfJ campaign, this minor scandal began to shake up the local Democrats and build support for the janitors.

Nevertheless, in 1995, in the absence of any coalition of Sacramento activists, the JfJ campaign was isolated and incapable of exercising influence over Somers, the building owners and HP, or elected officials. The Democratic Party leadership voiced disdain for the JfJ tactics and talked to the leaders of the building trades to pressure SEIU to abandon their contentious protests. The JfJ leaders from San Jose who were directing the campaign thought their reputation would be enough, combined with legal and regulatory pressure, to secure a contract. In a meeting between Somers directors and Local 1877 leaders in May 1995, SEIU handed the employer a packet of press clippings with stories about their campaign in Silicon Valley to impress them with their tough reputation and told Somers that they could make the DOL investigation, the lawsuits, and the NLRB charges disappear if they agreed to a card check procedure (U.S. House 1996, 67). Somers' directors were not moved and responded that they would not give in to SEIU's bullying.

While court cases and filings with the NLRB, which followed on the investigation of wage and hour violations, proceeded, the union went to the Sacramento City Council, asking for a resolution in support of the janitors' struggle for justice. At the March 1995 Council meeting, the Local's organizers presented an account of the livelihoods of low-wage workers, including testimony from one janitor, Estella Camarillo, about the harassment she had experienced at work. The councilors were not impressed by the union presentation, and were swayed by the response from a Somers director. They wanted statistics showing that the janitors represented a general problem.

Even the supportive councilors, such as Darrell Steinberg, found it difficult to help the union, because they could not find a justification for that support. Eventually the council decided to vote down the resolution, because they did not want to get in the middle of a dispute between a politically well connected employer and its employees. Without broader community support, JfJ was merely another labor dispute, not a social movement addressing a social problem. Until Local 1877 became part of the political context and developed the relationships that made it possible to represent more than just their members, they were incapable of having any influence or getting the "audience" to participate in their fight, as Schattschneider (1960) would explain it.

Somers was able to exploit the political context and the isolation of Local 1877 as became obvious in the most serious challenge to the Justice for Janitors in California (see Fisk, Mitchell and Erickson 2000, 222–224). In August 1995, janitors cleaning HP buildings in Roseville reported to Local 1877 organizers that a union was being organized and supervisors were helping to collect cards for the union. Calling itself the Couriers and Service Employees Local 1, this new union signed up 232 workers as members in three weeks and was immediately recognized by Somers as their employees' union. This launched the JfJ campaign into a tumultuous year of court cases and statewide mobilizing of their allies to defeat what had all the markings of a company union. It also began a process of rethinking the tactics of the Sacramento campaign; the union began to refocus its organizing on downtown Sacramento rather than the isolated HP campus in Roseville. Throughout 1996 the union worked on winning the NLRB cases against Local 1, and in August 1996 the NLRB reached an out-of-court settlement with Somers which dissolved the contract and that union, and reimbursed employees for their dues (Robertson 1996; Rudy 2003).

In October of that year, in a conversation with a State legislator from Sacramento set up by local labor leaders, Local 1877 discovered that their campaign was still perceived as simply an employer-employee fight, and that it did not have any larger meaning or effect on local politics (memorandum, author's personal archive). From this meeting the local developed a comprehensive plan to create a crisis for building owners and for local politicians, replicating the strategy that had succeeded in San Jose. The first major outcome of that planning was the organizing of another accountability session, in March 1997, entitled "Working but Poor." To prepare for this, the union brought in a new staff person who was responsible for developing a community coalition. Her work developed a coalition that was especially strong among local church leaders. They also secured more solidarity from various other SEIU locals, including the large SEIU Local 1000, California State Employees Association. By the time of the accountability session, the union also had more support among local politicians who attended and listened to the testimony, mostly from workers. Unlike in Silicon Valley, those at the head table did not include Sacramento's Latino Mayor Joe Serna, though several city councilors did attend, including Steve Cohen and Darrell Steinberg.

In a series of demonstrations geared to make the city politicians pay attention and cost the city money, the campaign escalated during the summer of 1997 with weekly demonstrations on the pedestrian K Street Mall, one block away from the state Capitol building and the recipient of perpetual efforts to make downtown a shopping and entertainment center. The target was one of the signature buildings in Sacramento, popularly known as the "Darth Vader" building because of its black reflective glass exterior, owned by local developer Joseph Benvenuti. At each of these demonstrations, a local religious leader blessed the crowd and the campaign. More local groups participated, including neighborhood organizations, various international solidarity coalitions, many churches, as well as Latino civil rights groups. Especially helpful were unionized state employees and their Latino caucus who collected signatures on petitions and provided groups of people to picket and demonstrate. The culmination of these demonstrations on K Street was on August 27, 1997 when Sacramento police arrested thirty protesters who were performing civil disobedience by sitting on the light-rail tracks that run down the middle of the mall. Among those arrested were Jim Murphy, head of the Sacramento Building Trades, Art Pulaski, Secretary-Treasurer of the California Federation of Labor, and Bill Camp, lobbyist for the California Labor Federation. Instead of citing the protesters and releasing them as SEIU assumed would happen, city police held them in jail for eight hours that night, while local labor activists and even members of the legislature frantically called Mayor Serna, who was out of town, to get the protestors released. Serendipitously, Serna's electoral campaign was fundraising that night and once news spread about the arrest of the labor leaders, the Mayor's campaign was met with refusals to contribute to his campaign. According to one union organizer who told me the story, Serna lost several thousand dollars in campaign contributions as a result of the eight-hour jail visit.

The fallout from the arrests in August 1997 was the beginning of the end for Somers. The constant pressure on the police and the downtown real estate and retail interests from the weekly demonstrations had produced an outcome that JfJ had not exactly planned. The zealous enforcement of city laws by the police had created the crisis for the political leadership that transformed the janitors' struggle at Somers into an issue that required elected officials' attention. In early September, the city council passed a resolution in support of the Justice for Janitors goals, and the mayor unenthusiastically announced that he would act as mediator between the union and Somers. In mid-September, a huge demonstration and parade through downtown Sacramento brought together Local 1877, numerous other SEIU locals, as well as President Arturo Rodriguez and a large contingent from the United Farm Workers. Mayor Serna's political biography touted his early association with the UFW, and this demonstration was directed at sustaining pressure on him to live up to his political posture and his persona as the first Latino mayor of Sacramento. Then, during December, the union staged a one week fast for justice in the recently renamed Cesar Chavez Park across from City Hall. Two janitors and one community activist fasted for the whole week and they were joined during the week by other janitors, community supporters, and labor leaders from Sacramento and California.

In January 1998, Mayor Serna ended his effort at mediation, concluding that "the company wasn't ready to negotiate in good faith" (Bizjak 1998). This was a coup for the union. In the first place, by agreeing to mediate, the Mayor had admitted that the fight between the janitors and their employer was no longer merely a private matter, but was a public issue. To use Schattschneider's concepts (1960), SEIU was able to change the scope of the conflict and socialize it, defeating the employer's effort to define it as a private conflict. In resigning, Serna was clearly blaming the employer for being recalcitrant and perpetuating the fight. At the same time, the support the janitors were receiving from local churches, especially the Cathedral of the Blessed Sacrament, which was the main Catholic church downtown, was upsetting building owners and Somers, because it was eroding the moral basis of their positions. This was eminently clear when the head priest at the Cathedral was pressured by these businessmen to back out of his support for the JfJ campaign, as I heard at a couple of organizing meetings in early 1998.

Local 1877 continued to build support for the janitors' struggle and demonstrate their strength and resolve to Somers and their clients with a pilgrimage from Sacramento to HP headquarters in the Silicon Valley in February 1998. HP was still using Somers to clean its buildings in Roseville, and the pilgrimage was timed to coincide with HP's shareholders meeting. This event was also designed to build more regional support for the union and the janitors, as well as build up the determination of the janitors themselves. Over ten days the janitors walked through the El Niño rains along the Highway 80 corridor and through the San Francisco Bay Area to San Jose, being housed and fed by MEChA groups, churches, and other unions each evening. For Local 1877 leaders like Mike Garcia, the "caminata," modeled after the famous Delano to Sacramento "peregrinación" of the UFW, was a tremendous success and showed Somers that they had organizational strength and resilience.

Within a few months, the union and Somers were beginning to meet and talk about the possibilities of a contract. The public demonstrations and marches died down for the rest of 1998 as the two sides met with help from local political officials. A contract was finally signed and then announced on the steps of City Hall in March 1999. Included at that event, in addition to a representative from Somers and the leaders of Local 1877, were the Mayor and two City Councilors, as well as a few church leaders and Jim Murphy of the building trades and Jim Hard of SEIU Local 1000. The gathering was clear evidence of the importance of the coalition of community groups that was central to the new contract between this employer and its workers.

CONCLUSION

While in both urban regions the JfJ campaigns successfully won major new contracts and were able to build on these contracts to win union representation for a majority of the areas' janitors, the trajectories of the campaigns and the outcomes were largely determined by the political context of the organizing. In San Jose, the JfJ campaign was part of a longer series of labor struggles, and these helped move the campaign more quickly to a resolution. By 1994 when Local 1877 represented a majority of the janitors and turned its attention to organizing Sacramento, the labor movement in the South Bay was moving to a new level with the selection of Amy Dean to head of the Central Labor Council. Under her leadership, the Silicon Valley became a place of innovative labor politics which, among other things, produced one of the best living wage ordinances in the state. The political context had truly been transformed by the mid-1990s, and JfJ had helped in that process.

By contrast, in Sacramento, because the Justice for Janitors was the first serious public political campaign for labor rights, transforming the political context was much more difficult. As a result of Local 1877's contentious repertoires, new options opened up for labor. Changes in the local labor movement meant that the building trades were no longer as dominant, and leadership in the Central Labor Council shifted to the service unions, led by SEIU. Simultaneous campaigns by health care workers in SEIU Local 250, as well as the new found activism among state workers in the civil service division of SEIU Local 1000, produced a new activist politics in Sacramento's labor movement. The living wage campaign that came out of the series of labor campaigns, and the support from a new coalition of community groups dismayed at the growing disparity of income, was partly the result of the new activism among workers and their unions. Labor also was the lead group in promoting one of the two city councilors who ran for mayor, although the campaign they ran ultimately flopped.

More widely, the lessons from the JfJ campaigns in these two California cities speak to the importance of building a community of support, among trade unions and with social movement groups. Among workers in service occupations that are rooted in specific geographical locations, the political context of organizing campaigns is especially important (see Gordon 1999 and Cobble 1996). Abundant resources, talented staff using rank-and-file intensive tactics, a supportive International, and workers who are willing and able to take risks to organize a union are not sufficient when the political context of that organizing is ignored. Union organizing is a form of political action that contests contemporary neoliberal political premises in the United States. As such, in organizing to improve the livelihoods of workers, the relationship of municipal players to how a union campaign interacts with them must be included in the strategizing. Moreover, as was the case when the JfJ moved from San Jose to Sacramento, that strategizing and analysis must be conducted in each new venture. What needs further research is how SEIU made mistakes in Sacramento and yet was creative enough to learn from the mistakes and adjust its practices. The most innovative organizing means taking risks and inevitably making mistakes, out of which better organizing and better union organizations might develop.

6

AGAINST THE TIDE

PROJECTS AND PATHWAYS OF THE NEW GENERATION
OF UNION LEADERS, 1984–2001

Marshall Ganz, Kim Voss, Teresa Sharpe, Carl Somers, and George Strauss

John Sweeney's election to the presidency of the AFL-CIO in 1996 sparked a major effort by American unions to "reinvent" themselves. Concurrent with the "Sweeney revolution," a dramatic generational turnover occurred in the leadership of major unions, labor councils, and state federations. Andrew Stern, 52, a graduate of and student activist at the University of Pennsylvania, rose to lead America's largest union, the Service Employees International Union (SEIU). Similarly, John Wilhelm, 56, the president of the Hotel Employees Restaurant Employees Union (HERE), a graduate of Yale, also came to labor as a student activist. A similar generational shift took place at the state and local level. Miguel Contreras, 50, the son of migrant farm workers and a former organizer for Cesar Chavez's United Farm Workers, began to lead the Los Angeles Federation of Labor in 1998. Josie Mooney, 48, a college-educated, former community organizer, leads the Bay Area public workers union and serves as president of the San Francisco Labor Council; she is the first woman to occupy those posts. Members of this generation are also responsible for new efforts to bring young people into the labor movement, such as college-educated apprentices recruited by the AFL-CIO Organizing Institute and Union Summer and, to a lesser degree, new immigrants who have been mobilized through campaigns like "Justice for Janitors."

Where did this new generation of California union leaders come from? Why did they join the union movement? How have their careers unfolded? And where are they today?

These questions are intriguing, because this generation came to work for unions in the 1970s, a time when organized labor was shrinking and offered few opportunities for advancement. Unions were no longer at the center of a social movement either. In fact, some unions' responses to the Civil Rights Movement and the Vietnam War led many political activists to see them as "part of the problem, rather than part of the solution." Yet some activists like Stern and Wilhelm did enter the labor movement. What led them to union work? And what effect have they had? Many observers have reported on the influence of members of this "'60s generation" on other American institutions (Katzenstein 1998; McAdam 1988; Klatch 1999). What about their influence on unions?

Existing scholarship on union leadership is of little help in answering these questions; it neither looks at this generation of union leaders nor grapples with questions of how the reasons people come to work for unions shapes their subsequent careers. Previous scholars have tended to limit their studies to successful union leaders selected at one moment in time. This method fails to observe the processes by which some sustained their commitment while others fell by the wayside or why some leaders have had more influence than others (Mills 1948; Quaglieri 1988). Moreover, existing research is frequently more descriptive than explanatory and therefore provides little theoretical guidance for understanding how career paths develop over time. Recently, a few researchers have begun to investigate the retention of union staff, but their focus has been on brand new recruits rather than those with a demonstrated long-term commitment to union work (see Rooks; Bunnage and Stepan-Norris, both in this volume).

This study is the first to focus on the generation of leaders currently heading the American labor movement. Rather than learning only about those who have become top leaders, we study a broad range of union leaders. And instead of focusing on a single moment, we use a longitudinal approach that allows us to investigate how careers evolve over time. Our research draws on a unique database of 68 California men and women who were first interviewed in 1984 when they were selected for study as rising young labor leaders. We interviewed them again in 2001 and 2002.

Studying California labor leaders is particularly useful for understanding attempts to revitalize unions. Not only do California unions represent 15 percent of all American union members today, but they were also especially active during the period of this study (BLS 2002). Significant attempts at union renewal in California, for example, include SEIU's "Justice for Janitors" campaigns, the Los Angeles Federation of Labor's grassroots political program, and unionization of 100,000 home health care providers.

MOVING BEYOND DEMOGRAPHICS

Many scholars of union leadership have followed in the footsteps of C. Wright Mills, who published his very influential portrait of American union leaders in 1948. It was a time when unions were growing and accumulating political power, and Mills located those leaders in the larger social and political context of post–Second World War American society. The leaders Mills studied were a newly empowered group of strategic actors; understanding their social origins, education, party ties, and the like were of interest in and of themselves. Mills demonstrated that most union leaders were self-made men. He did not inquire in any depth about their motivation for joining the labor movement, assuming their incentive was self-evident: these men of humble social origins entered union work because unions were a source of power and upward mobility.

When scholars focused on demographics, they assumed unionists' motivations rather than asking about them.[1] This emphasis made sense when unions were growing and gaining influence, and when unions were dominated by workers who came up from the ranks. Investigating motivation not only seemed unnecessary, but also was out of step with a focus on structure that has held sway in social science thinking in recent years. To the extent that students of leadership in the arenas of management (Hollander 1978; Bass 1990), political science (Kellerman 1986), and social movement theory (Oberschall 1973; Wickham-Crowley 1992) examine motivation at all, they do so primarily in terms of class background, education, and personality—and the relationship of those factors to the kind of work leaders do. Since the 1970s, however, it has been less self-evident that anyone, including rank-and-file workers, would be attracted to union work as a means of gaining social power. This makes the question of motivation—and what difference it might make—more relevant.

Moreover, sociologists have become much more interested in the role that agency plays in social life and how intentionality and purpose shape social action. This approach is rooted in a sociological tradition originating with Weber, Mead, and Schutz, and linked recently with narrative theory by Mische and others (Emirbeyer and Mische 1998; Mische 2003). In this view, an individual's choices unfold through a narrative process that situates motives for present action within a context of past recollection and future projection (Bruner 1990). Therefore, one's "project" is his account of where he hopes to go (his goals), why he wants to get there (his motivations), and how he thinks he can arrive at his destination (his means).[2] Paying attention to purpose then does not suggest individuals end up where they do because of random caprice. Choices are neither entirely spontaneous nor entirely predictable, but adaptive (Bandura 1990).[3]

Since projects are the outcome of this narrative process, they are not fixed. They are constructed and reconstructed as circumstances change and actors "continually reassess future possibilities in the face of past experiences" (Mische 2003). Sometimes our goals work out, and sometimes they do not. Sometimes we persist in finding new ways to pursue them, but other times we change them. Thus, career pathways can be viewed as devised rather than followed.

However, actors' projects and career pathways unfold in interaction with organizational settings (Barley 1989; Gunz 1989). To the extent that organizations pursue collective projects, an individual's project may be more or less dissonant with that of his or her organization and thus more or less aligned with its financial, political, and status incentives. Intention itself is influenced by organizational settings, "shifting with changing structures of interest and attention" (Mische 2003). So we would expect the projects of individuals within particular organizations to converge through processes of selection and adaptation: people leaving and people changing.[4] But how, then, do organizations change? Is it solely a matter of changes in the environment, or do people's projects have an influence? If so, what kinds of projects? And under what conditions? In this paper we study the role of projects systematically by analyzing what people say and how they say it, and comparing the results across individuals, organizations, and outcomes.[5]

HOW WE LEARNED ABOUT UNION LEADERSHIP

The initial data for this study comes from a set of interviews with 130 California union leaders, conducted in 1984 by Marshall Ganz and Scott Washburn. These interviews were designed to provide insight into the future direction of the California labor movement. With the support of California labor organizations and a number of small foundations, Ganz and Washburn targeted a set of younger, full-time union leaders. Most of these leaders had organizing experience, had earned positions of responsibility in their unions, and had built reputations among their colleagues for a commitment to union revitalization. The interviewees were broadly representative of the full range of California unions, industries, and regions. However, special emphasis was placed on organizers, women, people of color, those who were 30 to 45 years of age at the time, and those with records of success. Eighty-six people in the original sample were between the ages of 30 and 45. They worked for unions active in the public sector, services, manufacturing, building trades, and transportation. Each two to three hour interview was extensive and focused on the respondent's family background, career to date, mentoring, views of organizing, beliefs about leadership, and expectations for the future. The findings

were never published, except in presentations made to union leaders in
1985–86 and in a few article references (Kuttner 1987). Instead, the notes sat
in a trunk in a Salinas, California, warehouse until 2001.

The present study builds on the data collected in 1984. We re-interviewed
the original respondents to compare their positions in 1984 with their current
positions and to learn how they got there. Our first task was to locate the original cohort—a search that got underway in the spring of 2001. When we found
most of them, we conducted a set of two to three hour semi-structured interviews, tape-recorded and transcribed them, and met regularly as a research
team of five to discuss and analyze the data.

In each interview, we explored the individual's successes and failures, the
opportunities and barriers they encountered, and how they dealt with them.
We asked specific questions about key choices, probing why they did what they
did. And we compared these responses within the context of the broader narrative in which these choices were embedded, trying to get purchase on the
whys behind each person's choices. The risks of retrospective sense making are
obvious, but less problematic to the extent that we focused on actual choices.
These risks are also balanced by drawing data from two interviews, seventeen
years apart, comparing actual choices with inquiries about the choices, and
our own practice as skilled interviewers, paying attention to affect, context,
and metaphor.

Coding the interviews was a multi-step process. First, we reconstructed
profiles of each person's career path based on data drawn from both interviews. We focused on the choice points in their careers, how they accounted
for their choices, and what the outcomes were. And we began to discern narrative accounts of what we call projects: accounts of where one hopes to go
(goals), why one wants to get there (motivations), and how one thinks he can
arrive at his destination (means). We then evaluated the utility of people's
projects in understanding their patterns of behavior, the findings of which we
present here.

In this paper, we look only at the people in the original sample who were
between 30 and 45 years of age when they were first interviewed in 1984, a
total of 86. As table 6.1 shows, of these we were able to contact 75 (87 percent).
At least 2 of the 11 we could not contact were deceased[6]. Of those we could
contact, 48 (64 percent) were still working for a union, 3 (4 percent) had
retired from a union, and 24 (32 percent) had left union work before retiring.
Our study is based on those interviewed as of the writing of this paper—68
(91 percent) of the total interviewees available to us.

TABLE 6.1
Union leaders interviewed in 2001

Original Group	86
Deceased	2
Percent of Original Group Still Living	98%
Total Living	84
Found	75
Percent Found	89%
Working for Union	48
Percent of Those Found Working for Union	64%
Retired from Union	3
Percent of Those Found Retired from Union	4%
Left Union	24
Percent of Those Found Who Left Union	32%
Retired After Leaving	0
Percent of Those Found Who Retired After Leaving Union	0%
Interviewed	68
Percent of Those Found Interviewed	91%

BACKGROUNDS

Who were these 68 union leaders? Table 6.2 gives the broad picture. Perhaps accurately reflecting the makeup of mid-level union leadership in 1984, only 14 (21 percent) were women. Ethnically, the vast majority were non-Hispanic Caucasians. Eleven (16 percent) were Hispanics, a significant group that played an important role in the recent revival of California unionism. Fifteen (22 percent) were immigrants or had at least one immigrant parent. Despite considerable efforts to find rising African American union leaders to inter-view, Ganz and Washburn found only two in the 45-and-under age group and we were unable to interview either one again in 2001–2002.

With regard to religious background, half were raised Roman Catholic, one-quarter Protestant, one-fifth Jewish, and the remaining 5 percent claimed no religion. Only a minority had what might be called a devoutly religious upbringing, but a small and interesting proportion of these had attended a religious seminary or given serious thought to a religious career.

Traditionally, union leaders had working-class parents, a high school (or, rarely, college) education, and began their union careers as rank-and-file members of the unions they later represented. This standard path appears to be changing—more so in some unions than in others—with the nature of the change already dramatically apparent in the demographics of the leaders we interviewed. A bare majority came from working-class parents; indeed 47 percent were classified as having middle-class background. In considerable contrast to earlier generations of union leaders, only one-third of the entire group interviewed had union parents (Mills 1948). Reflecting the dramatic

TABLE 6.2
Union Leaders Interviewed in 1984 (30–45)

Individual and Organizational Characteristics		Number	Percent
Positions	CEOs	31	46%
	Other Elected Full Time Officers	0	0%
	Organizers & Organizing Directors	12	18%
	Other Appointed Directors	3	4%
	Business Agents	11	16%
	Business Agent-Organizers	8	12%
	Others	2	3%
How Selected?	Elected	26	38%
	Appointed	42	62%
Directing Staff?	Yes	38	56%
	No	30	44%
Organizing Experience	Some Organizing Before 1984	51	75%
	Organizing Responsibility in 1984	20	29%
Union Sector	Federation	8	12%
	Public	15	22%
	Service	16	24%
	Craft	13	19%
	Industrial	16	24%
Region	Los Angeles County	24	35%
	Orange County	4	6%
	San Diego County	4	6%
	Bay Area	26	38%
	San Jose	5	7%
	Central Valley	5	6%
	Inland Empire	0	0%
Gender	Male	54	79%
	Female	14	21%
Ethnicity	White	57	84%
	Hispanic	11	16%
Class	Working Class	36	53%
	Middle Class	32	47%
Religion	Roman Catholic	34	50%
	Protestant	18	26%
	Jewish	13	19%
	None	3	3%
Family Background	Union Family	23	34%
	Immigrant/Immigrant Family	15	22%
Education	College Completed When Went to Work for Union	38	56%
	College Not Completed When Went to Work for Union	30	44%
Marital Status in 2001	Ever Married by 2001	64	94%
	Married Only Once by 2001	29	43%

Recruitment		Number	Percent
Experience Prior to Recruitment	Activism	36	53%
	Military	10	15%
Source of Recruitment	From Inside the Workplace	46	68%
	From Outside the Workplace	22	32%

expansion of higher education among working-class youth in the 1960s and 1970s, a majority of our interviewees were college graduates, and a considerable number of those had done some graduate work. Far from incidentally, most of our college-graduate leaders were in college during the civil rights and anti-war movements of the 1960s and early 1970s. Many reported being radicalized in college, and some even participated in anti-war activities in high school. A majority (53 percent) were political or social activists in community or political organizations prior to their union employment. Again, in contrast to previous leadership generations, one-third (32 percent) were hired directly from "outside," without having first been a member of the union for which they worked.

WHY THEY CAME TO WORK FOR UNIONS

In our interviews, we asked people how they came to do union work, why they kept doing it, and, when relevant, why they left to do something else. From these accounts, we coded the projects each person had when they began working in the labor movement. We distinguished four broad projects: social reform, community leadership, personal advancement, and union building.

Social Reformers. These people were drawn into union work as a means of pursuing social reform. Motivated by their commitment to social justice, they generally believed political work was the best way to make the world a better place. For them, union work provided an opportunity to achieve goals that were even broader than those of the union.

Community Leaders. Community leaders hoped to improve the lives of the members of their community through union work. These leaders defined their communities based on ethnicity, kinship, or work place—often in combination. They were motivated by identification with their communities and believed they could best serve those communities by representing their interests and acting on their behalf. They often indicated willingness to assert community interests over union interests.

Union Builders. Union builders viewed union work as an end in itself. Often having had direct experience with the difference a union can make in one's life, they were motivated by the desire to improve the lives of others in the same way. They articulated that the best way of achieving that goal was to negotiate good contracts, win grievances, organize, and service members.

Personal Advancement. A number of interviewees got involved with union work with the objective of improving their individual lives. For some, union work offered the prospect of upward mobility; for others, a more interesting job; and for still others, a way to achieve influence and power. They looked for work based on the opportunity it offered, expressed themselves in

TABLE 6.3
First union projects

Project	Number	Percent
Social Reform	36	53%
Community Leadership	10	15%
Union Building	11	16%
Personal Advancement	11	16%
Total	68	100%

non-ideological terms, and typically considered union work as one option among others.

Table 6.3 shows the number of labor leaders who came into the movement with each project. The largest single group, some 54 percent, had social reform projects when they first began working in the labor movement. The remaining 46 percent of those interviewed were divided among community leaders (16 percent), personal advancement seekers (16 percent), and union builders (13 percent).

Social Reform

Chart 6.1 presents the class background, education, source of recruitment, and activist experience of the 36 people who came to the labor movement with a social reform project. More than half of the social reformers came from middle-class backgrounds and were college educated. Almost another third were college graduates from working-class homes. Regarding recruitment, the social reform group is split evenly between those who were hired from the outside the union and those who were promoted from within. They include men and women.

As column 4 indicates, prior activism is the common thread connecting those interested in social reform. Regardless of class background, education, gender, or recruitment method, every social reformer, save one, had been actively involved in social movements before coming to work for a union.

In our interviews, we explored people's early activism and tried to understand how it led to union work. We discovered three types of activism that brought social reformers into the labor movement; each type of activism was associated with a different pathway into union work. One type, which we label "unaffiliated," involved participation in the social movements of the 1960s and 1970s without membership in a vanguard political group. A second type of activism, "faith-motivated" activism, was rooted in religious commitments. A third variety, "vanguard" activism, entailed membership in a vanguard political group. No path to social reform was the exclusive route of any one

Chart 6.1. Social reform as first project by class, education, source of recruitment, and activist experience

Name	Class	Education	Recruited?	Activist?	1st project
Sam Hoffman	MC	C+	Out	Y	SR
Karen Emory	MC	C+	Out	Y	SR
Neil Rosen	MC	C+	Out	Y	SR
George Kaufman	MC	C+	Out	Y	SR
Sam Rosenberg	MC	C+	Out	Y	SR
Eli Altman	MC	C+	Out	Y	SR
Clem Donlevy	MC	C+	Out	Y	SR
Nancy Masterson	MC	C+	Out	Y	SR
Tom Nussbaum	MC	C+	Out	Y	SR
Laura Feirman	MC	C+	Out	Y	SR
Ulrich Darden	MC	C+	Out	Y	SR
Nick Martin	MC	C+	In	Y	SR
Kevin Rogers	MC	C+	In	Y	SR
Rob Harrington	MC	C+	In	Y	SR
Tom Weinberg	MC	C+	In	Y	SR
Charles Keaton	MC	C+	In	Y	SR
Vic Robinson	MC	C+	In	Y	SR
Ralph Reeves	MC	C+	In	Y	SR
Liam O'Reilly	MC	LC	Out	Y	SR
Dianne Burton	MC	LC	In	Y	SR
Norm Dunn	MC	LC	In	N	SR
Henry Carl	MC	LC	In	Y	SR
Ellen Atwood	WC	C+	Out	Y	SR
Nydia Elizondo	WC	C+	Out	Y	SR
Colin Gordon	WC	C+	Out	Y	SR
Karl Stephens	WC	C+	Out	Y	SR
Neil Eaton	WC	C+	Out	Y	SR
Carol Lewin	WC	C+	Out	Y	SR
Lloyd Callahan	WC	C+	Out	Y	SR
Henry Podack	WC	C+	In	Y	SR
Eric Marcovich	WC	C+	In	Y	SR
Kathrine McCarthy	WC	C+	In	Y	SR
Charles Harris	WC	C+	In	Y	SR
Linda Davis	WC	LC	Out	Y	SR
Rudy Del Castillo	WC	LC	In	Y	SR
Rom Giannini	WC	LC	In	Y	SR

KEY MC = Middle Class   Out = Hired from outside the union
WC = Working Class   In = Promoted from within the union
C+ = College degree or more   Y = Activist before joining union
LC = Less than college degree   N = Not activist before joining union
SR = Social Reform

class; people from both the working class and middle class traveled all three paths.

Social reformers were a diverse group, and their pathways into the labor movement led in different directions depending on the specific nature of their activist backgrounds. However, they all shared a commitment to broad social and political change, and they all saw their union work as a way to advance this larger project rather than as an end in and of itself.

Unaffiliated Social Reformers

Those with an unaffiliated social reform project, the largest group, typically became activists in high school or college. Most were spurred to action by the anti-war movement, but some were drawn in by the civil rights movement or community activism instead. Colin Gordon's story of anti-war activism, which began in high school, is characteristic.

> There was a feeling in the air in those times, and the draft, really, [was] the single biggest motivating factor in my developing of my thinking . . . I was reading about the war in Vietnam. But I was also reading about everything else. I remember reading about—was it in the summer of '67? —the riots in Newark and numerous other places. And, I remember a Life magazine cover with the guy killed by the National Guard for carrying a case of beer out of a liquor store that was being looted. And [they] had his bloody corpse on the cover of *Life* magazine. And I remember arguing with my father, saying, "You can't kill people for a case of beer." And my father took the other view, as lots of people did.

Gordon soon began to mobilize other students for anti-draft and anti-war activities. He continued this work when he went to college and joined Students for a Democratic Society (SDS). When approached by more sectarian groups, however, he "didn't opt to engage."

> I went to some of the meetings, some of the study groups, and I read the books. And it seemed odd. I remember thinking, "This is such a great idea that these people have, if everybody would just work together and cooperate and share, this is like such a brilliant idea. But their approach is, like, they're never going to reach the people in the U.S. that it's aimed at. They're not gonna come close."

Instead, Gordon's college involvement with social movements centered on non-sectarian, anti-war mobilization. He was also caught up in the larger activist milieu, which included "symbolic support for black activists who were being attacked by the government in '69 and '70 and '71." In his senior year, he supported a wildcat walkout of the cafeteria workers in the student center. However, that support ended when, "some guys in suits came up and told [the workers] to go back to work."

The "guys in suits"—union representatives—did not leave a favorable impression. When he graduated from college, Gordon had a social reform project, but unions were not the obvious place to look to pursue that project. He was typical of the unaffiliated social reformers with whom we spoke. Like most in the New Left, unaffiliated social reformers tended to view unions as undemocratic upholders of the status quo and the war effort. Making union work even more unlikely was the fact that most unions were opposed to hiring "outsiders"—people who did not come up from the workplace. How then did social reformers like Gordon come to do union work?

Here, too, Gordon's path is similar to that of many other unaffiliated activists. He came to union work only through involvement in a "bridge" organization, one that linked movement groups and labor unions. In his case, it was the United Farm Workers (UFW), which Gordon got involved with not because it was a labor organization but because it was part of a larger movement for social justice and civil rights.

> It would have been, like, June of '73, in *Time* magazine. There had been a little article, and it was on the [modern-day] *Grapes of Wrath*. It was about the fights between the Teamsters and the farm workers in Coachella. And, it said, "We're in the same place that Steinbeck used to write about. In the dusty fields, farm workers are being subjected to this violence . . ." I read that article, and that was the first time that I really thought about the farm workers when I read that article that summer. And, then after that, I ended up in the [San Francisco] area. And then when I met them [again] I said, "God this is an amazing struggle." And, I was talking to my friends from Fordham about it, and they're saying, "Look, they need people. They're trying to get people to work full time with them and support them. You were always Mr. Protest and making us go to demonstrations and everything. Why don't you go work with them?"

Gordon began by volunteering with the UFW and went on to become a field representative and the assistant field office director. He stayed for six years. When he left, he "knew that [he] was going to continue in the labor movement," largely because he realized that he could carry out his social reform project by doing union work. He eventually ran into an "old farm worker contact" who had gone to work for the HERE local in San Francisco. Gordon asked if there were any jobs, and he was hired to run a picket line. He has done union work ever since, because, "if everybody did a better job organizing their co-workers, we could make the working people and the poor people have a lot better share of what there is."

Another organization that bridged the world of activism with that of labor movement was the Citizens Action League (CAL), a membership advocacy group battling the public utilities in California for reforms like lifeline rates for poor people. CAL's founders, Mike Miller and Tim Sampson, were profoundly influenced by Saul Alinsky and worked with unions like SEIU on community organizing. Some of the social reformers, particularly those whose activism involved community organizing, came to the labor movement following involvement with CAL.

Clem Donlevy, for instance, became committed to a social reform project as a result of his experiences in the Peace Corps in Tanzania. After he left the Peace Corps, he spent a few years getting his master's degree in urban planning and then working as a well-paid urban planner for the city of Boston, which he hated. Donlevy came to the Bay Area and began working for CAL, doing community organizing for a subsistence wage of $60 per week. During these years, he never thought about working for a union. However, by the time he was ready to leave community organizing—because he "had learned what he was going to learn from [community organizing]"—his thinking had changed. Union work "was just sort of a natural progression," after working with people in labor while at CAL.

A few of the unaffiliated social reformers began working for unions without previous involvement with a bridging organization like the UFW or CAL. Some in this group came from working-class backgrounds and became more radical in college because of contact with radical professors. Carol Lewin told us:

> I really got radicalized in college. There was this history professor who taught Marxism and [explained] my whole life . . . My dad was a salesman, and he worked really hard. He would leave at 6:30 or 7 in the morning, and what he did was go to poor neighborhoods and sold household items that he had in the back seat of his car, like everything from toasters and irons to blankets and pots and pans. And people would buy it on a payment plan. And so then he would go back every week and collect $5 toward the toaster or whatever, and that was his job. But, there were some people in my family who had, now I sort of realize they were, like, doing well. Not rich, but they were doing well. And so there was . . . I just saw the difference, and mainly I saw how my dad felt about himself, because about, like, his own sense of himself and dignity. And so then when I went to college and learned about Marxism and the alienation of labor and how people get their sense of themselves through work, it just, like, totally . . . I just felt this amazing [sense of belonging]. . . . It was like my family.

Another interviewee, Lloyd Callahan, came from a similar working class background and talked about two of his professors—one a Marxist and the other an "anti-communist Socialist." Their teachings "made sense" of his father's life, offered him some pride of class, and a "philosopher's stone" to understand the world.

Once they had been radicalized, Lewin and Callahan entered union work more directly than Gordon and Donlevy. All it took was exposure to an organizing campaign or a job lead. Lewin, for example, had a summer internship in Washington, D.C., while she was still in college. While there, she roomed with someone who was working on an organizing campaign at the AFL-CIO.

I went there originally to work in the Health and Human Services, because I thought I wanted to go into public health. But I went there and it was during the Reagan years, and I can still remember this little cubicle I had at that office. And it was really boring. But I lived in this house with all these women who had all different jobs. And one of them had a job working for the AFL-CIO for the Food and Allied Service Trades, FAST. And so I remember she came home one night and said, "Tonight I have to go out at 2 in the morning to meet these waitresses at the Watergate Hotel. And, then I have to be up at 6 in the morning to leaflet a cleaners." And I went, "Oh my God! That's what I want to do." So I just quit. I got the internship also with AFL-CIO.

When I was at Berkeley, I was in the New American Movement, and I definitely knew that capitalism sucked . . . but I didn't know what you could do about it . . . because no one really talked about unions. But I studied all about gigantic corporations screwing over Third World countries. And then I knew that some people made all the money in the world but never spend it, and other people couldn't afford anything. And I felt like that about my family . . . but didn't know what to do . . . So then when I went to Washington, and I saw that people were doing that, I went, "God that's what I should do." And I remember thinking, "I can't believe that I could actually do this and have it be a job! . . . And so then when I left there and went back to [San Francisco], I looked up Local 2. And that was the job I got.

Similarly, Callahan submitted a resume when he heard that the American Federation of Government Employees (AFGE) was looking for organizers. In both cases, Lewin and Callahan seemed more predisposed than middle-class unaffiliated social reformers to think of unions as vehicles for social change. Job opportunities were also necessary for other unaffiliated social reformers— but so was participation in a bridging organization where they learned that unions could be vehicles for social change.

Another path by which some unaffiliated social reformers entered the labor movement was social work, which in the early 1970s was a target of aggressive organizing campaigns by the SEIU and the American Federation of State, County, and Municipal Employees (AFSCME). Social work was a rapidly expanding occupation in the late 1960s and early 1970s. It attracted large numbers of social reformers because it seemed to deal directly with the problem of poverty in American society. Before 1968, California public sector workers had no legally protected right to unionize. The situation changed with the 1968 passage of the Meyers-Milias-Brown Act, a law that guaranteed public employees the right to unionize and bargain collectively. A few of our interviewees entered union work as a result of organizing drives in their units; some determined that joining the union was a good way to protect themselves from managers who objected to their activist agendas.

One example is Rudy Del Castillo, who went to work as a welfare eligibility worker in southern California after being involved in anti-war and Chicano groups at a University of California campus. He discovered that Hispanic welfare applicants were disadvantaged because the Spanish translation of their applications was so inept that deserving people did not get public support. He helped organize social workers, clients, community people, and Chicano activists from the local university to agitate for better translations. They won, but managers soon retaliated against the social workers, who in turn organized a union that affiliated with SEIU. When Del Castillo was fired for his activities, he took a staff job with SEIU.

Faith-Motivated Social Reformers

Some social reformers found their way into the labor movement through their religious convictions. All of these activists were Roman Catholic, and all but one trained to be a nun or a priest before becoming involved in the labor movement. Their belief in social reform was profoundly shaped by faith. Liam O'Reilly, for example, joined the UFW boycott with other seminarians. He soon took a year off from the seminary to work for the UFW. One of his schoolmates asked, "Why are you doing that?" O'Reilly responded, "Building the union is like building the church without the crutch of religion."

After a year, O'Reilly left the UFW but found his way to HERE. When we asked him how he sees his union work today, he echoed his earlier views that the union "gives people hope, gives people a way to be heard, gives a chance for there to be justice, or something resembling justice. Something resembling fairness, and a way for people not to be powerless . . ."

Just as it was for many of the unaffiliated social reformers, the UFW was a common point of entry into the labor movement for those who arrived at their social reform project through religion. For the unaffiliated social reformers, the UFW bridged the divide between the social movements of the 1960s and unions because it was a way to fight for civil rights. However, for the social reformers motivated by faith, the UFW was a bridge between a religious vocation and the secular world. For example, one woman in this group, Linda Davis, remembered her father telling her that Cesar Chavez was "a modern day saint." Faith-motivated social reformers joined the UFW because of the union's profound religious content. After becoming active, they came to view union work as a means of carrying out their commitment to social justice.

Vanguard Social Reformers

The third way social reformers entered the labor movement was through activism linked with membership in a vanguard political group, such as the International Socialist Organization. For these people, union work was a very different undertaking than it was for either the unaffiliated or the faith-based activists. Political activists took jobs in factories and offices as "colonists," with the intent to remake unions. For example, when we asked Ralph Reeve why he came to work for a union, he told us:

> I had decided that I wanted to try to apply my politics in the labor movement. That was sort of a place you could go to foment social change, and that's what I wanted to do. So, why the Post Office in particular? I just sort of fell into that. But, I wanted to get into a blue collar, industrial setting of some sort, and that was what I landed.

Asked if he was affiliated with any group that shaped his politics, he replied, "For a while, I was a member of something called 'The New American Movement' and, after that, International Socialists." He went to work for the Post Office after graduating from Swarthmore. His goal was to "reform the unions . . . The view was that the unions were terrible; they were corrupt; they were bureaucratic. We were going to transform the unions and remake them so that they would be workers' unions."

After landing a job as a mail carrier in California, Reeves volunteered to be a shop steward. A year later he ran for recording secretary of the local American Postal Workers Union and took an active part in a movement to merge several branches. A few years later, he successfully ran for the presidency of the merged local.

Other vanguard activists took a similar "colonist" path to union work. This partially explains the large number of social reformers who entered union work from the workplace. Of the 17 social reformers who were recruited from within the workplace in chart 6.1, seven had gone to the shop floor with a radical political agenda.

Chart 6.2. Community leadership as first project by class, education, source of recruitment, and activist experience

Name	Class	Education	Recruited?	Activist?	1st project
Linda Donatello	MC	C+	In	N	CL
Don Bertlesman	MC	LC	In	N	CL
Nicolas Manriquez	WC	LC	In	N	CL
Rick Borjas	WC	LC	In	N	CL
Dick Lara	WC	LC	In	N	CL
Karl Norman	WC	LC	In	N	CL
Carlos Sanchez	WC	LC	In	Y	CL
Bob Alcala	WC	LC	In	Y	CL
Cal Lopez	WC	LC	In	Y	CL
Oscar Herrara	WC	LC	In	Y	CL

KEY   MC = Middle Class   Out = Hired from outside the union
      WC = Working Class   In = Promoted from within the union
      C+ = College degree or more   Y = Activist before joining union
      LC = Less than college degree   N = Not activist before joining union
                                        CL = Community Leadership

Community Leadership

As chart 6.2 shows, we interviewed ten people whose initial project was community leadership. All but two of them were from working class backgrounds, and only one finished college. Seven of the ten (70 percent) were Latinos whose work for the union was an extension of prior, ethnic community leadership.

Bob Alcala, a Chicano community leader, joined the Laborers' union after his uncles helped him find work in the trade. Before becoming active in the union, Alcala had taken part in Chicano community fights over police brutality and public parks. He gained visibility in the union as a critic of the established leadership and acquired a following through his position as a union foreman. After Alcala helped the bargaining committee with a particularly tough set of negotiations, the incumbent leaders invited him to serve as a business agent. Alcala made his decision whether to accept the offer very carefully.

> So . . . when the negotiations were finalized, the business manager told me, "I want you to come to work for me." So I said, "Let me think about that." I mean, I had people; I was building a political base. And I'm thinking, "What are they going to think? That I sold out?" So I told them, "This is what we want, and this is the way I see it. I can go to work for them and try to do some good from the inside, or stay out here and fight them from the

outside. You guys make the decision." So that's how I ended up working for them as business agent.

Before going to work for the union, Alcala had built a political base among the membership whose views he had to take into consideration when deciding his next move. Later, he led his own slate to victory. What he liked about union work was helping people like himself. He said that he enjoyed, "just dealing with people that had the same common problems and the same things that [he] went through in [his] work. Being able to help them with these problems."

Two of the seven Latino community leaders were new immigrants from Mexico. One, Carlos Sanchez, had become active in the new immigrant community and later found work in a unionized bakery. Sanchez said:

I think that the main thing is that you want to help the people . . . I form a social club for people from Acambaro, Guanajuato. I started meeting people from there and say, "You know somebody else?" "Yes, yes, yes." So, I get all together, and we make a social club to help the people there. It was before [I got involved with the union work] . . . Probably a couple of hundred [people were involved]. We had parties. Saturdays, we had all to collect the money to buy things, to send the money to the Red Cross.

Sanchez became active in the union after the union "defended" him, and he began "defending" other workers as an extension of his "community":

They told me that I was going to be demoted to part time. And, I say, "Wait a minute. Why didn't you tell me? You didn't give me any notice, any warnings." They have a preference, because somebody was a friend of somebody. So, I went to the shop steward, and I told him. He said, "No, no, no. Call the union." I said, "OK." So, I called the union. They were there. They had a meeting. They said, "No, you cannot demote him." So, they leave me there. From there, I decide these guys are really something, and I start defending people. I called the union and tell them this is happening here, and this is not fair. I was translating to the people and helping the people. At that time, JB [the business agent] says, "What is this guy? He's good." I was helping the people, [so] the people talked to the shop steward there, to make me another shop steward for them.

Sanchez later worked for the union full time as a business agent and organizer.

As the excerpts above demonstrate, community leaders—most of whom came from working-class backgrounds, did not finish college, and are linked

Chart 6.3. Union building as first project by class, education, source of recruitment, and activist experience

Name	Class	Education	Recruited?	Activist?	1st project
Van Sanders	MC	LC	In	N	UB
Ken McHenry	MC	LC	In	N	UB
Sam Hendricks	WC	C+	In	N	UB
Ellen Gardner	WC	C+	In	N	UB
Sean Reardon	WC	C+	In	N	UB
Sid Lang	WC	LC	In	N	UB
Wendy Martinez	WC	LC	In	N	UB
Karen Williams	WC	LC	In	N	UB
Ernie Fredricks	WC	LC	In	N	UB
Edward Schneider	WC	LC	In	N	UB
Dick Gonsalves	WC	LC	In	Y	UB

KEY   MC = Middle Class   Out = Hired from outside the union
       WC = Working Class   In = Promoted from within the union
       C+ = College degree or more   Y = Activist before joining union
       LC = Less than college degree   N = Not activist before joining union
                                       UB = Union Building

to their co-workers by ethnic, kinship, or other ties—saw their project as one of advancing the interests of their community.

Union Building

For eleven of the labor leaders we interviewed, their project was "building the union." As shown in chart 6.3, nine came from working-class backgrounds, and eight lacked college degrees. They entered union work from the inside, as volunteer leaders (stewards, organizers, etc.), and most won their first full-time positions through election. Both union builders and social reformers served as volunteer activists prior to union employment—union builders inside the union, and social reformers outside it. Union builders, however, described "awakenings" to the union in terms of personal experiences in which the union played an important role. Their stories often began with a successful stand against an injustice, usually in the form of a grievance, rather than with an account of values, commitments, or community responsibility.

Wendy Martinez, for example, grew up in an immigrant, working-class, union family. When she finished high school, she took a job at the phone company and began to move up. Although she belonged to the Communications Workers of America (CWA), from the time she began to work for the phone company, an incident in which she was personally involved turned her into a union activist.

I had this supervisor [who] is the reason I got active in the union . . . [S]he observed me for a whole day, and then she says to me, "You've got the highest production in the group. You've got the highest quality in the group. You're going places. I'm going to recommend you to get into . . . management. Oh, I'm just so pleased." She really just couldn't say enough about what good job I was doing.

As a person who cared deeply about respect for her work, Martinez hoped this would earn her the opportunity to become a manager.

It was not to be. When she challenged her supervisor, her supervisor turned on her, and the union became her line of defense. The union contract provided that workers could be required to work an extra 30 minutes in an emergency. If one worker in the unit had to work, all had to work until the job was completed. But the day that Martinez's supervisor took two of her co-workers to lunch, she applied the rule in an arbitrary way, angering Martinez. This incident brought her into contact with the union.

After they were gone [to lunch] for two to three hours, the supervisor . . . comes back . . . and says, "You have to work your half-hour." We had to work a half-hour to make up for their three-hour lunch. So I say, "OK. I'm working my half-hour, but I'm sure everybody has to work their half hour." But the minute the first [worker] got up to leave . . . I went to the supervisor's desk, and I said, "Excuse me . . ." Now this took a lot . . . because I was very [shy]. But it was not right . . . It motivated me out of my shyness. I went to her and said, "Excuse me, I have a question. It's my understanding that the union says that if one of us has to work a half-hour, we *all* have to work a half hour" [. . .] She was very good at turning people against each other. So she turns to the other [worker] who hadn't quite made it out the door and says, "Oh, you're going to have to stay and work your half hour because of Wendy Martinez."

Martinez felt taken advantage of and protested. But the supervisor who had told her she was a candidate for management now reprimanded her.

Well, the next thing, the supervisor summons me to the conference room. She's got all these binders in front of her, which were all my job evaluations. She's kind of leafing through them, and she looks me right in the eye, and she says, "You know, Wendy, you've always been a very good employee. I hope that's not going to change." Very intimidating. She says, "I know you want to get into management." And I really had aspirations, because it was more money. She says, "But you know, one of the most important management attributes is flexibility." And I am seething inside. I am, like, so horrified.

I looked at her, and now I'm crying. But she didn't know I was crying from rage. I was so indignant that she had done this, and I'm crying, and I looked at her, and I said, "You know, I thought that we were adults, and I thought that if I had a question I could come and ask you. But, it's obvious that that isn't what's happening. You're trying to intimidate me because I'm a union member. And you know what? The next time that I have a question, my union steward will be in to talk to you." I didn't even know who that was! [As] soon as I used the magic words "union steward," [as] soon as I said that, she closed up all her books, and she said, "Oh! I certainly wouldn't want you to get *that* impression. That's not what I'm doing. And, by the way, you don't have to work your half-hour anymore" [laughing]. She left the room. I had to compose myself because I was like a blubbering idiot.

Martinez then took her first steps along a pathway to union leadership.

As soon as she walked out the door, I left that office . . . There was a union steward down in the basement . . . And I'm asking people, . . . "Where's the union steward?" So I go down there, and I find myself standing in front of this woman, . . . the elected secretary of the local . . . and I said, "Hi, my name is Wendy Martinez, and I want to be a union steward. Because if I'm going to stand up for my rights, I should at least know what they are!"

The disrespect she experienced on the job, her own gumption, and access to the union turned Wendy Martinez into a union builder; she saw the union as a means of turning her anger into action and of becoming the person she wanted to be.

For many union builders, an important moment is one in which they come to see what they once had perceived as an individual problem to be a collective one. Ellen Gardner grew up in a working-class family, finished college, and became a social worker. She joined the union, became active during a strike, and was elected a steward. She came to see union work as an extension of what brought her to social work in the first place.

I saw my job to be an advocate for the client. But that was more on a one-by-one basis. . . . I saw the role of being involved in the union as being an advocate for my co-workers as a collective group. And, at the same time, my clients as a collective group. . . . Eventually, I was in the job long enough to come to the conclusion that, as an individual social worker, I could certainly have an impact on the individuals that I ran into. But I came to believe that I could have a much larger and more comprehensive impact on what it was like for me to be a social worker and what it was like for me to be in this system trying to achieve something. I could have a bigger impact if I came

at it from a collective perspective. And I don't know. I believe that this is
true in any labor situation.

Unlike social reformers, community leaders, and those seeking personal
advancement—all of whom saw the union as a means to a greater end—union
builders saw building a strong union as worthy in its own right. Like Wendy
Martinez, they could become the kind of people they wanted to be by helping
to make it happen.

Personal Advancement

Despite the weakened state of unions in the 1970s, eleven of the people we
interviewed entered union work as a vehicle for personal advancement. As
shown in chart 6.4, six came from middle-class backgrounds, and five came
from working-class backgrounds. Both groups had nearly equal numbers of
college graduates and non-college graduates. Except for two of the college
graduates, all were recruited from within the work place. Almost half of this
group benefited from family connections that facilitated their election to or
hiring into a union position, a fact that distinguishes them from the social
reformers and union builders.

Dave Mills, for example, grew up in a middle-class family, married while
still in college, and joined a union local with help from his father-in-law, a

Chart 6.4. Personal advancement seeking as first project by class, education, source of
recruitment, and activist experience

Name	Class	Education	Recruited?	Activist?	1st project
Nathan Berman	MC	C+	Out	Y	PA
Eliot Rudnick	MC	C+	In	N	PA
Dave Mills	MC	LC	In	N	PA
Len Thomas	MC	LC	In	N	PA
Dan Landers	MC	LC	In	N	PA
Walter Brown	MC	LC	In	N	PA
Ken Brown	WC	C+	Out	N	PA
Debra Brown	WC	C+	In	N	PA
Sam Alioto	WC	C+	In	N	PA
Lionel Rivera	WC	LC	In	N	PA
Arnold Stokowski	WC	LC	In	N	PA

KEY   MC = Middle Class   Out = Hired from outside the union
         WC = Working Class   In = Promoted from within the union
         C+ = College degree or more   Y = Activist before joining union
         LC = Less than college degree   N = Not activist before joining union
                                                          PA = Personal Advancement

union officer. After finishing college, he was not sure what to do. He had a
family to support, so he continued driving a truck. By then, however, his co-
workers had begun to turn to him for help with their grievances. When they
elected him a steward, he began considering union work as a career option.
"I mean I kind of viewed the job as being like an attorney. Like many other
union leaders, Mills described his decision to run for union office as the result
of urging by others. But it was one option among many.

> People had suggested that I run—the election was coming up: guys I was
> working with, co-workers, . . . and my brother-in-law who was also working
> there. . . . The idea appealed to me, but I didn't know if I wanted to do that
> because the local was chaotic. [But] . . . I had to make a choice of what I
> wanted to do. I'd been going to school, back to UC. So I was kind of looking
> around, and I started looking into the union, and I started thinking, "Maybe
> I could do this. Maybe I could make some kind of a difference." But, the local
> was such chaos, and the BAs were all elected. But, I thought, "Well . . . you
> know, it's [a] pretty heady thing when your co-workers say, 'You ought to do
> this' and start pushing." Anyway, I ran, and I came in, I think, third or fourth
> out of 12 people that ran for BA . . . I put on *very* aggressive campaigns,
> much more aggressive than anything the local had seen before. So, anyway, I
> got elected. I couldn't believe it. The election ends, and geez, I got elected.

Mills carefully considered the options before taking the risk of running for
union office. Once he decided to take the risk, with his future at stake, he was
very committed to winning—which he did.

For others, union work offered the opportunity to find more meaningful
work. Ken Brown, for example, came from a working-class family, finished
college, got married, and began teaching high school. However, he was
unhappy in this work. Brown's father-in-law, a local union leader, recommended him to his union's organizing director, who needed organizers to take
advantage of the new state collective bargaining law. Brown saw an opportunity. He was already sympathetic to unions, and the promise of more satisfy-
ing work made the union an attractive job option.

> And so they said they were interested in hiring, like, twenty organizers
> statewide to do some work in the school districts. So I thought, "I'd like to
> try that for a while. . . . " I just thought it was exciting. It was challenging.
> [The organizing director was an] exciting guy. He just had a lot of energy.
> He was very tuned in to how to do things.

The search for opportunities for personal advancement is part of many
people's professional decisions. For those whose *project* was personal advance-

ment, however, they recounted it as their primary consideration. Although they had links to the union world, it had no claims on them until they saw that it offered them a way to pursue their own career goals.

WHAT HAPPENED TO THEM?

We have observed how people's projects influenced their decisions to go to work for unions. We turn now to learn how those projects unfolded over time and how this influenced those who stayed in the labor movement and those who left it. Chart 6.5 groups interviewees according to their first union project, and includes people whose projects were social reform, union building, personal advancement, and community leadership. The second column shows whether or not each person's project changed over the course of his or her work with a union. If it did change, the second column indicates the new project. The third column shows each person's final union project. If an interviewee still works for a union, the column indicates his or her current project; if the interviewee has left the union, the project he or she was pursuing at the time of departure is indicated. Finally, the fourth column indicates whether the interviewee still works for a union. If the interviewee works for a union, a project is indicated; if the interviewee does not, the space is blank.

Chart 6.5 shows the two important ways in which people's projects interacted with their union leadership careers over time. Most adapted their projects to union work or left the union. Indeed, we found that most of our interviewees became union builders, and most of the union builders continued working for unions. Only 11 people began as union builders, but 38 developed a union building project at some point in their union career. Most of those who did not become union builders left union work. Of the 7 people who developed new kinds of projects, all but 2 left. Those who placed family concerns first left, as did 2 of those who became entrepreneurs.

The major exception to this pattern of adaptation or exit, however, is that of the social reformers. Of the 36 original social reformers, 22 continue to work for unions. Thirteen of these remain social reformers. Only 8 became union builders.

Becoming Union Builders

How and why did most of those who continued to work for unions become union builders? The pathway people followed was influenced by their original project.

Chart 6.5. First project, transition, and final union project with who stayed and who left

Name	First project	Second project	Last project	In or out
Henry Carl	SR	CL	CL	
Linda Davis	SR	FAM	FAM	
George Kaufman	SR	FAM	FAM	
Tom Nussbaum	SR	FAM	FAM	
Ralph Reeves	SR	PA	PA	
Nick Martin	SR	UB	ENT	
Sam Hoffman	SR	UB	UB	
Eli Altman	SR	UB	UB	
Rom Giannini	SR	UB	UB	
Sam Rosenberg	SR	SR	SR	
Lloyd Callahan	SR	SR	SR	
Rudy Del Castillo	SR	SR	SR	
Norm Dunn	SR	SR	SR	
Laura Feirman	SR	SR	SR	
Ellen Atwood	SR	SR	SR	SR
Nydia Elizondo	SR	SR	SR	SR
Karen Emory	SR	SR	SR	SR
Carol Lewin	SR	SR	SR	SR
Nancy Masterson	SR	SR	SR	SR
Colin Gordon	SR	SR	SR	SR
Eric Marcovich	SR	SR	SR	SR
Liam O'Reilly	SR	SR	SR	SR
Neil Rosen	SR	SR	SR	SR
Kevin Rogers	SR	SR	SR	SR
Karl Stephens	SR	SR	SR	SR
Dianne Burton	SR	SR	SR	SR
Tom Weinberg	SR	SR	SR	SR
Ulrich Darden	SR	UB	ENT	ENT
Neil Eaton	SR	UB	UB	UB
Rob Harrington	SR	UB	UB	UB
Henry Podack	SR	UB	UB	UB
Kathrine McCarthy	SR	UB	UB	UB
Clem Donlevy	SR	UB	UB	UB
Charles Harris	SR	UB	UB	UB
Charles Keaton	SR	UB	UB	UB
Vic Robinson	SR	UB	UB	UB

Name	First project	Second project	Last project	In or out
Karen Williams	UB	UB	UB	UB
Ernie Fredricks	UB	UB	UB	UB
Dick Gonsalves	UB	UB	UB	UB
Sam Hendricks	UB	UB	UB	UB
Van Sanders	UB	UB	UB	UB
Edward Schneider	UB	UB	UB	UB
Wendy Martinez	UB	UB	UB	UB
Sid Iang	UB	UB	UB	UB
Sean Reardon	UB	FAM	UB	UB
Ellen Gardner	UB	UB	UB	
Ken McHenry	UB	UB	UB	
Debra Brown	PA	UB	UB	UB
Sam Alioto	PA	UB	UB	UB
Ken Brown	PA	UB	UB	UB
Nathan Berman	PA	UB	UB	UB
Eliot Rudnick	PA	UB	UB	UB
Lionel Rivera	PA	UB	UB	UB
Arnold Stokowski	PA	UB	UB	UB
Dave Mills	PA	UB	UB	UB
Dan Landers	PA	UB	UB	UB
Len Thomas	PA	UB	ENT	
Walter Brown	PA	PA	PA	
Linda Donatello	CL	UB	UB	UB
Don Bertlesman	CL	UB	UB	UB
Carlos Sanchez	CL	UB	UB	UB
Cal Lopez	CL	UB	UB	UB
Karl Norman	CL	UB	ENT	ENT
Rick Borjas	CL	CL	CL	CL
Bob Alcala	CL	CL	CL	
Oscar Herrera	CL	CL	CL	
Dick Lara	CL	CL	CL	
Nicolas Manriquez	CL	CL	CL	

KEY SR = Social Reform   UB = Union Building
CL = Community Leadership   FAM = Family Interests
PA = Personal Advancement   ENT = Entrepreneurship

From Personal Advancement to Union Building

For the 11 people who began union work as a way to advance their careers, 9 became union builders as their commitment grew and they began to find greater meaning in their work. For example, Dave Mills, who we discussed above, entered union work in order to "move up." Once elected local business agent, he derived satisfaction from doing his work well, and his job began to take on new meaning.

He earned a reputation for competence, as "the business agent who could win any grievance."

> I became known as the drunk's best friend and the crook's best friend. . . . Man, I became like an attorney. And if I could nail the employers on any-thing—a technicality or whatever—I would. I would nail them on it. . . . But the one thing [that] . . . going to college gave me [was] an idea of how to prepare some things—prepare cases and stuff like that. Oftentimes, I was dealing with terminal managers [who had] never gone to college, or super-visors who never had the experience. [These were people who] just came off a truck and became a supervisor. And the BAs didn't have much formal education. So I think that helped a lot. I had some very good decisions in cases I had. I organized workers. I mean, I did a lot of things. And so I got a pretty good vote.

After Mills won re-election to a second term, a regional union leader who had taken a liking to him asked him to become a full-time lobbyist for the union in Sacramento, the state capital. Mills had an interest in politics and took the job, even though he had to resign his elected position in the local. Although he learned a lot from the union's chief lobbyist, he became restive at having to follow someone else's orders. He also longed for "more direct contact with members."

Mills quit his lobbying job, went back to driving a truck, and began his campaign to be elected as secretary/treasurer of his local. He won a key posi-tion of local leadership and developed his union building project more fully.

> Yeah, one of the things I wanted to do was to get the collective bargaining straightened out. . . . I don't care who you were in the local union. We didn't like the outcome of the 1970 negotiations, and we wanted to change it in '73. So, that was one thing. Health care, getting the best health care program we could for members, and a retiree health care program—[we] wanted to do that. I emphasized and argued for more money and better pension program. . . . I wanted to get collective bargaining agreements for members

... reviving stewards meetings, getting members involved in the process
... establishing some kind of solid and secure financial position.

Mills went to work for a union, because it offered him an opportunity for personal advancement. As with other personal advancement seekers, however, Mills's project became one of union building, as he grew more successful, experienced the rewards that went with success, and relished the opportunity to make a difference.

From Community Leadership to Union Building

Linda Donatello exemplifies the five community leaders who became union builders and continued to do union work. She became active in the union as a leader of a small group of teachers organizing to protest the changes a new principal introduced. At this point, she was motivated by helping her co-workers win the grievance; she had a community leadership project.

> I was finding myself kind of fascinated by doing some of the background work for this particular grievance. And so I did it. And I clearly became the lead person. . . . Number one, it interested me. Two, I had the time to do it, and I was willing to do it. I did not see myself as taking that on for any other reason but that. I did not see the beginning of a new career [or] anything along that line.

After the teachers won their grievance, Donatello became more and more active in the union, and discovered she was skilled at the work.

> So anyway, I started becoming *extremely* active in the Grievance Committee, to the point that I began going to represent teachers at level one, which was the site level of the grievance hearing. [I] started out having the staff person with me . . . [and] graduated, so to speak, to doing it on my own. . . . So I began then being involved in helping prepare the cases to go to binding arbitration. And I became almost like an assistant to the staff person. Just clearly I was spending more and more and more of my time involved in doing that kind of thing, doing some other things within the organization, and maybe helping to write newsletters or articles for the newsletter. Then people found out I could write and make stuff clear.

Gradually, as Donatello devoted more of her energy to persuading others to join the union, the union came to occupy a more central role in her life. Her project became one of union building. The "clincher" came when the state union representative, looking for new leadership to revitalize a local that had been in an ongoing jurisdictional fight with another union, asked her to run for local president.

Donatello served as president of her local, which eventually included the entire city, for ten years. As is the case with many union builders, her greatest satisfaction comes from bargaining and representation:

> All through my time being involved in the organization, I had continued to be involved in grievance handling . . . preparing for arbitration, [and] working with lawyers when we took cases to arbitration. And that always was my life . . . But it was something I really liked and enjoyed, and I did it. . . . There's always the challenge coming up with a document that you can be proud of that does good things for teachers—that strengthens their rights. I used to say that we'd know when we'd gone as far as we could go in bargaining when all that was left to negotiate was the quality of the toilet paper that was in the teachers' restrooms. . . . Obviously, when you go to the bargaining table, you don't go as an individual; you go as a team. . . . [But] there are sections of the contract that I can [point to and] say, "I did that. That was mine." [. . .] [There are] things in there that I know I helped make teachers' lives better. . . . So *that* I'm very proud of [that]. . . . The whole idea of teacher self-esteem, self-respect—that's going to be a forever battle.

Donatello began her union work as leader of a workplace-based community. As she gained more experience, however, she earned more responsibility and became increasingly competent at her work. She came to redefine her project in more institutional terms of building a union to make a difference in the lives of its members.

From Social Reform to Union Building

Of the 22 social reformers who continued to work for unions, 8 did so as union builders. For Charles Keaton, the transformation of his broad social reform project into one of union building occurred around his decision to seek full time union work. A faith-based social reformer, Keaton found his way to the Carpenters Union via the UFW. After getting married and taking time off to travel around the world, he thought about returning to the UFW. Ultimately under the pressure of having to earn a living, Keaton decided that he could blend his social reform agenda with a career as a carpenter.

> I think I realized at the time, too, that a lot of activities could take place through rank-and-file carpenters. . . . People could still be involved in movement issues without necessarily working full time. . . . So I did a little shift in consciousness. . . . I became a journeyman. . . . We also had a group

called the "Concerned Carpenters." [. . .] Some people that were much more politically oriented—RCP [Revolutionary Communist Party] people and stuff like that—were involved. . . . They sort of pulled away. They got bored with the thing, but I kept it going. Well, we had meetings and mailing lists and putting out a newsletter every so often. There [was] probably a core group of six or seven of us [in different locals].

When he moved to Orange County so that his wife could attend medical school, he decided to seek full-time union work and plunged right into local union politics. "I had been active in the local," he said, "and by that time, I was very clear [as to] what I wanted to do. I knew . . . probably by, like, 1980. It was very clear that I wanted to work full time for the union."

As Keaton decided to seek full-time union work, he began to redefine his project from one of broad social reform to one of union building. In 1982, he launched an "insurgent" campaign to become a local business agent and won. Although he found that the "day-to-day work of the union" took more time than he had expected, he led an effort to organize new residential construction. He continued to organize, won re-election in 1985 and 1988, and became active in municipal politics. Although Keaton narrowly lost re-election in 1991, the council executive secretary appointed him as a full-time organizer. He continues in that role and draws his greatest satisfaction from "redirecting union resources into organizing."

When asked how his politics had changed since he began his career, Keaton articulated this vision of union building in this way: "I have found that what's good for labor is usually good for the country. Abraham Lincoln said, 'Any man that tells you that he loves America, yet hates labor, is a liar.' "

Henry Podack is another social reformer who found his way into a union as a social worker. After graduating from the University of California at Berkeley, he joined the AFSCME when it began organizing in the welfare department where he found work. His decision to enter union work, however, was not rooted in an ideology of social reform, but occurred almost casually. "I forget why," he said. There was an issue that came up that I ended up representing our side of the building there . . . and just continued on . . . I think I got lucky on my first grievance and decided I had talent." Podack was elected steward and later chief steward; he began to get a "fever" for union work when he began organizing and competing successfully with other public sector unions. "That was a very exciting organizing campaign," he recalled, "one of those where if you win your first one, you kind of get the fever."

After going to work for the union as a full-time organizer in another city, Podack returned home to establish a base. He built a regional council and was elected to lead it. Despite backing a losing candidate for International president, he won election to the national executive board of his union.

When asked about the satisfaction he had in his work, Podack described his excitement about what a union can do for people:

It's working directly with our members in some struggle. One was in Eureka in '96. We had a county strike there. And it's when you see the troops really get a sense that they have some power. I mean, even the grievance wins when they realize that if you fight about it and you persist, and you fight smart, you can win some of these things. It's watching them feel empowered, I think, [that] is the greatest thing for me. . . . Well, I love to get involved in this. I'd rather do this than sit in the office and shuffle papers. I'm not a good administrator. My title is director, and that to me is hilarious. I love to mix it up in the field.

For Podack, the union offered a pathway to a successful career; it provided him with opportunities to do work he loved and to act on his social reform impulse. When asked to compare his politics today with those of his "Berkeley years," he described his move toward pragmatism, particularly at the local level:

I will have to admit that I have fallen victim to the concept of pragmatism on many occasions where I just did not see a viable alternative. Nor did I feel that maintaining a real radical position [was prudent], outside of making myself feel good and allowing me to say I'm a radical. . . . I still think I'm closer to the radical than the conservative. . . . And I've been to and worked for this union [in] Africa and [in] Asia and places. And so I come back thinking, "You know, we don't worry about dysentery every day. And we don't worry about some of the things." [. . .] I think my politics have been influenced by just my appreciation for how things work. . . . A lot of the shift for me has been to more local politics than national.

Thus, many union leaders—whose projects had been personal advancement, community leadership, or social reform—became union builders. Although they placed different emphasis on acting on their values, serving their constituency, or developing as effective leaders, their concerns came together in the "larger" project of building the union.

Not everyone became a union builder, however. Most who did not found that sticking with their project required moving on—except for the social reformers.

Staying the Course and Staying In: Social Reformers

Those who found ways to pursue their initial projects within unions but without becoming union builders were almost all social reformers. How did they do that? Six of them became part of efforts to change their unions. Seven others found ways to "negotiate" free spaces within their unions in which to pursue their projects.

Four of the thirteen social reformers who stayed the course went to work for HERE and remain there today. No one in our sample who went to work for HERE ever changed his or her project. This pattern suggests that, rather than HERE changing the social reformers, the social reformers helped to change HERE. Indeed, each interviewee who went to work for HERE took part in efforts to transform that union from an old-time business union into a social movement union.

Interestingly, the stories HERE leaders tell about their careers in the union have certain common elements. They took part in a formative political struggle soon after going to work for HERE. In that struggle, they formed relationships with allies that continue to sustain their union work today.

For instance, Liam O'Reilly, the faith-motivated social reformer discussed above, got involved in a bitter election campaign a few years after he went to work for a HERE local. That election, he told us, was fundamentally a fight "about the future of the union." He supported "the only person who understood organizing" or who was committed to making wholesale changes in the way the local was run. His candidate won the election. However, the power struggle continued because some of the staff had been on the losing side of the election, and they fought tooth and nail against change. O'Reilly was part of the small group of staff and rank-and-file union members who began to meet in the evenings and after work—he called it the "night shift"—to "talk about where [they] needed to take the union." This small group organized others and eventually won broad support for transforming the local union. Today, O'Reilly is still in touch with people from this "leadership group" who helped to convert the local into the kind of organization that fights for "justice" and "fairness."

While O'Reilly's story offers insight into how social reformers contributed to the transformation of a single local, Colin Gordon's experiences illuminate ways in which they contributed to changing the national union. O'Reilly was hired by Gordon, the unaffiliated social reformer whose journey to HERE via the UFW is recounted above. Gordon's first job was as strike coordinator for the local, a job that brought him into contact with Vincent Sirabella, HERE's legendary organizing director, and John Wilhelm, HERE's current president.[7] After directing a large and successful hotel strike, Gordon became organizing director of the local and formed an organizing team that included O'Reilly. Two years after coming to work for the local, Gordon was recruited to join the International staff and eventually became part of Sirabella's national organizing team. As a member of this team, he helped to reorganize several locals that had been trusteed by the International union. Today, he is president of a major local, a position to which he was elected after helping to revi-talize the local while in trusteeship. When we asked him what he had done to turn around the local, he emphasized his tools for bringing about organiza-tional change: team development, membership involvement, and organizing. "The plan," he said, "was to build a team of people so that we could, first of all, involve the members in the union and put the union into their hands. And then figure out how to approach organizing." Gordon remains a social reformer, having helped to transform HERE into the kind of union where one can pursue a social reform project.

Other social reformers who "stayed the course" told us about their efforts to change their organizations. Although they tended to suffer more political reverses than HERE leaders, they continued to do union work because they found "free spaces" that allowed them to sustain their projects. They also were often tied to a social reform network through which they could sustain their commitment.

One example is Tom Weinberg, a vanguard social reformer who led a suc-cessful insurgency in his local union. About a year-and-a-half after joining, he ran successfully for steward and then the executive board. Frustrated with how little he was able to accomplish in those positions and looking for another way to have more influence, he started an underground newspaper. Targeting "workers, families, and customers," it afforded him a way to conduct "propa-ganda campaigns" to solve problems he could not solve under the contract. Two years later, he ran against the incumbent local president, using the news-paper to articulate his broader view of unionism. That campaign proved to be a formative political battle. On the slate with him were two women, one of whom was a black Latina; a "young Latino guy" who would become his closest ally in the union; and a Japanese man. Weinberg won the presidency, but the old guard, with support from the International, Red-baited him and got the election thrown out. So he ran a second campaign and won again.

Consolidating power took a while, however, because many of the people on the executive board still opposed Weinberg. He built support by doing a good job at union work, focusing on race and gender issues, and reaching out to women and minorities in the union and in the community. Although these priorities fit with the politics of his vanguard group, he turned them into prac-tical successes. He won a breakthrough private-industry pay equity agreement, ran a campaign to keep local pay offices open ("Save Our Services"), and mobilized community support to win Martin Luther King's birthday as a paid holiday. Success encouraged the International president to make peace with him; therefore, after eight years as local president, he accepted an offer to work for the international as a regional director. His early ally, the "young Latino guy," became the new local president. Three years later, the International president asked him to become the national research director, with the under-standing he was being groomed to be his successor.

The International president did not survive the next election; the fact that Weinberg's political prospects depended on this relationship ended his rise in the union. Although he still serves as national research director, Weinberg has little power to continue his efforts to transform the union. However, he remains a social reformer and, looking back on his career, describes himself as "an agitator" who continually "adapts to the situation in which he finds himself." He is fighting to get the labor movement to live up to its "responsi-bility to workers and working families," a responsibility he sees as extending far beyond "those people who are unionized." While serving on the Interna-tional staff, Weinberg has organized a coalition to fight deregulation, a fight he considers crucial.

Weinberg is a social reformer who stayed the course, even in the face of set-backs and disappointments. His early successes as a local president enabled him to align his social reform project and his union work. Remaining in close contact with members of the vanguard group with whom he originally trav-eled to southern California has supported that effort. Although his efforts to transform his union appear to be stymied, Weinberg has found a "free space" from which he continues to pursue his project.

Why Some Social Reformers Became Union Builders and Others Did Not

A lingering question is what differentiates the social reformers who found ways to pursue their projects within the labor movement from those who became union builders? Two differences stand out. First, the social reformers who became union builders tended to be recruited from inside the workforce (75 percent). In contrast, 9 of the 13 (70 percent) who remained social reform-ers were recruited from outside. More specifically, most of those who became union builders were unaffiliated social reformers employed in the work force represented by the union they went to work for. Only 30 percent of those who retained their project had been so employed.

A second difference relates to the kind of work people did early on in their union careers. Of the social reformers who became union builders, only 3 out of 8 (38 percent) had worked as full-time organizers for a substantial period of time prior to their 1984 interview. This is in contrast with the social reform-ers who stayed the course, 11 out of 13 (85 percent) who worked as full time organizers (3 of the 5 who left to pursue their social reform projects had also worked as full time organizers).[8]

This suggests that the social reformers who stayed the course may have brought a greater purposefulness with them into their union work, a purposefulness that led them to take the union job—organizer—that required the greatest commitment. And organizing in turn may have reinforced their belief that union work was a way to pursue broad social change. In contrast, social reformers who found their way to the union via the workplace may never have been as convinced about the contribution of union work to social reform.

Leaving the Union

Some of the labor leaders we interviewed left union work. Why did they leave? Research on the careers of union leaders of an earlier generation shows that many went into management. In this generation, however, most of those who left unions continued to do work broadly related to labor's mission. Why didn't they pursue this work within their unions?

We looked at several factors to see whether they were associated with staying and leaving—including gender, ethnicity, religion, class, education, family background, marital status, recruitment, first union job, and mentors and sponsors. We concluded that people's projects had the strongest impact on their decision to stay in or leave. As has been illustrated, people who became union builders stayed with the labor movement. With the exception of the social reformers, however, those who did not become union builders often left the movement. And most of those who adopted new projects, like prioritizing family first or the pursuit of entrepreneurial careers, also departed.

Chart 6.6 displays the projects of those who left, why they came to leave, and the kind of places to which they went. The chart indicates that, of the 22 people who left union work, four were social reformers who found they could not pursue their projects by working for unions, and ten were community leaders or union builders (and one social reformer) who left after losing a political fight.

Keeping One's Project and Leaving the Union

All but one of the social reformers who left union work did so after concluding that pursuing their projects required exiting the labor movement. They came to this conclusion after many years of doing union work. Like almost all social reformers, they had experience as activists before coming to the labor movement. Moreover, all those who left had been recruited from the outside. This may be one reason why they found that they could leave of their own volition.

Laura Feirman was a middle-class, college-educated, unaffiliated social reformer who entered union work after being a community and antiwar

Chart 6.6. Last project, reason for leaving, and what they do now

Name	Last project	Why left	Where now
Rudy Del Castillo	Soc Ref	can't do project	NGO
Laura Feirman	Soc Ref	can't do project	NGO
Norm Dunn	Soc Ref	politics	Back to work
Sam Rosenberg	Soc Ref	can't do project	Journalist
Lloyd Callahan	Soc Ref	can't do project	Politics/Journalist
Ken McHenry	U. Builder	politics	Business
Rom Giannini	U. Builder	politics	politics
Eli Altman	U. Builder	politics	Government
Sam Hoffman	U. Builder	politics	politics
Ellen Gardner	U. Builder	venue changes	politics
Bob Alcala	Comm Ldr	politics	Business
Dick Lara	Comm Ldr	politics	Business
Nicolas Manriquez	Comm Ldr	politics	Business
Oscar Herrera	Comm Ldr	politics	Education
Henry Carl	Comm Ldr	politics	NGO
Walter Brown	Personal Advancement	can't do project	Business
Ralph Reeves	Personal Advancement	project change	Government
George Kaufman	Family	project change	Education
Tom Nussbaum	Family	project change	Government
Linda Davis	Family	project change	Social Service
Nick Martin	Entrepreneur	project change	Business
Len Thomas	Entrepreneur	project change	Business

activist. She left the labor movement after eighteen years of trying to find a place where she could "create the kinds of changes that really need to happen." During those eighteen years, she worked for some of the more progressive unions in the labor movement—SEIU, the Screen Actors Guild (SAG), and the National Writers Union (NWU). In 1991, Feirman finally decided to find other work.

> A bunch of things happened. . . . National health care goes down the tubes, in part because the labor movement can't get itself behind some real reform. NAFTA gets passed, in part because the labor movement has killed off all

the left wing people in Central America who could have helped them defeat it. A number of things happened that really changed my feelings about the labor movement relative to the rest of the progressive world. And, that needed to be bridged. That whatever happened next was not going to happen either exclusively in the labor movement or exclusively in the community sector and that we had to reconstruct the way the movement looked if we were ever going to win any of the things we needed to win again.

And the other thing that happened to me [was] I went back to something that had been a lot more important to me earlier and realized that I never again wanted to work in an organization that was basically white. . . . Race was my preeminent passion, and . . . I was really tired of working with people who were there by privilege. And I just was not interested anymore in that, and I no longer wanted to work in a situation where white people were in charge by fiat.

A year and a half after leaving her union job, Feirman created a nongovernmental organization (NGO) with the mission of "advancing progressive organizing and supporting the people who do it." She is currently the full-time director, overseeing programs that support organizers from a range of progressive groups, including some unions.

The other three social reformers who left the labor movement told similar stories of years invested pursuing their projects in the labor movement and eventually concluded that in order to do what they wanted to do, they had to leave. One of these, who was similar to Feirman, started an NGO that supports the organization of low-wage workers, often in collaboration with unions. Another became a journalist, political consultant, and public official who works closely with unions. The third became a journalist who played a leading role in national debates on public policy.

Losing a Political Fight and Leaving the Union

Ten of the labor leaders we interviewed left the union movement after losing political battles. Five of them were community leaders, four were union builders, and one was a social reformer. All those who left after losing political fights had been recruited from inside the work place, perhaps making them more reluctant to leave on their own accord. After leaving, the paths of union builders and community leaders diverged, with most of the union builders making their way into state politics and most of the community leaders repositioning themselves in a local business or other local enterprise.

The number of community leaders who left is notable, because it is such a large proportion of all those who stuck with this project: five out of six people.

Four of the five are Latinos who had articulated their project in terms of ethnicity rather than workplace. None had completed college when they entered union work, and all but one came from a working-class background. This suggests that community leaders who did not make the transition into union building found themselves ill-equipped—in terms of organizational relationships beyond their local communities, shared projects, or alliances—to survive political reverses. This might also help to explain why they turned to local enterprises rather than state or local politics after leaving their union.

By contrast, three of the four union builders who left after losing political fights had middle-class backgrounds; two had finished college before starting union careers. They also represent a much smaller proportion of union builders than is the case with community leaders. This suggests that union builders were usually able to regroup after suffering political losses rather than leaving, as the community leaders did. It is likely that union builders were able to develop a broader set of relationships, shared projects, and alliances than could community leaders. This might also help to explain why they made their way into state politics rather than into local businesses.

Rom Gianinni, for example, was a union builder who began union work as a social reformer. He was recruited by a growing SEIU local that represented the municipal workers of a city in which he had found work painting street lines. With good sponsorship in a growing union, he rose quickly and became a dedicated union builder. When he came to the attention of the national union leadership, which was looking for people with whom to beef up its local unions, he was appointed trustee of major locals in southern and northern California and eventually earned election to the national executive board. But when he ran for president of his local, he lost. Deeply shaken by his defeat, Gianinni began to reconsider his project. The national union offered him a variety of positions, carrying him until he decided on what to do. They supported him in his decision to go to work for the speaker of the Assembly. Now he is a political consultant, closely connected to unions.

Dick Lara, by contrast, was a community leader who was a Chicano activist long before he entered union work. As an activist, he became active in AFSCME by organizing his work place, winning election as steward and, eventually, as vice-president of his local. He then accepted a full-time union representative position, a post in which he served for seven years. During this period, however, Lara devoted much of his energy to organizing and leading a city-wide, "Alinsky style" community organization, which was linked more to his experience as a Chicano activist than as a union official. When his AFSMCE unit was decertified, he moved to SEIU to work as a business agent for a local branch of one of its statewide locals. He supported the formation of a separate local—part of the national union agenda—but had conflicts with

the national staff who fired him for insubordination. Although he pursued his
project by remaining active in local community organizing, he was out of a
job and began to sell insurance to make a living.

For Gianinni, like other union builders, recovering from a political loss was
personally difficult but made easier by his ties to the union he had been building. For Lara, however, it was the case that when he fell out of favor with the
union leadership, he found himself out of a job and without a union base on
which to depend. But like other community leaders, Lara drew upon his community ties to find work, those ties being of real value.

Changing One's Project and Leaving the Union

Eleven of the people we interviewed left their unions after they changed projects and did not find ways to pursue them within the labor movement. Five
left while in pursuit of projects with which we are already familiar. One social
reformer, Henry Carl, who became a community leader, left under the same
circumstance as other community leaders: political loss. Three social reformers—Altman, Gianinni, and Hoffman—who had become union builders, also
left after political losses. The one social reformer, Ralph Reeve, prioritized personal advancement and left to pursue his career.

Six others left to pursue new projects, developed in the course of their
union work. Three social reformers—Nussbaum, Davis, and Kaufman—left
to prioritize their family lives. Four people developed projects as entrepreneurs: Darden, Norman, Martin, and Thomas. And two of them, Martin and
Thomas, left the labor movement. All four "entrepreneurs" passed through a
"union builder" transition from initial projects of social reform (two), community leadership (one), and personal advancement (one).

"Family First" Projects

Three of our interviewees left their unions because their projects became less
important than giving priority to the quality of their family life. These people
decided to sacrifice work with the union for family interests. They articulate
this change in their project as an explicit decision associated with having small
children, having to make choices about parenting, and so on.

Our interviews show that union leadership work often creates serious tensions between work and family. In three cases, these tensions were resolved
(though often at serious costs to family life) with project changes which were
in turn followed shortly thereafter by leaving the labor movement. All three
of those who made this transition were former social reformers, and two were
men. They came from middle-class families and had finished college. The

woman came from a working-class, union family but had not yet finished college when she began her union work.

Tom Nussbaum is a middle-class college graduate and social reformer who went to work for SEIU through a community organization with ties to the labor movement. He became the chief political operative of a major public sector local, a position of influence inside and outside of the labor movement. When he had two children, he became increasingly compelled by his role as a parent.

> I was fully involved in parenting, probably really just in terms of the joy of raising kids. It seems to be my particular passion. . . . I did a bunch of psychotherapy, which I found very powerful. I think my conclusion, after all is said and done, was that my family was first and foremost. Which isn't an unusual conclusion. But [I realized] that, on a personal level, I wasn't going to work 60 hours a week again—that I needed to find a different path.

He found a way to spend most of a year at home, doing part-time work and focusing on parenting. He then returned to work part time as community liaison for a major university.

Two other former social reformers, George Kaufman and Linda Davis, also left union work to put their families first. One continued to work with unions, but as an educator attached to a university rather than as an active union leader. Davis found her life "transformed" by motherhood, returned to school, and became a child therapist. Thus, although these three social reformers found they could not reconcile the priority they wanted to give to family life with a career in the labor movement, they did find ways to pursue public service careers.

Entrepreneurial Projects

Four interviewees—two of whom left union work—developed entrepreneurial projects. These people turned their energies to initiating and developing their own enterprises—including, but not limited to, private businesses. For them, union work created the opportunity for new pursuits outside the union.

When compared with studies of earlier generations of union leaders who left unions, it is remarkable that so few in this generation turned to entrepreneurship. Although two had begun as social reformers, a third as a community leader and a fourth seeking personal advancement, all of those who developed entrepreneurial projects passed through a union building period. They had been successful in their union building, but it seems to have left them dissatisfied.

They also seem to have been well equipped to pursue new projects of their own. Three had come from middle-class families and two had finished college.

In the course of their union work, they all had acquired new skills, relationships, or resources that served them well in their new ventures.

Len Thomas's project trajectory went from personal advancement to union building to entrepreneurialism. Growing up in a troubled, middle-class family, he dropped out of high school and earned his high school equivalency degree in the Army, where he learned rocketry. Upon discharge, he found work in an aerospace plant represented by the UAW. The union steward recruited him, and the union offered him a way up by "getting people together to make things work better." As a "union builder," Thomas organized a new local, was elected president, and joined the UAW regional staff as an International representative. His "union building" project was shaken, however, when he was laid off due to industry cutbacks. He then tried his hand at politics. His candidate lost but asked him to join him in a business venture in Taiwan. The venture did not succeed, so he returned to the plant when recalled. When he was assigned to NUMMI, the joint General Motors/Toyota enterprise in Freemont, California, Thomas developed a deep interest in the Toyota system, "interdependent industrial enterprise." This became his new "entrepreneurial" project. He briefly headed a joint labor-management training program. Thomas then pursued it as a Vice President with a major aircraft firm, responsible for training in the new system. While there, he earned his MBA, despite having never attended college. When he parted ways with management, he continued his project by joining a consulting firm as a passionate advocate of the Toyota system.

For Thomas, then, the union offered him an avenue for personal advancement and a union building career during which he could acquire new skills, relationships, and commitments. These enabled him to become a dedicated advocate of a new industrial design system—his "entrepreneurial" project— that opened new opportunities for him outside the union. The other entrepreneur who left attended Harvard Business School, held a high post in the Clinton Labor Department, and began his own internet start-up company.

CONCLUSION

We began this paper by asking where the current generation of California union leaders came from. What are their backgrounds? Why did they come to work for unions in an era in which unions seemed neither a way up nor at the heart of a social movement? Why did union work change some? Why did some work to change their unions? Why did many stay? And why did others leave?

Drawing on a unique longitudinal data set, we discovered that many of the demographic variables often used to explain social action—and the career choices of earlier generations of union leadership—did not, in themselves, explain much about this current generation of labor leaders. Instead, what mattered were their projects; that is, how they conceived what they were trying to do. Projects help us understand the diversity of reasons why people came to work for unions, how those reasons evolved, and why, in some cases, they became reasons to leave.

Why Did They Come?

Some came to work for unions for traditional reasons. For some, it was because the union had made a big difference in their lives, and they came to believe that "building" the union was a goal worthy of their commitment. Others came seeking personal advancement, or a "way up." Some were leaders of communities—usually working-class and, in most cases, Latino. They thought unions could provide opportunities to serve those communities effectively. And some came on a mission of social reform, motivated by commitments to their faith, to vanguard politics, or to broad social change goals articulated via the movements of the 1960s and 1970s.

However, except for those from working-class families who were radicalized in college, few of those pursuing social reform found their way directly into the labor movement. Most passed through "bridging organizations," such as the United Farm Workers, the Citizen's Action League, or some other activist group. Their goals, organizational alliances, and the networks they had forged ensured that these organizations bridged the world of "the movement" to that of organized labor. Without them, it is unlikely that most of the social reformers would have found their way to unions.

Why Did They Stay?

Our most interesting finding is the process by which some people's projects changed as they turned to union building as the project most consonant with that of their organizations, while others sustained their projects, finding ways to work at changing their unions.

First of all, we observed a process of adaptation. All of those who began as union builders remained union builders. Ninety percent of those who began seeking personal advancement became union builders, as did 50 percent of those who started as community leaders, and 36 percent of those who started as social reformers. However, we also observed a process of selection, as many of those who did not adopt a union building project left the labor move-ment—i.e., the one personal advancement seeker who did not "convert," 50 percent of those who started as community leaders, and 28 percent of those who started as social reformers.

But we also observed an exception to this pattern of convergence: the 13 social reformers, or 36 percent of the social reformers who were included in this study, remained committed to social reform and found ways to stay in the labor movement. Some became part of a concerted and successful effort to change their unions. Others found organizational "free spaces" in which they could trade pursuit of their projects for work the organization required.

It is also interesting to note that although social reformers—both those who became union builders and those who did not—made valuable contri-butions to the unions, the unions did not make any social reformers.

As we explain above, the common thread that runs through the back-grounds of the middle class social reformers is their prior activist experience and bridging organizations. For working class youth going to college and encounters with radical faculty seems to have played a similar role. It may well be that the formation of their project with respect to work at a time of life that scholars associate with the formation of political identity (Kinder and Sears 1987; Plutzer 2002) occurred in those settings. So the project of social reform was something they brought with them into the labor movement, especially those who came to work from the outside, thereby giving them a stronger predisposition to persist. In contrast are those, the union builders, who defined their work project in the labor movement. The personal advance-ment seekers seemed to have no clearly formed project with respect to work, coming to the union more as a matter of opportunity or convenience. They developed their union building project after becoming successful. Commu-nity leaders were most like social reformers in conceiving their work project in the context of their community, rather than in the organization of which they became a part, their union.

Why Did They Leave?

Only a minority of the people in our study left union work: 22 out of 68 (32 percent). Those who did leave rarely did so because of "burn out." About half of those who left lost political fights and either could not or did not regroup. The other half left because they could not pursue their projects while working for a union. For some, it was their original projects—as with the social reform-ers and community leaders who left—that pulled them away. For others, it was a new project—as with those who decided to prioritize their family lives or pursue entrepreneurial endeavors. Regardless of the reason, most who left did not turn against the labor movement but went on to do work broadly consistent with its goals. In reflecting on this finding, however, it is important to note that the people interviewed in this study had many years of service as leaders behind them.

For scholars of the labor movement, social movements, organizations, and leadership, our findings demonstrate the value of studying agency systematically. Although data drawn from interviews, especially when retrospective, has its limitations, it nonetheless offers valuable insights into how people's intentions influence their actions, how these intentions change over time, and how intentions interact with the organizations within which people work. It can never be enough to assume undefined "interests" as a theory of motivation; this is particularly important when considering organizations like unions, which are rooted in non-economic values. It is important to note that this approach makes visible the relationship—and the tensions—between individual and organizational change. Finally, given the work of leaders in the lives of organizations, learning how agency works is essential for understanding how leaders develop.

We also hope that our study is valuable for union leaders. It will, no doubt, be interesting to the people we interviewed. More importantly, however, we hope they will contribute some valuable insights on why people work for unions. Indeed, our study suggests that it may be more fruitful to focus on why people stay in the labor movement than on why they leave it.

Perhaps reflecting on their own experiences, leaders of today's unions have reduced their reliance on "bridge organizations." They have committed themselves to direct outreach to today's generation of social reformers through the Organizing Institute, Union Summer, Living Wage campaigns, and the like. But it takes more than social reformers to build a union. It takes union builders, too. Our study underscores the fact that these union leaders often came from the workplace. They are people whose direct experience persuaded them of the difference a union can make in one's life. Those who came to work for "personal advancement" reasons also became union builders—as their skills, relationships, and commitment to their organizations developed. In fact, for almost everyone, the union building project was related not only to his or her initial union experiences but also to the extent to which the union offered opportunities for their ongoing professional development.

A major concern is the high proportion of community leaders who could not find a place within the labor movement, particularly because of their roles in the Latino community. This may no longer be true. It may simply have been a consequence of the particular time period that our study covers. But it should give us pause.

If people leave their unions in order to pursue other goals, they are likely to continue their support of the labor movement. Union leaders would be wise to wish them well. If they leave after suffering political losses, this too may be an unavoidable cost of contested elections. Fortunately, opportunities for staff to move between unions have expanded, so those who lose their jobs in one union may find work in another. However even when losing an election ends a career, these costs remain part of a critical accountability mechanism in America's largest—and most egalitarian—representative organizations.

7

STICKING IT OUT OR PACKING IT IN?

ORGANIZER RETENTION IN THE NEW LABOR MOVEMENT

Daisy Rooks

I came away from the three-day with a sense that [organizing] was more of a devotion, than a job . . . [I thought that] it was similar to going into the Peace Corps, or entering the priesthood. I [told my mother]: This is a commitment. This is something that needs to happen and I am going to give it my all. I need to marry this occupation for as long as it suits me.

(ARLENE, ORGANIZED 1 YEAR)

Some hardcore organizers [who have been] doing it for 20 years would argue that [organizing] is not a job, it's a calling. [They argue] that you have to be willing to give your soul to do this kind of work. . . . They would say that you shouldn't even try [to be an organizer] if you have a family, but that's bullshit. If you are good at your job and like it, why not fix it so that you can keep those good people?

(JUNE, ORGANIZED 10 MONTHS)

In 1995, John J. Sweeney was elected president of the AFL-CIO in the first-ever contested election in the federation's history. Determined to reverse several decades of union decline, Sweeney pledged to infuse new life into the American labor movement by re-committing the movement to organizing massive numbers of unrepresented workers in a number of expanding industries across the country.

Sweeney's blueprint for revitalizing the labor movement had two central components. First, Sweeney urged affiliates to develop aggressive organizing programs that used militant tactics and strategies. There was strong support for these tactics among the unions that already used them, but other union leaders were quite skeptical. Sweeney countered this skepticism by referring to his own record as President of the Service Employees International Union (SEIU). While many unions suffered serious membership losses throughout the 1980s and early 1990s, Sweeney's SEIU grew rapidly. Sweeney argued that this success was due to the union's use of militant tactics and strategies.

Second, Sweeney challenged affiliate unions to commit 30% of their annual resources to support new organizing initiatives. He did not specify exactly how these resources were to be spent, but most unions used these resources to fund salaries for organizing staff,[1] developing and printing communications materials used in organizing drives, and organizers' travel expenses. This last category is often quite substantial—many organizers travel extensively, often living and working out of hotels for a substantial portion of the year.

As unions that supported Sweeney's change mandate began initiating scores of new organizing drives, it became painfully clear that they did not have the human resources necessary to staff these campaigns. Frustrated by this lack of skilled organizers, many unions turned to the AFL-CIO's Organizing Institute (OI) training program for help.

Established in 1989, the OI is responsible for annually recruiting hundreds of individuals to work as full-time union organizers.[2] The OI was founded to develop a cadre of organizers fiercely loyal to the militant organizing tactics and strategies later touted by Sweeney. Using specially developed materials, OI staff train new organizers in the mechanics of aggressive organizing, and educate them about the need to focus their efforts on recruiting vulnerable[3] workers most in need of union protections (see appendix).

The OI was originally a semi-autonomous entity of the AFL-CIO, and as such was funded largely by individual unions.[4] Soon after becoming President of the Federation, Sweeney merged the Institute into the AFL-CIO's new Organizing Department and dramatically increased its budget (Foerster 2000). This move acknowledged organizers' central role in the process of union change, and solidified Sweeney's commitment to supporting affiliate union's organizing efforts.

To date, the AFL-CIO and its affiliates continue to spend the majority of their organizing resources on maintaining organizing staff and funding their campaigns. Few unions devote any resources to providing the kind of training and mentoring necessary to insure the long-term retention of their organizing staff. Many argue that this failure to provide training and mentoring has resulted in high turnover rates among organizers and that high turnover rates have negative consequences for unions' organizing agendas (Early 1996 and 1998; Erem 2001; Feekin and Widenor 2000, 2001). Few would disagree that experienced, well-trained organizers are more effective than new organizers, and those with minimal training.

Given the clear link between retention and organizing efficacy, it is surprising that no systematic data on organizer turnover exist. No local or International unions have collected statistics on organizer retention, nor has the Organizing Institute compiled retention statistics about its graduates. Until such quantitative data on retention is available, it is impossible to accurately assess the extent of turnover among organizers, or know with any certainty what the average tenure for organizers is, or whether this has changed significantly over time.

In the meantime, qualitative research can address the issue of why some organizers leave and others remain in the job. This paper asks two questions: first, what factors motivate organizers to leave during their first year-and-a-half in the field? And second, what conditions facilitate enduring commitment among those who stay?

TURNOVER AND RETENTION IN "JUSTICE JOBS"

While little research has been conducted on union organizing as an occupation, there is a rich literature that examines turnover and retention trends among workers employed in occupations that I refer to as "justice jobs." Such jobs include poverty law, social work, human service provision, community organizing, and the like. These jobs share several important characteristics. First, workers are motivated by a basic commitment to helping others by providing basic services in under-served communities. Second, because practitioners work closely with disadvantaged clients in crisis situations, justice jobs are both emotionally draining and stressful. Last, because they are employed by non-profit organizations with limited resources, workers in justice jobs often receive low salaries and limited training, and have limited opportunity for promotion (Azar 2000; Katz 1978; Paquet, Deslauriers and Sarrazin 1999; McNeely 1989).

The general literature on occupations attributes turnover to demographic characteristics such as youth and life cycle, and occupational characteristics such as low salary and lack of prestige. In contrast, individual characteristics such as commitment and idealism and organizational characteristics such as limited training and mentoring are more likely to impact turnover in justice jobs (Azar 2000; Cannon 1998; Farber 2000; Grosch and Olsen 2000; Katz 1978; McDuff and Mueller 2000; Starr, Mizrahi and Gurinsky 1999; Wagner 1989; Weiss 1999).

Individual Characteristics

The literature on justice jobs suggests that idealism and expectation can have both a positive and negative effect on retention. On the positive side, it is crucial for recruiting individuals into justice jobs that offer low salaries and little prestige. Many workers are motivated by a sense of "idealistic altruism," a vague desire to help others or make the world a better place (Csikai and Rozensky 1997). Among the clergy, this social commitment is called a "calling" (Farber 2000; McDuff and Mueller 2000).

Idealism also strengthens workers' long-term commitment to justice jobs. The literature suggests that turnover is high among justice jobs. Many workers become frustrated by the long hours, lack of organizational support, and stressful working environments that characterize justice jobs, and quit. However, research has shown that many of these workers are subsequently employed by socially oriented, service-providing organizations (McDuff and Mueller 2000). Scholars refer to this trend as "global commitment," and acknowledge that idealism plays a significant role in cementing workers' long-term commitment to justice jobs (Becker 1992; Hunt and Morgan 1994).

Idealism can have a negative effect on retention as well, primarily by creating unrealistic expectations. Although many workers enter justice jobs with a strong belief in their individual ability to affect change, many quickly confront individual barriers to achieving their goals, such as waning patience and inability to manage stress effectively. Unable to affect the quantity or quality of change that they initially believed possible, many workers are unable to sustain their initial idealism and become frustrated. This frustration leads many to leave their jobs (Azar 2000; Reisch and Wencour 1986).

Aside from a belief in their individual ability to make change, workers routinely bring several other expectations to justice jobs. Many enter the field expecting to receive high quality training and mentoring on the job. However, due to limited organizational (staff and material) resources, many non-profit and social service organizations are unable to meet these expectations (Katz 1978). The literature also suggests that individuals enter justice jobs with a strong commitment to specific tactics and strategies for achieving change. Many expect that their employer organization will share their commitment to these tactics and strategies, but this is not always the case. The frequency with which workers' expectations are not met is an important cause of turnover in justice jobs (Reisch and Wencour 1986).

Although scholars acknowledge that structural factors often cause this tension between expectation and reality, many still propose individual-level solutions. Some suggest that individuals scale back or adopt more "reasonable" expectations to limit frustration and disillusionment (Azar 2000; Farber 2000; Koeske and Kirk 1995; Mondros and Wilson 1990; Starr, Mizrahi and

Gurinsky 1999). Others claim that aging will naturally correct for unrealistic expectations. They argue that as workers age and accumulate more occupational experience, they often adopt more realistic expectations. As a result, turnover tends to decrease with age (Farber 2000; Csikai and Rozensky 1997).

Demographic Characteristics

Research also shows that young workers and workers without family responsibilities are over-represented in justice jobs. The literature on traditional occupations would argue that young workers' prevalence in justice jobs reflects their general tendency to work in high-turnover jobs. Some argue that young workers are concentrated in low-wage, low-prestige and emotionally draining jobs because they are unqualified for jobs that are higher-wage, more prestigious and less taxing (Miller 1984; Newman 2000; Simpson et al. 1982; Tannock 2001). Others suggest that young workers seek these types of jobs because they are inherently resistant to occupational commitment (Miller 1984). Advocates of this position argue that as workers age and are better able to commit, they move into jobs with less turnover. Still others have attributed this phenomenon to labor market discrimination, claiming that high turnover is a direct response to employers' routine violation of young workers' rights (Newman 2000; Tannock 2001).[5]

The literature offers a variety of different explanations for the high concentration of youth in justice jobs. First, some scholars argue that youth are attracted to justice jobs because they are more idealistic than their older counterparts (Farber 2000; Csikai and Rozensky 1997). Others contend that young workers are concentrated in justice jobs because they are well positioned to cope with the emotional and temporal demands of the work. As workers age, they accumulate family and community responsibilities that often conflict with the extensive demands of justice jobs (Azar 2000).

The literature offers several suggestions for how older workers can balance this tension between work and family responsibility. Some older workers cope with this tension by leaving these occupations altogether in search of less demanding work. Others move off the "front lines"—away from direct service-provision and into supervisory roles. This strategy allows workers to minimize occupational stress and reduce work hours without abandoning their "global commitment" to justice jobs (Azar 2000).

Occupational Characteristics

Although the literature on traditional occupations argues that status and salary concerns cause most job turnover, the literature on justice jobs rejects such economic reductionism (Koeske and Kirk 1995; McNeely 1989; Paquet,

Deslauriers and Sarrazin 1999; Weiss 1999). Workers in justice jobs earn significantly less than individuals employed in the for-profit or business worlds.
Lower salaries, limited benefits and heavy reliance upon unstable funding
sources marks most of these jobs low-status. However, the literature on justice
jobs challenges the assumption that low status and low pay are the primary
cause of high turnover.

As mentioned above, few workers in justice jobs remain with a single
employer during their entire career, although many maintain a "global commitment" to social justice work (Becker 1992; Hunt and Morgan 1994).
However, changing jobs rarely improves workers' compensation, because most
justice jobs offer modest salaries. Research indicates that workers are most
likely to leave justice jobs to escape restrictive organization policies, improve
their working conditions, and so on. (Katz 1978; McDuff and Mueller 2000).
This suggests that structural factors such as working conditions, organizational structure, and working environment are equally, if not more important
than status and salary, in determining turnover.

ORGANIZATIONAL CHARACTERISTICS

The literature argues that although training and mentoring positively impact
worker retention, they are rarely available to workers in justice jobs. Many who
work in justice jobs are employed by organizations with limited resources.
This lack of resources renders them unable to adequately support their staff
(Azar 2000; Cannon 1998; Weiss 1999). Lack of adequate training undermines
workers' competence. These feelings of incompetence exacerbate occupational
stress, which often induces staff turnover (Farber 2000). Lack of training also
undermines workers' ability to affect the nature and quality of change they
had expected. As mentioned above, frustration about their inability to make
change often drives turnover.

Although mentoring is important for most workers, it is essential for surviving the stressful, emotionally draining work that is typical in justice jobs.
Because so few of these workers have no access to formal mentoring or
support, many workers turn to informal support networks to sustain them in
the face of the frustration and disappointment common to justice jobs.
Although these support networks are positive, their effectiveness is undermined by the high staff turnover that marks justice jobs. High turnover
reduces the number of experienced staff members available to mentor and
support new employees (Katz 1978).

Organizing as a Justice Job

Before applying the insights of this literature to union organizer retention, it is important to assess whether union organizing is indeed a justice job. As noted above, justice jobs share three characteristics; workers are motivated by a basic commitment to helping others, the work is quite stressful and emotionally draining, and workers often receive low salaries, limited training, and have limited opportunity for promotion.

There are many similarities between justice jobs and union organizing. Like workers in justice jobs, union organizers are motivated by a strong commitment to helping others.[6] Union organizers demonstrate this commitment by playing a variety of roles during organizing drives. They are responsible for recruiting, educating, motivating and "inoculating"[7] workers throughout organizing drives. They recruit, train and supervise a core committee of dedicated union supporters who are responsible for organizing their co-workers to support union representation. Organizers also document abuses during the campaign, in some instances filing legal actions against offending employers (Erem 2001; Lopez 2000; Markowitz 1999; Russo 1993).

Some have described unions as "greedy institutions" that make excessive demands on organizers (Franzway 2000). In the middle and later stages of an organizing campaign, union organizers work between 70 and 80 hours per week. Once an election date has been established, organizers are "on-call" virtually 24 hours a day (Erem 2001; Franzway 2000). This is necessary because campaigns rarely follow a predictable trajectory; pro-union workers are often fired during the organizing drive, employers routinely violate workers' rights, and union support fluctuates in relation to the intensity of employers' anti-union campaigns.

Like justice jobs, union organizing is quite emotionally demanding work. One reason for this is that unions lose more than half of their organizing campaigns, on average (Bronfenbrenner 1997; Bronfenbrenner and Juravich 1998). The hopelessness and inefficacy that organizers feel in the face of these losses often causes them to question their enthusiasm for the work. Many organizers also travel extensively, which isolates them from the emotional support of their friends and family (Erem 2001). Constant travel also routinely undermines organizers' efforts to establish support networks that could sustain them in the face of this disappointment.

Having demonstrated that there are many similarities between justice jobs and union organizing, this paper will apply the insights of this literature to understanding organizer retention and turnover. In particular, this paper will adopt a structural focus, in response to the literature's finding that structural characteristics of the workplace impact turnover in justice jobs. Second, this paper will evaluate the literature's claims that several specific factors impact

TABLE 7.1
Respondent characteristics by retention status

Characteristic	Stayers	Leavers	Total
Gender			
Male	4	5	9
Female	12	10	22
Race			
African American	2		2
Asian	2	2	4
Latino	2	3	5
White	11	10	21
Recruitment Status*			
External	12	13	25
Internal	4	2	6
Relationship Status			
Single	6	4	10
Coupled	9	9	18
Not sure		3	3

* "Recruitment status" indicates whether respondents were rank and file union members prior to becoming union organizers. "Internal recruits" were rank and file members and "external recruits" were not. Many "external recruits" were student, community, peace or environmental organizers before becoming union organizers.

turnover, such as idealism and expectation, life cycle, status, and training and mentoring.

METHODS

Respondent Interviews

This paper is based on in-depth interviews with 31 current and former union organizers and 12 individuals involved in the recruitment, training, and retention of staff organizers. Table 7.1 shows the characteristics of the first group of respondents, half of whom stayed and half of whom left the labor movement. All organizers in this sample completed the OI's entire field training program, which consists of three stages: a three-day classroom training on basic organizing skills, a ten-day field internship,[8] and a three-month apprenticeship (see appendix). Staff interviewed included local and International union organizing directors and current and former staff of the OI, as shown in table 7.2.

I located potential respondents using several methods. As a former employee of the OI, my personal contacts enabled me to gain access to program graduates across the country. I also contacted OI graduates whom I

TABLE 7.2
Organizing director and OI staff characteristics

OI staff	
Present	2
Former	6
Organizing directors	
Local Union	2
International Union	1
Other	1

TABLE 7.3
Post-Organizing occupations of respondents who were not
retained (N = 15)

Subsequent job	Number of leavers
Community organizing	2
Graduate or professional school	2
Homemaker or stay-at-home parent	1
Non-profit or social service sector	4
Other labor movement jobs (research, representational work, etc.)	3
High school teacher	1
Other	2

had recruited and/or worked with in the field during the time I was employed by the OI. Finally, I developed a "snowball sample," asking each respondent to recommend other OI graduates for me to interview. The combination of these methods proved quite successful, turning up far more leads than I was ultimately able to pursue.

Retention Measure

This paper uses a retention measure of one-and-a-half years. Organizers who remained working on new organizing campaigns longer than one-and-a-half years are classified as "stayers" and those who left within their first one-and-a-half years in the field are classified as "leavers." This year-and-a-half includes the three-and-a-half months spent in the OI field training program. Many of the stayers in this sample are currently organizing, and the rest organized for several years before leaving.

Most of the fifteen "leavers" left the labor movement entirely when they quit organizing. However, three retained a strong "global commitment" to the labor movement and are now employed as union researchers, OI staff, business reps, internal organizers or community and political organizers for unions (see table 7.3). Although internal organizers perform many of the same job duties as business agents or field reps, they focus on assisting workers organize collectively to solve shop-floor problems, instead of relying exclusively on the grievance procedure. Internal organizers do not organize new workers—that is the job of external organizers.

Despite the similarities between internal and external organizing, I classify internal organizers as "leavers," because internal organizing is noticeably less intense than external organizing.[9] Regardless of their global commitment, I also classify individuals employed in non-organizing jobs in the labor movement as "leavers." It is appropriate to make this distinction, because this paper explores the causes of turnover and retention among external organizers and is less concerned with documenting individuals' "global commitment" to the labor movement.

Interview Structure

Interviews generally lasted between forty-five minutes and two hours, and focused primarily on individuals' experiences during the recruitment and training process of the OI. Interviews also explored where respondents had worked since completing the program, emphasizing why they left the labor movement, if in fact they had. Respondents were also asked to share their perceptions about recruitment and retention trends within their unions and among their colleagues.

I asked the organizing directors and OI staff to describe their personal experiences in the OI program (where applicable), and comment more generally on a number of issues surrounding the recruitment and training of new organizers. I also asked long-term OI staff to reflect on changes that had taken place in the Institute since Sweeney's rise to power.

Of the organizers, sixteen of the interviews were conducted in person, taped and later transcribed. Fifteen of the organizers were conducted over the phone, simultaneously transcribed and not taped. Of the OI staff and organizing directors, four were conducted over the phone and eight in person. To preserve respondents' confidentiality, all proper names in the interviews have been replaced with pseudonyms. I deleted all references to specific local and international unions, geographic locations, and organizing targets for the same reason.

PACKING IT IN

Using the literature on justice jobs as a guide, this section will explore the impact of individual, demographic, organizational and occupational characteristics on union organizer retention. Because approximately half of the organizers in this sample do remain, the second part of this section explores three conditions that facilitate commitment: (a) compromise, (b) peer support groups, and (c) organizing success.

INDIVIDUAL CHARACTERISTICS

As anticipated by the literature on justice jobs, expectations influence organizers' occupational decisions. All of the organizers in this sample described a mismatch between their expectations about organizing and the reality they confronted in the field. This section will describe the three most common expectations with which organizers entered the field: (a) that "the new labor movement" is substantially different from its predecessors, (b) that increased diversity has resulted in more open discussions about race and racism within the movement, and (c) that new labor's emphasis on militant organizing tactics translates into true worker empowerment.

A New Labor Movement

Most individuals in this sample were initially attracted to union organizing because they believed that labor was undergoing a re-birth of sorts. Individuals who had been active in social movements during the 1990s were inspired by labor's re-emergence as a progressive, diverse, and militant force for social change. Carissa was attracted to organizing once she heard a "buzz" about the "new labor movement" at the progressive think tank where she was a summer intern.

> When I started hearing about the OI . . . it seemed like there was something new going on. A new movement was taking place, a turnover, a readjustment in the ways that people were thinking about things. Regardless of what had happened historically, it seemed like something really valid and exciting to get involved in. (Carissa, organized 4 months)[10]

Others, such as Kylie, were first exposed to "new labor" when an organizer spoke in their college class. The militant, worker-driven organizing model that the organizer described was drastically different than the model of unionism that she had been exposed to as support staff at a local union.

> I remember that [the presentation got] me thinking, "Wow, there's shit like this happening out there? It certainly isn't happening at my local. I can do

this!" We watched some videos about the Janitors and I got totally sparked watching them block doors . . . Civil disobedience seemed like the right thing to be doing. I liked the idea of it. (Kylie, former OI staff, organized 1-1/2 years)

In addition to an understanding that big changes were afoot in the labor movement, many entered the OI expecting that they would play a critical role in labor movement transformation. Carrie, an OI graduate and current Institute staff member, describes her reaction to early OI recruitment materials.

I just remember [that the original OI] literature said "the labor movement is in crisis." My [interpretation of] the message was "come save the labor movement because it's run by a bunch of idiots and dolts who don't know what to do." (Carrie, OI staff, organized 6 years)

Many middle class, college-educated recruits were initially hesitant to get involved, worried that their "outsider" status would undermine the contribution that they wanted to make. Although she initially had misgivings about organizing, Erin was ultimately convinced by the message that the new labor movement was in desperate need of people like her to help transform itself.

I feel like the labor movement is in a place right now . . . where we are in a tough fight. It's a life or death fight, and we need all hands on deck. We need commitment and talent wherever it exists. . . . In general that's the message. (Erin, former OI staff, organized 6 years)

Many organizers entered the field convinced of their centrality to efforts to reform labor, and expecting union staff and leadership to welcome them with open arms. They encountered a somewhat different reality, though.

New Labor and Diversity

In addition to believing that labor had been truly transformed, new organizers also entered the field with an expectation that "new labor" would be more diverse than its predecessor. This is true in two senses. First, new labor's organizing agenda has recruited many non-white (especially immigrant) workers into the movement. Second, Sweeney's administration has advocated for greater diversity among union staff and elected leadership.[11] The OI has helped diversify new labor's staff by recruiting organizers from several historically black colleges and by focusing efforts upon campus groups and community organizations with mostly non-white membership.[12]

Encouraged by these changes, many organizers of color such as Ryan entered the labor movement with an expectation that unions were a mechanism of empowerment for workers of color.

> After my internship with UNITE, I thought that labor was a really cool thing. [Initially] my take on labor was personal—I identified with it by way of racial empowerment rather than empowerment on the job. (Ryan, organized 4 months).

Although many new organizers were initially hopeful about new labor's potential to empower workers of color, they soon realized that new labor had adopted new methods for dealing with race and racism within its ranks. Organizers identified two main areas of stasis. First, despite pledges to organize more workers of color and confront racism in the workplace, unions still insisted that race remained tangential to class. Second, despite significant increases in the number of organizers of color, unions were still unwilling to candidly discuss racism within their ranks.

Emma describes how deeply embedded the belief that race is tangential to class is in union culture.

> There's definitely a school of thought in labor that if you are not dealing with labor issues, you are not doing anything. If you are dealing with race or other issues, you are off the program. [Race] is tangential to the party line . . . (Emma, former OI staff, organized 2 years)

Janet offers another example of this phenomenon. When she voiced her frustration about racism within the local's membership, she was instructed to try to unite members around their common class identity.

> [When I left] I was really depressed [because] I thought that the challenges of racism were just unconquerable . . . At our local—the Chinese were really against the blacks, and the blacks against the Filipinos, and the Filipinos wanted to be on their own. That kind of prejudice doesn't go away [by saying] "Come on guys, we need to stick together for the greater good!" (Janet, organized 1 year)

Although she tried to implement the union's strategy, Janet was deeply frustrated by its ineffectiveness, and by the union's unwillingness to honestly confront this racism. Ultimately, this frustration led her to leave organizing altogether.

Organizers were also quite frustrated by new labor's refusal to confront issues of racism within its own ranks. Nathan argues that unions' unwillingness to address racial tensions among staff undermines their ability to foster trust and respect among staff, which in turn undermines their ability to function efficiently.

> [Union folks are] stronger than most, but we could be so much stronger if somehow we honestly dealt with the diversity factor in the union itself. I think that we don't like to talk about it just like society itself [doesn't like to talk about it]. We think that just because we are in the union we are automatically above [racism], but we're not. It saps a lot of our energy. (Nathan, organizing 2-1/2 years)

While Nathan claims that unions passively neglect issues of race, Emma claims that unions consciously refuse to acknowledge racism in their midst. She claims that when non-white organizers discuss racism, their commitment to the labor movement is often questioned.

> I can think of one really blatant example where an Asian American intern tried to raise issues [about racism] with the lead organizer, and he was really rude to her and made her cry. He said, "That's not what we're concerned about here." (Emma, former OI staff, organized 2 years)

The OI has been instrumental in developing a diverse cadre of new organizers for the movement and the Sweeney administration has pushed for greater diversity within the rank and file and elected leadership of the movement. Inspired by these changes, new organizers enter the movement with high hopes about the diversity and openness of new labor. But they are often disappointed when they confront a labor movement that refuses to facilitate frank discussion about race and racism. As predicted by the literature on justice jobs, this frustration often leads organizers to leave organizing altogether.

Worker Empowerment

A third expectation that many new organizers bring to the field is that union organizing truly empowers workers. Many an organizers' decision to organize is rooted in a desire to empower workers. For female and non-white organizers, this desire to empower has a personal dimension. Having confronted discrimination in their own lives, many people of color such as Carrie become union organizers to help others confront discrimination.

> My experience [growing up] in West Virginia as a person of color was that fucked up things would happen to me, and that people were racist and hateful. [Working as an] organizer enabled me to empower people of color. (Carrie, OI staff, organized 6 years)

Although some organizers in this sample believe that they have been able to empower workers to fight oppression on the job, others are more ambivalent. Emma argues that unions rarely make good on the claims that they make about empowerment during organizing drives.

> [During the] organizing we always talk about leadership development and empowering workers, but the reality is that that doesn't necessarily happen . . . Once people join the union, they don't necessarily get the opportunity to take power and develop as leaders . . . (Emma, former OI staff, organized 2 years)

Others struggled to empower workers during the initial organizing drive. When Elsie and her co-workers' began to implement a democratic organizing strategy, their efforts were met with hostility and resistance from their host union.

> [When people in the regional] union office met some of the committee members and saw them interact . . . [they made it clear that] (a) this was not a committee that they are used to working with and (b) they don't really like working with committees like this. . . . It was pretty clear that we had really screwed up in putting a committee together that was empowered enough to assert itself and direct the campaign . . . From what we could see we hadn't screwed anything up. It seemed to be going really well. (Elsie, organizing 1-1/2 years)

Because the OI trains new organizers in worker-intensive organizing models, organizers expect to implement these strategies in the field. However, many host unions resist organizers' attempts to implement this model in the field, preferring that power be centralized in the staff organizers. Facing this mismatch between expectation and reality, many organizers tried to seek out placements where they would be able to implement this model. Elsie's commitment to worker empowerment influenced her to quit her job and seek out a position with a union that she believed shared her vision.

> [After my apprenticeship] the thought that this [participatory] strategy . . . was neither valued [by the union], nor something that was going to be part of any concerted program that I would do with them, made me hesitant to continue working for them. (Elsie, organizing 1-1/2 years)

Although labor's promise of worker empowerment appeals to new organizers, upon entering the field, many new organizers discover that many unions' organizing models do not truly empower workers.

Organizers' commitment to empowering workers and diversifying the "new labor movement" are examples of the expectations and commitments that new organizers enter the field with. This finding resonates with the literature on justice jobs by underscoring the importance of expectations and idealism in drawing new organizers to the work. Subsequent sections will demonstrate how organizers deal with the mismatch between their expectations and the reality that they confront in the field.

Demographic Characteristics

Young people tend to be concentrated in organizing jobs throughout the labor movement (Bensinger 1991; Bensinger and Porter 1993; Foerster 2000). This sample is no exception—many, though not all, of the organizers in this sample are relatively young (between the ages of 22 and 30) and only one was a parent. Although there is some disagreement on this point, many in the labor movement argue that young workers are concentrated in organizing due to the demanding nature of the work. This is consistent with the literature on justice jobs, which argues that younger workers are better equipped than older workers to satisfy the demands of organizing jobs because they have few personal/family responsibilities.

All of the organizers in this sample negatively describe the occupational demands placed on them. Kathryn claims that unions expect organizers to

> not have a life and put everything else aside, and make [organizing] absolutely the center of your life. . . . There's this theory out there that in organizing you [must] devote your entire life, and if you can't do that, you don't belong here. So there's a bit of that cowboy mentality. (Kathryn, organized 4 years)

Others, like June, criticized the negative impact that these demands have on organizers' families and personal lives.

> [My boss] puts in at least sixteen hours a day . . . He has three kids and he sees them every three or four months. That's it for them. He has not made them his priority . . . When (Laura, a former lead) was organizing, it said in her contact that the union would fly her home [every other weekend], but she wouldn't go most of the time. She had a husband in another state [when she started organizing, but] they were divorced within a year of being married. It just wasn't the most important thing to her. (June, organized 1 year)

Reflecting on the intensity of the work and the negative toll that it takes on organizers' personal and family lives, most in this sample were resigned to the fact that they would probably quit organizing when they start a family. Although many would prefer to remain organizing, their experiences in the field have convinced them that it is nearly impossible to be both a responsible parent and a good organizer.

> I would love to stay in the labor movement . . . but I can't be an organizer [because] I want to have a family and a life. I need to have regular hours. I'm going to be a mom and it's just too damn hard [to stay]. We only get four days off per month—that's what the contract says—and that's pretty common across the unions that are doing serious organizing . . . People who want to have a family, they get out of organizing. (June, organized 1 year)

While many are quite critical of these demands, others defend them. Erin argues that the difficulty of organizing necessitates the extreme demands placed on organizers. Instead of advocating that unions reduce their demands to accommodate parents, Erin argues that people should transition in and out of organizing in response to changes in their personal/family commitments.

> [Organizing is] a job that you have to be mentally available for 24–7. . . . That is determined by the fact that it's always an unfair fight. Management fights dirty, so we have to fight back. I want to be available and receptive for the people who are trying to organize, because they are enduring a real hard fight . . . My vision of how I want to do the job is not compatible [with being a parent]. . . . I do want to go back to [organizing] at some point when I can make myself available on those terms. (Erin, former OI staff, organized 6 years)

Erin's position is consistent with much of the literature on justice jobs, which suggests that workers "compensate" for these demands by moving off the front lines and into supervisory roles as they age and/or accumulate family responsibilities (Azar 2000). Contrary to the literature, though, organizing supervision does not offer a respite from these demands. To the contrary, it usually requires a more intense commitment of time and energy than front-line organizing positions.

Many leave organizing altogether as they age and/or begin families. As they age, organizers with strong "global commitment" to the labor movement move into jobs such as internal organizing, representational work, contract negotiations, member education, and so on. These jobs are indeed less stressful and less time-intensive than either organizing or supervising organizers, making them more attractive for older workers and those with children. Others leave the labor movement altogether, and find work in other socially conscious occupations such as teaching, community organizing, or social service (see table 7.3). The evidence presented above demonstrates that youth and life cycle are important factors that clearly impact organizer retention and turnover.

Occupational Characteristics

While the literature on justice jobs predicts that status and salary impact turnover, these factors are less salient for union organizers. Although entry-level union organizers earn significantly less than similarly qualified workers in the private sector, they earn more than workers in most justice jobs.[13] Entry-level union organizers begin at $24,000 with full health benefits, car insurance, a monthly allowance for car payments, and (in many cases) per diems when working away from home. After one year in the field, organizers make approximately $30,000 plus all benefits outlined above.[14] None of the organizers in my sample characterized their salary or benefits as inadequate, nor did any of the departed organizers claim that compensation compelled them to quit.

The issue of status is more complicated. Many argue that prior to the establishment of the OI organizers were the least respected, lowest paid and least valued of all union staff (Bensinger and Porter 1993; Foerster 2000). One long-term staff of the Organizing Institute describes organizers' low status prior to the Institute's establishment:

When [the OI started], organizing was a dumping ground where people [were put] who couldn't service or were a political liability. Unions were stacked to the gills with high-paid people who couldn't organize (Patricia, OI staff, organized 6 years).

Patricia explains that the OI was founded, in part, to correct this problem (Bensinger and Porter 1993).

> The OI was about creating a standard, about saying "you have to have a minimum level of skill to have an organizing job. This is not a job that you get demoted into. This is not an entry-level position. Instead, this is the hardest job in the union. . . ." (Patricia, OI staff, organized 6 years)

When asked whether the OI had been successful meeting this goal, the same former OI staff person replied,

> Yes, dramatically . . . [now] there's a career ladder within organizing by which people can be promoted. That gives [organizers] more resources and power and a voice within the union . . . (Patricia, OI staff, organized 6 years).

Many other staff (current and former) and OI graduates agree that organizers' status has improved significantly during the 13 years that the OI has existed. This reduces the likelihood that status is a central determinant of union organizer turnover. The limited impact of status and salary on union organizer retention represents the most significant departure from the literature on justice jobs. Although salary and status are real concerns for organizers, none in this sample reported leaving organizing in search of higher-paying or higher prestige work.

Organizational Characteristics

The literature on justice jobs suggests that the availability of quality training and mentoring influences workers' occupational decisions, and this research on union organizers supports this finding. As mentioned above, many new organizers enter the field with a strong belief (a) that the labor movement is in deep trouble, and (b) that their energy, talent, and commitment is necessary to reverse labor's downward spiral. By extension, many new organizers assumed that because they would play a central role in union transformation, unions would commit adequate resources to train and mentor them. Many were shocked when they encountered the direct opposite when they entered the field.

Kathryn, whose constituency group works closely with many new organizers, explains that many unions view new organizers differently than they expect.

> Some [unions] view the folks from the OI as cannon fodder. . . . It varies, but in most unions there's this feeling that [OI grads] are just college kids, and that they can always get more of them. (Kathryn, organized 4 years)

Vanessa describes how organizers experience this.

> At that point I felt like a commodity to the union, [even though] they weren't [paying] attention to me at all. It was like "you aren't worth having, but we're going to fight over you." (Vanessa, organizing 2-1/2 years)

Throughout her OI apprenticeship, Vanessa's host union relocated her repeatedly. At one point the union removed her from a campaign where she was receiving extensive training and mentoring and re-assigned her to solo probing missions.[15] She felt powerless to challenge these decisions. She was also disturbed that the union seemed to have no interest in her development as an organizer, nor did they seem particularly concerned about her general well-being.

Emma, a former OI staffer, explains how this view of new organizers as "cannon fodder" undermines unions' commitment to training and mentoring. She argues that if unions truly believed in organizers-as-change-agents—they would invest resources in the training and mentoring necessary to retain organizers. Instead, she claims,

> Unions are just interested in warm bodies. They don't really care about the training, they just want someone who they can . . . mold however they want to. (Emma, former OI staff, organized 2 years)

While a few unions invest significant time and (human) resources in developing and implementing high quality training for new organizers, research demonstrates that most do not (Feekin and Widenor 2000, 2001). Frustrated by this lack of support and shocked that most unions do not value them enough to train them properly, some organizers quit. This finding echoes the literature on justice jobs, which argues that training and mentoring do indeed impact organizer retention.

The previous sections demonstrate that a combination of individual, demographic, and organizational factors influence union organizer retention. However, knowing why organizers leave is only half the story. It is also crucial to understand why organizers stay on the job. The following section will examine the conditions that facilitate commitment among union organizers.

STICKING IT OUT

Although many new organizers leave, others remain (see table 7.1). This section examines three conditions that facilitate commitment among new organizers: compromise, peer support, and organizing success.

Compromise

The previous section demonstrated that there is a significant mismatch between organizers' initial expectations and the reality that they confront once they enter the field.[16] Responding to this mismatch between expectation and reality, some leave union organizing altogether. Others compromise their beliefs about the necessity of real empowerment, claiming that partial empowerment is better for workers than none at all.

Emma describes both the objective need for compromise and the difficulty that many women and organizers of color have making this compromise.

> If you want to stay involved in the movement, there is a lot of compromise involved, particularly for women of color. . . . If you were in a field campaign [where] most of those workers are women of color, and if you don't have a [plan] that actually develops those women as leaders, I don't know how you can justify it. I don't know how a woman of color can be on that campaign and not feel somewhat compromised. (Emma, former OI staff, organized 2 years)

Although many organizers, such as Betsy, recognize that unions offer workers only partial empowerment, they refuse to abandon labor. Although imperfect, they believe that unions are the best available option for workers.

> Is there another alternative that's better for workers? No, and that's what pisses me off. . . . There's no alternative at this point. People may think that there are alternatives, but in reality there aren't. [Having a] union is better than no union, regardless of how corrupt it is. (Betsy, OI staff, organized 4 years)

Nathan shares Betsy's commitment to the labor movement, however imperfect it may be. He argues that organizers must be honest with workers about the limitations of unions. He suggests that communicating a realistic vision of the labor movement to workers will better prepare them for the problems that they will encounter once they join unions.

> I let [the workers] know that the union is not a panacea. [Labor] has a lot of problems, but you are looking at one of the best vehicles out there to get rid of a lot of the ills that we have in society, and that helps bring people together. [For all its faults, labor] addresses a lot of the "isms" that separate us. (Nathan, organizing 2-1/2 years)

Many argue that the Institute must be more honest with potential organizers about the movement's imperfections. They believe that this will better prepare applicants for the inevitability of compromise. OI staff members such as Carrie argue that honesty will increase organizer retention by encouraging individuals to enter the labor movement with more realistic expectations.

> [We need to tell potential organizers that] it's going to be really fucked up when you get here, so don't be surprised that there's racism. You might be hit on. You will have to deal with the imperfections of the labor movement . . . (Carrie, OI staff, organized 6 years)

Organizers who make compromises do so because they believe that some union representation, however flawed, is always preferable to none at all. In order to remain organizing they must accept that some personal compromise is required to help workers gain access to the benefits of union representation. In the long run, many come to believe that the benefits that they help workers win outweigh the individual compromises that they must make. This finding echoes the literature, which argues both that high or unrealistic expectations often lead to turnover and that workers must adopt more realistic expectations in order to remain employed in justice jobs.

Peer Groups

The literature on justice jobs suggests that although mentoring and peer support play a crucial role in improving retention in justice jobs, few organizations systematically provide support to their employees (Katz 1978). Organizers in this sample supported this finding, consistently bemoaning the lack of mentoring and institutional support that they received in the field. Given the centrality of mentoring and support, it is not surprising that access to small peer support groups (2–3 people) was an important factor in determining organizer retention.

While these groups often develop during the OI field training, they also develop spontaneously in the field outside of the OI. These peer groups provide organizers with the support necessary to weather the isolating lifestyle and intense occupational demands of organizing. They do this by providing support that is sometimes emotional, sometimes tactical, and other times social. Lissa underscores the importance of peer groups in helping organizers tolerate the demanding nature of organizing.

[The organizing lifestyle] is built on strong groups. The staff at [my union] who have been there for a while, [are] very tight. They [don't] have any other friends who were not organizers. [People who do leave, do it] because they want to have a life. They've left not because they were disenchanted, but because they couldn't stand the lifestyle. It has been a hard lifestyle. (Lissa, organized 10 months)

Darren underscores the loneliness and isolation of organizing, implying that peer groups could mediate organizers' awkwardness when relating socially with non-organizers

I feel bored and weird [when I] try hanging out with students at a local college, because I don't feel like they are my peers. I don't have any fucking peers, I exist in this weird social gray area. It's tough to keep relationships with friends [who are not organizers, and so] it's important to keep a relationship with someone. (Darren, organizing 1-1/2 years)

Vanessa underscores the increasing importance of the social support provided by these peer groups, because the demands of organizing have eliminated all non-organizers from her life.

I don't have any friends who aren't organizers of some sort. As I [have been organizing] longer, I [have grown] apart from people who were doing other sorts of organizing, but I am still close to people who do [union organizing]. (Vanessa, organizing 2-1/2 years)

These small peer groups play several important roles. They provide peer contact and social outlets for organizers who are often isolated from their peers due by long hours and extensive travel. They also provide crucial emotional support during the devastating organizing losses that most organizers experience during their careers.[17]

Of the sixteen who stayed, fourteen had access to a peer support group (see table 7.4). Only two of those who stayed had no peer support group, and both were older and had far more work experience than most other organizers in the sample. One of these organizers had been a union member prior to going

TABLE 7.4
Peer groups by retention status

Peer group	Stayed	Left
No	2	5
Yes	14	10
N	16	15

through the OI and the other had been in the workforce for more than twenty years prior to entering the OI.

Because small peer groups generate trust and reliance among their members, it is understandable that members would influence each other to leave, as well as stay. Although five of the leavers had no peer support, the other eleven did. Among leavers with peer support, it was common for these groups to exert a negative effect. When one member left organizing, the other members of the small peer group tended to follow. This was true for eight of the eleven leavers with peer support. Only three leavers had peers in their support groups who continued organizing after they left. For two of these three, their peer group was a romantic relationship that continued long after they left organizing (see table 7.4).

While these peer support groups tend to develop spontaneously, further research is necessary to determine whether they are more likely to develop in response to certain conditions in the field, such as local union, type of organizing campaign, access to training and mentoring. The finding that these groups positively impact retention is important, given that neither the OI nor most host unions systematically provide peer support for new organizers.[18] Further research is needed to specify what impact their institutionalization would have on organizer retention.

Organizing Success

The third condition that facilitates organizer retention is campaign success. Although individuals who stayed experienced both success and failure, few organizers in this sample won a campaign and quit organizing within their first year-and-a-half (see table 7.5). This indicates that there is an important relationship between organizing outcomes and commitment.

Organizing defeat is a serious emotional blow to organizers and workers alike. Nathan's OI internship ended the day before workers voted for union representation. As soon as he got home, he called the union to find out the results of the election. He describes his reaction upon hearing of the union's failure.

TABLE 7.5
Organizing outcomes by retention status

	Success	Failure	Neither	Both
Stayed	7	5	4	
Left		5	6	4
N	7	10	10	4

When I called . . . the lady at the hotel said "the election is over." I said, "OK, what happened?" and she said, "the union lost by 13 votes." My heart went boom and I cried. . . . We had put so much into it, but it wasn't so much that. [It was that] I knew the hell these workers were going to catch when they went back [to work] . . . Some of the workers had become so bold, so brave. They were wearing their [union] caps and all that stuff. There were people who hated [the union] too, so retaliation was up the water. (Nathan, organizing 2-1/2 years)

Carissa also experienced a loss during her OI internship. The loss was quite painful for her and ultimately dampened her initial enthusiasm for organizing.

I was depressed when I found out that the [workers] didn't win. It's not that it made me think "well, now I don't want to be an organizer" at all, but . . . the ten-day went from something that I had been so invested in and excited about, to something that I [questioned]; "what good came out of it? Those people are totally flattened." (Carissa, organized 4 months)

These examples demonstrate that losing a campaign is quite depressing. Organizers such as Denice underscore the impact that failure can have on organizer retention.

We somehow need to learn how to win more. If we did, I think that more people would stay. [Losing is] very depressing. (Denice, organizing 2 years)

Denice's co-worker, Vanessa, explains that although organizers' lifestyle is intense and often unpleasant, organizing success can make it more bearable.

When I was winning, the lifestyle was more tolerable. As a local we haven't organized anybody for a year [so it's been quite depressing]. (Vanessa, organizing 2-1/2 years)

Seven of the sixteen who stayed experienced campaign success (and no failure) during their first year-and-a-half in the field. Five of those who stayed experienced failure only, and four experienced neither success nor failure. Of the "stayers," five experienced failure only, and six experienced neither success nor failure. Of the three "leavers" who had an initial victory, all suffered crushing defeats in later campaigns. These defeats undoubtedly dampened their initial enthusiasm for organizing (see table 7.5). There is not a perfect correlation between organizing success and retention, and this is not a perfect sample. Nevertheless, these findings suggest that there is a relationship between organizing success and retention, and that the more new organizers win, the more likely they are to remain organizing.

These three conditions—compromise, peer groups, and organizing success—provide a framework for understanding how individuals maintain commitment to organizing despite significant individual, demographic, and organizational obstacles.

CONCLUSION

As mentioned previously, little research on union organizers exists, and few scholars have systematically studied organizers' experience in John Sweeney's "new labor movement." Existing scholarship on the contemporary labor movement mentions the recent influx of OI-trained organizers in passing, if at all. Rarely, if ever, does it speculate about how organizer retention (or the lack thereof) has impacted the AFL-CIO's and individual unions' efforts to develop aggressive and effective organizing programs.

This paper attempts to fill this gap by rigorously examining organizers' experiences in the "new labor movement," and critically assessing the factors that influence their occupational decisions. My interviews with graduates of the Organizing Institute's training program uncovered several factors that influence organizers' occupational decisions. First, organizers enter the field with several dearly held expectations, such as (a) that "the new labor movement" is substantially different from its predecessors, (b) that increased diversity has resulted in more open discussions about race and racism within the movement, and (c) that new labor's emphasis on militant organizing tactics translates into true worker empowerment.

This research also exposed the intensity of the demands that unions placed on organizers once they enter the field. Because many of the organizers in this sample are young and few have significant family or personal responsibilities, they are initially able to meet these demands. However, many are critical of the demands placed on organizers and the ways that these demands exclude many qualified individuals. Most resign themselves to the fact that they will leave organizing once they decide to start a family, because these demands are generally incompatible with family life.

Lastly, this research demonstrates that organizers enter the field convinced that they will play a critical role in transforming the labor movement. Assuming that unions share this outlook, they expect that they will provide organizers with training and support. Most are shocked to find that most unions view them as "cannon fodder," and as a result do not provide them with the systematic training or mentoring necessary to maximize their effectiveness in the field.

Recognition of these issues often generates intense frustration and disillusionment among new organizers. Although this frustration leads some to leave organizing, others remain. This paper has shown that there are three conditions capable of facilitating commitment among organizers. When organizers have access to peer support networks, when they experience organizing success during their first year-and-a-half in the field, and when they are willing to compromise some of their expectations (especially about worker empowerment), they are more likely to remain organizing beyond their first year-and-a-half in the field.

These results echo many of the findings in the literature on the constellation of occupations that I refer to as justice jobs. Individual characteristics such as expectation and idealism, and organizational characteristics such as training and mentoring are both powerful determinants of retention and turnover among union organizers and workers employed in justice jobs. Demographic characteristics are important as well. The extensive demands and emotional intensity of both kinds of work limit the number of parents/older people employed, disproportionately concentrating young workers in both kinds of jobs.

Salary is not a key determinant of turnover in either field. However, another occupational characteristic, namely, status is relevant for justice jobs but not organizers. Although most justice jobs are considered low-status work, the status of organizing work has improved in the thirteen years that the Organizing Institute has existed. Given the central role that organizing has played in transforming the "new labor movement," it is no surprise that organizers are increasingly respected as a critical element of vital and aggressive unions.

This paper offers several important insights about the factors that influence turnover, as well as the conditions that facilitate commitment among union organizers. However, these findings should be interpreted with several caveats. First, the sample is relatively skewed toward external recruits, white organizers, and women. Further research utilizing a more balanced sample is necessary to understand whether the same conditions facilitate commitment for internal recruits, people of color, and men.

Second, the majority of unions that employed organizers in this sample meet Voss and Sherman's (2001) definition of "full innovator" unions.[19] Full innovator unions have more sophisticated organizing programs and higher organizing success rates than their partial and non-innovative counterparts. As a result, it is possible that increasing the variation in innovation among host unions could yield different findings about the impact of success rates on organizers' commitment.

Nonetheless, given the centrality of organizing and organizers to the "new labor movement," this research offers important insight into the motivation and working conditions of the individuals at the cutting edge of union transformation. Just as it has been influenced by the excellent work on "the new labor movement" that preceded it (Lopez 2000; Voss and Sherman 2001; Waldinger et al. 1997), I hope that this paper will inspire future research on the timely and important topic of union organizer turnover and retention.

APPENDIX 7.1

STRUCTURE OF THE ORGANIZING INSTITUTE PROGRAM

There are several separate components of the Organizing Institute Training Program.

THE THREE-DAY TRAINING

The Organizing Institute training program consists of a three-day weekend workshop in which recruits are taught basic organizing skills and strategy. Approximately half of all three-day participants are current union members who are interested in volunteering on organizing campaigns, but do not want to become full-time organizers. The rest of the three-day participants are members (internal recruits) and non-members (external recruits) who seek employment as full-time organizers (Organizing Institute 2000).

THE TEN-DAY ORIENTATION

Approximately one third of three-day participants interested in becoming organizers are invited to participate in the OI's ten-day orientation. During the orientation, training takes place in the field, on an active organizing campaign of a local union. OI trainers instruct between three and fifteen trainees on organizing strategy, labor history, and basic organizing skills (Feekin and Widenor 2000).

THE THREE-MONTH APPRENTICESHIP

After completing the ten-day, most OI trainees begin their three month apprenticeship. OI apprentices are placed individually with local unions and are assigned to active organizing drives underway at the local union. At the end of the apprenticeship, OI staff provide limited help to program graduates in securing employment.

TRAINING AND SUPERVISION

The amount of training and supervision that participants receive from their placement union varies wildly. Apprentices are assigned an OI tracker when they begin their apprenticeship, but for a variety of reasons these relationships rarely result in concrete mentoring or supervision. OI staff members are assigned to "track" OI apprentices, in addition to their other job duties at the Institute. They are supposed to be available for support, feedback, and mentoring as needed, but the depth of the mentoring that they can provide to apprentices varies widely, based on geographical proximity, the intensity of their other job demands, their commitment to mentoring, and the needs of the trainee (Feekin and Widenor 2001).

8

"OUTSIDERS" INSIDE THE LABOR MOVEMENT

AN EXAMINATION OF YOUTH INVOLVEMENT IN THE 1996 UNION SUMMER PROGRAM

Leslie Bunnage and Judith Stepan-Norris

Individual social movements exist within larger fields of activities oriented to social change. Alliances between movements and the crossing over of activists from one movement to another ebb and flow over time in response to changes in political opportunities, the emergence and management of issues, and the strategic plans of movement leadership (Meyer and Whittier 1994; della Porta and Rucht 1995). As a crucial component of its plan to revitalize the U.S. labor movement, the AFL-CIO top leadership recently decided to incorporate various non-labor activists into its organizing campaigns. Over a seven-year period, the AFL-CIO has reached out to college students, seniors/retirees, people training in seminaries and law schools, and community groups to obtain concrete assistance in their revitalized union organizing programs. A prominent part of this plan is the Union Summer program, which seeks to involve youth, mainly college students, in day-to-day union organizing drives in major U.S. cities during the summer months.

Yet the successful melding of two sets of social movement activists (those "inside" and those "outside" the movement) requires considerable thought and planning. Eighty-two percent of 1996 Union Summer participants were college students. While college students have many of the characteristics that make for good social activists, they are often unprepared for the realities of union organizing. Although college curricula normally include extensive course offerings on issues surrounding social inequalities, they do not ordinarily offer many (if any) courses on the labor movement in particular. And despite the opportunities available to students to build some organizing skills within student-based movements, they are not generally exposed to the specifics of union organizing. As a result, students rarely know much about how unions operate, their histories, or their current issues and concerns.

In this paper, we focus on the integration of "outside" activists into the first AFL-CIO Union Summer program in 1996. We begin with a description of the program, which works on the principle of students' total immersion in the union organizing process for a three-week period. We seek to understand the extent to which and how the Union Summer interns learned about the campaigns on which they labored, and how the processes of incorporation affected the overall success of their efforts on behalf of participating unions. Because we see gaining the support and commitment of the interns (who were working for a small stipend) as crucial to the success of the overall project, we emphasize here the ways in which the various union locals worked to incorporate student interns into their ongoing campaigns. We show how local unions' "strategic capacity" mattered for the ways the various programs were organized, and for their outcomes.

THE UNION SUMMER PROGRAM

The 1996 Union Summer program was one of the AFL-CIO "New Voice" leadership's first initiatives to recruit, train, and deploy young people to organize the unorganized. AFL-CIO President John Sweeney committed 20 million dollars to "support coordinated large-scale industry-based organizing drives," part of which went to the Union Summer program (Bronfenbrenner et al. 1998).

The program sought to recruit college-age activists because in some ways they match the demographics of the people that the labor movement wanted to organize. "They're our future," said Andy Levin, AFL-CIO 1996 Union Summer Director (cited in Cooper 1996: website 3). Union Summer interns were mainly from middle-income neighborhoods (with about a third coming from upper-income neighborhoods and 15 percent from lower-income neighborhoods); a little more than half (58 percent) were female, and half were members of a minority racial or ethnic group (22 percent Latino, 20 percent Black, 6 percent Asian, and 1 percent "Other"). Most traveled to Union Summer sites away from their home states. Of the vast majority that were college students (82 percent), most (57 percent) attended relatively prestigious colleges and universities (Bunnage 2002).

In order to secure the participation of unions and their locals, the AFL-CIO advertised the new program to International unions, local unions, and labor connected community groups. The word was put out to faculty contacts listed in the Organizing Institute's (OI) roster and advertised in AFL-CIO publications, AFL-CIO affiliate publications, and local union publications. The federation pursued particular unions that the leadership thought were likely to be interested in this new organizing strategy. For union locals, the appeal was that they would have access to a group of energetic and progressive young people to supplement the regular union staff.

In selecting host union and community groups, the AFL-CIO looked for organizations that would involve interns in a variety of organizing strategies; that were well organized and capable of successfully utilizing the interns; that had officials and organizers that reflected the racial, ethnic and gender diversity of union members; and that were run by people sympathetic to the activist vision of the new AFL-CIO leadership. Most participating organizations, either directly or indirectly through their parent organizations, made substantial contributions to the financial support of the program (AFL-CIO Union Summer Site Coordinator Manual 1998). In the end, fifty unions and community organizations participated in the 1996 Union Summer program. Of these, fourteen participated extensively.[1]

The AFL-CIO identified cities and locales for which a substantial group of unions responded to the call for participation. In the end, the 1996 program included 20 cities, along with Puerto Rico, and a Southern Bus Tour, which was modeled after the 1961 Freedom Rides in Mississippi. The bus traveled to several historic civil rights movement sites within the three-week period. Interns helped with ongoing voter registration drives and with an organizing campaign in a nursing home chain.

Interested students and workers responded to the Union Summer call by filling out an application. Program personnel reviewed the applications and decided whether or not to admit the applicants. The reject rate was very low; the main criteria involved having the necessary maturity and interest required of this program. Placement was accomplished by matching the program needs (bilingualism, workforce characteristics, and number of activists desired) with the applicants' desired location, time availability, and their ability to arrange for travel to that site.

In forty-three of the three week sessions that took place between the beginning of June and the end of August, interns worked on 185 labor movement campaigns. Student interns directly witnessed the struggles of workers and their families. Many observed first-hand battles over union recognition in which employers blatantly violated workers' legal rights to organize.

Union Summer internship periods or "site waves" during 1996 included anywhere from 5 to 44 activists. Although most of the unions that participated in Union Summer put interns to work on activist tasks, a few unions saw this program as an opportunity to secure free labor to accomplish more bureaucratic goals (e.g., working on local newsletters, sending notices regarding upcoming meetings, and so forth).

STUDENTS AS UNION ORGANIZERS

Students bring a host of beneficial characteristics to any movement they join. These include the boost gained through youthful energy, students' structural availability, their life course position, and the tactics they are competent to utilize. The AFL-CIO's decision to recruit young people who were primarily students was based on its understanding that youth participation in social movements has been a critical component of past successful social movements.

Zald and Useem (1987) consider the role of college students in their larger exploration of "organization intellectuals." They assert that those who are "well educated" are strong candidates for social movement participation, because they are likely to possess social change oriented values. These authors also highlight the fact that students who are often relatively new to social movement activity are not "issue-satiated," leaving more room for focused participation (1987, 355).

But the Union Summer program was not created exclusively for the purpose of recruiting new activists. Andy Levin was quick to point out the multi-faceted agenda that involved an attempt to transform this population of student activists: "Put simply, we want to inject a massive dose of class consciousness into youth politics . . . we want to transform the politics of the next generation of activists" (quoted in Cooper 1996). Union Summer was developed in order to rectify what Levin and others perceived to be a monumental problem with youth social movement participation. Since the Vietnam War period, most young left-wing progressives had engaged in single-issue social movements (e.g., anti-war, anti-nuclear, environmental, etc.) or strict identity politics (e.g., women's movement, gay rights), largely ignoring labor struggles. Thus, the new AFL-CIO was interested in communicating its latest vision: "Our message is that labor is where it's at in the fight for social justice in the nineties" (Levin as quoted in Cooper 1996).

Zald and McCarthy also note that though students are often bogged down by academic responsibilities, their schedules can be flexible, allowing them to make accommodations for political action. In particular, highly concentrated participation is possible during summer breaks. Snow, Zurcher, and Ekland-Olson (1980) amplify this point in their research findings which show that some participate in social movements once they have been introduced to it, while others do not, partly due to potential activists' structural availability. Stemming from their exploration of the Nichiren Shoshu Buddhist movement, they found that some people are more "available" for movement participation because they have considerable free time and a flexible schedule, and because they have few "countervailing risks or sanctions" (1980, 793).

Once movements have recruited activists, they must attend to the issue of activists' skill sets. Movements use activists with certain skills and a "cultural-technological stock" that is an outgrowth of their tactical repertoires. Tactics can be taught and learned. However, each tactic involves a group of skills, people, and set of tools that may or may not be available to a group of activists (Zald 1987, 331). For instance, activists with a college background are likely to have strong skills in the development and execution of certain forms of activity, such as research (particularly internet-related), demonstrations (beyond picket line collective action), and surveys (both the construction and administration of them).

Immediately after the first summer, participating unions and Union Summer staff commented on the particular importance of recruiting youth. A 1996 Union Summer intern, who was recruited to be a program staff member later that summer, discussed the importance of reaching out to college students: "Colleges are the perfect place to get the young involved because they are radical, thirsty for social change, and love to be involved. TRUST ME! This is the outlet they've been looking for."

Participating union representatives also commented on the benefits of youthful activists. A representative from a Boston-based service workers' union wrote: "Because of the large facilities [we were organizing], numbers were needed to cover entrances. Youth [were] important because they had a lot of energy." An Atlanta manufacturing union representative indicated the way in which young activists affected the workers: "Young adults were very convincing to older workers about changing, taking control over their lives. [Their] energy and dedication is so much a plus." Representatives from other participating unions also commented on the ways younger interns were able to connect with and "relate" to younger employees (Boston staff).

UNIONS AND STRATEGIC CAPACITY

The literature we reviewed up to this point emphasizes the role of the students in contributing to the programs' success. Yet social movement organizations, in this case, mostly unions, are also obviously implicated in the success of the campaigns. What union level factors are important in creating successful campaigns? The resource mobilization literature emphasizes that resources available to the social movement organization are the most important factor. Yet some newer studies have found that organizations without conventional resources can compensate in various ways to achieve successful outcomes. Most unions have considerable conventional resources compared to other social movement organizations, but tactical, effective use of resources is another matter.

Marshall Ganz (2000: 1003) shows the ways in which "'strategic capacity' can explain how resourcefulness can compensate for lack of resources." By strategic capacity, he means "leaders' access to salient information about the environment, heuristic use they [make] of this information, and their motivation." As mentioned previously, student interns bring a new body of salient information to union campaigns. They often know how to use computers, interact with businesses, and conduct systematic research. Their ideological orientations are also likely to differ from those of union activists due to their generally higher levels of education and their structural locations. Motivation affects "the focus actors bring to their work . . . , their ability to concentrate for extended periods of time . . . , their persistence . . . , their willingness to take risks . . . , and their ability to sustain high energy" (Ganz 2000: 1014 [internal parenthetic cites omitted here]). Students often have a high level and different type of motivation than workers. During the summer, they have approximately three full months to concentrate their energies on non-school related activities. And in general, young people are characterized as open to riskier activities and have high levels of energy. When students organize as "outsiders," as is typically the case in Union Summer, they are not exposed to the same risks as workers. They aren't agitating at their own workplaces and thus are not at risk of creating tension in their work environments, agitating their co-workers, or losing their jobs. And for the most part, they don't have families to support, so monetary concerns are not as important.

While student interns brought a new set of resources to the union organizing efforts, they lacked salient information about the structure, history, and environment of the specific campaigns on which they were expected to work. Their integration and incorporation into the existing campaigns occurred only when particular care was given to a true partnership between the union officials and the interns. Our data suggest that the willingness of the interns to fully immerse themselves in these efforts was contingent upon the union's willingness to mentor them and incorporate their suggestions in the planning process. This took concerted attention and planning both prior to and after the arrival of the interns. When this happened, both union personnel and Union Summer interns had a better experience, and they tended to accomplish more.

The labor movement isn't the first social movement to attempt to employ "outside" organizers in its primary mission. The legendary organizer, Saul Alinsky (1972, 65–66), notes that a common problem with activists in general is that they often learn to organize in their own particular communities and are unable to translate their organizing skills to different settings. Some "campus activists . . . could organize a substantial number of students—but they were utter failures when it came to trying to communicate with and organize lower-middle-class workers" (Alinsky 1972: 66). Training that takes into account the specifics of the local people, traditions, and culture is crucial for overcoming these limitations.

Several organizations have the primary aim of helping social movements educate their participants for the necessary work. Training at the Highlander School in Tennessee has historically constituted what Aldon Morris (1984, 139–40) calls a "movement halfway house." It provided targeted training for activists seeking to work with various social movements. For instance, its training has been invaluable to labor insurrections (particularly to the Congress of Industrial Organizations [CIO] struggles in the 1930s and 1940s) and to the civil rights movement.

The Highlander School also aided the Student Non-violent Coordinating Committee (SNCC) during the 1960s. SNCC put a great deal of thought into the types of mobilization in which it engaged. For instance, its leaders consistently and creatively responded to problems and situations that arose in the field. Trouble-shooting and strong training programs were critical components of their extensive and largely successful mobilization process (Payne 1995).

Organizer activity was crafted to accomplish SNCC's multiple goals simultaneously. The goal of voter registration necessitated training around literacy, process and basic citizenship rights. SNCC set up an innovative program that addressed these needs at the same time it empowered the community, and recruited and developed leadership. Septima Clark, co-developer of the program (and not a student), thoughtfully took into account the recruitment aspect of this work: "The basic purpose of the Citizenship Schools is discovering local community leaders . . . and stay[ing] in the local picture only long enough to help in [their] development" (Payne 1995, 75). One SNCC training document makes it clear that organizers put a great deal of thought into this multi-faceted agenda via the use of many tactics, including role-plays (Payne 1995, 248).

Another non-student SNCC organizer, Ella Baker, fought to prioritize mass-based inclusion in the movement, with the understanding that many types of actors can make useful contributions. Payne summarizes this idea well: "Just as one has to be able to look at a sharecropper and see a potential teacher, one must be able to look at a conservative lawyer and see a potential crusader for justice" (Payne 1995, 89). Baker also ran highly effective training conferences which were both "skill-enhancing and consciousness-raising" (Payne 1995, 89) for the diverse body of participants.

Civil rights worker Bob Moses, who at the time of his participation in SNCC was a teacher in Harlem, felt that despite their lack of community connections, "outsiders" like him had the ability to spearhead campaigns by getting a critical mass of local people involved. He described the process that made this possible:

> One of the things that happened in the movement was that there was a joining of a young generation of people and an older generation that nurtured and sustained them . . . it's almost literally like you're throwing yourself on the people and they have actually picked you up and gone on to carry you so you don't really need money, you don't really need transportation. (Payne 1995, 128)

The intergenerational sharing of experience, through good training, made it possible for "young recruits [to go] into the field armed with as much vicarious experience as the older activists and Highlander could make available to them" (Payne 1995, 144).

A number of college students spent their spring break working with SNCC in Greenwood in 1963. One student activist's report on this experience illustrated the diversity of tasks and quickened pace of events. A sample of the activities in which she participated in the course of one week illustrates the movement's impressive ability to incorporate her specific skills: office work, salvaging office records in response to the office being burned down, receiving citizenship school teacher certification, attending and organizing nightly mass meetings, participating in a protest in response to a shooting, helping move and setting up temporary headquarters, registering several people, and teaching a citizenship class (Payne 1995, 167–70).

SNCC demonstrated its strategic capacity by an impressive ability to use outsiders. The outsiders brought a set of skills and labor to the rural South, and their deficits were overcome by comprehensive training that enabled them to adapt their assets to this setting. In particular, the pairing of older more seasoned organizers with younger people demonstrated this dynamic.

Another civil rights movement program, Freedom Summer, had a very effective strategy of incorporating students into its ongoing local project. Existing staff members were incredibly immersed in the campaigns on which they had been working for several years. They served as a point of inspiration for the volunteers during the orientation sessions and motivated them to fully commit themselves to the work at hand.

Officially, the Council of Federated Organizations (COFO), a coalition of civil rights groups formed in 1962 to oversee voter registration activities in the South, was responsible for running Freedom Summer. Yet in reality, SNCC was the major force that directed all aspects of the Freedom Summer program, from its most nascent planning stages to nearly all aspects of its execution.

Indeed, the program was essentially a response to several particular strategic problems experienced by SNCC: the propensity of police to abuse black activists, the fact that they lacked the funds to subsidize the program for volunteers, and limitations due to the local focus of their efforts. They accomplished these goals by making various strategic choices and by overseeing the recruitment process (and they also did a good deal of the participant interviewing themselves). For example, SNCC found that when white activists were involved, police abuse drastically declined. Also, white wealthier volunteers were much better able to support themselves over the summer. This resulted in an increase in the number of white volunteers from elite schools. Even though SNCC did not have much money, it contributed approximately 95 percent of the funds for the program, provided 95 percent of the central state headquarters staff, and managed four out of five of the state's Congressional districts (the Congress of Racial Equality, or CORE, staffed the remaining one). (Sellers 1973, 96; Sutherland 1965, 35; as quoted in McAdam 1988, 28–29.) The campaigns included voter registration, freedom schools, and attention to media coverage, all of which reveal SNCC's stamp on the project.

The Freedom Summer program was a creative response to emerging issues in the struggle for racial equality. SNCC took the lead and utilized its "strategic capacity" to develop new approaches to overcome the obstacles confronting it. These strategic decisions themselves served to bring a new and energetic class of activists (white students from elite schools) powerfully into play. But SNCC was a new and informal organization that was riding the tide at the peak of the civil rights movement back in the '60s. The labor movement in the '90s, on the contrary, is highly institutionalized and situated at the bottom of the trough of union decline. Can such movements experience a similar use of strategic capacity?

Needless to say, the contemporary union movement is very different from SNCC during the 1960s. The AFL-CIO is an umbrella organization that has considerable resources, but has little input into the everyday activities of member unions. Yet there is also a precedent for parent organization involvement in member unions. During the massive organizing drives of the 1930s and early 1940s, the CIO entered into partnerships with member unions in which they shared in the costs as well as the decision-making of organizing drives. In this way, the CIO put its resources (along with constraints, which where in some cases substantial) into the hands of resource poor unions. In the current period, the AFL-CIO has attempted to spread its own revitalization from the top down to member unions. One avenue for this is the Union Summer program, which uses innovative ideas and outside participants in order to push traditional unions in more productive directions. But whether that cue leads to more effective organizing programs is another question.

We now turn to a description of the sample and our analysis of how the local unions that participated in the 1996 Union Summer program worked to integrate and incorporate student interns into their ongoing campaigns.

ABOUT THE SAMPLE

The primary unit of analysis in this study is the campaign within the Union Summer site wave. We gleaned information from three forms produced and disseminated by the program on each of the 185 campaigns. Union Summer site coordinators filled out the *Union Summer Final Wave Report* and the *Union Summer Field Staff Opinion Survey*. A representative from the participating union or community organization filled out the *Union Summer Evaluation Form for Participating Unions*. We have maintained the confidentiality of the participating union locals and site coordinators by referring to them only by the city in which the campaign occurred.

ANALYSIS: UNION SUMMER ORIENTATION AND TRAINING

Key to the success of the Union Summer program was the extent to which a given union local committed itself to the process of incorporating the interns. The Union Summer intern orientation and educational programs were important for cultivating the interns and giving them a feel for the work. According to Ganz, deliberative processes, resource flows, and accountability structures of organizations have an impact on their levels of strategic capacity, or the use they are able to make of the resources they have. The ways in which union leaders develop, the mix of participants involved in the union, and the organizational structure are relevant in determining a union's strategic capacity.

With regard to the Union Summer organizing program, we found that certain unions were better prepared to receive and effectively utilize the interns that were assigned to them. These unions had been engaged in progressive organizing efforts prior to the arrival of the interns, and their staff had already been working to accomplish similar goals. This is most evident in the case of the SEIU. Of all the unions in our sample, the SEIU is the one that most closely approximates what Voss and Sherman (2000) call a "fully revitalized" union. In their formulation, fully revitalized locals are those "that had shifted away from servicing current union members to organizing the unorganized and that used unconventional disruptive tactics in these organizing campaigns" (Voss and Sherman 2000, 316). Many SEIU locals were engaged in aggressive and innovative organizing efforts, and the intensity of their efforts was extremely high. When asked to participate in the Union Summer program, union locals like those from the SEIU were able to develop strong organizing programs that effectively incorporated interns, because they had already begun such endeavors on their own. They had a panoply of contacts, and were utilizing a social movement mindset. For these unions, the Union Summer program brought in "outsiders" to help with ongoing efforts, and they were able to maximize the utility of these new activists. This is clearly demonstrated in the fact that Union Summer site coordinators most often mentioned SEIU locals as having good programs. Site coordinators classified twenty-four of the Union Summer campaigns as good, and seven of these were with SEIU locals.

To be effective in using Union Summer interns, unions needed not only good programs, but also the insight and creativity to incorporate the interns. An SEIU local official highlighted the challenge involved in incorporating interns. "Unlike Freedom Summer, this was not structured in a way that allows people to come into something that is already in place." According to Ganz, contacts with a range of constituents tend to build incorporation skills. What is needed here was a good understanding of young people, and students in particular, as well as their concerns and motivations. The SEIU and other fully revitalized unions were able to incorporate the interns, make them feel at home, and tap into their creative ideas. This ability contributed to the ultimate success of their endeavors.

In 1996, most AFL-CIO unions had been operating under the traditional model, often referred to as business unionism, that emphasized established practices. This model is the one that is in part responsible for the almost fifty years of labor movement decline. Their organizing programs were not suited to the current environment, and they were stuck in ineffective patterns. They had lower levels of strategic capacity and were not well positioned to develop it. Hence, they were not able to develop strong organizing programs to which the Union Summer program could contribute. The Boston coordinator for all three waves elaborated on the mixed implications of exposing interns to poorly organized campaigns. "As we explained to interns we can't invent good organizing drives. The question is, can we find them? Even I was shocked at how badly most organizing had been done, even by 'progressive' unions."

Business unions were functioning with a more traditional union-organizing model, which predominantly used existing internal resources. They were hard-pressed to figure out how to effectively use the influx of a group of outside organizers. They also tended to be unfamiliar with what Ganz calls "deviant" points of view that bring new and divergent ways of thinking into play, which in turn, lead to greater effectiveness. These unions also tended to be less concerned with the students' own goals and orientations. This, in part, is also attributable to their more insular perspectives and practices.

During the first year of the Union Summer program, these unions and community organizations did not meet the challenge to engage the interns (and some failed miserably). Site coordinators classified ten campaigns as having weak programs. For the most part, these were community groups, which were less well suited to the type of aid offered by Union Summer interns. These community organizations often times asked interns to engage in voter registration and living wage campaigns. Such tasks were not emphasized in the training sessions, and many interns thought that the voter registration campaigns should not be included in the Union Summer program. Some of the more radical interns felt that working within the two party political system was a futile endeavor. In addition, these campaigns were often disorganized, had little oversight, and involved monotonous tasks for interns. The interns perceived the living wage campaigns as valuable, but they also saw them as disorganized. These organizations rarely mobilized their resources to engage the Union Summer interns.

In light of the incredible success of the Freedom Summer orientation program, the AFL-CIO modeled its Union Summer training sessions after them. Freedom Summer sessions, which took place over a one week period, included section meetings, general assemblies and work groups that addressed the background of the civil rights movement, logistics of the local situations, the specifics of the organizing work the volunteers would be engaged in, and the role of the media in the campaign (McAdam 1988).

The Union Summer program held both orientation and educational sessions. The orientation session took place during the first two days of the program. The training manual[2] delineates fifteen potential components to the orientation session, with a clear description of how to enact them. Site coordinators were also provided with most of the materials necessary to put these sessions into play. The components included exercises involving issues and actions such as ice breakers and introductions, the visions and goals of Union Summer, union history and information on basic union structures, organizing basics, site specific information, introductions to the unions and their ongoing campaigns, and the civil rights movement's Freedom Summer as a model. The site coordinators often envisioned the orientation as "a starting point for the students to know each other and share opinions and values about the labor movement" (Los Angeles site).

Several site coordinators suggested a need for more integration of training with campaign activities and union staff presence. A Los Angeles coordinator wrote, "we need to integrate actions with the orientation training and include role plays." The Seattle coordinator not only stressed the importance of action, but also the difficulties that arose because of the brevity of the program. He indicated that "in three weeks we can either *teach* about the labor movement or *do* the labor movement, but not both."

Union Summer educational sessions took place throughout the program, mainly in the evenings after a day of organizing work. They included segments on one-on-one communication (including role playing exercises), labor history (and its relationship with immigrant workers, women workers, the civil rights movement, and community organizations), power analysis, diversity workshops, AFL-CIO history and structure, and the basics of NLRB and non-NLRB campaigns. Although a few site coordinators suggested making several of the more important sessions mandatory (site coordinators were free to select from among the modules in the manual), the majority favored allowing site coordinators to select and tailor modules to their specific campaign and group dynamic needs.

According to a coordinator in Los Angeles, the educational sessions should get down to the basics: "training modules should be skill centered . . . Send USAs [Union Summer activists] with the skills to be fearless and the knowledge to be confident when dealing with the unorganized."

In order for interns to be legitimate in the eyes of the unions and their members, they needed to be aware of the circumstances and obstacles involved in the specific campaigns they joined. As we explained previously, information on specific campaigns was structured into the orientation and educational sessions. But many site coordinators felt that there were far too little of these kinds of activities. The vast majority of the union locals did not participate in either the educational sessions or the orientation sessions. As described by a Chicago coordinator, "The biggest problem was getting union staff and members to help [with training.]" A San Jose coordinator reported that "Issues surrounding the training of the interns, staff, and affiliates came up in almost every evaluation session. The desire for more or better training was expressed by everyone involved." A Boston coordinator wrote, "Some USAs got the impression the AFL-CIO throws money at problems to solve them. Most importantly, [the program] needs to develop a political base for this work at all levels of the labor movement and make it a year-round orientation so that they stop calling USAs 'kids.'" However, when union officials were able to participate, the outcome was positive. A San Jose site coordinator appreciated the impact of the training session on women in the labor movement that was led by several female union presidents. That combination of participants helped the contents of the module come across more strongly.

Without concerted local union involvement in the orientation and educational sessions, interns were left without important detailed information on the campaigns. Several coordinators, including those in Miami and Watsonville, noticed this void. In the words of the latter: "I think the most effective orientation would involve the *specifics* of campaigns they'll be working on, and use the details to teach about skills, strategies, etc."

Impact of Union Participation in Orientation and Educational Sessions

We found that the more a union local was involved in the overall Union Summer training experience, the more successful it was. This is true in terms of achieving victories as well as in attracting post-Union Summer volunteers and paid personnel. We define a major victory as concrete accomplishments that were codified in a formal way, e.g., a successful election, contract, negotiation, trial, or union recognition. We also consider the recruitment of volunteer and paid organizers for the post-Union Summer period to be a successful outcome. We collected information on these variables from the Union Summer Final Wave Report (see table 8.1).

Local unions that participated in the Union Summer educational sessions were significantly more likely to hire Union Summer interns in the aftermath of Union Summer. Twenty-five percent of the participating union locals hired interns, whereas only 8 percent of the educational session non-participants did. The participants were also significantly more likely to experience a major victory during the campaign. Twenty-three percent of those who participated in the session had victories, compared to 8 percent of those that did not.

Similarly, local unions that participated in the Union Summer orientation were significantly more successful in attracting post-Union Summer volunteers (19 percent of the participants in the orientation sessions versus 6 percent of the non-participants had volunteers stay on immediately after the Union Summer program). They were also significantly more likely to have a major victory than the non-participants (17.5 percent of the participants versus 6.5 percent of the non-participants had a major victory).

Not only is there a need for orientation prior to interns' work on campaigns, but many site coordinators also expressed the need to debrief interns. The Southern Bus Tour coordinator suggested that "Unions need to meet the needs of *our* program [by taking] time to train, time to debrief . . . and be open to input." These activities would demonstrate the commitment the unions have towards the interns and help interns feel that they have a stake in the enterprise. This, in turn, solidifies their commitment and willingness to continue their work in the movement.

Characteristics of the Local Union Campaigns

The Union Summer site coordinators made extensive comments about their views on the strengths and weaknesses of some of the union campaigns. They were asked: "Among the locals that participated in this wave, did any have particularly strong organizing programs? Particularly good organizing directors? Particularly good organizing staffs? Leadership particularly committed to organizing? Please list each such local and explain." They commented on 60

TABLE 8.1
Union Involvement in the Union Summer program by successful outcomes (Percents, N's in parentheses)

		Volunteer Organizer		Paid Organizer		Major Victory	
		Volunteer Organizer	No volunteer organizer	Paid organizer	No paid organizer	Yes	No
Local union Involved in Educational Sessions	Yes	8.3% (1)	91.7% (11)	25% (3)	75% (9)	23.1% (3)	76.9% (10)
	No	18.5% (22)	81.5% (97)	8.3% (9)	91.7% (99)	8.3% (10)	91.7% (110)
Spearman Correlation		−.019		.167*		.147*	
Local union Involved in Orientation Sessions	Yes	19.4% (7)	80.6% (29)	11.1% (4)	88.9% (32)	17.5% (7)	82.5% (33)
	No	6.0% (5)	94.0% (78)	9.6% (8)	90.4% (75)	6.5% (6)	93.5% (86)
Spearman Correlation		.205*		.022		.169*	

* Significant at .05 level.

of the 184 campaigns. In the analysis below we utilize these comments to assess what worked and what didn't work in these campaigns in conjunction with the Union Summer program.

The site coordinators' assessments, positive and negative, are associated with the actual accomplishments of the campaigns. Of the campaigns that received positive remarks by the site coordinators, 18 percent experienced victories (as opposed to 9 percent of the entire sample), 16 percent had volunteers stay on after the program (as opposed to 9 percent of the entire sample), and 20 percent hired interns on after the program (as opposed to 11 percent of the entire sample). By looking closely at these comments, we can see what rank-and-file Union Summer staff thought of the strengths and weaknesses of various unions.

Several themes emerged from a reading of the site coordinators' written comments. Most of the comments praised the campaigns and the unions that the interns worked with (site coordinators had positive things to say about 50 of the 60 campaigns on which they remarked). But there were also a considerable number of negative comments (site coordinators made negative remarks regarding 20 of the 60 campaigns).[3] Site coordinators made both positive and negative remarks with regard to 10 of the 60 campaigns.

The most common positive remark had to do with the quality of the staff. More than half (34) of the 60 site coordinators praised the dedication and effectiveness of particular union staff members and their work with the interns. Forty percent mentioned a good organizing program, 30 percent mentioned good training for the Union Summer interns, 25 percent stated that the work the unions gave the interns was particularly well-suited to them (encouraged and involved them in the projects); and without prompting on this particular issue, 7 percent volunteered that the union's active membership played a crucial role in the campaign and its success.

The most common negative comment complained of a bad program (17 percent of the 60 mentioned this). Fifteen percent mentioned problematic staff (usually a particular person who exhibited offensive [e.g., sexist, racist, insensitive] behavior), 10 percent mentioned inappropriate use of interns, and 5 percent complained of a bad training program for the interns.

In table 8.2, we examine how these remarks relate to success, specifically major victory; attracting post-Union Summer volunteers; and paid organizers. (See table 8.2.)

Good Programs and Good Training

Those locals identified by a site coordinator as having a good program were generally more successful: they were significantly more likely to attract a post-Union Summer volunteer (25 percent of those with good programs versus 8

TABLE 8.2
Qualities of union campaigns by successful outcomes (Percents, N's in parentheses)

		Volunteer Organizer		Paid Organizer		Major Victory	
		Volunteer Organizer	No volunteer organizer	Paid organizer	No paid organizer	Yes	No
Good program	Yes	25% (6)	75% (18)	25% (6)	75% (18)	20.8% (5)	79.2% (19)
	No	8.3% (3)	91.7% (33)	13.9% (5)	86.1% (31)	13.9% (5)	86.1% (31)
Spearman Correlation		.229*		.141		.091	
Good training	Yes	16.7% (3)	83.3% (15)	27.8% (5)	72.2% (13)	27.8% (5)	72.2% (13)
	No	14.3% (6)	85.7% (36)	14.3% (6)	85.7% (36)	11.9% (5)	88.1% (37)
Spearman Correlation		.031		.160		.195†	
Active union members	Yes	0% (0)	100% (4)	50% (2)	50% (2)	50% (2)	50% (2)
	No	16.1% (9)	83.9% (47)	16.1% (9)	83.9% (47)	14.3% (8)	85.7% (48)
Spearman Correlation		-.112		.219*		.239*	
Problematic programs	Yes	0% (0)	100% (10)	0% (0)	100% (10)	10% (1)	90% (9)
	No	18% (9)	82% (41)	22% (11)	78% (39)	18% (9)	82% (41)
Spearman Correlation		-.188†		-.212*		-.080	

* significant at .05 level.
† significant at .10 level.

percent of those without a positive mention of their programs), a little more likely to hire interns on as organizers (25 percent versus 14 percent), and to have a major victory (21 percent versus 14 percent). Similarly, locals with good training had significantly more victories (28 percent versus 12 percent), and somewhat more interns hired on for pay (28 percent versus 14 percent).

Several of the site coordinators' comments call attention to the importance of adequate training and a mindful incorporation of interns. A St. Louis coordinator stressed the value of a union official who "conducted trainings well and worked with us to provide a meaningful experience for the interns." Many of the site coordinators emphasized that "a responsible and committed staff to supervise and mentor the interns is necessary." The unions "have to be conscientious about training and exciting interns about the labor movement" (Watsonville site coordinator). A Sacramento coordinator commented that some of the staff they worked with "were like family and teachers to us and *never* tired of our numerous questions." When well trained and incorporated into the planning of the campaigns, the interns felt that they were a meaningful part of the process and had a stake in the outcomes. These reactions also reflect accountability to interns, and are crucial for attracting them to subsequent union work.

Good union organizing programs use a well thought-out and extensive plan that is appropriate for the workers in the industry. Some effective staff members were able to turn situations in which interns lacked work into productive experiences. The St. Louis coordinator mentioned a campaign in which a union official "bent over backwards to help us when we didn't have enough work for participants and came up with creative work plans to involve the interns in a full Union Summer experience."

We found evidence that some union staff served as an inspiration for the interns. Several site coordinators mentioned the dedication and effectiveness of union staff. The lives of these union organizers provided concrete examples of dedicated activism, which included nurturing the interns through the Union Summer sessions. Although the importance of these activists did not seem to rival that of the activists in the Freedom Summer program (largely due to the dramatic nature and circumstances of the latter campaign),it was definitely an important factor.

These comments stress how various tasks were combined and laid out for the interns, and the effectiveness of the people who coordinated the work. Good union organizing programs, good training for the interns, and effective staff members were important parts of making the Union Summer experience successful. Also important were the specific set of tasks the interns completed and the feelings they experienced while engaged in these activities.

On the whole, Union Summer interns were motivated when the union campaigns revealed to them the grave injustices and inequality workers faced.

A Washington D.C. site coordinator stated that all of the campaigns in that site wave "included very compelling components: incredibly stark working conditions, courageous and inspiring workers, logical and creative organizing strategies, and women, immigrants, and people of color on the move." Interns' exposure to campaigns that made a difference with regard to existing inequalities made lasting impressions and in some cases had life-changing ramifications. Two interns from the Washington D.C. site wave experienced these types of changes in their lives as a result of their participation. The site coordinator described the way these two interns were later perceived by the AFL-CIO Organizing Institute personnel: "They were unanimously considered the strongest participants there by the seasoned organizers who ran the training. One of the two graduates is a sophomore in college who has decided to drop out of school because he believes he has found his calling in the struggle for workers' rights." Not only were these two interns motivated to continue working with the labor movement, but, as emphasized by the site coordinator, "I strongly believe we transformed the lives of a majority of the participants in our group, and if other sites mirror D.C. at all, I think the AFL-CIO is seriously setting a foundation of what could become a vibrant pro-labor youth movement."

A New York coordinator contrasted the experiences of interns who did the more routine tasks with those whose comfort zones were challenged:

> Even though our USAs helped the labor movement with their computer skills, the ability to call government offices, etc., I don't think many of them were really challenged or confronted with the real work at hand, organizing the unorganized. Now that is the challenge of a life time! The USAs that were able to work on organizing campaigns and do house visits and building site visits really were moved personally and intellectually. They felt that we challenged their comfort zones and opened their eyes in a non abstract way to the struggles of unorganized workers in this country.

When successfully incorporated into a "comprehensive rank-and-file approach to organizing," the most effectual approaches to union organizing involve "personal contact, leadership development, and a combination of aggressive and creative internal and external pressure tactics" (Bronfenbrenner and Juravich 1998). In a related study (in progress), we found that the interns liked these types of tasks best. Yet even when interns were doing work that was appropriate, effective and what they considered to be most enjoyable, that didn't insure their continued involvement in the labor movement. For example, we found no relationship between work assignments deemed particularly suitable by the site coordinators and major victories. And although there was a weak positive association between such assignments and post-

Union Summer paid organizers, we found a negative and significant relationship between these assignments and post-Union Summer volunteers.

Active Membership

The value of an active membership was an issue that several site coordinators raised. Although only four mentioned this factor, there is a significant and very strong relationship between its mention and both a major victory (50 percent versus 14 percent) and interns staying on for pay (50 percent versus 16 percent). However, none of the campaigns with active union members attracted post-Union Summer volunteers, whereas 16 percent of those with no mention of the activity level of the membership did. Yet, since the numbers are so small, we can't make much of this.

Site coordinators often described an active union membership as more important than a solid organizing program, because the latter were hard to find. A Seattle coordinator, for example, indicated that "If we only worked with unions that have effective 'organizing programs,' then we will eliminate 95 percent of all locals." He emphasized supervision and highlighted the importance of "campaigns that matched interns with worker-organizers and that maximize contact with workers."

Problematic Union Programs

When in alliance or partnership with another movement, participants are dependent upon the competence of their partners. The site coordinators were mindful that they relied on existing union campaigns. Many coordinators identified vibrant and effective campaigns, some didn't mention the campaign's effectiveness, and still others noted problematic campaigns. Those local union campaigns and community programs identified by site coordinators as problematic tended to be much less successful. The ten local union campaigns and community programs identified as having bad programs had no post-Union Summer volunteers or paid organizers, and only one achieved a major victory (10 percent compared to 18 percent of all others; see table 8.2).

Ineffective integration of the interns was seen as a problem for a number of site coordinators. A St. Louis coordinator stated, "We worked with [a community group] and although we all believed in the mission . . . it was hard working with them because of their inflexibility and inability to work with the Union Summer plan. They didn't seem to care about the USAs and were single-mindedly trying to accomplish their goal, and not to provide a meaningful, well-rounded experience for the USAs."

When interns were not properly incorporated into the campaigns, they felt alienated from the union organizing process and, in the words of a Chicago coordinator, "People sometimes felt like they didn't get enough supervision and they [began] to question strategy—no input or explanation was given." Also in Chicago, USA interns worked with a community organization that had them post-carding for three weeks on street corners and "they were not involved in planning or even in how strategy was developed . . . On the last wave they were supervised by an intern with one month experience himself." These experiences were frustrating for the participants.

Several coordinators mentioned inefficient coordination and timing between the Union Summer program and the union locals as an issue. One Los Angeles site wave suffered from a lack of timely coordination on the part of the Union Summer central staff. The site coordinator wrote: "If someone had contacted unions months in advance to set up programs, there could have been a lot of strategizing on campaigns and projects for the students . . . My situation was cold calling unions less than a week before the interns started. In that time, it's no wonder that things were a little unstructured."

Problematic union programs sometimes had long lasting negative effects on the interns' desire for continued involvement in the labor movement. A Los Angeles coordinator emphasized that "Some unions did not have much to do with the USAs, this was negative in two big ways: (1) it took away credibility for the labor movement in the eyes of USAs, (2) it was a waste of useful help which other unions could have used for their big campaigns." Part of the disorganization had to do with the lack of coordination on the part of Union Summer central staff. For instance, a number of coordinators commented that, upon arrival, they were unexpectedly charged with selecting the unions to participate in their site wave. This situation created turmoil for several reasons. First, it put a bigger responsibility on the site coordinators, and it prevented unions from thoroughly planning their campaigns, their supervision, their use of interns, and every other aspect of their participation in the program. So even if union locals had a high degree of "strategic capacity," these problems of coordination between programs could prevent successful outcomes.[4] This is an issue that relates to Union Summer in general, as opposed to the individual unions.

Impact on Interns

We don't have any systematic evidence of the extent to which Union Summer transformed interns' way of looking at the world, yet we can offer several observations about this. Interns experienced an intense three-week session in which they worked with various unions for approximately 50 hours a week.

If they had been previously unfamiliar with unions and their work, after these sessions, they undoubtedly had a good feel for union culture, organizing drives, strikes, and the like. For the vast majority of interns, knowledge of unions increased dramatically.

Interns liked doing house calls more than any other activity. This suggests that they felt a connection to the workers they were organizing and empowering. Such concern and affinity with workers is a necessary precondition for class consciousness, as is an understanding of the realities of exploitation, another goal of much of the training. Together, these aspects of the Union Summer program exposed the interns to a practical class analysis. Although we can't definitively say that interns left the program with enhanced class consciousness, we can say that they left equipped with the knowledge and experiences that are the building blocks of class-consciousness. Immediately after the program's first summer, site coordinators were unsure about how successful the program was at increasing class-based consciousness among the interns. A Boston staff member wrote: "Most important factor is, will this build class consciousness among youth and lead to more activism on campus this year? I think that with all our problems the answer is yes."

DISCUSSION AND CONCLUSIONS

The materials from the first Union Summer program give us rich insight into the types of issues and obstacles associated with social movement alliance work and crossover of movement activists. In this paper, we have focused on the rationale behind the association between youthful (mainly college student) interns and the labor movement, and how the Union Summer participants were integrated or incorporated into the ongoing local union campaigns. The task of integration was not an easy one, nor was there a clear understanding of what needed to be accomplished.

Although we did not focus on students' later incorporation into labor organizing, we can make a few observations about how their Union Summer experiences affected their willingness to continue their union involvement. In order for students to want to continue in this line of work, they need to have proper preparation, a sense of efficacy and overall positive experiences. In the student reports, we noted a range of both positive and negative aspects of the Union Summer training and orientation sessions: many commented on how those sessions equipped them to work in the field; others commented on the gaps in their knowledge and understanding of union-related issues or the repetition of information that they already knew. Since interns and trainers had varying levels of prior preparation and enthusiasm for the tasks they were asked to complete, training scenarios most likely had different rates of success for different interns.

Some interns found the sessions to be overly monotonous. These interns were sometimes more knowledgeable about the topics, but more often they disliked the format of the sessions or the mismatch of the topics covered with the necessary skills for the job. An intern from Detroit (white, college student, daughter of a union member) said the orientation session was "a gripe session with most of the day taken up with people complaining. Focus was not brought to the task at hand." This intern was critical of the AFL-CIO and its programs, but expressed an interest in continuing with progressive politics in general. Another intern from Chicago (white college student, daughter of a union member) said: "More emphasis should have been placed on role playing, team building, and a better introduction into what we would be doing—perhaps bringing in the locals and having them run part of the orientation. Everyone came in at different levels but possibly a stronger history/movement training before we started would have been helpful." This intern expressed a strong interest in continuing with the labor movement, but had some criticisms of the Union Summer program. Others thought the sessions were too intense. A different Chicago intern (African American college student, daughter of a union member) explained: "By the end of the day everyone (including the site coordinators) was too tired to absorb information. We were given readings that were [not useful], ineffective, and/or outdated. A lot of the information was only briefly touched upon and so it went in one ear and out the other." She did not express an intention to continue with the labor movement.

Much of the student feedback on the educational and orientation sessions was positive and many interns expressed that the sessions were "inspirational." This was especially the case for several sites involving farm workers. An intern in Miami (Latina college student, daughter of a union member) said: "The briefings on the campaigns were great. I got really excited after I heard them and I wanted to work with every group." Another intern (Latina college student) said: "The orientation was intense, but it prepared us well for the task on hand. Not only did we learn about the strawberry campaign and our role in the campaign, but we also learned about the labor movement, and about the UFW, from campaigns to the workings of the UFW . . . This program has influenced me greatly. I now know that I want to be involved with the labor movement. I also know that I can make a difference . . ." A Detroit intern (white college student, daughter of a union member) expressed: "The meeting with [the union organizer] was stimulating in that it challenged me to think about how workers' fear is the biggest barrier to unionizing and it helped to offer solutions to that problem. The speakers were all inspirational and helped to bring unionism down to a real, interpersonal, attainable level . . . I hope to remain involved in the labor movement. I'd love to organize to fight the good fight." A Chicago intern (white college student, son of a union member) who mentioned that he intended to continue in the labor movement and to set up a Student Labor Action Coalition [SLAC] on his campus related: "The orientation was great. I feel like it provided me the background I needed." But he added that the three-week Union Summer session itself would be strengthened by a longer timeframe: "This would allow for people to get more involved with their particular campaigns and therefore gain more experience and be more beneficial to the movement." So the educational and orientation sessions were part of a larger experience that cumulatively worked towards integrating interns into a lifestyle of work with the labor movement. It was one step (albeit an important one) in the process of moving them in this direction.

Another important issue that we haven't addressed here is what happened to the Union Summer class of 1996? Have they remained active in the labor movement? Have they become involved in progressive political causes? Leslie Bunnage has pursued these questions in a related research project. She has uncovered evidence that many 1996 Union Summer interns became important initiators of campus-based anti-sweatshop activities, and has noted that almost half of the 1996 cohort reported an interest in participating in (and/or forming) student labor groups. In addition, almost half reported an interest in working with a union campaign in the future (Bunnage 2003).

Students were only one of the AFL-CIO's target groups, and in retrospect, seem to have been the most successful "outsiders." As emphasized in the social movement literature and mentioned earlier, they are characterized by social change oriented values, the lack of issue satiation, flexible schedules and large blocks of time in which to concentrate social movement activities, a higher threshold for risk, and high energy levels. In light of the victories and recruitment of Union Summer activists in the aftermath of the 1996 program, and despite some of the problems that arose, Union Summer represents a relatively effective and successful use of "outside" activists.

The Union Summer program modeled itself after the civil rights movement's Freedom Summer program, and did an excellent job of amassing a comprehensive set of orientation and training materials for the site waves. Yet there was no way to cover all of these materials in the two days (and various evenings throughout the program) that were allotted to these activities, and the program found it difficult to enlist the participation of the local union officials. The latter, especially, was a major downfall.

In order to overcome the lack of resources needed to accomplish the enormous task of organizing the American labor force, the AFL-CIO leadership endeavored to use both its strategic capacity and that of its constituent unions. This came through in a number of new and innovative local union campaigns, many of which were included as part of the Union Summer site activities.

A crucial component of strategic capacity involves the gathering of information on the environment and its effective use in the organizing campaign. For a program like Union Summer, this is contingent upon effectively communicating detailed information to student interns. For interns to be successful in their organizational activities, they had to be competent on the specifics of the local campaigns, and the needs and desires of the workers involved. Although this information many times was delivered briefly on the spot, the most useful approach was to have formal presentations where interns could get to know union staff beforehand, ask them questions, and think about the issues prior to entering the field.

In fact, we found that when unions participated in the orientation and educational sessions, they were significantly more likely to experience a favorable outcome. They were more likely to win a tangible victory and more likely to attract post-Union Summer interns to both volunteer and paid positions.

Unions already engaging in innovative and progressive organizing campaigns also tended to be the ones best suited to understand the needs and orientations of the student interns. This, in turn, allowed them to organize effective and participatory tasks in which the interns could contribute. When interns sensed that their efforts and ideas mattered in the conduct of the campaigns, they were drawn in and tended to be more successful than when they were merely told what to do. They were also more likely to continue their work in the labor movement after Union Summer.

Solid organizing programs, good training, and an active union membership stood out as the most important specific factors in influencing successful outcomes. Dedicated union organizers served as inspiring examples for the interns, but we didn't find them to be systematically related to successful outcomes. Despite what an intuitive understanding of youth activists' motivations might suggest, work that was exciting and enjoyable to them was not what led to interns' continued involvement in the labor movement. Rather, what mattered most was the witnessing of injustice and participation in effective campaigns that had the potential to enact important social change.

EPILOGUE: CHANGES IN THE UNION SUMMER PROGRAM SINCE 1996

Union Summer has been repeated every year since the first. In 1996 the program broadly focused on the goal of increasing labor activism on campus. While more recent Union Summer programs still target college students and seek to increase campus labor activism, they now emphasize preparing interns to be full-time organizers. A series of programmatic changes were made in accordance with the new concentration on union organizer recruitment and training (Stewart 2003). Only those students closer to graduation (juniors and seniors) are now eligible to participate. This change is advantageous for the program, since it immerses students who are preparing to make life-long career decisions in the midst of labor struggles that are likely to have a strong impact on them.

The Union Summer program has also reduced significantly the average size of its site waves (to approximately six interns). The program is much more selective of its applicants now than it was in prior years, and as a result, the caliber of the interns is now generally regarded as higher. A tightly knit group of dedicated interns is likely to make for a better experience (for both interns and unions) than a larger group of interns with various levels of attachment to the program.

Working with smaller numbers of interns both in the individual site wave groups and in the overall program also means that Union Summer can be more selective with respect to host union and community groups. The sheer size of the 1996 program was unwieldy, and as we noted earlier in this chapter, finding strong union campaigns for interns' participation was a tremendous challenge. At its current size, Union Summer has less difficulty finding host organizations doing substantive, interesting and engaging work. Matching dedicated interns with strong union organizing programs is beneficial for both intern recruitment and successful outcomes.

In order to give interns more intensive experience and training, both the program and the initial orientation period have been expanded. There is a single one-week nation wide training session in which all interns participate simultaneously. There is also a day-long nation-wide debriefing session at the end of the program. With these additions, the duration of the program has increased to five weeks. These changes make for a more encompassing and comprehensive orientation program more akin to that of Freedom Summer.

But according to our analysis, the comprehensiveness of the orientation session is only one of two important aspects of successful orientation and training. Our findings indicate that local union participation in the orientation and educational sessions is also crucial. While conserving important staff resources, centralized training decreases the likelihood of individual *local* union participation in the process. Hence, interns are less likely to get the details of the specific campaigns and miss the opportunity to meet and converse with the local union staff with whom they will be working. Unless coupled with site-specific orientations that entail substantial local union participation, the national training is likely to miss an important component of a successful training process.

9

UNIONISM IN CALIFORNIA AND THE UNITED STATES

USING REPRESENTATION ELECTIONS TO EVALUATE THEIR IMPACT ON BUSINESS ESTABLISHMENTS

John DiNardo and David S. Lee

Interest in the impacts of unions spans literatures in industrial relations, political science, sociology, and indeed virtually every area of inquiry in the "social sciences." An arguably distinctive aspect of the approach of "modern labor economics" is the concern with the following fundamental question of whether labor market institutions, especially those which ostensibly serve the interests of workers, have a "distortionary" impact on the allocation of resources and the level of economic activity. One of the leading examples of this concern has been the question of whether or not unions primarily act as a cartel for labor services in which wage gains for union workers come at the expense of non-union workers.

Perhaps because of a paucity of credible estimates on the effect of unions on employment or establishment survival, the few shreds of evidence that exist suggest there is no "consensus" view on virtually any aspect of the "labor economics" of labor unions. In a study of the views of 65 labor economists from "Top 40" economics departments, for example, responses indicated wide disagreement on the desirability of all the policy proposals for which opinions were solicited and little correlation between these opinions and views about the relevant "policy parameters" (Fuchs et al. 1998). When asked to rate on a scale of 0 to 100 (from "strongly opposed" to "strongly favor") the degree of their support for a proposal that would increase the fraction of workers covered by a collective bargaining agreement, the median score was a 48, and there was a wide dispersion of responses.[1] While the survey did not ask specifically about union impacts on establishment survival, estimates of the union effect on productivity—which might be expected to be related to beliefs about the effect of unions on establishment survival—ranged from 0 to a positive 10 percent with a mean of about 3 percent.

Nonetheless, in part because of its simplicity, the analytic framework most frequently used to analyze the employment impacts of labor unionism is the so-called "monopoly union" model. In this model, unions are assumed to negotiate "above market" wages for their members. Faced with a higher price for their input, profit maximizing employers substitute away from unionized labor. The consequence is lower employment for workers in the union sector, even though those union members who are still employed command higher relative wages. The primary concern for economists is that this outcome would be "inefficient": that is, employers would like to hire extra workers at a lower wage, and at the same time there are workers who would be willing to work at that lower wage, but who are nonetheless "crowded out" or underemployed due to the "above market" wage. This perspective of unions is a staple of economics textbook treatments of unionization. Even in Freeman and Medoff's (1984) wide-ranging review of the economic impacts of unionization (which inter alia highlights the potential for allocation improvements under unionization), Freeman and Medoff essentially stipulate the existence of such a welfare loss, while noting that their estimate of this loss is small.[2]

However, while this view of the impacts of unions on the economy is widespread among economists, there is a literature within modern labor economic analysis that explores another possibility: that employers do not substitute away from unionized labor in response to an "above market" wage negotiated by the union. In the so-called "efficient-contracts" view of unionism, the union and management bargain, either implicitly or explicitly, over both the level of wages and the level of employment. In this view, the "monopoly union" outcome is not in the best interest of either management or the union. If management is willing to hire more labor when the wage is slightly lower, and if unions also care about the level of employment for their members, then both parties should be able to find a combination of wages and employment that is strictly more agreeable to both sides. Thus, in this view, it is possible that unions do not lead to lower employment, but merely redistribute the economic "pie" produced by the firm.[3]

UNION ANALYSIS: THE IMPORTANCE OF LARGE-SCALE DATA COLLECTION AND ANALYSIS

Ultimately, whether or not unions make business establishments more likely to fail is an empirical question. The core issue is that of the fundamental problem of causal inference. That is, in any isolated case, although we can observe the level of employment and wages at an establishment that employs union workers, we do not and cannot ever know what the employment and wages would have been in the absence of the union. Therefore, it is impossible to learn whether unions cause a change in employment, relying upon our knowledge of an isolated case of a union-management relationship.

While we do not mean to imply that all (or even most) important issues regarding an institution like the American labor union can be addressed by the type of approach we adopt here (see Thacher 2001 for one recent discussion of some of the limitations in the context of police research), it would appear that progress on questions such as "in the present context, do labor organizing victories lead to establishment failures?" is unlikely without the use of large-scale databases that contain information on a large number of employers, employees, and unions.

Addison et al. (2002) observe, however, that "there is remarkably little evidence as to union impact on plant closings." Moreover, much of the literature they cite has had to rely heavily on regression adjustment to try to make the comparison of unionized and non-unionized establishments informative about a causal effect of unionization. The inadequacy of regression adjustment in this context has been apparent and has even led to contradictory estimates from the same data.[4]

Some previous research has used NLRB or FMCS data, using a variety of methods to approximate a valid comparison between union and non-unionized establishments. For example, Lalonde, Marschke, and Troske (1996) combine NLRB representation election data with the Bureau of the Census' Longitudinal Research Datafile (LRD) to examine the impact of union victories in NLRB certification elections on wages, employment, and shipments. They essentially use a "difference-in-difference" approach to account for selectivity, assuming that the outcomes (e.g. employment growth, expressed as deviations from establishment-specific trends) of establishments experiencing union losses in organizing drives are adequate representations of what would have happened for those that experience a union victory, had the union not won.

Freeman and Kleiner (1999) conduct their own survey of establishments that experienced organizing drives, as well as a "control" sample of establishments (determined by asking managers of the establishments in the first sample who their "closest" non-union competitor was). Using these matched pairings, they compare wage and employment changes for those establishments experiencing union victories to the experience of their matched "competitor." Freeman and Kleiner (1999) use FMCS data, although they observe that "lacking an appropriate control group, [they] can only approximate the extent to which ... closure rate[s] might be attributable to unionization."

One message that comes through from this research is the vital importance of a research design that allows us some confidence that we are comparing establishments that are similar in all other ways (besides union status). The more confident we can be that this *ceteris paribus* condition is satisfied, the more confident we can be that differences in the outcomes represent a true impact of unionism.

Our approach relies on a distinctive aspect of the unionization process in American union certification elections, that is, the fact that in most establishments workers become unionized as a partial consequence of a secret ballot among the workers. In principle, a simple majority vote in favor of the union leads to the unionization of an establishment. In the analysis, we examine the short and long term survival rates of establishments, where NLRB representation elections were held. Focusing on this sample of establishments, we compare the survival rates of businesses where the union prevailed in the election to those where the union lost. Since it could be argued that establishments where the union won a representation election may not be otherwise similar to establishments where the union lost, we also examine the differences among elections that were either barely won or lost (as measured by the actual vote count) by the union.

Using data on more than 27,000 union certification elections between 1983 and 2000, we find that: (1) certification elections in which a union wins a simple majority of the workers, as might be expected, increases the likelihood that workers in an establishment will have a collective bargaining agreement; and (2) the effect of unionization on establishment survival is a fairly precisely estimated "zero"—establishments whose workers have unionized are neither more nor less likely to survive.

Under the assumption that the firms begin with identical survival probabilities, and that the treatment effect of unionization is a constant across firms, our 95 percent confidence interval includes an estimate of the average treatment effect of unionization that ranges from an increase in the probability that an establishment will survive an additional year of .006 of a percent to a decrease in the probability that an establishment will survive an additional year of .5 of a percent. This can be compared to a base rate of establishment death of about 15 to 20 percent during a typical year in our data.

THE INDUSTRIAL RELATIONS CLIMATE AND THE NLRB ELECTION PROCESS: INSTITUTIONAL BACKGROUND

Since most new unionization occurs as a consequence of an NLRB election, and the "selection" of firms at risk for unionization in our sample includes only those firms that have faced such an election, it is useful to provide a brief synopsis of the process and the context in which these elections occur.

The NLRB is the most significant administrative agency to be a consequence of the National Labor Relations Act (NLRA)—the Wagner Act—of the 1930s. The law has been changing continuously since its enactment, most notably with the passage of Taft-Hartley Act in 1947 (which, among other things, provided for temporary government seizure of struck facilities in the event of a strike that creates an "emergency") and the Landrum-Griffin Act of 1959 (which, for example, outlawed a number of successful union tactics including "secondary boycotts"). In principle, the NLRA provides a neutral setting in which the right for workers to bargain collectively is enforced.

A fundamental reason for certification elections, however, and the resulting complexity of the process is employer opposition to unions. American law gives workers the right to unionize, but an NLRB election is not required. In most instances, nothing prevents an employer from recognizing a union without the formalities of an election. However, voluntary recognition of a union is rare. Moreover, with data on firms who faced NLRB elections in the early 1990s, Bronfenbrenner (1994) documents that most employers used multiple tactics to delay or deny a collective bargaining agreement; this included holding "captive meetings", firing union activists, hiring a management consultant, and the like.

In the case of graduate students at universities, for example, employers have often attempted to argue—sometimes successfully—that graduate student employees are not "employees" but "students receiving financial aid." Another example is employers arguing that its employees are not workers but "independent contractors" who are not covered by the provisions of NLRA.

Against this backdrop of employer opposition to unionization, it is perhaps not surprising that there is no single path to an NLRB election and eventual recognition of the union by the employer. Nonetheless, it is useful to describe a common scenario that results in an establishment agreeing to bargain with its workers through a labor union:

1. A group of workers decide to try to form a union. These workers contact a labor union and ask for assistance in beginning an organizing drive.

2. In collaboration with the union, the employees begin a "card drive." The purpose of the card drive is to be able to petition the NLRB to hold an election. Unions generally seek to get cards from at least 50 percent of the workers in the 6 month period of time usually allowed (although in principle, only 30 percent is required to be granted an election by the NLRB).

3. After the cards have been submitted, the NLRB makes a ruling on whether the people the union seeks to represent have a "community of interest"—basically form a coherent group for the purposes of bargaining. The NLRB makes a determination of which categories of employees fall within the union's "bargaining unit."

4. Next, typically within 30 days from the card submission, the NLRB holds an election at the work site (with exceptions to account for such things as the vagaries of employment seasonality). A simple majority of those voting for one union is all that is required to win.

5. Within 7 days after the final tally of the ballots, parties can file objections to how the election was conducted or to specific ballots.

6. If after all this, a union still has a simple majority, then the employer is, in principle, obligated to negotiate "in good faith." Again, even at this state, however, there is no guarantee that the firm will recognize the union, or that a contract secured by collective bargaining is inevitable. Indeed, analysis by the "Dunlop Commission" found that only 55 percent of those unions who win elections eventually get a first contract. We discuss this issue in more detail below.

THE DATA

For a more detailed discussion of our data, see DiNardo and Lee 2002. Here we will sketch only the most salient features of our data. Our point of departure is our sample of all NLRB elections from 1983 to 2000. We limit ourselves to NLRB certification elections, which comprise the overwhelming majority of elections conducted by the NLRB.

We merge data from the Federal Mediation and Conciliation Service (FMCS), which we received through a Freedom of Information Act (FOIA) request. The FMCS is an independent agency whose creation was mandated by Congress by the Taft-Hartley Act "to promote sound and stable labor-management relations." Our data is the FMCS census of all notices that a collective bargaining agreement has expired. For our purposes, a desirable feature of the law is the legal requirement that firms and unions report an impending contract expiration.

For our analysis, it would be ideal to obtain more detailed information on whether unions that prevailed in NLRB representation elections were able to secure an initial contract. Such data is, in principle, available from the FMCS, and was used to create some summary statistics for the Dunlop Commission report (see table 9.1). It would be interesting to examine whether the proba-

TABLE 9.1

Estimates of the outcome of certification cases as tabulated by the FMCS

	Fiscal year 1986 to fiscal year 1993	
	Number of cases	Percent of cases
Number of certifications	10,783	100.0%
Reason for closing the case		
Agreement reached	6,009	55.7
Diverse factors for closing	488	4.5
Question of representation	580	5.4
Referred to NLRB	563	5.2
Plant closed	341	3.2
Other	2,802	26.0
Strikes of certification cases	356	100.0%
Agreement reached	191	53.7
Diverse factors for closing	3	0.8
Question of representation	18	5.1
Referred to NLRB	27	7.6
Plant closed	8	2.2
Other	109	30.6

bility that such an initial agreement is reached is at all related to the strength of support for the union (as measured through the NLRB vote count).

Nevertheless, we use our data on contract expirations to provide a rough measure of whether workers at an establishment are covered by a union contract. Again, this is not an ideal measure: most limiting for some of our analysis is the fact that we can only observe a contract expiration if an establishment survives until the end of the first contract. Put differently, our "unionization" variable is potentially "censored".

The NLRB and FMCS data are additionally merged with our third source of data—a marketing research database maintained by InfoUSA, Inc. This is a comprehensive database of business establishments in existence as of May, 2001. We use this data to measure "survival." A firm is denoted as surviving when an establishment with the same name and the same address is identified in the InfoUSA data base.

An inherent limitation of this data is that our matches are imperfect, because of miscoding and related problems. Consequently, we end up treating some firms as having "died," when instead we have simply been unable to match them. On a case-by-case basis, this is obviously a problem, but such idiosyncratic errors are likely to be "averaged out" by looking at the summary statistics of the sample.

METHODS AND ANALYSIS

We begin our discussion with a simple comparison of differences between the unionized and non-unionized establishments in our sample. Throughout we perform an analysis of California and the rest of the nation.

Table 9.2 tabulates a series of outcomes associated with establishments located in California at the time of their NLRB election. We divide our firms into two categories—those for whom we have an FMCS contract expiration notice (which we label "union" establishments), and those for whom we do not have such a notice (which we label "non-union" establishments).

In the first three columns we consider the proportion of firms in our data who survived until 2001—the focus of our attention in much of the analysis below. As expected, the later the election the more likely we observe the firm. Of establishments who faced elections in 1984, for example, only 26 percent of them had survived to 2001. Of those who faced elections in 1999, approximately two thirds survived until the year 2001.

Also worthy of note is the fact that union establishments generally have higher survival rates than their non-union counterparts. With the exception of those establishments who faced elections in 1985, the union/non-union survival gap is positive and ranges from 1 percent in 1999 to 15 percent for those establishments who faced elections in 1991, although averaged over all firms in all years the difference is not significantly different from zero.

An inference that should not be taken from these numbers is that unions help establishments survive longer. This may or may not be true, but these numbers do not address the issue satisfactorily for two reasons. First, our measure of union status only exists if the firm survives long enough to have a first contract expire. If, for instance, the firm "died" before the first contract ended, it would be categorized as "non-union" in our analysis. More importantly, we have reason to suspect that "union" establishments may be very different from "non-union" establishments where unions lose elections. In other words, these simple comparisons of means fail to identify the true "causal" effect of unionization.

The next set of columns display similar comparisons for mean employment levels, treating a firm death as a case of zero employment. Here the comparison is even more striking—the union/non-union gap employment in 2001 generally is large and positive—from a low of 58.6 for those establishments that faced elections in 1987 up to a high of 278.5 for those establishments that faced elections in 1999.

The final set of columns, labeled "mean log of employment," takes the natural logarithm of employment for those firms who survived. This is a convenient way of assessing differences in unionized and non-unionized establishments that survived. While the relatively small sample of establishments

TABLE 9.2

Establishment outcomes by presence of union, as of 2001: NLRB elections, 1983–1999, California

Year of election	Proportion survived as of 2001				Mean employment as of 2001				Mean log of employment as of 2001			
	All	No union	Union	Diff.	All	No union	Union	Diff.	All	No union	Union	Diff.
1983	0.268	0.246	0.353	0.107	30.9	33.3	21.4	−11.9	3.80	3.97	3.28	−0.70
1984	0.257	0.248	0.286	0.037	39.8	40.9	35.8	−5.1	4.13	4.06	4.34	0.27
1985	0.392	0.409	0.317	−0.092	38.6	41.3	27.2	−14.1	3.91	3.88	4.07	0.19
1986	0.261	0.250	0.303	0.053	21.3	22.2	18.1	−4.1	3.63	3.68	3.49	−0.19
1987	0.329	0.328	0.333	0.005	49.4	40.3	98.8	58.6	4.28	4.16	5.00	0.84
1988	0.335	0.316	0.413	0.097	47.8	41.9	72.5	30.6	4.50	4.49	4.51	0.01
1989	0.330	0.317	0.400	0.083	57.9	57.7	58.7	0.9	4.40	4.49	4.01	−0.48
1990	0.367	0.353	0.448	0.095	47.5	45.5	59.4	13.8	4.28	4.24	4.47	0.23
1991	0.390	0.365	0.516	0.151	68.6	68.2	70.9	2.6	4.27	4.29	4.20	−0.09
1992	0.431	0.417	0.500	0.083	69.3	47.1	175.2	128.1	4.07	3.85	4.83	0.98
1993	0.399	0.394	0.419	0.025	50.7	49.3	56.5	7.2	4.06	4.14	3.69	−0.45
1994	0.448	0.416	0.652	0.236	67.9	56.6	146.8	90.1	4.25	4.21	4.42	0.21
1995	0.496	0.491	0.526	0.035	82.5	72.2	139.1	67.0	4.39	4.32	4.71	0.39
1996	0.549	0.542	0.593	0.050	135.7	96.0	369.2	273.2	4.44	4.32	5.08	0.76
1997	0.492	0.487	0.524	0.036	94.5	86.0	166.9	81.0	4.46	4.48	4.26	−0.22
1998	0.646	0.631	0.900	0.269	97.8	97.3	109.4	12.1	4.26	4.28	3.88	−0.41
1999	0.657	0.657	0.667	0.010	89.2	73.1	351.7	278.5	4.16	4.09	5.38	1.29
All	0.410	0.405	0.437	0.031	64.0	58.2	95.7	37.5	4.24	4.22	4.35	0.13
	(0.009)	(0.010)	(0.023)	(0.025)	(3.7)	(3.5)	(14.0)	(14.4)	(0.04)	(0.05)	(0.12)	(0.13)
Obs.	2951	2486	465		2811	2374	437		1071	896	175	

Note: Standard errors in parentheses. Entries are outcomes, as of 2001, of establishments that experienced an NLRB certification election in a given year. Zero is assigned to the employment of "dead" establishments. "Union/No Union" Indicates whether or not the establishment's location appeared in the FMCS contract expiration notice, implying the presence of a union.

accounts for much of the variation in the union/non-union gap, over the entire period there is virtually no difference in the size of surviving unionized and non-unionized firms.

Table 9.3 repeats the analysis for the rest of the country. Perhaps surprisingly, the pattern, although not identical, is very similar to that of California. This suggests that an analysis based on experiences in the rest of the country may be useful for learning something about the California experience. The main difference in table 9.3 is that the large sample allows more precise inference. Indeed, the "union advantage" in firm survival is large and precisely estimated as is the "union advantage" in mean employment levels. Conditional on employment, the difference between unionized and nonunionized firms is essentially a precisely estimated zero.

COMPARING WINNERS AND LOSERS

We next turn to a descriptive analysis of firms, this type divided by whether the union won or lost the representation election. As before, the California case (table 9.4) and the case for the rest of the country (table 9.5) are remarkably similar. The first row of each table shows the survival rate of firms for the full sample, for the sample of establishments where the union lost, and for the sample of establishments where the union won the representation election. Both for California and the rest of the country, establishments that faced union wins were slightly less likely to survive than those where the union lost. The situation is more dramatic if we look at sales volume in the year 2001 where there is a highly significant "union deficit"—union winners have much lower sales volume than union losses. Again, there is good reason to resist interpreting this as evidence that unions have an adverse effect on establishment survival. Indeed, the rest of the table makes it clear that "all else is not the same" at firms where the union won the representation election and establishments where the union lost.

Both in California and in the rest of America, unions are much less likely to be in manufacturing firms, and much more likely to be in services. For example, in California about a third of the firms where unions lost their representation elections were in manufacturing; that figure is closer to 28 percent for union winners. Perhaps reflecting the successes of such unions as the SEIU, a third of the union winners were in the service sector compared to only 24 percent of the union losers. Moreover, union wins tend to occur in smaller elections—the average number of eligible voters was 88 among union wins and 106 where the union lost.

TABLE 9.3

Establishment outcomes by presence of union, as of 2001: NLRB elections 1983–1999, rest of U.S.

Year of election	Proportion survived as of 2001				Mean employment as of 2001				Mean log of employment as of 2001			
	All	No union	Union	Diff.	All	No union	Union	Diff.	All	No union	Union	Diff.
1983	0.308	0.310	0.302	−0.007	69.8	71.1	64.7	−6.4	4.41	4.51	4.04	−0.46
1984	0.280	0.262	0.343	0.081	63.9	49.6	114.3	64.7	4.41	4.37	4.49	0.11
1985	0.301	0.275	0.415	0.140	60.1	42.6	136.0	93.5	4.43	4.37	4.57	0.20
1986	0.313	0.293	0.391	0.097	56.1	47.6	89.4	41.8	4.37	4.36	4.42	0.07
1987	0.327	0.322	0.344	0.022	58.2	50.3	84.9	34.6	4.40	4.44	4.29	−0.15
1988	0.364	0.345	0.427	0.082	71.7	65.0	94.8	29.9	4.42	4.44	4.37	−0.07
1989	0.379	0.344	0.524	0.180	78.8	65.5	136.1	70.6	4.40	4.44	4.31	−0.13
1990	0.396	0.367	0.517	0.150	68.5	59.9	104.7	44.8	4.25	4.32	4.05	−0.28
1991	0.414	0.395	0.496	0.101	87.0	75.6	136.3	60.7	4.38	4.39	4.36	−0.03
1992	0.432	0.395	0.582	0.187	81.1	71.8	119.6	47.7	4.43	4.44	4.40	−0.04
1993	0.418	0.389	0.550	0.161	77.6	58.5	164.8	106.3	4.40	4.38	4.47	0.09
1994	0.467	0.435	0.618	0.183	109.7	86.5	217.8	131.4	4.56	4.52	4.68	0.16
1995	0.510	0.485	0.631	0.146	109.5	95.4	181.1	85.7	4.60	4.58	4.70	0.12
1996	0.519	0.488	0.691	0.203	103.6	85.3	207.4	122.2	4.47	4.44	4.59	0.15
1997	0.581	0.571	0.656	0.085	137.9	114.4	309.0	194.6	4.58	4.57	4.63	0.06
1998	0.563	0.556	0.653	0.097	122.4	117.8	176.8	59.0	4.46	4.50	4.04	−0.46
1999	0.569	0.557	0.735	0.178	118.4	102.2	343.7	241.6	4.45	4.40	5.00	0.60
All	0.418	0.401	0.497	0.095	85.7	73.7	141.6	67.9	4.45	4.45	4.44	−0.01
	(0.003)	(0.003)	(0.008)	(0.008)	(1.9)	(1.7)	(6.6)	(6.8)	(0.02)	(0.02)	(0.04)	(0.04)
Obs.	24671	20293	4378		23544	19381	4163		9194	7234	1960	

Note: Standard errors in parentheses. Entries are outcomes, as of 2001, of establishments that experienced an NLRB certification election in a given year. Zero is assigned to the employment of "dead" establishments. "Union/No Union" Indicates whether or not the establishment's location appeared in the FMCS contract expiration notice, implying the presence of a union.

TABLE 9.4

Means of establishment and election outcomes and characteristics, by representation election outcome, 1983–1999, California

	N	Full sample	Union loss	Union win	Difference
1 Survival (Indicator Variable), 2001	2951	0.410 (0.009)	0.420 (0.012)	0.399 (0.013)	−0.021 (0.018)
2 Employment, 2001	2811	64.0 (3.7)	67.9 (4.8)	59.5 (5.7)	−8.3 (7.4)
3 Log of employment, 2001	1071	4.24 (0.04)	4.32 (0.06)	4.14 (0.07)	−0.18 (0.09)
4 Sales volume, 2001	2771	12026.1 (840.2)	14517.5 (1400.3)	9132.5 (801.1)	−5385.0 (1613.2)
5 Log of sales volume, 2001	1031	9.16 (0.05)	9.28 (0.07)	9.01 (0.08)	−0.28 (0.11)
6 Presence of union post-election (indicator variable)	2951	0.158 (0.007)	0.080 (0.007)	0.247 (0.012)	0.167 (0.014)
7 Presence of union pre-election (indicator variable)	2951	0.090 (0.005)	0.073 (0.007)	0.111 (0.009)	0.039 (0.011)
8 Number of eligible voters	2951	97.6 (2.3)	105.5 (3.4)	88.4 (3.0)	−17.1 (4.5)
9 Log of eligible voters	2951	4.19 (0.01)	4.25 (0.02)	4.13 (0.02)	−0.12 (0.03)
10 Number of votes cast	2951	82.5 (1.9)	91.3 (2.9)	72.3 (2.4)	−19.0 (3.7)
11 Log of votes cast	2951	4.04 (0.01)	4.11 (0.02)	3.95 (0.02)	−0.16 (0.03)
12 Manufacturing sector (indicator variable)	2951	0.303 (0.008)	0.326 (0.012)	0.276 (0.012)	−0.050 (0.017)
13 Service sector (indicator variable)	2951	0.278 (0.008)	0.235 (0.011)	0.328 (0.013)	0.093 (0.017)
14 Trucking voting unit (indicator variable)	2951	0.191 (0.007)	0.206 (0.010)	0.173 (0.010)	−0.034 (0.014)

Note: Standard errors in parentheses. Presence of union post-election (pre-election) indicates whether or not a union at the location of the establishment filed a contract expiration between the election date and 2001 (between the beginning of the FMCS data and the date of the election). Details of the merged data from the NLRB, FMCS, and InfoUSA are described in DiNardo and Lee 2002.

FROM SIMPLE COMPARISONS TO CAUSALITY

The key to making a causal analysis is to compare establishments where the union won its representation election to establishments where the union lost its representation election, *holding everything else constant*. In other words, it would be desirable for the winners and losers to appear comparable on all dimensions, except with respect to whether or not the union ultimately won the election. As we have shown above, however, when we compare winners and losers, they do not appear otherwise "identical."

However, we argue that a valid comparison can be made if we examine establishments where the NLRB election happened to be *close* (as measured by the eventual vote count). That is, if there is some uncertainty *ex ante* about

TABLE 9.5

Means of establishment and election outcomes and characteristics, by representation election outcome, 1983–1999, rest of United States

	N	Full sample	Union loss	Union win	Difference
1 Survival (indicator variable), 2001	24671	0.418 (0.003)	0.431 (0.004)	0.401 (0.005)	−0.031 (0.006)
2 Employment, 2001	23544	85.7 (1.9)	90.6 (2.4)	79.0 (2.9)	−11.6 (3.8)
3 Log of employemt, 2001	9194	4.45 (0.02)	4.53 (0.02)	4.31 (0.02)	−0.22 (0.03)
4 Sales volume, 2001	22948	14490.8 (345.6)	16445.0 (479.5)	11814.1 (487.9)	−4630.8 (684.1)
5 Log of sales volume, 2001	8598	9.36 (0.02)	9.50 (0.02)	9.15 (0.03)	−0.35 (0.04)
6 Presence of union post-election (indicator variable)	24671	0.177 (0.002)	0.088 (0.002)	0.299 (0.004)	0.211 (0.005)
7 Presence of union pre-election (indicator variable)	24671	0.103 (0.002)	0.077 (0.002)	0.139 (0.003)	0.062 (0.004)
8 Number of Eligible voters	24671	104.9 (0.9)	114.3 (1.2)	92.0 (1.2)	−22.3 (1.7)
9 Log of eligible voters	24671	4.23 (0.01)	4.29 (0.01)	4.14 (0.01)	−0.16 (0.01)
10 Number of votes cast	24671	92.8 (0.8)	103.1 (1.1)	78.8 (1.0)	−24.3 (1.5)
11 Log of votes cast	24671	4.11 (0.01)	4.19 (0.01)	4.00 (0.01)	−0.20 (0.01)
12 Manufacturing sector (indicator variable)	24671	0.390 (0.003)	0.431 (0.004)	0.333 (0.005)	−0.098 (0.006)
13 Service sector (indicator variable)	24671	0.273 (0.003)	0.216 (0.003)	0.350 (0.005)	0.135 (0.006)
14 Trucking voting unit (indicator variable)	24671	0.145 (0.002)	0.170 (0.003)	0.112 (0.003)	−0.059 (0.004)
15 Log of state employment, election year	24671	14.92 (0.00)	14.91 (0.01)	14.93 (0.01)	0.02 (0.01)
16 Log of state employment, 2000	24671	15.03 (0.00)	15.02 (0.01)	15.04 (0.01)	0.01 (0.01)
17 Change in log emp. (2000— election year)	24671	0.111 (0.001)	0.113 (0.001)	0.108 (0.001)	−0.005 (0.001)
18 State unemployment rate, election year	24671	6.15 (0.01)	6.16 (0.02)	6.13 (0.02)	−0.03 (0.02)
19 State unemployment rate, 2000	24671	4.03 (0.01)	4.00 (0.01)	4.06 (0.01)	0.05 (0.01)
20 Change in UR (2000— election year)	24671	−2.12 (0.01)	−2.16 (0.01)	−2.08 (0.02)	0.08 (0.02)

Note: Standard errors in parentheses. Presence of Union post-election (pre-election) indicates whether or not a union at the location of the establishment filed a contract expiration between the election date and 2001 (between the beginning of the FMCS data and the date of the election). Details of the merged data from the NLRB, FMCS, and InfoUSA are described in DiNardo and Lee 2002.

the final outcome of the election, then firms just above and below 50 percent are likely to be very similar. In those close cases, it is plausible that the determination of whether the union won or lost the election is unpredictable, as if determined by the flip of a coin. One implication of this "unpredictability" is

Figure 9.1. Probability of post-election union presence, California

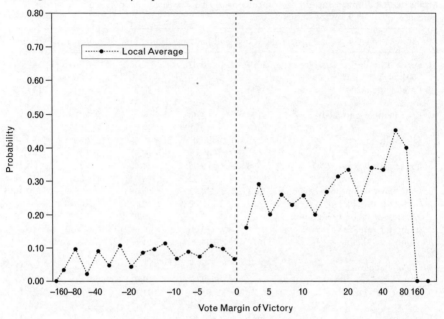

Figure 9.2. Probability of post-election union presence, rest of U.S.

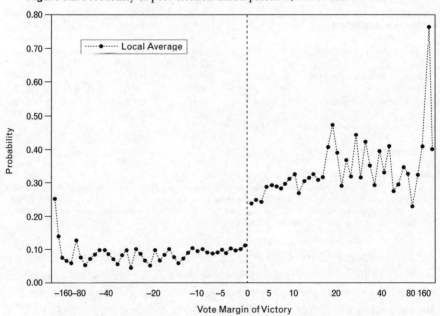

that we should expect to see that the winners and losers of close elections appear to be similar in every way we can measure. Finding that near-winners and near-losers are the same in ways we can observe does not prove, of course, that near-winners and near-losers are the same in unobservable ways also, but would appear to be a necessary pre-requisite for a credible analysis of the effect of unionization on establishment survival.

GRAPHICAL ANALYSIS

Figures 9.1, 9.2, 9.3, and 9.4 give a simple graphic version of our analysis. Including the California data, figure Ia graphs the probability that we observe an FMCS expiration notice (our measure of union "presence") against the actual vote margin of victory in the NLRB representation election. Negative and positive numbers on the horizontal axis refer to cases where the union lost or won. Each point in the graph is a proportion, calculated within intervals for the vote margin. While the relatively small size of the sample makes the graph a bit "bumpy," it is clear that there is a sharp break at zero—if the union wins by one vote, there is nearly double the possibility that we detect "union presence" at the establishment thereafter. When we use data for the rest of the country in figure 9.3, the figure is almost identical, except that the estimated gap at the 50 percent threshold is much more precise. This demonstrates that the union vote is not merely a "chimera"—winning by one vote clearly raises the probability that the firm will ultimately recognize a union (via a contract) at the establishment.

Having shown that union presence is greatly augmented by having won a union representation election, we next turn to see whether the outcome of the election has any effect on survival. The logic of our analysis is simple. If unions have a significant impact on the survival probability of establishments, we should see graphs similar to figures 9.1 and 9.3, except for the outcome of whether or not the establishment closed. Figures 9.2 and 9.4 report the results of such an analysis—in both cases it is clear that there is no sudden "break" at the point where narrow union losses become narrow union wins. While the results for California in 9.2 are somewhat noisy (again, due to the smaller sample size) the results are qualitatively similar to the more precise estimates we report for the rest of the country in figure 9.4

In other words, although the likelihood of the establishment being unionized rises discontinuously moving from a narrow union loss to a narrow union victory, we detect little or no change in the establishment's survival probability. What we conclude from this analysis is that among the types of establishments we analyzed, there is no evidence that unions lower or raise the survival probability of an establishment.

Figure 9.3. Probability of establishment survival by 2001, California

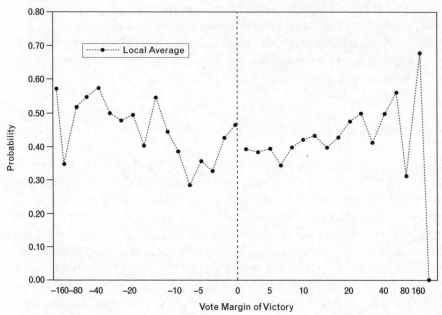

Figure 9.4. Probability of establishment survival by 2001, rest of U.S.

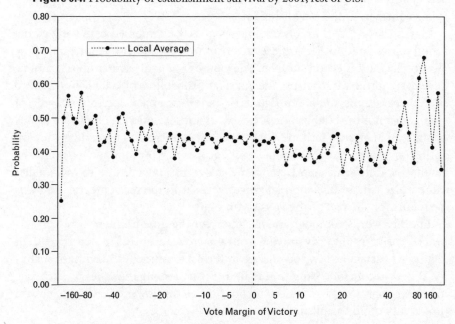

FURTHER EVIDENCE ON THE RESEARCH DESIGN

Tables 9.6 and 9.7 present tabular versions of the graphic analysis discussed above. However, in addition to the results on the presence of a union after the election and the survival of the firm, we also compare a number of different pre-election characteristics, such as the number of voters, the numbers of votes cast, and the sector that the establishment is in (manufacturing, service, or trucking). These differences address the credibility of our conclusion that establishment survivorship probabilities are unaffected by a union victory in an NLRB election.

In the first three columns, we compare union winners and losers for the entire sample—essentially repeating the analysis we did in table 9.4 and table 9.5 where we verified that winners and losers were not "otherwise identical." The strength of our approach can be seen as we go across the columns in tables 9.6 and 9.7—each time restricting our analysis to "closer" elections. Consider first the case for California in table 9.6. For example, in the full sample the number of eligible voters is 17 percent lower in establishments where the union lost the election; when we restrict our focus to establishment where the margin of victory (or loss) was 8 (or 7) votes, this difference falls to less than 1 percent.

A similar pattern is found when we consider the rest of the United States. Again focusing on the number of eligible voters, establishments where unions win are 16 percent smaller, on average, in the full sample; when the elections are restricted to those that were decided by less than 8 votes, this difference shrinks to 3 percent, and the difference further falls to 2.2 percent when we restrict the analysis to those decided by 2 votes.

Roughly the same pattern is observed for the other variables we can measure. Focusing on California in table 9.6, for example, winners are 9 percent more likely to be in the service sector than the union losers, and the difference is highly statistically significant—as we examine close elections, the difference falls—to an insignificant 3 percent for vote margins between −7 and 8, and to a smaller −1.9 percent when we look at the closest of elections. Furthermore, in our larger non-California sample, the difference in the likelihood of being in the service sector falls from a very large 14 percent in the full sample to a much smaller 5 percent in our narrowest window.

The fact that firms where unions barely lost appear to be similar to those where the union barely won on a large number of different characteristics lends some credibility to the analysis on establishment survivorship. It should be noted that it is impossible to rule out the possibility that there are unobserved differences between "bare-winners" and "bare-losers" that confound the analysis.[5]

TABLE 9.6

Establishment survival, union presence, and pre-determined characteristics, by margin of victory (loss) in California NLRB election

	Full sample			$-7 \le$ Margin ≤ 8			$-1 \le$ Margin ≤ 2		
	Loss	Won	Diff.	Loss	Won	Diff.	Loss	Won	Diff.
Survival, 2001	0.420	0.399	-0.021	0.374	0.377	0.003	0.454	0.384	-0.070
	(0.012)	(0.013)	(0.018)	(0.019)	(0.019)	(0.027)	(0.036)	(0.037)	(0.052)
Union present post-election	0.080	0.247	0.167	0.085	0.218	0.133	0.066	0.163	0.096
	(0.007)	(0.012)	(0.014)	(0.011)	(0.016)	(0.019)	(0.018)	(0.028)	(0.033)
Union present pre-election	0.073	0.111	0.039	0.082	0.111	0.029	0.056	0.087	0.031
	(0.007)	(0.009)	(0.011)	(0.010)	(0.012)	(0.016)	(0.016)	(0.022)	(0.027)
Eligible voters	105.500	88.357	-17.143	58.164	57.532	-0.632	52.801	51.971	-0.830
	(3.403)	(2.953)	(4.505)	(2.406)	(2.258)	(3.360)	(3.372)	(3.721)	(5.011)
Log (elig. voters)	4.247	4.129	-0.118	3.822	3.812	-0.011	3.757	3.715	-0.043
	(0.021)	(0.020)	(0.029)	(0.023)	(0.024)	(0.034)	(0.041)	(0.047)	(0.062)
Votes cast	91.274	72.316	-18.958	50.238	49.687	-0.551	47.245	46.256	-0.989
	(2.884)	(2.394)	(3.748)	(1.990)	(1.951)	(2.837)	(3.136)	(3.312)	(4.564)
Log (votes cast)	4.114	3.949	-0.165	3.688	3.673	-0.016	3.645	3.609	-0.036
	(0.020)	(0.020)	(0.028)	(0.022)	(0.023)	(0.033)	(0.041)	(0.045)	(0.061)
Manufacturing	0.326	0.276	-0.050	0.250	0.258	0.008	0.240	0.221	-0.019
	(0.012)	(0.012)	(0.017)	(0.017)	(0.017)	(0.024)	(0.031)	(0.032)	(0.044)
Service sector	0.235	0.328	0.093	0.287	0.318	0.031	0.260	0.279	0.019
	(0.011)	(0.013)	(0.017)	(0.017)	(0.018)	(0.025)	(0.031)	(0.034)	(0.046)
Trucking	0.206	0.173	-0.034	0.200	0.210	0.009	0.189	0.209	0.021
	(0.010)	(0.010)	(0.014)	(0.015)	(0.016)	(0.022)	(0.028)	(0.031)	(0.042)
Number of obs.	1585	1366		684	639		196	172	

Note: Robust standard errors in parentheses. Entries are means and differences by election outcome, in three different samples.

TABLE 9.7

Establishment survival, union presence, and pre-determined characteristics, by margin of victory (loss) in NLRB election, of the rest of the United States

	Full sample			$-7 \le$ Margin ≤ 8			$-1 \le$ Margin ≤ 2		
	Loss	Won	Diff.	Loss	Won	Diff.	Loss	Won	Diff.
Survival, 2001	0.431	0.401	-0.031	0.428	0.409	-0.019	0.429	0.417	-0.013
	(0.004)	(0.005)	(0.006)	(0.006)	(0.007)	(0.009)	(0.012)	(0.013)	(0.018)
Union present Post-election	0.088	0.299	0.211	0.095	0.269	0.174	0.104	0.241	0.136
	(0.002)	(0.004)	(0.005)	(0.004)	(0.006)	(0.007)	(0.008)	(0.011)	(0.013)
Union present Pre-election	0.077	0.139	0.062	0.080	0.117	0.037	0.089	0.114	0.024
	(0.002)	(0.003)	(0.004)	(0.003)	(0.004)	(0.005)	(0.007)	(0.008)	(0.011)
Eligible voters	114.314	92.027	-22.287	56.436	58.819	2.382	53.536	54.413	0.877
	(1.228)	(1.168)	(1.748)	(0.698)	(0.825)	(1.074)	(1.402)	(1.486)	(2.042)
Log (elig. voters)	4.294	4.139	-0.155	3.810	3.840	0.031	3.747	3.769	0.022
	(0.007)	(0.008)	(0.011)	(0.007)	(0.008)	(0.011)	(0.015)	(0.016)	(0.022)
Votes cast	103.123	78.781	-24.342	50.806	52.204	1.398	48.629	49.100	0.472
	(1.101)	(0.997)	(1.544)	(0.610)	(0.726)	(0.942)	(1.275)	(1.294)	(1.820)
Log (votes cast)	4.192	3.995	-0.197	3.709	3.727	0.017	3.656	3.675	0.019
	(0.007)	(0.007)	(0.011)	(0.007)	(0.008)	(0.011)	(0.015)	(0.015)	(0.021)
Manufacturing	0.431	0.333	-0.098	0.392	0.357	-0.035	0.395	0.364	-0.031
	(0.004)	(0.005)	(0.006)	(0.006)	(0.007)	(0.009)	(0.012)	(0.013)	(0.018)
Service sector	0.216	0.350	0.135	0.227	0.303	0.076	0.228	0.279	0.051
	(0.003)	(0.005)	(0.006)	(0.005)	(0.006)	(0.008)	(0.011)	(0.012)	(0.016)
Trucking	0.170	0.112	-0.059	0.187	0.135	-0.052	0.172	0.137	-0.035
	(0.003)	(0.003)	(0.005)	(0.005)	(0.005)	(0.007)	(0.009)	(0.009)	(0.013)
Number of obs.	14233	10438		6459	5242		1589	1426	

Note: Robust standard errors in parentheses. Entries are means and differences by election outcome, in three different samples.

CONCLUSION

We believe there are some important lessons to be drawn from the analysis summarized here. First, our analysis of a large-scale database on union elections and establishments leads us to conclude that the outcome of an NLRB election has little or no impact on the probability that an establishment survives subsequent to the election. This does not mean that elections do not have an impact on workers along other dimensions. Our analysis does not address the potential effects of union recognition on wages, working conditions, and employment levels. It is our view that systematic research regarding these effects can be in the interest of the public, especially to the extent that labor and management's diametrically opposed opinions are the natural consequence of both parties' ultimate uncertainty as to the true impacts of unionization.

Finally, and most importantly, our analysis illustrates both the value and need for more and better quality, data on the performance of business establishments, and the presence of unions. For example, while much is known about union membership in the population of individual workers (via studies using the Current Population Survey, for example), almost nothing is known about unionism at the level of the business establishment. What proportion of establishments have some union presence among the workers? To what extent are union members concentrated among small or large establishments? Is a successful organizing drive more likely after an establishment experiences good or bad economic times? How have these things changed over time? What are the current trends? These questions are impossible to answer without representative, quality data on even such simple things as union presence by business establishment. In the absence of an improvement in public access to such data, and increased willingness to provide it by all the parties involved in collective bargaining, answers to such questions may be a long time in coming.

NOTES

1. Changing to Organize, by Kate Bronfenbrenner and Robert Hickey

1. The study focuses on units with fifty or more eligible voters because data on bargaining unit demographics, company and union characteristics, and union and employer tactics are much more difficult to reliably analyze in units with only a small number of voters.
2. Although this study is limited to NLRB private sector certification election campaigns and does not include either private sector card check and voluntary recognition organizing campaigns or organizing campaigns in the public sector, qualitative studies of private sector non-NLRB campaigns by Waldinger et al. (1998), Juravich and Hilgert (1998), and Lewis and Mirand (1998), along with Juravich and Bronfenbrenner's quantitative research on public sector certification and voluntary recognition campaigns (1998), confirm that our model is also applicable in the non-NLRB organizing environment.
3. See appendix 1.1 for definitions for each of the ten elements in the model.
4. Although, according to our model, the ideal union campaign would use all ten, or close to ten, of the elements of our comprehensive organizing strategy, we were unable to use the higher standard since only a small percent of the unions in our sample use more than six tactics (3 percent) and none of the unions in our sample used more than eight.
5. Although in previous studies union win rates were found to decline as unit size increased, we hypothesize that that was no longer true by the mid-1990s when unions began to more aggressively go after larger units.
6. We hypothesize a positive relationship between ownership change and election outcome, because companies where ownership changes occur before the union campaign are much more likely to make negative changes in wages, benefits, safety, job duties, workload, and work pace, driving workers to seek more voice and power in their workplace.
7. Although profitable companies have more money available to spend on their anti-union campaigns, the combination of worker resentment, caused by the refusal of many of these companies to share their economic windfall with their employees, coupled with the greater economic security in a profitable company, can undermine the negative effect of a more aggressive company campaign and increase the positive effect of the union campaign.
8. Sixty percent or more women and 60 percent or more workers of color are used rather than simple continuous variables, because union win rates are highest when a clear majority of

the unit are women or workers of color, but are slightly higher in all-male units or all-white units than in units where women or workers of color represent a minority of the unit, since in these more homogeneous units the employer is less able to play one group against the other (Bronfenbrenner 1993).

9. The key here is that the resources should be both adequate and appropriate. We would hypothesize that adequate resources alone would not be associated with higher win rates, because if the union fails to use the appropriate resources (e.g., brings in lots of green organizers with no knowledge of the industry or connections in the community) or fails to tie the resources to an effective strategy (e.g., spending money on lots of glossy mass mailings) then throwing money at a campaign could end up having an adverse rather than a positive impact on election outcome.

10. These findings suggest that the signing of a union card can not be used as a measure of pre-campaign worker propensity to vote for the union, since in the majority of the campaigns today, the circulation or "dropping" of cards occurs much later in the campaign, often after the workers have been exposed to several months of employer and union campaigns. It also confirms that worker pre-campaign propensity to vote for a union is a poor predictor of election outcome because of how both worker and employer tactics can change work attitudes toward unions during the course of the campaign.

11. Although we included six comprehensive organizing tactics in each group, there were several cases where unions used only a maximum of five out of the six comprehensive tactics during the campaigns.

12. Some elements of the model, such as targeting, choosing issues that resonate, using benchmarks and assessments, using member volunteers, having a representative committee, and building for the first contract during the organizing campaign are all strategic choices that could end saving money rather than costing the union additional resources. For example, strategic use of benchmarks keeps the union from moving ahead with the campaign before the workers are ready; choosing the right issues can garner community support that restrains the employer campaign; building for the first contract can prevent lengthy and expensive delays; and both member volunteers and representative committee members, when trained and used effectively, cost less than paid full-time staff.

13. Financial condition was determined by a combination of criteria that include annual revenues, net profits, credit rating, earned price per share, newspaper and trade journal articles, and organizer interviews.

14. Union cities include Atlanta GA, Cincinnati OH, Cleveland OH, Houston TX, Los Angeles CA, Madison WI, Milwaukee WI, New York NY, Quad Cities IA, San Diego CA, San Jose CA, Seattle WA, Syracuse NY, and Washington DC.

15. We did not include the Union Cities variable in our regression model because the relationship between Union Cities and election outcome is also somewhat circular in that CLCs where member unions are winning and running more comprehensive campaigns are more likely to have the commitment to work toward meeting the criteria to become a Union City, and because Union Cities exist in only a handful of communities nationwide.

16. Although the majority of unions do continue to run fairly weak campaigns when faced with aggressive employer opposition, these data also show that union campaigns are more, rather than less, aggressive in the context of more aggressive employer campaigns. This then discounts the argument that unions would be likely to put fewer resources into campaigns or run less aggressive campaigns when faced with greater employer opposition and a greater likelihood of a loss. Our data suggest the contrary, namely, that the intensity of union campaigns increases in response to the intensity of employer opposition, but, in most cases, not to the extent necessary to overcome the employer campaign.

17. The fifteen unions listed individually in tables 1.5 and 1.6 account for 79 percent of all elections in units with fifty or more eligible voters in 1998–1999. Because of our high response

rate (69 percent) for most of the unions the proportion of the elections in the sample is within a few percentage points of their proportion in the population, and win rates are within five percentage points of the population win rate. However, for five of the unions the difference between the sample and population win rates is at least 10 percent. The population win rates for these unions are as follows: UNITE (57 percent), UAW (46 percent), IAM (52 percent), LIUNA (41 percent), and IBEW (35 percent for the population). Because our focus here is on the relationship between the number and combination of tactics used by each union and election outcomes, these differences do not undermine the validity of this analysis.

18. The only exceptions are AFSCME, CWA/IUE, and the UFCW, in which win rates are lower in campaigns where more than five comprehensive tactics are used than they are in campaigns where the union used five or fewer tactics. The results for AFSMCE and CWA are explained by the fact that the union used more than five comprehensive tactics in only two AFSCME campaigns (one of which was lost) and one CWA campaign (which was lost). In the case of the UFCW, which faces some of the most intensive employer opposition, there were only four campaigns where the union used more than five comprehensive tactics, and, in the three that were lost, the employer ran an aggressive campaign using more than ten anti-union tactics.

19. We use binary logistic regression because the dependent variable is dichotomous (loss = 0, win = 1). In binary logistic regression the odds ratio is used to predict the impact of a single unit change in each of the independent variables on the odds of the union winning the election (the probability of the union winning the election divided by the probability of the union losing the election). These findings differ from ordinary linear regression in which coefficients can be used to predict the impact of independent variables on the probability of a union win (Hosmer and Lemeshow 1989; Menard 1995).

20. Standard measures for statistical significance of models in binary logistic regression, such as the model Chi-square and Hosmer and Lemeshow's Goodness-of-Fit test statistic, support the appropriateness of both models.

21. Our analysis of the importance of these three elements would be enhanced if we were able to test a model by comparing the effects of an additive variable using just those three elements, and an additive variable that would equal zero if all three of those elements were not included, with the effects of the additive variable we used in model B. Unfortunately, because only 2 percent of the campaigns in the sample (eight cases) used all three elements, we were unable to test those effects. However, based on our earlier analysis of the various combinations of six tactics, we know that there were campaigns where all three of those tactics were used that had lower win rates than campaigns where all three were not used. Because win rates increased in six of the cases in which the union used those three tactics plus one additional tactic, and win rates stayed the same for the remaining two cases, we believe that the positive effects of the additive union tactic variable would be even stronger if those three elements were a required component of the variable.

22. While some might argue that resources are a proxy for all other tactics, as we explained earlier, this is not borne out by either the descriptive statistics or regression findings. Not only are several of the tactics not associated with higher resource costs, but there are numerous examples in our data of unions that lost elections because they failed to tie those resources to an effective strategy.

23. Although the percent negative impact on the odds of an election win appears to be significantly greater for the union tactics (−34 percent) versus the employer tactics (−13 percent), this difference may be partially due to the fact that union comprehensive organizing tactics are actually clusters of tactics, while employer tactics are individual tactics, albeit very effective ones. Instead, our data show that both union and employer tactics play a major role in determining election outcome; however, because union campaigns continue to be less com-

prehensive, sophisticated, and intensive than employer campaigns, there is a great potential for union strategies to have a much greater positive impact on election outcome than they do at this time.

24. The lack of statistical significance for these variables in model A is likely to be a function of multicollinearity between these demographic variables and two of the individual comprehensive tactic variables, adequate and appropriate resources and active representative committee, that each have one component related to race and gender representation on either the staff or the committee. Multicollinearity for these variables is no longer an issue in model B, because we are estimating the effect of the number of comprehensive organizing tactics used rather than any individual comprehensive tactic.

25. The odds ratio is problematic as a measure of the relative effects of independent variables because of its asymmetry (a decrease the odds ratio can vary only from 0 to .999, while an increase in the odds ratio can vary from 1.001 to infinity). As recommended by Selvin (1991), because SPSS does not generate standardized logistic coefficients, we used an alternate method of ranking the independent variables in which we multiplied the unstandardized logit coefficients by their respective standard deviations to gain an estimated standardized coefficient for each statistically significant variable in both our models. As reported in tables 1.10 and 1.11, for each of the independent variables in our model, these rank-ordered estimates report the change in the log-odds of winning the election for a one standard deviation change in the independent variable.

26. Some researchers have begun to examine this important question (see Voss and Sherman 2000), but more research is needed to understand why only a limited number of unions have begun the difficult transformation of building organizing capacity and developing a comprehensive organizing strategy.

27. The employer tactics included in the employer scale variable include: employer used outside consultant; employer held five or more captive audience meetings; employer sent five or more anti-union letters; employer distributed five or more anti-union leaflets; employer made plant-closing threats; workers were discharged for union activity and not reinstated before the election; employer engaged in other harassment or discipline of union activists; supervisors campaigned one-on-one at least weekly; employer gave wage increases; employer made unilateral changes in benefits; workers were laid off during the campaign; employer used the media; employer used bribes; employer used electronic surveillance; employer assisted the rank-and-file anti-union committee; employer set up an employee involvement program after the petition was filed; employer held social events; employer made changes in management structure and personnel; employer threatened to report workers to INS; employer involved community leaders and politicians; and employer used other tactics such as union promise coupon books, raffles, videos, e-mails, or distributed pay stubs with union dues deducted. We have not clustered employer tactics in the same way we did union tactics, because unlike union tactics, individual employer tactics are effective both in isolation and in combination with other individual anti-union tactics (Bronfenbrenner and Juravich 1998).

2. Union Democracy and Successful Campaigns, by Teresa Sharpe

I thank Sam Davis, Amy Hanswer, Isaac Martin, Kim Medina, Ruth Milkman, Lynn Rivas, Barrie Thorne, Youyenn Teo, Jonathan Van Antwerpen, Kim Voss, and Margaret Weir for valuable comments and suggestions. A special thanks to the workers, leaders, and staff of HERE Local B.

1. I changed the name of the local union (not the International), the hotel, and all individuals. I spent nineteen months working with Local B on the Bayview organizing campaign,

primarily as an active member of the worker organizing committee. I also worked inside the hotel as a hostess, cocktail waitress, and restaurant server. I met with dozens of Bayview workers in their homes to talk about the union, usually with a staff organizer or another committee member present. I attended weekly organizing staff meetings at which the organizers met to discuss organizing plans. I also attended "Bayview Strategy Sessions," where organizers, researchers, the union president and sometimes the International Union's organizing director met (via conference call) to discuss the campaign. Neither of these meetings was open to Bayview workers. As the campaign progressed, my field work expanded to include regular rallies outside the hotel, worker presentations at labor-friendly churches and city council meetings, and boycott delegations to local businesses.

3. Workers against Unions, by Robert A. Penney

1. Names and places have been changed in order to protect the anonymity of the participants.
2. Bronfenbrenner (1994) found that the presence of anti-union committees seriously jeopardizes the union's chances of victory. The percentage of union votes in campaign election with anti-union committees declines by 20 percent. While Bronfenbrenner (2000) found that employers assisted the anti-union campaigns, it is unclear if even more committees existed but were "unsupported" by management. In any case, Bronfenbrenner's work points to the commonality of anti-union mobilization in union organizing campaigns.
3. The cases included a union success and failure across two occupational categories—service and maintenance workers and Registered Nurses. Seventy-seven semi-structured qualitative interviews, including twenty-nine with anti-union activists or adherents, were conducted to explore the ideological foundations of anti-union leadership and their motivations for action. The hospitals had comparable numbers of beds and workers and were situated in similar market positions and faced with the same industry pressures of managed-care transitions. Each campaign was organized by different locals, but the same International Union conducted all four campaigns; thus, while individual tactics varied, the same general strategy of organizing was used in each case. In addition, each hospital hired outside labor-management consultants to run their anti-union campaigns, so that the strategies and tactics of resistance were also very similar in each case.
4. In one campaign, the anti-union workers acted more independently of each other, rather than forming a coherent organization. The reasons for the lack of organizational form will be discussed in more detail later in this chapter.
5. Collective action frames are "interpretive schemata" that identify and highlight social injustices and challenge hegemonic understandings of situations and experiences (Gamson 1992; Snow and Benford 1988; Tarrow 1994). Frames are a conceptual tool to explain the formation and power of collective identities in social movement organizations and collective action.
6. This is not to imply that "strong-arm" tactics such as firing, demoting, and suspending workers involved in organizing drives does not occur frequently (Bronfenbrenner 1997, 2000).
7. "Created" in that of the three cases that formed formal organizations, the leaders recounted that they met fellow anti-unionists and then began the process of creating a committee. The committees seemed to form as a result of interpersonal networks of friends and acquaintances that slowly grew in size and shape.
8. Counter-movements are "networks of individuals" that may share many of the same issues as the originating movement, but "make contrary claims simultaneously to those of the original movement" (Meyer and Staggenborg 1996, 1632). As movements make demands and

open space for the possibility of change, counter-movements develop, grow and force reactions by the original movement.

4. Overcoming Legacies of Business Unionism, by Steven H. Lopez

This research was conducted with funding from the University of California at Berkeley. The author would like to thank Michael Burawoy, Dan Clawson, Ruth Milkman, Sean O'Riain, Rachel Sherman, Eddy U, Kim Voss, Margaret Weir, and the staff and members of the SEIU Local A.

1. A pseudonym.
2. This election was held under the terms of an expedited election agreement between the SEIU and the nursing home chain, which allowed for an expedited, non-NLRB procedure administered by an independent arbitrator. Under the terms of the agreement, the employer agreed to schedule an election within four weeks of the union's petition; promised not to begin any anti-union campaign until after the petition for election had been filed with the arbitrator; and agreed not to engage in any "negative campaigning." Both sides also agreed to accept the decisions of the arbitrator as binding and forewent any recourse to court appeals.
3. Local A leaders and staff took me on as an intern with the explicit understanding that I was conducting research for a doctoral dissertation on service-sector union organizing. They were unanimously open toward my research and eager to help. Several staff members eventually read all or part of the dissertation and offered insightful comments.
4. On this point, Fantasia (1988) relates a wonderful story about a survey research study at an English auto plant concluding that "class consciousness was practically nonexistent" (7). While the study was at the printer, the workers got hold of a copy, along with a report of company profits. Two days of "wild rioting" ensued (7).
5. This claim was fully supported by the Department of Health's investigation.
6. The administrator's note to McMurray was probably an unfair labor practice, because it is illegal for an employer to ask a worker about their union activity. But in the scheme of things, this was not a major violation, and Hardy did not make a formal complaint to the arbitrator.
7. I have deliberately avoided citing the relevant newspaper articles, because there is no way to do so without revealing the identity of Rosemont Pavilion to anyone who wanted to look up the articles.
8. Sexism and racism are deeply rooted in the labor movement in southwestern Pennsylvania. The 1996 documentary film "Struggles in Steel," by Tony Buba and Ray Henderson, documents how the United Steelworkers Union collaborated with metal-industry employers throughout the postwar period to keep African Americans in the worst, lowest-paid positions, and women out of the plants altogether. The USWA's discriminatory practices persisted well into the 1970s, when a lawsuit filed by a group of African American workers against both the union and the major steel companies finally resulted in a federal consent decree mandating affirmative action for minorities and women. See also M. M. Fonow on women in the USWA (Fonow 1978).
9. A pseudonym.

5. Justice for Janitors, by Preston Rudy

1. Unless otherwise indicated, I have used pseudonyms for people I interviewed and people's real names when referring to public events reported in the press.
2. This is a situation in which as one worker wakes to go to work, another returns home from his shift and goes to bed in the recently vacated, and still warm, bed.

3. All names are pseudonyms unless otherwise indicated. This account comes from files at the union's offices.

4. Though Sawyer was exonerated of any violations by a DOL investigation, political pressure from the House of Representatives over the appearance of collusion with SEIU resulted in his being relieved of his position (see U.S. House 1996 for a full account).

6. Against the Tide, by Marshall Ganz, Kim Voss, Teresa Sharpe, Carl Somers, and George Strauss

This research was supported by the Institute for Labor and Employment at the University of California, the Nathan Cummings Foundation, and the Center for Public Leadership and Hauser Center for Non-Profit Organizations at the John F. Kennedy School of Government at Harvard University.

1. Union leaders do not begin at the top, but instead work their way up organizational ladders. A focus on top national leaders reveals little about the careers of the thousands of other elected and appointed local, state, and national leaders who do the work of the union. Moreover, a focus on national leaders reveals little about why some rise to the top and others do not. Although scholars have examined unpaid rank-and-file leaders (Strauss and Sayles 1952, 1953; Peck 1963; Chaison and Andiappan 1987), few studies of the full-time people responsible for day-to-day union leadership have been conducted in America since the 1960s. Yet, in 1984, some 2,000,000 union members in California alone supported 5,000 full-time business agents, elected leaders, and organizers who coordinated the work of an estimated 26,500 volunteers.

2. Mische describes projects as "evolving, imaginatively constructed configurations of desired social possibility, accompanied by an implicit or explicit theorization of personal and/or collective capacity to act to achieve that possibility" (Emirbeyer and Mische 1998, 46–47; Mische 2002, 14).

3. Bandura describes this as "emergent interactive agency," which he distinguishes from agency as purely autonomous or as a mechanical response to environmental changes (Bandura 1989). This cognitive distinction is quite similar to the relational distinction Granovetter makes between "undersocialized" and "oversocialized" agency—actors as entirely autonomous individuals or as mere extensions of social groups, classes, or other collectivities. In sociology, a number of scholars make distinctions quite similar to that of Bandura (cf. Powell and DiMaggio 1989; Banaszak 1996; Zerubavel 1997; DiMaggio 1997).

4. Mische writes that collective projects can be defined as public narratives of proposed interventions by groups or collectivities (Mische and Pattison 2000; Mische 1996). Such narratives clearly have a projective dimension, in that they "embed identities in time and place" (Somers 1992); they give a sense of where a society and an organization have come from, while also delimiting where actors think, hope, or fear they may be going. Sometimes those collective projects encompass the youths' own "projects-in-formation"; sometimes they expand or challenge them; and sometimes they conflict with or cause internal dissension in an activist's perceived sense of direction and possibility.

5. From a psychological point of view, relying on verbal accounts to assess goals and motivations, as we do here, might be suspect. Similarly, sociologists would point to factors that can have an influence on career outcomes that have little to do with intentionality, such as the structure of leadership opportunities. To the contrary, attending to what people say about what they want in relation to what they actually did (which is what we do here) can teach us about the relationship between the two.

6. It is entirely possible that those we couldn't find differed significantly from those that we did.

7. Although we interviewed neither of them, Sirabella's "project" may have been one of union building, recognizing that "social reformers" can make a valuable contribution to organizing. Other labor leaders have from time to time recognized this—as in the legendary account of John L. Lewis's response to criticism for hiring Communists for the CIO organizing drive in the 1930s: "We'll see who winds up with the bird—the hunter or the dog."

8. Union Leadership Project.

7. Sticking It Out or Packing It In? by Daisy Rooks

1. In this paper the use of the term "organizing staff" includes field organizers, campaign coordinators or lead organizers, local union organizing directors and strategic research staff. Although strategic research plays a crucial role in new organizing, not all local unions have their own research staff. Larger local unions usually have several researchers on staff. Smaller local unions, or more centralized international unions, tend to centralize research staff either at the International union's headquarters or in regional "research shops" that service a number of local unions.

2. Throughout its history, both union members and non-members have participated in the OI. "Internal recruits" are union members who leave their jobs in the shop to work as full-time union organizers. OI founders welcomed the participation of "internal recruits," citing their unique ability to convince workers to join the union by citing their own experiences as union members. The Institute's founders also recognized the ways that non-members could contribute to the movement. Many of these non-members, or "external recruits," had been activists in the progressive movements of the '80s and '90s, such as student organizing, affirmative action, environmental justice, etc. The OI valued these "external recruits" both because of their experience with disruptive organizing tactics, and because they were a source of commitment, inspiration, and energy for the flailing movement (Bensinger and Porter 1993; Voss and Sherman 2001). This recruitment of radical labor organizers has a historical equivalent. In the 1930s, John J. Lewis hired scores of young communists to organize for his union. Although controversial, Lewis defended his decision by citing their organizing skills and willingness to do the work at a time when few others were (Milkman 1998; Zeitlin and Stepan-Norris 1989).

3. "Vulnerable workers" are usually defined as immigrant workers, women, low-wage and young workers.

4. The OI was originally funded by five International unions: SEIU, Union of Needletrades, Industrial and Textile Employees (UNITE), United Food and Commercial Workers (UFCW), American Federation of State, County and Municipal Employees (AFSCME) and the United Steelworkers of America (USWA).

5. Tannock (2001) argues that employers treat young workers differently than adult workers, routinely offering them lower wages, fewer work hours, and less benefits than their adult counterparts.

6. It is important to note that the ideological content of this commitment and the preferred strategies for achieving social change is often different between both groups of workers. Perhaps the most salient example of the difference between the two is the fact that union organizers are committed to changing the balance of power both in the workplace and in society, while workers in justice jobs are more focused on providing relief (often temporary) to people in need.

7. "Inoculating" refers to preparing workers for employer resistance and the harassment of union activists that too often accompanies organizing efforts. Well-inoculated workers are better equipped to face adversity and successfully resist the impulse to drop out of the effort when the "going gets tough."

8. During their interviews, some respondents refer to the internship as a "three week." Prior to 1998, the OI internship lasted for three weeks. During this time a higher number of OI participants were accepted for the internship, and the field training component of the internship was used to "screen" participants out of the program when trainers did not think that they were ready to organize. Since the OI implemented the 10 day, fewer participants are accepted for the internship and trainers rarely "screen out" participants at this stage of the program.

9. Here "intensity" refers to hours worked per week, emotional intensity, travel requirements, etc.

10. When identifying quotes I use the word "organized" to indicate the length of time that someone organized before they quit. Use of the word "organizing" indicates that the person in question is still organizing and specifies for how long.

11. During Sweeney's administration, Linda Chavez-Thompson was both the first woman and first Latina Executive Vice President of the Federation and Arturo Rodriguez, President of the United Farm Workers Union, was the first Latino elected to the AFL-CIO Executive Board.

12. Although many would like to see the OI recruit even more non-white organizers, even its most vocal critics are likely to agree that the OI has done more to diversify the ranks of paid organizers than any other organization in the movement.

13. National Organizers' Alliance website (http://www.gadgetfarm.com/noa/jobbank).

14. The AFL-CIO Organizing Institute website (http://www.aflcio.org/aboutunions/oi/training.cfm); The Service Employees International website (http://www.seiu.org/work/findjobs.cfm); The United Farm Workers of America website (http://www.ufw.org/jobs.htm); and Union Jobs Clearinghouse (http://unionjobs.com).

15. When "probing," organizers search for organizing leads by making initial contacts with workers at targeted shops to ascertain their level of interest in organizing.

16. The literature on justice jobs indicates that institutions, such as the Organizing Institute that are responsible for recruitment and training, play a central role in developing appropriate expectations for new staff. Due to the tremendous variation that exists among OI trainers and recruiters, new recruits enter the field with widely different expectations about organizing, the labor movement, and their role in creating change within unions. Furthermore, factors such as amount of job experience, previous social movement activism, and prior exposure to the labor movement can shape new recruits' expectations about organizing. Because these other factors also influence new organizers' expectations, it is inaccurate to simply blame the Organizing Institute or its staff for creating unrealistic expectations among new organizers. Rather than focusing on the source of inaccurate expectations, this paper explores the content of these expectations and demonstrates how they can impact on organizer retention and turnover.

17. The following section details the impact of organizing success and failure on organizer retention.

18. SEIU's WAVE program is the exception to this rule. WAVE recruits and trains new organizers in small cadres in order to facilitate peer support. Initial classroom training on organizing is provided centrally, and unlike the OI, "WAVERs" receive a full year of field training in small groups. Service Employees International Union website (http://www.weiu.org/work/seiu_wave_organizing_jobs/join.cfm).

19. A full innovator union is one that has fully integrated new labor's organizing agenda into its mission and operations. These unions allocate minimum of 30% of their resources toward organizing, employ an organizing staff of internal and external recruits, and routinely use militant tactics in new organizing campaigns.

8. "Outsiders" Inside the Labor Movement, by Leslie Bunnage and Judith Stepan-Norris

1. These include: ACORN, AFSCME, Carpenters Council, HERE, IAM, IOUE, Jobs with Justice, SEIU, Teamsters, UAW, UFCW, UFW, UNITE, and USWA.
2. We have access to the 1998 training manual, which contains materials from the 1996 and 1997 Union Summer program. Although the basic structure of the training programs in 1996 through 1998 were the same, some of the details may have changed, and sessions added in response to feedback on what was missing.
3. As displayed above, the question posed to the site coordinators asked about positive and not about negative aspects of the unions and union staff with whom they worked. Nevertheless, a considerable minority mentioned negative features of the campaigns.
4. Our data report on the inception of this program; therefore, some of these problems have been rectified in subsequent years.

9. Unionism in California, by John DiNardo and David S. Lee

1. The standard deviation of responses were more than one half the maximum standard deviation possible (if 50 percent of the labor economists had reported 0 and 50 percent had reported 100, the standard deviation would have been 50).
2. The "Harberger triangle" is merely one-half the product of the union wage effect, the consequent decline in employment in the union sector, the fraction of the workforce unionized, and the fraction of total costs associated with labor. Assuming an elasticity of demand for labor of $-2/3$, upper bound to the union wage effect of 25 percent, a union share of the workforce of 25 percent in 1981, and a labor share of GNP of .75 their estimate is merely $-0.5 \times 0.20 \times 0.13 \times 0.25 \times 0.75 = 0.0040$. They go on to observe that their estimate is very close to the calculations in Rees (1963).
3. See MacDonald and Solow (1981), Brown and Ashenfelter (1986), Pencavel and MacCurdy (1986), Card (1986), Abowd (1989), for a more thorough discussion and debate on the issue.
4. See the debate, for example, in the *Economic Journal* between Blanchflower et al. (1991) and Machin and Wadhwani (1991).
5. For example, pure double-blind randomized trials which are the "gold standard" for analyzing the efficacy of medications and treatments suffer the same limitation. Even if we perfectly randomize, we can never rule out the possibility in any one analysis that those who received the treatment were different in some important but unobservable way. The reason analysts randomize (and the reason we focus on close winners and losers) is because one then minimizes the likelihood that there are important but unobserved confounding influences.

REFERENCES

Abowd, John M. 1989. "The Effect of Wage Bargains on the Stock Market Value of the Firm." *American Economic Review* 79:774–800.

Acuff, Stewart. 1999. "Expanded Roles for the Central Labor Council: The View from Atlanta." In *Which Direction for Organized Labor?* edited by B. Nissen, 133–42. Detroit: Wayne State University Press.

Addison, John T., Lutz Bellmann, and Arnd Kölling. 2002. "Unions, Works Councils and Plant Closings in Germany." Institute for Employment Research (IAB), Nurember (April): Discussion Paper No. 474.

AFL-CIO. 1998. Union Summer Education Manual.

———. 1998. Union Summer Site Coordinator Handbook.

———. n.d. Union Summer Training Materials. AFL-CIO Union Summer Program.

———. Union Summer website, Union Summer in Review. http://www.bctd.workingfamilies.com/unionsummer/inreview.htm

———. 2000. "Union Membership Shows Biggest Growth in Over 20 Years, According to New Government Data." Press Release. 19 January.

Alinsky, Saul. 1972. *Rules for Radicals: A Practical Primer for Realistic Radicals.* New York: Vintage Books.

Alvarado, Jaime, Mark Sharwood, Lisa Soto, and Al Traugott. 1991. "The Rich, the Poor, and the Forgotten . . . in Silicon Valley." Study prepared for the Cleaning Up Silicon Valley Coalition. San Jose: SEIU Local 1877.

Armbrister, Trevor. 1980. *Act of Vengeance.* New York: Warner Books.

Aronowitz, Stanley. 1992. *False Promises: The Shaping of American Working Class Consciousness.* Durham, N.C.: Duke University Press.

———. 1998. *From the Ashes of the Old: American Labor and America's Future.* Boston: Houghton Mifflin.

Azar, Sandra. 2000. "Preventing Burnout in Professionals and Paraprofessionals Who Work with Child Abuse and Neglect Cases: A Cognitive Behavioral Approach to Supervision." *Journal of Clinical Psychology* 56(5):643–63.

Bailey, Brandon. 1991. "Chavez Calls for an Apple Boycott." *San Jose Mercury News,* 18 November: 5B.

Banaszak, Lee Ann. 1996. "Why Movements Succeed or Fail: Opportunity, Culture, and the Struggle for Woman Suffrage." In *Princeton Studies in American Politics*, edited by I. Katznelson and T. Skocpol. Princeton: Princeton University Press.

Bandura, A. 1989. "Human Agency in Social Cognitive Theory." *American Psychologist* 44(9):1175–84.

Banks, Andy. 1991. "The Power and Promise of Community Organizing." *Labor Research Review* 18:17–31.

Barbash, Jack. 1954. *Taft-Hartley in Action, 1947–1954*. New York: League for Industrial Democracy.

Barley, Steve. 1989. "Careers, Identities, and Institutions: the Legacy of the Chicago School of Sociology." In *Handbook of Career Theory*, edited by M. Arthur, D. Hall, and B. Lawrence, 41–65. Cambridge: Cambridge University Press.

Bass, Bernard M., and Ralph Stogdill. 1990. *Bass and Stogdill's Handbook of Leadership: Theory, Research, and Managerial Applications*. New York: Free Press.

Becker, Thomas. 1992. "Foci and Bases of Commitment: Are They Distinctions Worth Making?" *Academy of Management Journal* 35(1):232–44.

Belkin, Lisa. 1996. "Showdown at Yazoo Industries: Representing the Last Best Chance for Labor, The Union Kids Come to Town." *New York Times Magazine*, 21 January: 26–69.

Bensinger, Richard. 1991. "Committed to Organizing: An Interview with Richard Bensinger, Director, AFL-CIO Organizing Institute." *Labor Research Review* 18:82–91.

Bensinger, Richard, and Allison Porter. 1993. "Labor at the Crossroads." *Boston Review* 18(5). http://bostonreview.mit.edu/BR18.5/laboratcross.html.

Bizjak, Tony. 1998. "Serna Ends Janitor Mediation." *Sacramento Bee*, 24 January: B3.

Blanchflower, David, Andrew Oswald, and Neil Millward. 1991. "Unionism and Employment Behaviour." *Economic Journal* (July): 815–34.

Bluestone, Barry, and Bennett Harrison. 1983. *The Deindustrialization of America: Plant Closings, Community Abandonment, and the Dismantling of Basic Industry*. New York: Basic Books.

BNA PLUS. 2000. *Database of NLRB Elections in Units with 50 or More Eligible Voters, 1998–1999*. Washington: Bureau of National Affairs, Inc.

———. 2001. *Database of NLRB elections 1997–2000*. Washington: Bureau of National Affairs, Inc.

Bramble, T. 1995. "Deterring Democracy? Australia's New Generation of Trade Union Officials." *Journal of Industrial Relations* 37:401–26.

Bronfenbrenner, Kate. 1993. "Seeds of Resurgence: Successful Union Strategies for Winning Certification Elections and First Contracts in the 1980s and Beyond." PhD diss., Cornell University.

———. 1994. "Employer Behavior in Certification Elections and First Contracts: Implications for Labor Law Reform." In *Restoring the Promise of American Labor Law*, edited by S. Friedman, R. Hurd, R. Oswald, and R. Seeber, 75–89. Ithaca: Cornell University Press.

———. 1997. "The Role of Union Strategies in NLRB Certification Elections." *Industrial and Labor Relations Review* 50(2):195–212.

———. 1997a. "The Effects of Plant Closing or Threat of Plant Closing on the Right of Workers to Organize." Supplement to *Plant Closings and Workers Rights: A Report to the Council of Ministers by the Secretariat of the Commission for Labor Cooperation*, 1–56. Dallas: Bernan Press.

———. 1997b. "Organizing in the NAFTA Environment." *New Labor Forum* 1(1):50–60.

———. 2000. "Uneasy Terrain: The Impact of Capital Mobility on Workers, Wages, and Union Organizing." Supplement to *The U.S. Trade Deficit: Causes, Consequences, and Recommendations for Action*. Washington: U.S. Trade Deficit Review Commission.

———. 2002. "The American Labor Movement and the Resurgence in Union Organizing." In *Trade Union Renewal and Organizing: A Comparative Study of Trade Union Movements in*

Five Countries, edited by P. Fairbrother and C. Yates. London: Cassell Academic/Mansell Imprint.

Bronfenbrenner, Kate, James Burke, et al. 2001. *Impact of U.S.-China Trade Relations on Workers, Wages, and Employment: Pilot Study Report*. Commissioned research paper submitted to the U.S. Trade Deficit Review Commission. 30 June.

Bronfenbrenner, Kate, Sheldon Friedman, Richard W. Hurd, Rudolph A. Oswald, and Ronald L. Seeber. 1998. *Organizing to Win: New Research on Union Strategies*. Ithaca: Cornell University Press.

Bronfenbrenner, Kate, and Robert Hickey. 2002. *Overcoming the Challenges to Organizing in Manufacturing*. Report submitted to the AFL-CIO.

Bronfenbrenner, Kate, and Tom Juravich. 1995. *The Impact of Employer Opposition on Union Certification Win Rates: A Private/Public Sector Comparison*. Economic Policy Institute Working Paper No. 113. Washington, D.C.

——. 1998. "It Takes More than House Calls: Organizing to Win with a Comprehensive Union-Building Strategy." In *Organizing To Win: New Research on Union Strategies*, edited by K. Bronfenbrenner, S. Friedman, R. Hurd, R. Oswald, and R. Seeber, 18–36. Ithaca: Cornell University Press.

Brown, James N., and Orley Ashenfelter. 1986. "Testing the Efficiency of Employment Contracts." *Journal of Political Economy* 94:S40–87.

Brown, Randall. 1996. "Organizational Commitment: Clarifying the Concept and Simplifying the Existing Construct Typology." *Journal of Occupational Behavior* 49(3):230–51.

Buba, Tony, and Ray Henderson. 1996. *Struggles In Steel: A Story of African American Steelworkers*. Documentary Film. Pittsburgh: Braddock Films.

Budnick, Nick. 1996. "Dirty Pool? The Feds Dive into Sacramento's Janitorial Labor War." *Sacramento News and Review*, 8 February.

Buhle, Paul. 1999. *Taking Care of Business: Samuel Gompers, George Meany, Lane Kirkland, and the Tragedy of American Labor*. New York: Monthly Review Press.

Bunnage, Leslie. 2002. "Freshman Organizers: Can Union Summer Become a Year-Round Vocation?" *New Labor Forum* (fall/winter):92–97.

——. 2003. "Labor Movement Transformation and Revitalization: An Organizational Case Study of the Efficacy of the Union Summer Program." Unpublished manuscript.

Burns, James MacGregor. 1978. *Leadership*. New York: Harper and Row.

Callus, Ron. 1986. "Employment Characteristics of Full-time Union Officials in New South Wales." *Journal of Industrial Relations* 28:410–27.

Cannon, Debra Franklin. 1998. "Better Understanding the Impact of Work Interferences on Organizational Commitment." *Marriage and Family Review* 28(1/2):153–66.

Card, David. 1986 "Efficient Contracts with Costly Adjustment: Short Run Employment Determination for Airline Mechanics." *American Economic Review* 76:1045–71.

Carroll, Amy. n.d. *Savvy Troublemaking: Politics for New Labor Activists*. http://solidarity.igc.org/SavvyTroublemaking.htm.

Chaison, Gary, and P. Andiappan. 1987. "Profiles of Local Union Officers: Females vs. Males." *Industrial Relations* 26(3):284–91.

Chen, May, and Kent Wong. 1998. "The Challenge of Diversity and Inclusion in the AFL-CIO." In *A New Labor Movement for the New Century*, edited by G. Mantsios, 185–201. New York: Monthly Review Press.

Clark, Paul F. 1989. "Organizing the Organizers: Professional Staff Unionism in the American Labor Movement." *Industrial Labor Relations Review* 42(4):584–99.

——. 1992. "Professional Staff in American Unions: Changes, Trends, Implications." *Journal of Labor Research* 8(4):381–92.

Clawson, Dan. 1999. "What Happened to the United States Labor Movement? Union Decline and Renewal." *Annual Review of Sociology* 25:95–119.

———. 2003. *The Next Upsurge: Labor and the New Social Movements*. Ithaca: Cornell University Press.

Cobble, Dorothy Sue. 1996. "The Prospects for Unionism in a Service Economy." In *Working in the Service Economy*, edited by C. MacDonald and C. Sirianni, 333–58. Philadelphia: Temple University Press.

Cohen, Larry, and Steve Early. 1999. "Defending Workers' Rights in the Global Economy: The CWA Experience." In *Which Direction for Organized Labor? Essays on Organizing, Outreach, and Internal Transformations*, edited by B. Nissen, 143–64. Detroit: Wayne State University Press.

Cohen, Larry, and Richard W. Hurd. 1998. "Fear, Conflict, and Union Organizing." In *Organizing to Win: New Research on Union Strategies*, edited by K. Bronfenbrenner, S. Friedman, R. Hurd, R. Oswald, and R. Seeber, 181–96. Ithaca: Cornell University Press.

Cooke, William N. 1983. "Determinants of the Outcomes of Union Certification Elections." *Industrial and Labor Relations Review* 36:402–13.

Cooper, Mark. 1996. "The Boys and Girls of (Union) Summer." *Nation*.

Cornfield, Dan, Holly McCammon, Darren McDaniel, and Dean Eatman. 1998. "In the Community or in the Union? The Impact of Community Involvement on Nonunion Worker Attitudes about Unionizing." In *Organizing To Win: New Research on Union Strategies*, edited by K. Bronfenbrenner, S. Friedman, R. Hurd, R. Oswald, and R. Seeber, 247–58. Ithaca: Cornell University Press.

Cornfield, Daniel. 1999. *Shifts in Public Approval of Labor Unions in the United States, 1936–1999*. Gallup Organization Guest Scholar Series. http://www.gallup.com/poll/guest_scholar/gs990902.asp.

Csikai, Ellen, and Cindy Rozensky. 1997. "'Social Work Idealism' and Students' Perceived Reasons for Entering Social Work." *Journal of Social Work Education* 33(3):529–38.

Delgado, Hector. 2000. "The Los Angeles Manufacturing Action Project: An Opportunity Squandered?" In *Organizing Immigrants: The Challenge for Unions in Contemporary California*, edited by R. Milkman, 225–38. Ithaca: Cornell University Press.

Della Porta, Donatella, and Dieter Rucht. 1995. "Left-Libertarian Movements in Context: A Comparison of Italy and West Germany, 1965 to 1990." In *The Politics of Social Protest: Comparative Perspectives on States and Social Movements*, edited by C. Jenkins and B. Klandermans, 229–73. Minneapolis: University of Minnesota Press.

Delp, Linda, and Katie Quan. 2002. "Homecare Worker Organizing in California: An Analysis of a Successful Strategy." *Labor Studies Journal* 27(1):1–23.

Diamond, Virginia R. 1992. *Organizing Guide for Local Unions*. Washington: Labor's Heritage Press.

Dickens, William T. 1983. "The Effect of Company Campaigns on Certification Elections: Law and Reality Once Again." *Industrial and Labor Relations Review* 36(4):560–76.

DiMaggio, Paul. 1997. "Culture and Cognition." *Annual Review of Sociology* 23:263–87.

DiNardo, John, and David S. Lee. 2002. "The Impact of Unionization on Establishment Closure: A Regression Discontinuity Analysis of Representation Elections." National Bureau of Economic Research Working Paper No. 8993. http://www.nber.org/papers/w8993.

Dubofsky, Melyvn, and Warren Van Tine. 1977. *John L. Lewis, a Biography*. New York: Quadrangle/New York Times Book Company.

Early, Steve. 1996. "New Organizing Should Be Membership-based." *Labor Notes* 205:12.

———. 1998. "Membership-Based Organizing." In *A New Labor Movement for the New Century*, edited by G. Mantsios, 82–103. New York: Monthly Review Press.

Ecklein, Joan L. 1972. *Community Organizers and Urban Planners*. New York: Wiley.

Eisenscher, Michael. 1999. "Critical Juncture: Unionism at the Crossroads." In *Which Direction for Organized Labor? Essays on Organizing, Outreach, and Internal Transformations*, edited by B. Nissen, 217–46. Detroit: Wayne State University Press.

Emirbeyer, Mustafa, and Ann Mische. 1998. "What is Agency?" *American Journal of Sociology* 103:962–1023.

Erem, Suzan. 2001. *Labor Pains: Inside America's New Union Movement*. New York: Monthly Review Press.

Fantasia, Rick. 1988. *Cultures of Solidarity: Consciousness, Action and Contemporary American Workers*. Berkeley: University of California Press.

Farber, Barry. 2000. "Introduction: Understanding and Treating Burnout in a Changing Culture." *Journal of Clinical Psychology* 56(5):589–94.

Farber, Henry, and Bruce Western. 2001. "Accounting for the Decline of Unions in the Private Sector, 1973–1998." *Journal of Labor Research* 22:459–85.

Feekin, Lynn, and Marcus Widenor. 2000. "Organizer Training in Two Hemispheres: The AFL-CIO Organizing Institute and the Australian Council of Trade Union's Organizing Works." Unpublished paper.

——. 2001. "Helping New Organizers Survive and Thrive in the Field: The Essential Role of Training and Mentoring." Unpublished paper.

Fellner, Kim. 1991. "Time for an Organizers Association: An Overhaul for the Long Haul." *Labor Research Review* 18:92–103.

——. 1993. "Reintegrating Our Movement: What's Our Vision?" *Social Policy* (winter):51–58.

——. 1998. "Hearts and Crafts: Powering the Movement." *Shelterforce* (September/October): 20–22.

——. 2000. "Hearts on Fire: How Do We Keep Them From Burning Out?" Unpublished paper.

Fine, Janice. 1998. "Moving Innovation from the Margins to the Center." In *A New Labor Movement for the New Century*, edited by G. Mantsios, 119–45. New York: Monthly Review Press.

——. 2001. "Building Community Unions." *The Nation* (January):18–22.

Fink, Gary M. 1984. "The American Labor Leader in the Twentieth Century: Quantitative and Qualitative Portraits." In *Biographical Dictionary of American Labor*, edited by Gary M. Fink. Westport, Conn.: Greenwood Press.

Fiorito, Jack, Paul Jarley, and John Thomas Delaney. 1995. "National Union Effectiveness In Organizing: Measures and Influences." *Industrial and Labor Relations Review* 48:613–35.

Fisk, Catherine L., Daniel J. B. Mitchell, and Christopher L. Erickson. 2000. "Union Representation of Immigrant Janitors in Southern California: Economic and Legal Challenges." In *Organizing Immigrants: The Challenge for Unions in Contemporary California*, edited by R. Milkman, 199–224. Ithaca: Cornell University Press.

Fletcher, Bill, and Richard Hurd. 1998. "Beyond the Organizing Model: The Transformation Process in Local Unions." In *Organizing to Win: New Research on Union Strategies*, edited by K. Bronfenbrenner, S. Friedman, R. W. Hurd, R. A. Oswald, and R. L. Seeber, 37–53. Ithaca: Cornell University Press.

——. 1999. "Political Will, Local Union Transformation, and the Organizing Imperative." In *Which Direction for Organized Labor? Essays on Organizing, Outreach, and Internal Transformations*, edited by B. Nissen, 191–216. Detroit: Wayne State University Press.

——. 2001. "Overcoming Obstacles to Transformation: Challenges on the Way to a New Unionism." In *Rekindling the Movement: Labor's Quest for 21ˢᵗ Century Relevance*, edited by L. Turner, H. Katz, and R. Hurd, 99–128. Ithaca: Cornell University Press.

Foerster, Amy. 2000. "Transformation of a Social Movement Organization: The Case of the AFL-CIO Organizing Institute." PhD diss., Cornell University.

Fonow, Mary Margaret. 1978. "Women in Steel: A Case Study of Women in Trade Unions." University Microfilms International.

Franzway, Suzanne. 2000. "Women Working in a Greedy Institution: Commitment and Emotional Labour in the Union Movement." *Gender, Work, and Organization* 7(4):258–68.

Freeman, Richard B. 1985. "Why Are Unions Faring Poorly in NLRB Representation Elections?" *Challenges and Choices Facing American Labor*, edited by T. Kochan, 45–64. Cambridge: MIT Press.

Freeman, Richard B., and Morris M. Kleiner. 1990. "Employer Behavior in the Face of Union Organizing Drives." *Industrial and Labor Relations Review* 43(4):351–65.

——. 1999. "Do Unions Make Enterprises Insolvent?" *Industrial and Labor Relations Review* 52(4):507–24.

Freeman, Richard B., and James L. Medoff. 1984. *What Do Unions Do?* New York: Basic Books.

Freeman, Richard B., and Joel Rogers. 1999. *What Workers Want.* Ithaca: Cornell University Press.

Friedman, Milton. 1962. *Capitalism and Freedom.* Chicago: University of Chicago Press.

Friedman, Sheldon, Richard Hurd, Rudolph Oswald, and Ronald Seeber, eds. 1994. *Restoring the Promise of American Labor Law.* Ithaca: ILR Press.

Fuchs, Victor R., Alan B. Krueger, and James M. Poterba. 1998. "Economists' Views about Parameters, Values, and Policies: Survey Results in Labor and Public Economics." *Journal of Economic Literature* 36:1387–1425.

Gamson, William. 1992. "The Social Psychology of Collective Action." In *Frontiers in Social Movement Theory,* edited by A. D. Morris and C. M. Mueller. New Haven: Yale University Press.

Ganz, Marshall. 2000. "Resources and Resourcefulness: Strategic Capacity in the Unionization of California Agriculture, 1959–1966." *American Journal of Sociology* 105(4):1003–62.

Gapasin, Fernando, and Howard Wial. 1998. "The Role of Central Labor Councils in Union Organizing in the 1990s." In *Organizing to Win: New Research on Union Strategies,* edited by K. Bronfenbrenner, S. Friedman, R. W. Hurd, R. A. Oswald, and R. L. Seeber, 54–68. Ithaca: Cornell University Press.

Goldston, Linda. 1991. "INS Audit of Janitorial Firm Protested." *San Jose Mercury News,* 6 May:1B, 3B.

Gordon, Colin. 1999. "The Lost City of Solidarity: Metropolitan Unionism in Historical Perspective." *Politics and Society* 27:561–86.

Grenier, Guillermo. 1987. *Inhuman Relations: Quality Circles and Anti-Unionism in American Industry.* Philadelphia: Temple University Press.

Grosch, William, and David Olsen. 2000. "Clergy Burnout: An Integrative Approach." *Journal of Clinical Psychology* 56(5):619–32.

Gruelle, Martha. 2000. "Members Protest Service Employees Dues Hike: Dues to Nearly Double for Many by 2005." *Labor Notes* 259:15.

Gruelle, Martha, and Mike Parker. 1999. *Democracy is Power: Rebuilding Unions from the Bottom Up.* Chicago: Labor Notes.

Gunz, Hugh. 1989. *Careers and Corporate Cultures: Managerial Mobility in Large Corporations.* New York: Basil Blackwell.

Hermanson, Jeff. 1993. "Organizing for Justice: ILGWU Returns to Social Unionism to Organize Immigrant Workers." *Labor Research Review* 20:52–97.

Hirsch, Barry T., and David A. Macpherson. 2003. *Union Membership and Earnings Data Book: Compilations form the Current Population Survey.* Washington: Bureau of National Affairs.

Hochwarter, Wayne, Pamela Perrewe, Gerald Ferris, and Rachel Guercio. 1999. "Commitment as an Antidote to the Tension and Turnover Consequences of Organizational Politics." *Journal of Vocational Behavior* 55(3):277–97.

Hoerr, John. 1997. *We Can't Eat Prestige: The Women Who Organized Harvard.* Philadelphia: Temple University Press.

Hollander, Edwin P. 1978. *Leadership Dynamics: A Practical Guide to Effective Relationships.* New York: Free Press.

Hosmer, David, and Stanley Lemeshow. 1989. *Applied Logistic Regression.* New York: Wiley and Sons.

Howley, John. 1990. "Justice for Janitors: The Challenge of Organizing Contract Services." *Labor Research Review* 15:61–75.

Hunt, Shelby, and Robert Morgan. 1994. "Organizational Commitment: One of Many Commitments or Key Mediating Construct?" *Academy of Management Journal* 37(6): 1568–87.

Hurd, Richard W. 1998. "Contesting the Dinosaur Image: The Labor Movement's Search for a Future." *Labor Studies Journal* (winter):5–30.

Hurd, Richard W., and John Bunge. 2003. "Unionization of Professional and Technical Workers: The Labor Market and Institutional Transformation." In *Labor Market Institutions for the 21st Century*, edited by R. Freeman, J. Hersch, and L. Mishel. Chicago: University of Chicago Press for NBER.

Hurd, Richard W., and Adrienne McElwain. 1988. "Organizing Clerical Workers: Determinants of Success." *Industrial and Labor Relations Review* 41:350–73.

Hurd, Richard W., and Joseph Uehlein. 1994. "Patterned Responses to Organizing: Case Studies of the Union-Busting Convention." In *Restoring the Promise of American Labor Law*, edited by S. Friedman, R. W. Hurd, R. A. Oswald, and R. Seeber, 61–75. Ithaca: ILR Press.

Jarley, Paul, and Jack Fiorito. 1991. "Unionism and Changing Employee Views toward Work." *Journal of Labor Research* 12(3):223–29.

Johnston, Paul. 1994. *Success While Others Fail: Social Movement Unionism and the Public Workforce*. Ithaca: ILR Press.

Juravich, Tom, and Kate Bronfenbrenner. 1998. "Preparing for the Worst: Organizing and Staying Organized in the Public Sector." In *Organizing to Win: New Research on Union Strategies*, edited by K. Bronfenbrenner, S. Friedman, R. Hurd, R. Oswald, and R. Seeber, 263–82. Ithaca: Cornell University Press.

———. 1999. *Ravenswood: The Steelworkers' Victory and the Revival of American Labor*. Ithaca: Cornell University Press.

Juravich, Tom, and Jeff Hilgert. 1999. "UNITE's Victory at Richmark: Community-Based Union Organizing in Communities of Color." *Labor Studies Journal* 24:27–41.

Katz, Jack. 1978. "Lawyers for the Poor in Transition: Involvement, Reform, and the Turnover Problem in the Legal Services Program." *Law and Society* 12:275–300.

Katzenstein, Mary, 1998. *Faithful and Fearless: Moving Feminist Protest Inside the Church and Military*. Princeton: Princeton University Press.

Kaufman, Bruce, and Paula E. Stephan. 1995. "The Role of Management Attorneys in Union Organizing Campaigns." *Industrial and Labor Relations Review* 48(4):439–54.

Kellerman, Barbara. 1986. *Political Leadership: A Source Book*. Pittsburgh: University of Pittsburgh Press.

Kelley, John, and Edmund Heery. 1994. *Working for the Union*. Cambridge: Cambridge University Press.

Kiefer, David, and Immanuel Ness. 1999. "Organizing Immigrant Workers in New York City: The LIUNA Asbestos Removal Workers Campaign." *Labor Studies Journal* 24:12–26.

Kirton, M. J., and R. M. McCarthy. 1988. "Cognitive Climate and Organizations." *Journal of Occupational Psychology* 61:175–84.

Klandermans, Bert. 1984. "Mobilization and Participation: Social-Psychological Extensions of Resource Mobilization Theory." *American Sociological Review* 49:583–600.

Klandermans, Bert, and Dirk Oegema. 1987. "Campaigning for a Nuclear Freeze: Grassroots Strategies and Local Government in the Netherlands." In *Research in Political Sociology*, edited by R. Braungart, 305–37. Greenwich, Conn.: JAI Press.

Klatch, Rebecca. 1999. *A Generation Divided: The New Left, the New Right, and the 1960s*. Berkeley: University of California Press.

Kochan, Thomas, Harry C. Katz, and Robert B. McKersie. 1994. *The Transformation of American Industrial Relations*. New York: Basic Books.

Kochan, Thomas, Robert B. McKersie, and John Chalykoff. 1986. "The Effects of Corporate Strategy and Workplace Innovations on Union Representation." *Industrial and Labor Relations Review* 39(4):487–501.

Koeske, Gary F., and Stuart A. Kirk. 1995. "The Effect of Characteristics of Human Service Workers on Subsequent Morale and Turnover." *Administration in Social Work* 19(1):15–31.

Kusnet, David. 1987. "Labor-Saving Devices: Unions Try the Soft-Sell." *Commonweal*, 526–29.

Kuttner, Robert. 1987. "Will Unions Organize Again?" *Dissent* (winter).

Lawler, John. 1990. *Unionization and Deunionization*. Columbia: University of South Carolina Press.

Leiter, Michael, and Kimberly Ann Meechan. 1986. "Role Structure and Burnout in the Field of Human Services." *Journal of Applied Behavioral Science* 22(1):47–52.

Lerner, Stephen. 1991. "Let's Get Moving: Labor's Survival Depends on Organizing Industry-Wide for Justice and Power." *Labor Research Review* 18:1–15.

———. 1996. "Strategic Labor Organizing: How to Win Against the Odds." *Dollars and Sense* 205:32–38.

———. 1998. "Taking the Offensive, Turning the Tide." In *A New Labor Movement for a New Century*, edited by G. Mantsios, 79–94. New York: Garland.

———. 2001. Presentation on "Organizing Strategies for the 21st Century." Conference on "The New Economy and Union Responses." University of California, Institute for Labor and Employment, Los Angeles, March 9. Summary of Proceedings: http://ucop.edu/ile/conferences/march_conf/index.html

———. 2003. "An Immodest Proposal: A New Architecture for the House of Labor." *New Labor Forum* 12(2):9–30.

Levander, Michelle. 1994. "U.S. Warns Tech Firms to Clean Up Janitorial Contracts." *San Jose Mercury News*, 22 January:10D, 14D.

Levitt, Martin Jay, with Terry Conrow. 1993. *Confessions of a Union Buster*. New York: Crown.

Lewis, H. Gregg. 1963. *Unionism and Relative Wages in the United States*. Chicago: University of Chicago Press.

Lewis, Janet, and Bill Mirand. 1998. "Creating an Organizing Culture in Today's Building and Construction Trades: A Case Study of IBEW Local 46." In *Organizing to Win: New Research on Union Strategies*, edited by K. Bronfenbrenner, S. Friedman, R. Hurd, R. Oswald, and R. Seeber, 297–308. Ithaca: Cornell University Press.

Lichtenstein, Nelson. 2002. "A Race between Cynicism and Hope: Labor and Academia." *New Labor Forum* 10:71–9.

Lopez, Steven H. 2000. "Contesting the Global City: Pittsburgh's Public Service Unions Confront a Neoliberal Agenda." In *Global Ethnography: Forces, Connections, and Imaginations in a Postmodern World*, edited by Michael Burawoy et al., 268–98. Berkeley: University of California Press.

Lopez, Steven H. 2000. "Reorganizing the Rust Belt: Social Movement Unionism and the SEIU in Pennsylvania." PhD diss., University of California, Berkeley.

Lynn, Monty, and Jozell Brister. 1989. "Trends in Union Organizing Issues and Tactics." *Industrial Relations* 28(1):104–13.

Macdonald, Ian, and Robert M. Solow. 1981. "Wage Bargaining and Employment." *American Economic Review* 71:886–908.

Machin, Stephen, and Sushil Wadhwani. 1991. "The Effects of Unions on Organisational Change and Employment." *Economic Journal* 101(407):835–54.

MaCurdy, Thomas, and John Pencavel. 1986. "Testing the Efficiency of Employment Contracts." *Journal of Political Economy* 94:S3–S39.

Mantsios, Gregory, ed. 1998. *A New Labor Movement for the New Century*. New York: Garland.

Maranto, Cheryl L., and Jack Fiorito. 1987. "The Effect of Union Characteristics on the Outcome of NLRB Certification Elections." *Industrial and Labor Relations Review* 40:225–41.

Markowitz, Linda. 1995. "Union Presentation of Self and Worker Participation in Organizing Campaigns." *Sociological Perspectives* 38:437–54.

———. 1999. *Worker Activism after Successful Union Organizing*. Armonk, N.Y.: M. E. Sharpe.

McAdam, Doug. 1988. *Freedom Summer*. New York: Oxford University Press.

McDuff, Elaine M., and Charles W. Mueller. 2000. "The Ministry as an Occupational Labor Market: Intentions to Leave an Employer (Church) versus Intentions to Leave a Profession (Ministry). *Work and Occupations* 27(1):89–116.

McNeely, R. L. 1989. "Gender, Job-Satisfaction, Earnings, and Other Characteristics of Human-Service Workers During and After Midlife." *Administration in Social Work* 13(2):99–116.

Medina, Michael. 1991. "Civic Leaders Hear Testimony of Janitors' Work Woes." *El Observador*, 12 June.

Menard, Scott. 1995. *Applied Logistic Regression Analysis.* Series: Quantitative Applications in the Social Sciences, No. 106. Thousand Oaks, Calif.: Sage Publications.

Meyer, David, and Suzanne Staggenborg. 1996. "Movements, Countermovements, and the Structure of Political Opportunity." *American Journal of Sociology* 101(6):1628–60.

Meyer, David, and Nancy Whittier. 1994. "Social Movement Spillover." *Social Problems* 41:277–98.

Meyerson, Harold. 2001. "California's Progressive Mosaic." *American Prospect* 18 June, 17–23.

Milkman, Ruth. 1998. "The New Labor Movement: Possibilities and Limits." *Contemporary Sociology* 27(2):125–29.

———. 2000. "Immigrant Organizing and the New Labor Movement in Los Angeles." *Critical Sociology* 26(1/2):59–81.

Milkman, Ruth, ed. 2000. *Organizing Immigrants: The Challenge for Unions in Contemporary California.* Ithaca: Cornell University Press.

Milkman, Ruth, and Daisy Rooks. 2003. "California Union Membership: A Turn-of-the-Century Portrait." In *The State of California Labor 2003*, 1–33. Berkeley: University of California Press for the UC Institute for Labor and Employment.

Milkman, Ruth, and Kent Wong. 2001. "Organizing Immigrant Workers: Case Studies from Southern California." In *Rekindling the Movement: Labor's Quest for 21st Century Relevance*, edited by L. Turner, H. Katz, and R. Hurd, 99–128. Ithaca: Cornell University Press.

Miller, Robert A. 1984. "Job Matching and Occupational Choice." *Journal of Political Economy* 92(6):1086–120.

Mills, C. Wright. 1940. "Situated Actions and Vocabularies of Motive." *American Sociological Review* 5(6):904–13.

———. 1948. *The New Men of Power: America's Labor Leaders.* New York: Harcourt Brace.

Mines, Richard, and Jeffrey Avina. 1992. "Immigrants and Labor Standards: The Case of California Janitors." In *The U.S.-Mexico Relations: Labor Market Interdependence*, edited by J. A. Bustamante, C. W. Reynolds, and R. A. Hinojosa Ojeda, 429–48. Stanford: Stanford University Press.

Mische, Ann. 1996. "Projecting Democracy: The Formation of Citizenship across Youth Networks in Brazil." *International Review of Social History* 40(Supplement 3):131–58.

———. 2002. "Crosstalk in Movements: Reconceiving the Culture-Network Link." In *Social Movement Analysis: The Network Perspective*, edited by M. Diani and D. McAdam. New York: Oxford University Press.

Mische, Ann, and Philippa Pattison. 2000. "Composing a Civic Arena: Publics, Projects, and Social Settings." *Poetics* 27:163–94.

Mondros, Jacqueline B., and Scott M. Wilson. 1990. "Staying Alive: Career Selection and Sustenance of Community Organizers." *Administration in Social Work* 14(2):95–109.

Moody, Kim. 1988. *An Injury to All: The Decline of American Unionism.* New York: Verso.

———. 1997. "American Labor: A Movement Again?" *Monthly Review* 49:63–80.

Morris, Aldon. 1984. *The Origins of the Civil Rights Movement.* New York: Free Press.

Mort, Jo-Ann, ed. 1998. *Not Your Father's Labor Movement: Inside the AFL-CIO.* New York: Verso.

National Organizers Alliance. 2001. "Practicing What We Preach: The National Organizers Alliance Report on Policies and Practices of Justice Organizations." Washington, D.C.: NOA.

Newman, Katherine S. 2000. *No Shame in My Game: The Working Poor in the Inner City.* New York: Random House.

Nissen, Bruce, and Seth Rosen. 1999. "The CWA Model of Membership-based Organizing." *Labor Studies Journal* 24:73–88.

Oberschall, Anthony. 1973. *Social Conflict and Social Movements*. Englewood Cliffs, N.J.: Prentice-Hall.

Olson, Mancur. 1965. *The Logic of Collective Action: Public Goods and the Theory of Groups*. Cambridge: Harvard University Press.

Organizing Institute. 2000. "Criteria for Union Organizers: Recruiter Training Manual."

Paquet, Renaud, Jean-Pierre Deslauriers, and Marc Sarrazin. 1999. "Unionization of Community Workers." *Relations Industrielles-Industrial Relations* 54(2):337–64.

Payne, Charles. 1995. *I've Got the Light of Freedom: The Organizing Tradition and the Mississippi Freedom Struggle*. Berkeley: University of California Press.

Peck, Sidney. 1963. *The Rank and File Leader*. New Haven: College and University Press.

Penney, Robert. 2002. "Organizing the Unorganized: The Construction of Consciousness and Action in Worker Mobilization." PhD diss., University of Michigan.

Peterson, Richard B., Thomas Lee, and Barbara Finnegan. 1992. "Strategies and Tactics in Union Organizing Campaigns." *Industrial Relations* 31(2):370–81.

Phillips, Henry. 1997. "An (Ex) Staffers Story." *Savvy Troublemaking: Politics for New. Labor Activists*. Detroit: Solidarity.

Piore, Michael. 1994. "Unions: A Reorientation to Survive." In *Labor Economics and Industrial Relations*, edited by C. Kerr and P. D. Staudohar, 512–41. Cambridge: Harvard University Press.

Piven, Frances Fox, and Richard Cloward. 1977. *Poor People's Movements: Why they Succeed, How they Fail*. New York: Random House.

——. 2000. "Does the Electoral Path Work for Labor?" *Working USA* 4:8–18.

Polletta, Francesca. 1998. "Contending Stories: Narrative in Social Movements." *Qualitative Sociology* 21(4):419–46.

Powell, Walter W., and Paul J. DiMaggio. 1991. *The New Institutionalism in Organizational Analysis*. Chicago: University of Chicago Press.

Puette, William J. 1992. *Through Jaundiced Eyes: How The Media Views Organized Labor*. Ithaca: ILR Press.

Putnam, Robert D. 2000. *Bowling Alone: The Collapse and Revival of American Community*. New York: Simon and Schuster.

Quaglieri, Philip. 1988. "The New Men of Power: The Backgrounds and Careers of Top Labor Leaders." *Journal of Labor Research* 9(3):271–84.

Rafferty, Carole. 1993. "It's a Dirty Business . . ." *West Magazine*, 12 September.

Reed, Thomas F. 1989. "Do Union Organizers Matter?: Individual Differences, Campaign Practices, and Representational Election Outcomes." *Industrial and Labor Relations Review* 43(1):103–19.

——. 1990. "Profiles of Union Organizers." *Journal of Labor Research* 11:73–80.

Rees, Albert. 1963. "The Effect of Unions on Resource Allocation." *Journal of Law and Economics* 6:69–78.

Reisch, Michael, and Stanley Wencour. 1986. "The Future of Community Organization in Social Work: Social Activism and the Politics of Profession Building." *Social Service Review* 6(1):70–93.

Robertson, Kathy. 1996. "Janitors' Union Claims A Victory, Sort Of." *Business Journal (Sacramento)*, 19 August: 1.

Rogers, Joel. 1997. "'The Folks Who Brought You the Weekend': Labor and Independent Politics." In *Audacious Democracy*, edited by S. Fraser and J. Freeman, 247–61. New York: Houghton Mifflin.

Rondeau, Kris. 1993. "Finding Their Voice." *Boston Review* 18(5). http://bostonreview.mit.edu/BR18.5/findingvoice.html

Rose, Joseph B, and Gary N. Chaison. 1990. "New Measures of Union Organizing Effectiveness." *Industrial Relations* 29:457–69.

Rudy, Preston. 2003. "Labor, Globalization and Urban Political Fields: A Comparison of Justice for Janitors in Three California Cities." PhD diss., University of California, Davis.

Russo, Monica. 1993. "This World Called Miami: ACTWU Approaches Union-Building in a Multicultural Framework." *Labor Research Review* 20:36–49.

Savage, Lydia A. 1998. "Geographies of Organizing: Justice for Janitors in Los Angeles." In *Organizing the Landscape: Geographical Perspectives on Labor Unionism*, edited by A. Herod, 225–52. Minneapolis: University of Minnesota Press.

Saxenian, AnnaLee. 1989. "In Search of Power: The Organization of Business Interests in Silicon Valley and Route 128." *Economy and Society* 18(1):25–70.

Schattschneider, E. E. 1960. *The Semi-sovereign People: A Realist's View of Democracy in America.* New York: Holt, Rinehart, and Winston.

Sciacchitano, Katherine. 1998. "Finding the Community in the Union and the Union in the Community: The First Contract Campaign at Steeltech." In *Organizing to Win: New Research on Union Strategies*, edited by K. Bronfenbrenner, S. Friedman, R. Hurd, R. Oswald, and R. Seeber, 150–63. Ithaca: Cornell University Press.

Selvin, Steven. 1991. *Statistical Analysis of Epidemiologic Data.* New York: Oxford University Press.

Shaw, Randy. 1999. *Reclaiming America: Nike, Clean Air, and the New National Activism.* Berkeley: University of California Press.

Sherman, Rachel, and Kim Voss. 2000. "Organize or Die: Labor's New Tactics and Immigrant Workers." In *Organizing Immigrants: The Challenge for Unions in Contemporary California*, edited by R. Milkman, 81–108. Ithaca: Cornell University Press.

Siegmann, Ken, and Don Clark. 1991. "Janitor Dispute Enlivens Apple's Annual Meeting." *San Francisco Chronicle*, 31 January: Business Section.

Simpson, Ida Harper, Richard L. Simpson, Mark Evers, and Sharon Sandomirsky Poss. 1982. "Occupational Recruitment, Retention, and Labor Force Cohort Representation." *American Journal of Sociology* 87(6):1287–313.

Skocpol, Theda. 2003 *Diminished Democracy: From Membership to Management in American Civic Life.* Norman: University of Oklahoma Press.

Slaughter, Jane. 1998. "From the Bottom Up: Only the Rank and File Can Bring Real and Lasting Change." *Sojourner* 27(5):38–42.

Snow, David A., and Robert D. Benford. 1988. "Ideology, Frame Resonance, and Participant Mobilization." *International Social Movement Research* 1:197–217.

Snow, David A., Louis A. Zurcher, and Sheldon Ekland-Olson. 1980. "Social Networks and Social Movements: A Microstructural Approach to Differential Recruitment." *American Sociological Review* 45:787–801.

Somers, Margaret. 1992. "Narrativity, Narrative Identity, and Social Action: Rethinking English Working Class Formation." *Social Science History* 16:591–629.

Starr, Rose, Terry Mizrahi, and Ellen Gurinsky. 1999. "Where Have All the Organizers Gone? The Career Paths of Community Organizing Social Work Alumni." *Journal of Community Practice* 6(3):23–48.

Stewart, Julia. 2003. Personal Conversation with Leslie Bunnage. 21 August.

Strauss, George. 1956. "Control by the Membership in Building Trades Local Unions." *American Journal of Sociology* 61(6):523–35.

———. 1957. "Business Agents in the Building Trades." *Industrial and Labor Relations Review* 10:237–51.

Strauss, George, and Leonard R. Sayles. 1952. "The Unpaid Labor Leader." *Harvard Business Review* 30(3):91–101.

Tannock, Stuart. 2001. *Youth at Work: The Unionized Fast-Food and Grocery Workplace.* Philadelphia: Temple University Press.

Tarrow, Sydney. 1994. *Power in Movement: Social Movements, Collective Action, and Politics.* Cambridge: Cambridge University Press.

Thacher, David. 2001. "Policing Is Not a Treatment: Alternatives to the Medical Model of Police Research." *Journal of Research in Crime and Delinquency* 38(4):387–415.

Trounstine, Philip J., and Terry Christensen. 1982. *Movers and Shakers: The Study of Community Power*. New York: St. Martin's Press.

Turner, Lowell. 1998. "Rank and File Participation in Organizing at Home and Abroad." In *Organizing To Win: New Research on Union Strategies*, edited by K. Bronfenbrenner, S. Friedman, R. Hurd, R. Oswald, and R. Seeber, 123–34. Ithaca: Cornell University Press.

U.S. Bureau of Labor Statistics. 2002. *Union Affiliation of Employed Wage and Salary Workers by State*. Washington, D.C.: U.S. Bureau of Labor Statistics. http://www.bls.gov/news.release/union2.t05.htm.

——. 2002. *Database of Employment, Hours and Earnings from the Current Employment Statistics Survey*. Washington: U.S. Department of Labor, Bureau of Labor Statistics.

U.S. Bureau of the Census. 1990. Census of Population and Housing, Summary Tape File 3.

U.S. House of Representatives. 1996. Committee on Economic and Educational Opportunities. Subcommittee on Oversight and Investigations. *Hearing on Abuse of Power at the Department of Labor*. 104th Congress, 2nd Session, 25 April. Washington: U.S. Government Printing Office.

Voss, Kim. 1998. "Claim-Making and the Interpretation of Defeats: The Interpretation of Losses by American and British Labor Activists, 1886–1895." In *Challenging Authority: The Historical Study of Contentious Politics*, edited by M. Hanagan, L. Page Moon, and W. T. Brake, 136–48. Minneapolis: University of Minnesota Press.

Voss, Kim, and Rachel Sherman. 2000. "Breaking the Iron Law of Oligarchy: Union Revitalization in the American Labor Movement." *American Journal of Sociology* 106(2):303–49.

Wagner, D. 1989. "The Fate of Idealism in Social Work: Alternative Experiences of Professional Careers." *Social Work* 34(5):389–95.

Waldinger, Roger, Chris Erickson, Ruth Milkman, Daniel J.B. Mitchell, Abel Valenzuela, Kent Wong, and Maurice Zeitlin. 1998. "Helots No More: A Case Study of the Justice for Janitors Campaign in Los Angeles." In *Organizing to Win: New Research on Union Strategies*, edited by K. Bronfenbrenner, S. Friedman, R. W. Hurd, R. A. Oswald, and R. Seeber, 102–19. Ithaca: Cornell University Press.

Waldinger, Roger, and Claudia Der-Martirosian. 2000. "Immigrant Workers and American Labor: Challenge . . . or Disaster?" In *Organizing Immigrants: The Challenge for Unions in Contemporary California*, edited by R. Milkman, 49–80. Ithaca: Cornell University Press.

Walsh, Edward J., and Rex H. Warland. 1983. "Social Movement Involvement in the Wake of a Nuclear Accident: Activists and Free Riders in the TMI Area." *American Sociological Review* 48(6):764–80.

Warren, Mark R. 2001. *Dry Bones Rattling: Community Building to Revitalize American Democracy*. Princeton: Princeton University Press.

Weikle, Roger, Hoyt Wheeler, and John McClendon. 1998. "A Comparative Case Study of Union Success and Failure." In *Organizing To Win: New Research on Union Strategies*, edited by K. Bronfenbrenner, S. Friedman, R. Hurd, R. Oswald, and R. Seeber, 197–212. Ithaca: Cornell University Press.

Weinbaum, Eva. 1999. "Organizing Labor in an Era of Contingent Work and Globalization." In *Which Direction for Organized Labor? Essays on Organizing, Outreach, and Internal Transformations*, edited by B. Nissen, 37–58. Detroit: Wayne State University Press.

Weiss, Eileen. 1999. "Perceived Workplace Conditions and First-Year Teachers' Morale, Career Choice Commitment, and Planned Retention: A Secondary Analysis." *Teaching and Teacher Education* 15(8):861–79.

Wells, Miriam. 2000. "Immigration and Unionization in the San Francisco Hotel Industry." In *Organizing Immigrants: The Challenge for Unions in Contemporary California*, edited by R. Milkman, 109–29. Ithaca: Cornell University Press.

Wickham-Crowley, Timothy P. 1992. *Guerrillas and Revolution in Latin America*. Princeton: Princeton University Press.

Williams, Jane. 1999. "Restructuring Labor's Identity: The Justice for Janitors Campaign in Washington, D.C." In *Transformation of U.S. Unions: Voices, Visions, and Strategies from the Grassroots*, edited by R. M. Tillman and M. S. Cummings, 203–17. Boulder, Colo.: Lynne Rienner.

Wimberly, James W. 1996. "Union Summer Is Here." *Bobbin Live*. http://www.bobbin.com/media/96august/summer.htm.

Ybarra, Michael. 1994. "Janitor's Union Uses Pressure and Theatrics to Expand Its Ranks." *Wall Street Journal*, 21 March.

Zald, Mayer, and Bert Useem. 1987. "Movement and Countermovement Interaction: Mobilization, Tactics, and State Involvement." In *Social Movements in an Organizational Society*, edited by Mayer Zald and John D. McCarthy. New Brunswick, N.J.: Transaction.

Zeitlin, Maurice, and Judith Stepan-Norris. 1989. "'Who Gets the Bird?' or, How the Communists Won Power and Trust in America's Unions: The Relative Autonomy of Intraclass Political Struggles." *American Sociological Review* 54(4):503–23.

Zerubavel, Eviatar. 1997. *Social Mindscapes: An Invitation to Cognitive Sociology*. Cambridge: Harvard University Press.

Zlolniski, Christian. 1994. "The Informal Economy in an Advanced Industrialized Society: Mexican Immigrant Labor in Silicon Valley." *Yale Law Journal* 103:2305–35.

http://www.aflcio.organize/orginst/program.htm

http://www.seiu.org

http://www.seiujobs.org/brochure

http://www.ufw.org/o.htm

http://www.unionjobs.com/staff/ca/HEREINT.html

CONTRIBUTORS

LESLIE BUNNAGE is a Ph.D. candidate in Sociology at the University of California, Irvine. She is the author of "Freshman Organizers: Can Union Summer Become a Year-Round Vocation?" *New Labor Forum* (Fall/Winter 2002). In 1998 she served as a Union Summer Site Coordinator in Los Angeles.

KATE BRONFENBRENNER is Director of Labor Education Research at Cornell's School of Industrial and Labor Relations. She received her Ph.D. from Cornell in 1993 and worked for many years as an organizer and union representative. She is the co-author and editor of several books, including *Organizing to Win: New Research on Union Strategies* (1998) and *Ravenswood: The Steelworkers' Victory and the Revival of American Labor* (1999) and writes extensively on union and employer behavior in organizing and bargaining campaigns and on the impact of global trade and investment policy on workers and unions.

JOHN DINARDO is Professor of Economics and Public Policy at the University of Michigan, Ann Arbor, and a Research Associate of the National Bureau of Economic Research. A labor economist and applied econometrician, he is currently studying the efficacy of federal mediation between new unions and employers, as well as systematic biases in pre-election U.S. presidential "horse race" polls.

MARSHALL GANZ is Lecturer in Public Policy at the Kennedy School of Government, Harvard University. After 28 years organizing with SNCC, the United Farm Workers, and union, electoral, and advocacy groups, he completed a Ph.D. in sociology at Harvard in 2000. He teaches leadership, organizing, and advocacy at the Kennedy School, has published in the *American Prospect, American Journal of Sociology*, and *American Political Science Review*. His book on the United Farm Workers, *Why David Sometimes Wins*, will be published by Oxford University Press.

ROBERT HICKEY is a Ph.D. student in Collective Bargaining, Labor Law, and Labor History at Cornell's School of Industrial and Labor Relations and a graduate research associate in the Office of Labor Education Research. Prior to coming to Cornell, he worked for many years as an organizer and union representative for the International Brotherhood of Teamsters. He received his MS degree from Cornell in 2003 and is the author and co-author of several articles and monographs on union bargaining and organizing strategies in the global economy.

DAVID S. LEE is Assistant Professor of Economics at UC Berkeley. His research interests include wage inequality in the United States, political economy and Congressional voting behavior, applied econometrics, and labor unions.

STEVEN H. LOPEZ is an assistant professor of sociology at The Ohio State University and a former Robert Wood Johnson Scholar in Health Policy Research at the University of Michigan. He is the author of *Reorganizing the Rust Belt: An Inside Study of the American Labor Movement,* published by the University of California Press in 2004. His previous research includes studies of route sales drivers and auto workers. Currently, he is working on a study of work organization in the nursing home industry.

RUTH MILKMAN is Professor of Sociology at UCLA and Director of the UCLA Institute of Industrial Relations. She served as director of the UC Institute for Labor and Employment from 2001 to 2004. Her research and writing has ranged over a variety of issues surrounding work and labor organization in the U.S. Her publications include *Gender at Work: The Dynamics of Job Segregation during World War II* (1987) and *Farewell to the Factory: Auto Workers in the Late 20th Century* (1997).

ROBERT A. PENNEY is an Assistant Professor of Sociology at George Washington University. He received his Ph.D. from the University of Michigan in 2002 where his doctoral thesis was on healthcare worker organizing. He worked as a union organizer with the Service Employees International Union before entering his graduate program. His research interests include working-class collective action, union-community coalitions, and working-class collective identity.

DAISY ROOKS is a graduate student in Sociology at UCLA. Her research focus is on job retention and turnover among staff organizers in the contemporary U.S. labor movement. Recent publications include "The Cowboy Mentality: Organizers and Occupational Commitment in the New Labor Movement" in *Labor Studies Journal* (2003).

PRESTON RUDY recently completed his Ph.D. in sociology at the University of California, Davis. His research focuses on the relationship of labor, globalization and the state. He continues to be involved with Sacramento's labor and social movements.

TERESA SHARPE is a Ph.D. candidate in the Department of Sociology at the University of California, Berkeley. Her dissertation seeks to explain organizational change and union revitalization in the SEIU and HERE.

CARL SOMERS is a graduate student in Sociology at the University of California, Berkeley. His research focuses on labor, social movements, and health care policy in Latin America.

JUDITH STEPAN-NORRIS is Professor of Sociology at the University of California, Irvine. She is the author of two books (co-authored with Maurice Zeitlin): *Talking Union* (University of Illinois Press) and *Left Out: Reds and America's Industrial Unions* (Cambridge University Press) and several award-winning articles concerning politics and democracy in CIO unions. Her most recent work examines (1) Victories in the AFL-CIO's Union Summer campaign; (2) the effects of workplace, religious, and ethnic/racial spatial groupings on neighborhood politics; and (3) workplace friendship networks.

GEORGE STRAUSS is an emeritus professor of Business Administration and former Director of the Institute of Industrial Relations at the University of California, Berkeley, as well as a former president of the Industrial Relations Research Association. Beginning with *The Local Union: Its Place in the Industrial Plant* (1953) and *Unions in the Building Trades* (1957), much of his work has focused on the internal life of unions. "What's Happening in U.S. Unions Today: Democracy and Union Politics" is among his recent articles. He has also written on workers' participation in management and comparative international industrial relations. Currently he is at work on a book about recent changes in the union movement in collaboration with Lois Gray (Cornell) and Paul Clark (Penn State), and with the assistance of Lynn Williams, former president of the United Steel Workers Union.

KIM VOSS is Associate Professor of Sociology and Associate Director of the Institute of Industrial Relations at the University of California, Berkeley. She is the author of *The Making of American Exceptionalism: The Knights of Labor and Class Formation in the Nineteenth Century* (Cornell University Press, 1993), and is co-author of *Inequality by Design: Cracking the Bell Curve Myth* (Princeton University Press, 1996) and *Hard Work: Remaking the American Labor Movement* (University of California Press, 2004).

INDEX